IFIP Advances in Information and Communication Technology 752

IFIP Advances in Information and Communication Technology

The IFIP AICT series publishes state-of-the-art results in the sciences and technologies of information and communication. The scope of the series includes: foundations of computer science; software theory and practice; education; computer applications in technology; communication systems; systems modeling and optimization; information systems; ICT and society; computer systems technology; security and protection in information processing systems; artificial intelligence; and human-computer interaction.

Edited volumes and proceedings of refereed international conferences in computer science and interdisciplinary fields are featured. These results often precede journal publication and represent the most current research.

The principal aim of the IFIP AICT series is to encourage education and the dissemination and exchange of information about all aspects of computing.

More information about this series at https://link.springer.com/bookseries/6102

Walter Seböck · Thomas J. Lampoltshammer ·
Julie Dugdale · Ingeborg Zeller
Editors

Information Technology in Disaster Risk Reduction

9th IFIP WG 5.15 International Conference, ITDRR 2024
Krems an der Donau, Austria, October 14–16, 2024
Revised Selected Papers

Springer

Editors
Walter Seböck
University for Continuing Education Krems
Krems an der Donau, Austria

Thomas J. Lampoltshammer
University for Continuing Education Krems
Krems an der Donau, Austria

Julie Dugdale
University Grenoble Alps
Saint-Martin-d'Hères, France

Ingeborg Zeller
University for Continuing Education Krems
Krems an der Donau, Austria

ISSN 1868-4238 ISSN 1868-422X (electronic)
IFIP Advances in Information and Communication Technology
ISBN 978-3-031-97114-3 ISBN 978-3-031-97115-0 (eBook)
https://doi.org/10.1007/978-3-031-97115-0

This Springer imprint is published by the registered company Springer Nature Switzerland AG
The registered company address is: Gewerbestrasse 11, 6330 Cham, Switzerland

Preface

The Great East Japan Earthquake and Tsunami struck a vast coastal area of northern Japan's main island, including Iwate Prefecture, on Friday, March 11, 2011. Our experiences aiding a part of the affected area through Information Technology for crisis response and disaster management inspired us to explore the research field of Information Technology in Disaster Risk Reduction (ITDRR). When we presented this research domain at the IFIP General Assembly in Vienna in 2014, it received high praise. For Blagovest Hristov Sendov (February 8, 1932 –January 19, 2020), who served as IFIP President from 1989 to 1992 and was an Honorary Member, it was a novel revelation to learn about the application of IT in disaster management.

In contrast, traditional research topics in IT and disaster were confined to the technical aspects of networking, simulation, risk evaluation, and management. In 2016, we established a Domain Committee on Information Technology in Disaster Risk Reduction (ITDRR) within IFIP, which evolved into a working group under Technical Committee 5, WG 5.15, in 2020. Due to recent global climate change, natural disasters such as floods, tornadoes, and wildfires have risen worldwide. Major earthquakes have also occurred more frequently in various parts of the world. Unfortunately, these trends suggest that natural disasters and their associated damage will continue escalating. Moreover, man-made disasters, including terrorism and international conflicts, can have potentially devastating effects, underscoring the importance and urgency of research in information technology to mitigate such damage. After the COVID-19 pandemic, there remains concern that an unknown infectious disease could spark a new pandemic on a global scale. ITDRR serves as an interdisciplinary research area aimed at tackling these urgent issues.

WG 5.15 currently comprises 32 members from 16 countries. Since 2016, we have hosted an annual ITDRR conference to advance the research domain of ITDRR within the IFIP community. The 9th IFIP WG 5.15 Conference on Information Technology in Disaster Risk Reduction (ITDRR 2024) took place in a hybrid format from October 14-16, 2024, at the University for Continuing Education Krems in Austria. We had 35 participants, which included three keynote speakers, eighteen paper presentations, and a poster session. The Program Committee received 21 paper submissions. Each paper was assigned at least three reviewers and underwent a single-blind review process, resulting in the acceptance of 18 papers. The volume editors express their special gratitude to the Program Committee members and the numerous paper reviewers for their commitment to producing this volume. ITDRR 2024 selected the following submissions for the Best Paper Award, the Best Student Paper Award, and the Best Poster Award based on the review outcomes:

- The ITDRR 2024 Best Paper Award: Lucia Castro Herrera, Ingimar Ari Jensson, and Terje Gjøsæter; Between Early Warning and Fatigue: Exploring Evacuation and Crisis Management in the 2023/24 Volcanic Eruptions in Iceland

- The ITDRR 2024 Best Student Paper Award: Kunihiro Nakahara and Michinori Hatayama; Toward the Realization of Resident-led Tsunami Evacuation Simulation Creation for the Promotion of Community-based Countermeasures
- The ITDRR 2024 Best Poster Award: Daniel Jefimov, Stella Polikarpus, and Kärt Reitel;Online Version of Field Exercise of Railway Accident

We hope these awards will encourage the awardees and future candidates to submit their research work to our upcoming conferences.

April 2025

Walter Seböck
Thomas J. Lampoltshammer
Julie Dugdale
Ingeborg Zeller

Organization

Honorary General Chair

Ingrid Schaumüller-Bichl	Austrian Computer Society, Austria

General Chairs

Walter Seböck	University for Continuing Education, Krems, Austria
Ingeborg Zeller	University for Continuing Education Krems, Austria

Program Committee Chairs

Walter Seböck	University for Continuing Education Krems, Austria
Thomas J. Lampoltshammer	University for Continuing Education Krems, Austria
Julie Dugdale	Université Grenoble Alpes, France
Ingeborg Zeller	University for Continuing Education Krems, Austria

Program Committee Members

Reem Abbas	Auckland University of Technology, New Zealand
Ahmed A. Abdelgawad	University of Agder, Norway
Victor Bañuls	Universidad Pablo de Olavide, Spain
Marcos R. S. Borges	Universidade Federal do Rio de Janeiro, Brazil
Tadeusz Czachorski	Institute of Theoretical and Applied Informatics – PAS, Poland
Ioannis Dokas	Democritus University of Thrace, Greece
Julie Dugdale	Université Grenoble Alpes, France
Terje Gjøsæter	University of Agder, Norway
Rob Grace	University of Cincinatti, USA

Igor Grebennik	Kharkiv National University of Radio Electronics, Ukraine
Kei Hiroi	Kyoto University, Japan
Deepak Khazanchi	University of Nebraska Omaha, USA
Thomas J. Lampoltshammer	University for Continuing Education Krems, Austria
Tim A. Majchrzak	University of Agder, Norway
Yutaka Matsuno	Nihon University, Japan
Kenny Meesters	Tilburg University, The Netherlands
Tilo Mentler	Trier University of Applied Sciences, Germany
Ophélie Morand	Conseil & recherche, France
Bjørn Erik Munkvold	University of Agder, Norway
Yuko Murayama	Tsuda University, Japan
Benny B. Nasution	Politeknik Negeri Medan, Indonesia
Erich Neuhold	University of Vienna, Austria
Duygu Pamukcu	Providence College, USA
Sofie Pilemalm	Linköping University, Sweden
Jaziar Radianti	University of Agder, Norway
Mihoko Sakurai	International University of Japan, Japan
Jun Sasaki	Yamato University, Japan
Hans Jochen Scholl	University of Washington, USA
Walter Seböck	University for Continuing Education Krems, Austria
A Min Tjoa	Vienna University of Technology, Austria
Denis Trcek	University of Ljubljana, Slovenia
Osamu Uchida	Tokai University, Japan
Keisuke Utsu	Tokai University, Japan
Dimiter Velev	University of National and World Economy, Bulgaria
Christian Webersik	University of Agder, Norway
Kayoko Yamamoto	University of Electro-Communications, Japan
Christopher Zobel	Virginia Tech, USA

Local Organization Chairs

Ingeborg Zeller	University for Continuing Education Krems, Austria
Stephanie Amon	University for Continuing Education Krems, Austria
Irene Lehr	University for Continuing Education Krems, Austria

Contents

Information for Disaster Management

Identifying Bottlenecks for Information Flow with an Explorative Information Trading Zone Framework in Emergency Management

Kjetil Rustenberg(✉)

University of Agder, Centre for Integrated Emergency Management (CIEM), Kristiansand, Norway
Kjetil.rustenberg@uia.no

Abstract. This paper examines how to identify Information Flow Bottlenecks during a full-scale Emergency Management (EM) exercise involving a vessel collision off Norway's shore, necessitating collaboration between emergency responders and municipalities. It also investigates factors that amplify or mitigate these. Using surveys, qualitative interviews, and socio-technical network mapping, the paper identifies key barriers and analyse the interplay between Norway's collaborative SAMVIRKE doctrine and the structured Command and Control (C2) approach. It proposes a research model that employs an explorative framework to identify Information Trading Zones (ITZ), categorizing information trading into Enforced, Fractionated, Shared Representation, and Subversive zones. The impact of information exchanges in each zone on the Common Operational Picture (COP) and, consequently, Situational Awareness (SA) is explored, revealing how different information trading dynamics influence crisis response effectiveness. Through findings, the paper offers recommendations for enhancing information flow, balancing SAMVIRKE's collaborative ethos with C2's structure, and potentially improving COP presentation, thus contributing to more effective EM operations.

Keywords: Exercise · Situational Awareness · Information Trading Zones

1 Introduction

Norway has the second longest coastline in the world, stretching 100 915km, including all islands, and has one of the world's largest offshore markets. Over the last decades, severe maritime incidents have occurred with a fairly low frequency. Still, the handling of these incidents is complex. It requires a multi-agency response where traditional Emergency Management (EM) organisations are involved, and non-EM organisations such as municipalities and volunteer organisations must also contribute. In Norway, this collaborative effort is called SAMVIRKE. The more significant the incidents are, the more complex collaboration is needed, involving multiple stakeholders not accustomed

Published by Springer Nature Switzerland AG 2026
W. Seböck et al. (Eds.): ITDRR 2024, IFIP AICT 752, pp. 3–18, 2026.
https://doi.org/10.1007/978-3-031-97115-0_1

to collaborating across organisational borders. This creates a high demand for information and information flow between stakeholders with individual information needs to create a shared situational understanding [1]. This article is written based on a large-scale maritime exercise inspired by the *Viking Sky* incident. In 2019, the cruise ship *Viking Sky* experienced an engine failure off Norway's coast. This triggered a large-scale rescue operation involving numerous organizations. The operation became Norway's largest helicopter rescue, with 479 of the 1,373 persons on board (POB) airlifted to safety. Sixteen were hospitalized, three with severe injuries, but no fatalities occurred. Despite being deemed a success, the incident report highlighted areas for improvement. Key challenges included poor coordination, fragmented communication platforms, unclear messaging across stakeholders, and a lack of shared understanding of roles and responsibilities. The report emphasized aligning collaboration with Norway's SAMVIRKE doctrine to enhance Shared Situational Awareness (SSA) [2, 3]. The *Viking Sky* incident required complex coordination between various actors, which is uncommon. The report suggests conducting full-scale exercises to simulate such collaboration. Based on experiences from the incident, key elements in such an exercise should include the activation of various coordination functions, such as the Norwegian Joint Rescue Coordination Centres (NJRCC), the rescue leadership at the local rescue centre (LRC), and the coordination functions of the Directorate for Civil Protection (DSB) and the County Governor. In literature, there is an ongoing debate about the added value of larger-scale collaborative exercises compared to drills focused on enhancing an individual's knowledge within a single organizational field (such as police work or ambulance services) and strategic exercises where an event is simulated to examine the outcomes of various interventions [4–6]. In a Norwegian context, evaluation reports after major events repeatedly point out that organisations struggle to learn from both real events and exercises [7]. Information sharing, Team Situational Awareness (TSA) [3], and role understanding are recurring challenges. Still, despite clearly identifying problem areas, the different organisations do not absorb the lessons, which does not lead to real change. This challenges the preparedness for future incidents [2, 8–11].

In September 2023, the author participated as one of three researchers in a full-scale maritime EM exercise. This article presents findings from extensive data collection and describes information flow bottlenecks, e.g., factors limiting or slowing down information flow between stakeholders (4.1.) in the collaborative effort. Further, I use an explorative Information Trading Zone (ITZ) framework to dissect how information flows between various actors. By applying the framework in combination with a socio-technical mapping of the whole exercise, I intend to provide insights into the obstacles preventing information from reaching key stakeholders. Based on this, I have formulated the following Research Question (RQ): *How do information flow bottlenecks occur in a Maritime Emergency Management exercise, and what factors amplify or mitigate these?*

2 Theoretical Frameworks

The theoretical approach in this paper is twofold. First, I will explain how the ITZ framework is appropriate for identifying and detailing the information trading process between stakeholders in an EM setting and, thus, barriers to information flow, e.g. information flow bottlenecks. Second, I will elaborate on the doctrinal perspectives on Crisis Governance and argue that these perspectives add to the understanding of how the bottlenecks can be seen as an emerging phenomenon from the collaboration that cannot be described independently of contextual, governing elements.

2.1 Information Trading Zones and Common Operational Picture

Galison [13] used the 'Trading Zones' metaphor to describe how physicists and engineers worked together to build complex particle detectors. They had to develop a 'creole', or reduced common language, that allowed them to reach a consensus on design changes [13]. Trading Zones, in the context of EM, can be defined as a space where various actors "trade" their ideas about the relevance of available crisis information, as they involve collective sensemaking with actors from other disciplines. This can relate to exchanging information and ideas, legitimating decision-making processes, and political dynamics. From this perspective, it is recognised that actors in ITZ give different meanings to the same information based on their experiences and knowledge [14]. In previous studies, the metaphorical use of ITZ is often mentioned in connection with a Common Operational Picture (COP) [15, 16]. A COP can be defined as a collection of available information units [17] or as a "centralized information display system" [18], presenting situational and operational information from various sources relevant to the involved stakeholders [1]. In this perspective, ITZ are necessary as they enable negotiations to develop collective sensemaking of information from a COP [16]. As a contribution to the Hawaii International Conference on System Science (HICSS) in 2024, I presented an exploratory framework (Fig. 1) for identifying characteristics of ITZ in an EM setting [12]. The framework is based on findings from a literature review, a workshop with EM experts, and an exploration of whether the framework was suitable for a major wildfire exercise. The framework is evolutionary and demonstrates what characterizes the diffusion of information in different zones. Key indicators are whether information negotiation occurs heterogeneously or homogeneously and whether it is based on collaboration or a degree of coercion.

2.2 Crisis Governance Doctrines: Command and Control vs. Collaboration

A doctrine is a set of principles, beliefs, or teachings that guide and inform actions, decisions, and policies within a particular context or domain. It serves as a framework for understanding and addressing complex issues, providing a structured approach to problem-solving and decision-making [19, 20]. Høiback (2016) argue that "A doctrine is an approach to make the total greater than the sum of its parts, to have the best team without having the best players, so to speak". Doctrines often reflect established norms, practices, and values within a given field, organization, or society, and they may evolve over time in response to changing circumstances, challenges, and priorities. In Crisis Governance, doctrines outline overarching strategies, principles, and approaches to effectively prepare for, respond to, and recover from crises. And, as Høiback argues "A viable doctrine makes collaboration and teamwork possible among a huge number of people who do not know each other or talk the same language" [20].

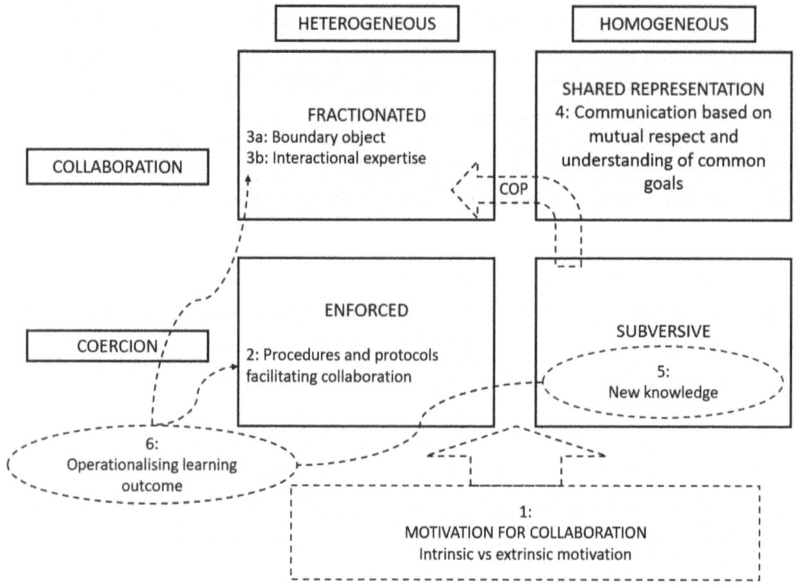

Fig. 1. Explorative Information Trading Zone Framework [12]

In this paper, I argue that Norway's SAMVIRKE principle is, in fact, a doctrinal approach to EM. It differs from the Command and Control (C2) doctrine and aligns more with the Integrated Emergency Management (IEM) doctrine, as it is presented by the Federal Emergency Management Agency (FEMA) [21, 22]. The Command and Control (C2) doctrine represents the idea that crises cause chaos and require Command and Control to restore society to a normal situation [14]. It uses a military analogy where disasters are the enemy that must be fought down [23]. The institutional structure is often paramilitary, as it presupposes that this form of organization will be most effective in combat [24]. C2 is often criticized for being hierarchical and bureaucratic, and the predefined formal chain of command usually associated with the model can limit the effective use of volunteers and necessary improvisation when handling crises and collaborating [25]. Hierarchical organisations with long decision channels tend to prevent collaboration [5]. Diffusion of information from a C2 perspective will be dominated by a quest to obtain a full overview and present a complete COP of the situation so that the correct decisions can be made. Doctrines with a collaborative focus acknowledge that crises create a certain form of turmoil but not complete chaos and panic. In this doctrine, collaboration and coordinated efforts are central. IEM, adopted by EM in the early 1980s, represents an all-threat approach to directing, controlling, and coordinating disasters, regardless of location, size, or complexity [21, 22, 26]. It emphasizes whole community preparedness and fosters a culture of unity of effort, transcending mere methodology to become a joint enterprise in emergency management. This approach aims to cultivate an organizational culture crucial for achieving unity of effort among government, community members, non-governmental organizations, and the private sector. Further, a central aspect of the doctrine is establishing mechanisms for effective coordination and collaboration among various actors, including authorities at all levels, voluntary organizations, the private sector, and international partners. An integrated crisis management doctrine should be flexible enough to adapt to different crises and changing circumstances. This may involve training personnel in various scenarios and regularly evaluating and updating emergency plans. Learning from past experiences and continuously improving the response is crucial for addressing new challenges and threats. The diffusion of information in an IEM perspective differs from C2 by acknowledging that the information available at any given time in a crisis can be incomplete, inadequate, and even incorrect. This necessitates that the information be negotiated and interpreted by the various actors in interaction, forming the basis for collective sensemaking. SAMVIRKE is a Norwegian term for a concept based on a form of organization that can be traced back several hundred years [27]. SAMVIRKE is a leading concept in emergency preparedness and rescue services in Norway. It is built on core values such as mutual trust, common situational understanding, voluntarism, and democratic values [28]. SAMVIRKE can be defined as working together towards a specific goal or purpose, described as a kind of universal solution where different actors with emergency responsibilities offer their expertise and resources so that events can be resolved in collaboration with others [29]. SAMVIRKE has been a guiding principle for the rescue services in Norway since the 1960s. Following a terrorist attack in Oslo and on Utøya in 2011 [11], the principle of SAMVIRKE became one of four national fundamental principles upon which all emergency preparedness work is based [27]; 1) The Principle of Responsibility states that organizations are accountable for emergency preparedness and managing extraordinary events within their area of expertise, assessing what constitutes acceptable risk, 2) the Principle of Similarity advises that crisis operations should closely resemble routine procedures to ensure efficiency, 3) the Principle of Proximity suggests that crises should be managed at the lowest appropriate organizational level to enhance response effectiveness, and, lastly, 4) the Principle of SAMVIRKE emphasizes that authorities, businesses, and agencies have an independent duty to ensure optimal cooperation with relevant actors in prevention, preparedness, and crisis management. Including SAMVIRKE as a principle ensures that Norway has "a consistent principle for types of crises and levels. At the same time, it becomes a responsibility for authorities, businesses, and agencies to ensure optimal cooperation with relevant actors and organizations in prevention, preparedness, and crisis management." The principle is expected to be reflected in the various organizations' plans, routines, and procedures.

3 Methodology

This article has a qualitative design. Data collected during the exercise is used to create a contextual foundation, and we demonstrate the appropriateness of using our ITZ framework as a lens to describe further the information flow bottlenecks we have identified through interviews and observations. Before the actual exercise, the exercise committee engaged us as researchers to work with them to develop exercise goals that could be traced throughout the exercise and evaluated afterwards. We also conducted a workshop to identify whether the different organisations' plans and procedures aligned. To set the stage for the next part of this paper, I will start with a scenario description and continue explaining the data collection.

3.1 Scenario Description

The exercise involved a full-scale collision between two medium-sized vessels in southern Norway's archipelago to test local collaboration. Such exercises are common in Norway. A total of 102 actors played shipwreck victims. The exercise began at 09:18 AM with a MAYDAY distress call intercepted by Coastal Radio, reporting a collision, water ingress on one vessel, and smoke and fire on the other. The Norwegian Joint Rescue Control Centre (NJRCC) notified police, fire, and healthcare services according to National Search and Rescue (SAR) Standard Operating Procedures (SOP) for a coordinated response [30]. Local tactical teams were alerted, and a common radio frequency was established for coordination. Each EM organization then followed individual SOPs to alert necessary resources. The Emergency Medical Control Centre (EMCC) alerted ambulances and doctors while the police led local operations and notified relevant parties (Fig. 2). Two ports were designated for the vessels, but only one made it; the other was simulated to have sunk, with passengers reaching nearby islets. The scenario included key actors and stressed the Norwegian Critical Communication Network (NCCN). The exercise ended at 1:00 PM. Individual organizations conducted Hot Wash evaluations, but no cross-organizational review occurred. Researchers distributed a survey and gathered input from observers [31].

3.2 Data Collection

Data from the exercise were collected in four different ways. 1) Seven individuals, including the author of this study, observed the exercise at various locations. At predetermined times, observations related to the exercise objectives were recorded using an observation guide to direct attention to predefined elements and minimize observation bias. 2) Following the exercise, a survey was distributed to approximately 200 respondents, of which 154 responded. The survey contained both closed and open-ended questions. 3) Selected findings from both observations and the survey have been followed up with qualitative interviews. A total of 13 interviews have been conducted. The interviews follow an interview guide to clarify respondents' role understanding, use of information systems, information sharing and communication, and experiences with evaluation and learning from exercises and real events. The length of each interview varies from 50 to 150 min. Interviews were transcribed and analysed using NVivo [32]. 4) Before the interviews, we mapped alerting sequences, information systems in use, communication channels, and SOPs using MindManager [33]. This commercial mind mapping program allows users to visualize information in mind maps and flowcharts. Together with the respondents, we enriched the initial mapping (3.3.). We created a network map that visualizes how information flows and how it is supported or not supported by adequate technical solutions and SOPs, thereby supporting TSA or creating barriers to TSA and, subsequently, information flow bottlenecks [31].

3.3 Co-Creation of Socio-Technical Network (STN) Mapping

Together with respondents, we conducted an STN mapping during our qualitative interviews (Fig. 2). This mapping covers the period from the exercise's inception until the notification phase ended and the work phase began. The aim was to understand information patterns and how technology supported human actors' situational awareness (SA), identifying both human and non-human actors, and the interplay between humans and technology. Our approach, inspired by Salmon et al. [34] on Distributed Situation Awareness (DSA) and the Delphi method [35], values expert opinions from practitioners. Using socio-technical network analysis in emergency management is common. For example, Houghton et al. [36] categorized networks in Command & Control contexts, showing the value of social network analysis in such studies. Mapping social networks and information systems is timely. We call our approach STN-mapping to emphasize connections between human and non-human actors, procedures, and communication pathways, distinguishing between Mapping and Analysis. The mapping is part of the analysis, not an analysis itself. In social networks, communication flows between human and non-human actors, like computers, are plotted as connections [36]. Our approach to STN mapping as a method is published in the following paper [31].

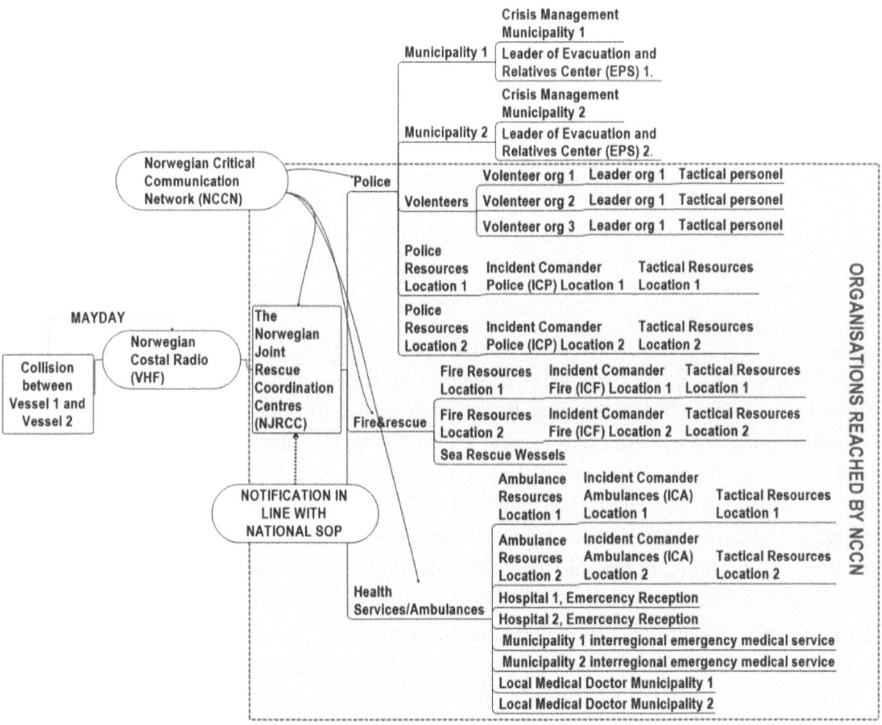

Fig. 2. Simplified STN map of exercise

4 Results

In this chapter, I will present findings categorized as Information Bottlenecks (IB) and use our ITZ Framework to detail the information flow and information trading process.

4.1 Information Bottlenecks (IB)

IB is used metaphorically to describe the factors that limit or slow down information from sender A to receiver B, thus creating a barrier for individual and/or Team Situational Awareness [37–40], and the sensemaking process that these processes necessitate. The author is aware of the IB method presented by Tishby et al. [38] and IB as related to Broadbent's Filter Theory [41]. Perspectives from both these theories are inspirational, but we do not commit to them. We have identified three main types of IBs from interviews and observations, as depicted in Table 1.

Table 1. Information Bottlenecks

Types of Bottlenecks	Description
Technological	Issues related to hardware, software, connectivity, and interoperability between different systems
Procedural	Inefficiencies in protocols, unclear communication lines, and information processing delays
Human Factors	Cognitive overload, miscommunication, and varying levels of training or familiarity with the technology

4.2 Enforced ITZ

In the Enforced ITZ, IBs primarily occurred due to the rigid structure of communication and procedures. When Coastal Radio intercepted the first MAYDAY distress call, it initiated an alerting sequence guided by SOPs and action cards. At this stage, the collaborative effort that was needed to handle the incident was heterogeneous, and a strict C2 approach was applied to onboard all the organisations. Coastal Radio is col-located at the same physical location as the NJRCC; thus, information was conveyed verbally via telephony, radio, and direct face-to-face to a liaison from the NJRCC. There was an early understanding of the severity of the incident that triggered a large-scale alerting of other potentially involved stakeholders in the proximity of the incident. The notification of all the established emergency response organisations followed National guidelines in the form of a SAR notification SOP [30]. The SOP refers to the notification between the police, fire and rescue and ambulance services and the NJRCC. This SOP is well-known and regularly drilled by all emergency response organisations, but not more peripheral organisations, like the municipalities. The use of the SOP is mandatory, and information flow is top-down, where the NRJCC takes a leading role in coordinating and structuring both the information trading and the communication process between the alerted resources. Initially, the information flow was one-way from the NJRCC to the other organisation, where the different organisations replied verbally that the message was copied and that resources would respond. The commitment to the SOP secured a shared situational awareness early on, where baseline information like the exact location and scale of the incident were clarified [42]. The alerting phase was supported by the NCCN, as well as procedures and protocols securing and detailing the correct use of the radio network. To be a NCCN user, all personnel must be certified and trained in using the radio equipment. We argue that the strict framing of information sharing and trading in this phase occurred in an Enforced ITZ. Still, using the NCCN, and even the procedural enforcement, can be seen as boundary objects in a Fractionated ITZ, moving the collaborative effort towards a Shared Representation ITZ. From the STN mapping and interviews we identified that the preliminary alerting phase and the information trading between the stakeholders conveyed by the national SOPs worked as intended. The first observed bottleneck emerged in the second alerting sequel, where internal procedures were utilized to inform more remote collaborating organizations. The EMCC conducted macro alerts, where predefined NCCN macros secured correct notification of all relevant healthcare resources. Other organisations relied more on predefined call lists where operators had to call each organisation manually. Due to the high workload in the initial phase, the municipalities and the voluntary organisations were only partially notified. The responsible operator thus became an IB where both human factors and procedural elements interplayed and slowed down the information flow. None of these organizations were included in the national alerting SOP; thus, they were blocked from participating in the information trading from an early onset.

4.3 Fractionated ITZ

In the Fractionated ITZ, IBs mainly occurred due to fragmentation of information and the magnitude of different communication systems in play (Table 2). From an ITZ perspective, we argue that there really was no boundary object (2.1.) that fully reached the whole collaboration during the exercise, but mere organizational silos that shared information with each other without entirely securing that every stakeholder got relevant and timely information, and the option to ask for more information if anything was unclear.

From the initial alert until the responding organisations were established on-scene, in the immediate proximity of the incident, the collaborative effort was heterogeneous in the sense that they were geographically dispersed. This created a need for technological support to unite them, enabling the negotiation of a shared understanding of the situation. The NCCN was the only communication system that all stakeholders could potentially use to obtain appropriate information. In this sense, it was the only possibility for the whole collaboration to obtain a boundary object that could cross organisational boundaries. One early example of an IB related to this was that the number of persons on board (POB) the two vessels was presented very early before all stakeholders were involved. Even though the NRJCC had a verified number of passengers and crew and communicated this on the radio in the early phase, this information disappeared as collaboration expanded and more stakeholders were introduced, compromising Shared Situational

Table 2. Communication Systems in use during exercise

Communication System	Description
Norwegian Critical Communication Network (NCCN)	National, secure, digital radio network for emergency response organisations
VHF Maritime	International, worldwide, very high frequency (VHF) radio band system of two-way radio transceivers. Installed on all large ships
Crisis Management System (CMS) 1	A national system currently being phased out. Employed by municipalities, but less frequently by established crisis organizations
Crisis Management System (CMS) 2	A national system currently in a rollout phase. Intended for use by municipalities, with no specified use beyond that
Crisis Management System (CMS) 3	A system primarily utilized by the fire service and the health sector. It is used, for example, to keep hospitals informed of the status during an incident
Instant Messaging Services	Platforms that enable real-time text and multimedia communication over the internet
Common Operational Picture (COP) 1	COP restricted to the JRCC
Common Operational Picture (COP) 2	COP restricted to the police
Common Operational Picture (COP) 3	COP restricted to the EMCC
Common Operational Picture (COP) 4	COP restricted to the Fire and rescue services
Other	E-mail, telephony, simple in-house systems

Awareness (SSA) [3]. When the exercise was close to ENDEX (finished) there were still organisations that did not have control over this essential piece of information. One leading cause for this was a lack of procedures that secured situational updates on a regular basis in a communication channel that could reach everyone. Respondents from municipalities argue that they were in charge of establishing centres for evacuees and relatives, in line with procedures. But they struggled to get relevant information, something that clearly hindered them in fulfilling their duties. Both response from interviews and observations point to several IBs related to the use and limitations of the NCCN. An important function of the NCCN is the ability to set up different call groups or "digital rooms." It is possible to set up several call groups, both agency-specific and cross-organizational, during one emergency operation [43]. In the initial phase, the first collaboration between the NRJCC and emergency responders was conducted in one call group (SAR 1). Since the rescue operation involved two separate locations, there was initiated a second call group (SAR 2). Even though this simplified the tactical work at the two locations, it challenged the operators at the emergency centres as they had to monitor two call groups with similar information. Since the NCCN infrastructure has user limitations, good practice argues that the local collaboration on a tactical level should occur radio to radio, in line of sight [30]. This is to limit the strain on the base station. While this reduced the workload on the base stations, it introduced new challenges as incident commanders (ICs) had to pass on information between tactical personnel and the operations centres, thus creating bottlenecks since they got overloaded with information. We observed ICs with two and even three radio terminals and mobile telephones in addition to managing the more interpersonal, face-to-face communication on site. COPs, as a centralized information display, presenting geospatial information in a map-based interface, were present, but not as an overarching COP that could reach the whole collaboration. The technical solutions used by the emergency responders enables the sharing of information from a technical point of view, but legislation and common practices limit this. We observed map-based information being shared internally in the organisations, e.g. from the EMCC to the ambulances, and between EM centres, but this information was not made accessible to the collaboration as a whole.

4.4 Shared Representation ITZ

In the Shared Representation ITZ, information flow is characterized by collaborative efforts where stakeholders work together to get a shared situational understanding, and ideally build a COP. This zone relies on open communication and the integration of information from multiple sources to enhance both a Shared Situational Awareness (SSA) and Team Situational Awareness (TSA) [3, 42]. Information Trading in this zone was mainly observed within organizational teams, e.g. at the police‘s Emergency Operations Centre or in close proximity to the incident, where ICs from the different emergency responder organizations collaborated. IBs in this zone were more related to Human Factors and the interplay between humans and technology. As the example from Sect. 4.3. Shows, ICs had to handle several radio terminals, along with managing mobile phone communication and interpersonal communication at the scene (see 4.3). They were constantly interrupted and disturbed, and external factors such as wind, rain, and noise from machinery in the area led to cognitive burdens and challenged the collaboration among the responders physically co-located. The joint effort lacked a COP across all organizations, and the shared NCCN's full potential was not utilized, leading to fragmented communication. Consequently, the foundation for a Shared Representation ITZ for the joint operation was missing. This resulted in confusion over even small details such as the gender of the individuals being searched after and the allocation of resources. Another example comes from the operational level, where respondents argue that that some operators had to leave their desk and the rest of the team to provide status updates to the management and staff in the next room. This practice was also observed by us. This caused them to lose track of the situation, and they had to spend time catching up on what had happened when returning to the control centre. The role of operators on an operational level is very central in information flow, as they should ideally verify all information before it is distributed to the rest of the collaboration. The shift in roles from leading the joint effort and providing situational status reports to the managerial level created stress and, thus, a Human Factors IB.

4.5 Subversive ITZ

Observed IBs in the Subversive ITZ relate to both technology and procedures. There was a lack of technological support for the shared distribution of information. The absence of interoperability between the various communication systems meant there was never a fully functional COP during the exercise. This prevented the creation of dynamic Subversive ITZs. As a result, misinformation was not adequately handled. For example, personnel in Municipality 1 were unsure about the POB. To address this, a firefighter was sent from the municipal crisis team to the patient reception area closer to the actual incident. He met someone he thought was the captain of one of the vessels and got a POB count. This number turned out to be wrong, but because there were no shared digital spaces available to verify the information, this was discovered too late. There were also no procedures for regular status updates. In other words, there was no way to correct information satisfactorily. The inconsistency between formal and informal information streams led to confusion and the dissemination of conflicting information. Trust issues also played a role, with personnel from the crisis team relying more on personal knowledge than the official communication hierarchy. Confusion of the POB count was also an issue between the different Emergency Control Centres. At a specific time, we, as researchers, asked the operators in each central to provide the number of POBs. Only one central provided the correct number, something that underscores the importance of regular cross-organizational updates to secure the quality of imperative information. Immediately after the exercise, some initiatives were launched for evaluation. However, the primary evaluation of the exercise was primarily set aside. As researchers, we are now involved in the evaluation, contributing to evaluation of findings in a Subversive ITZ, where the goal of information negotiation is to foster learning and thus change practices within individual organizations and to the collaboration. This exemplifies that a Subversive ITZ has a time-dynamic that is both valid in real-time during an incident, and in non-real time in post-incident evaluation [44].

5 Discussion

The use of ITZ to explain and detail information negotiation in EM, thus identifying IBs is promising. ITZs are dynamic, and it is important to note that reaching a Shared Representation ITZ is not an explicit goal, even though this best aligns with the SAMVIRKE doctrines. Each ITZ has its own peculiarities, and they are all necessary for the collaborating organizations to negotiate as accurate a representation of the real world as possible. Findings from our analyses of the Maritime EM exercise point to the fact that a C2 approach can be necessary early on, and we have highlighted the consequences of insufficient quality control in the notification and communication of peripheral organizations, such as municipalities, both at the procedural level and supported by adequate technology. Failing to acknowledge this can lead to certain organizations becoming isolated and valuable information not reaching those who need it. In this article, we have explored how IBs arise in an exercise and pointed out factors that support and weaken them. We believe that using the ITZ framework brings out the details of information diffusion between different actors and that this approach provides rich insights into how coordination in a larger exercise works and, to some extent, does not work. The exercise we followed was a SAMVIRKE exercise. The SAMVIRKE doctrine is based on values such as openness, mutual trust, and autonomy. In our analyses, we see that while this is an ideal to strive for, mechanisms we know better from C2 are necessary for cooperation in a larger incident to function, even in the preparatory phase. Top-down governance, control, and a certain hierarchy can be necessary in some cases. In the exercise, JNRCC took control early on and acted as a central authority that coordinated and directed actions. As the collaboration grew, the opportunities for this diminished, both due to technological challenges and information fragmentation, but also because procedural facilitation for common status updates was lacking. This is particularly evident when central information must be requested from the tactical level outside the established emergency actors. The high degree of autonomy and lack of top-down governance at a political level has led to a situation where a major incident in Norway must be handled with several technological communication systems that only, to a limited extent, are open for information sharing across organizational boundaries. Lack of interoperability can be a major challenge, and as we see in this exercise, it can result in the joint effort struggling to achieve an adequate, common situational understanding. C2 mechanisms, as we show they function initially in the exercise, seem necessary for a larger number of organizations to cooperate effectively. This is particularly evident regarding information sharing, where information bottlenecks pose a real threat to life and health and further escalate an incident. In an ideal setting, SAMVIRKE can provide flexibility and adaptation, which are necessary for organizations to handle both conceivable and inconceivable scenarios. On the other hand, these principles heavily challenge information flow, and C2 may prove necessary to contribute more structuring elements. These ideas align with a netcentric approach to EM, as it is implemented in e.g. The Netherlands [45].

6 Conclusion and Further Research

Evaluations of exercises and real incidents are demanding, and there are no quick fixes. We do not claim that our approach offers this. Evaluations are time-consuming, and it can be challenging to motivate various organizations to come together after incidents to review findings and learn from them. The use of the ITZ framework, complimented by the STN mapping, is fruitful. This is especially evident in the interaction between us from academia and practitioners. A visual representation of a collaborative effort (Fig. 2) opens dialogue, and information bottlenecks are visualized. Findings from our research are already subject to implementation, and we will continue engaging in EM exercises to validate the ITZ framework and the methodological approach presented in this paper.

7 Limitations

This study is limited to the context of a single exercise. The framework for identifying Information Trading Zones is experimental and requires more empirical data for validation. This article's findings, opinions, and conclusions result from the author's understanding and interpretations and do not necessarily reflect the informants' views. Some information revealed in the exercise is subject to high confidentiality. Certain details have been omitted to safeguard information security.

Acknowledgements. The author would like to thank the emergency management stakeholders participating in the described exercise for sharing their time and expertise. The author would also like to thank the participants from the PhD workshop on Governance and crisis handling held at the University of Berkeley, California 29. April -3 May 2024, where this paper was initially presented. Especially Prof. Trond Petersen, Prof. Gudmund Hernes, Prof. Morten Øgård and Connie Salvesen for organising and Dr Are Vegard Haug and Prof. Elin Wihlborg for taking the role as opponents.

References

1. Steen-Tveit, K., Munkvold, B.E.: From common operational picture to common situational understanding: an analysis based on practitioner perspectives. Saf. Sci. **142**, 105381 (2021)
2. DSB (Directorate for Civil Protection). Evaluation of The Viking Sky incident (2020)
3. Endsley, M., Jones, W.M.: A model of inter and intra team situation awareness: Implications for design, training and measurement. New trends in cooperative activities: Understanding system dynamics in complex environments. CA, pp. 46–67 (2001)
4. Berlin, J.M., Carlström, E.D.: Learning and usefulness of collaboration exercises: a study of the three level collaboration (3LC) exercises between the police, ambulance, and rescue services. Int. J. Mass Emergencies Disasters **33**(3) (2015)
5. Berlin, J.M., Carlström, E.D.: Why is collaboration minimised at the accident scene? a critical study of a hidden phenomenon. Disaster Prev. Manage. Int. J. **20**(2), 159–171 (2011)
6. Roud, E., et al.: Outcome of collaborative emergency exercises: differences between full-scale and tabletop exercises. J. Contingencies Crisis Manage. **29**(2), 170–184 (2021)
7. Henriksen, S.V.B., Torgeir; Hoel, Linda; Kruke, Bjørn Ivar; Myhrer, Tor-Geir; , *Evaluation of PST's and the police's handling in connection with the Kongsberg incident on 13th October 2021.* 2022
8. Borell, J., Eriksson, K.: Learning effectiveness of discussion-based crisis management exercises. Int. J. Disaster Risk Red. **5**, 28–37 (2013)
9. DSB (Directorate for Civil Protection). The Valdress Express: Evaluation of the authorities' handling of the November 2013 incident. (2014)
10. Halvorsen, J.: Evaluation: the rescue operation and the acute handeling of the crisis during the quick clay landslide at Gjerdrum (2021)
11. Sønderland, O.D., et al.: 22 July 2011: Evaluation of the police's efforts (2012)
12. Rustenberg, K., Radianti, J., Gjøsæter, T.: Adopting a Trading Zone Framework to Emergency Management. In: Proceedings of the 57th Hawaii International Conference on System Sciences | 2024 (2024)
13. Galison, P.: Image and logic: A material culture of microphysics. University of Chicago Press (1997)
14. Boersma, F., Wolbers, J.: Foundations of responsive crisis management: institutional design and information. Oxford Research Encyclopedia of Politics, p. 1–25 (2021)
15. Steen-Tveit, K.: From Common Operational Picture to Common Situational Understanding : A Framework for Information Sharing in Multi-Organizational Emergency Management. University of Agder: Kristiansand, Norway (2022)
16. Wolbers, J., Boersma, K.: The common operational picture as collective sensemaking. J. Contingencies Crisis Manage. **21**(4), 186–199 (2013)
17. Borglund, E.A.M., Granholm, M.: You Talk the Talk – But What Do You Talk About? In: Hughes, A., McNeill, F., Zobel, C.W. (eds.) 17th International Conference on Information Systems for Crisis Response and Management (ISCRAM 2020), pp. 295–302. Virginia Tech, Blacksburg, VA (2020)

18. Hwang, G.H., Yoon, W.C.: A new approach to requirement development for a common operational picture to support distributed situation awareness. Saf. Sci. **125**, 104569 (2020)
19. Høiback, H.: What is doctrine? J. Strateg. Stud. **34**(6), 879–900 (2011)
20. Høiback, H.: The anatomy of doctrine and ways to keep it fit. J. Strateg. Stud. **39**(2), 185–197 (2016)
21. FEMA. National Incident Management System, H. Security, Editor. FEMA: Washington, DC. p. x/156 (2008)
22. FEMA. National Response Framework, H. Security, Editor. FEMA: Washington, DC. p. iv/48 (2013)
23. Helsloot, I., Groenendaal, J.: Centralization in large scale emergencies: rarely needed, barely achievable (2023)
24. Monet, J.-P., et al.: Civil protection in Europe: Towards a unified command system? Lessons learned, studies and ideas about change management. In: Hughes, A., McNeill, F., Zobel, C.W. (eds.) 17th International Conference on Information Systems for Crisis Response and Management (ISCRAM 2020), pp. 315–325. Virginia Tech, Blacksburg, VA (2020)
25. Boersma, F., et al.: Incident command systems: a dynamic tension among goals, rules and practice. J. Contingencies Crisis Manage. **22**(1), 1–4 (2014)
26. McLoughlin, D.: A framework for integrated emergency management. Public Adm. Rev. **45**, 165–172 (1985)
27. Aasland, T., Braut, G.S.: Cooperation in Norwegian search and rescue services as seen by voluntary organizations (2019)
28. Aasland, T., Braut, G.S.: Independence, trust, and loyalty. The county governor's coordination of public and voluntary resources in crises in Norway. J. Contingencies Crisis Manage. **31**(1), 2–12 (2023)
29. Kristiansen, E., Johansen, F.H., Carlström, E.: When it matters most: collaboration between first responders in incidents and exercises. J. Contingencies Crisis Manage. **27**(1), 72–78 (2019)
30. Ly, J.M., Vangen, T., Olsen, S.: Felles sambandsreglement for Nødnett (Common Communications Regulations for Nødnett). T.N.P. Directorate, Editor (2022)
31. Rustenberg, K., et al.: Collaborative evaluation: mapping socio-technical patterns in an emergency exercise. In: ISCRAM Proceedings **21** (2024)
32. Beekhuyzen, J., Bazeley, P.: Qualitative Data Analysis with NVivo. SAGE Publications Limited (2024)
33. MindManager. Corel Corporation: Ottawa, Canada p. Computer Software (2021)
34. Salmon, P.M., Stanton, N.A., Jenkins, D.P.: Distributed situation awareness: Theory, measurement and application to teamwork (2017)
35. Linstone, H.A., Turoff, M.: The delphi method. Addison-Wesley Reading, MA (1975)
36. Houghton, R.J., et al.: Command and control in emergency services operations: a social network analysis. Ergonomics **49**(12–13), 1204–1225 (2006)
37. Endsley, M.R.: Toward a theory of situational awareness in dynamic systems. Hum. Factors. J. Hum. Factors Ergon. Soc. **37**(1), 32–64 (1995)
38. Endsley, M.R., Connors, E.S.: Situation awareness: state of the art. In: 2008 IEEE Power and Energy Society General Meeting-Conversion and Delivery of Electrical Energy in the 21st Century. IEEE (2008)
39. Endsley, M.R.: Situation Awareness in Teams: Models and Measures. In: Contemporary Research, pp. 1–27. CRC Press (2020)
40. Endsley, M.R., Jones, D.G.: Situation awareness oriented design: review and future directions. Int. J. Hum. Comput. Interact. 1–18 (2024)
41. Broadbent, D.E.: Perception and communication. London, Oxford: Pergamon Press (1958)
42. Nofi, A.A.: Defining and measuring shared situational awareness (2000)

43. Steen-Tveit, K., Radianti, J., Munkvold, B.E.: Using audio-logs for analyzing the development of a common operational picture in multi-agency emergency response. In: Proceedings of the 53rd Hawaii International Conference on System Sciences (2020)
44. Van De Ven, J., et al.: Network centric operations in crisis management, In: Fiedrich, F., van de Walle, B.A., (Eds), 5th International Conference on Information Systems for Crisis Response and Management (Proceedings of ISCRAM 2008). Information Systems for Crisis Response and Management, ISCRAM. pp. 764–773 (2008)
45. Wolbers, J., Treurniet, W., Boersma, F.K.: A Decade of Netcentric Crisis Management: Challenges and Future Development. In: Disaster Management and Information Technology: Professional Response and Recovery Management in the Age of Disasters, pp. 65–81. Springer (2023)

Performance Evaluation of An Orchestrator Framework for Disaster Cyber-Physical System

Kei Hiroi[1(✉)], Akihito Kohiga[2], Sho Fukaya[3], and Yoichi Shinoda[2]

[1] Disaster Prevention Research Institute, Kyoto University, Kyoto, Japan
hiroi@dimsis.dpri.kyoto-u.ac.jp
[2] Japan Advanced Institute of Science and Technology, Nomi, Japan
[3] Suwa University of Science, Suwa, Japan

Abstract. This paper proposes an orchestrator framework for reproducing complex disaster phenomena. Our orchestrator framework, based on the CyReal concept, integrates multiple simulators and systems through a federation bus, and enables effective collaboration and coordination among them using data exchange functions and time synchronization mechanisms. This framework allows for flexible integration of different types of simulators, enabling simultaneous modeling of diverse elements such as disaster phenomena, human behavior, and infrastructure conditions. The framework's performance was evaluated through load and scalability tests of a prototype, demonstrating its ability to handle increases in data volume and processing of multiple simulators with minimal impact. The prototype using simplified simulators represents a significant step towards creating a comprehensive cyber-physical system capable of addressing more complex disaster scenarios.

Keywords: federation · crisis management IT system component · cyber-physical system

1 Introduction

1.1 Background

The world is experiencing a steady increase in both the number of disasters and human casualties. This alarming trend is attributed to the complex interplay between changes in the global climate system and greenhouse gas-induced global warming[1]. Rapid urbanization is increasing the population in disaster-prone areas, exacerbating the risk. Among various natural calamities, flood disasters stand out as particularly devastating, claiming the highest number of human casualties.

[1] Intergovernmental Panel on Climate Change Fifth Assessment Report (AR5): https://www.ipcc.ch/report/ar5/.

Published by Springer Nature Switzerland AG 2026
W. Seböck et al. (Eds.): ITDRR 2024, IFIP AICT 752, pp. 19–34, 2026.
https://doi.org/10.1007/978-3-031-97115-0_2

Smart city technology is emerging as a promising solution for creating resilient urban environments. This innovative approach leverages Internet of Things (IoT) sensors to gather diverse urban data, including traffic flow, population movement, and weather patterns [Yamagata(2016)]. By harnessing the power of artificial intelligence, smart cities can analyze this data in real-time to determine and predict the needs and behaviors of urban residents. The ultimate goal of smart cities is to enhance the quality of life in high-risk urban areas by improving their resilience to disasters. The development of smart cities is being actively driven by advancements in various technologies, including cyber-physical systems, IoT, cloud computing, and other software innovations. These technologies enable the seamless integration of sensors, actuators, and other devices into the city's physical infrastructure through a range of computational techniques. Among these, simulation technology stands out as a cornerstone of smart city functionality, playing a crucial role in forecasting service demands in physical spaces and conducting predictive analyses in virtual environments.

1.2 Motivation

By incorporating cyber-physical systems into disaster prevention, the following applications and service developments can be anticipated:Simulation study, Development and performance testing for component technologies such as analysis methods and simulators, Operator training, evacuation drill, Damage prediction, evacuation guidance.

The primary objective of simulation studies in disaster management is to analyze results and gain comprehensive insights into various aspects of disasters. Traditional simulations that focus on a single factor essentially conduct analyses under the assumption that all other factors remain constant, thus excluding their potential influences.

However, the reality of disaster damage is complex, involving the interplay of multiple factors including the disaster event itself, affected infrastructure, human behavior, and information dissemination. Conventional simulators typically focus on a single factor or a limited subset, which falls short when considering the holistic perspective required for an urban cyber-physical system. We argue that overcoming these limitations is crucial for developing truly effective cyber-physical systems for disaster management.

This cyber-physical system is based on the system we have been continuously developing. We have developed prototypes to verify the concept [Hiroi(2023)] and have built functions that enable simulation studies and development and performance testing for component technologies [Hiroi(2024)]. In this paper, we will describe these functions in detail and conduct basic performance verification, considering the utilization as a cyber-physical system.

2 Literature Review

We now describe the literature on what simulators address single or partial factors related to disaster damage and how they handle their interaction. One of the simulation techniques is physical simulation for reproducing disaster phenomena; for flood damage, this means a flood analysis simulator that estimates the occurrence of flood damage and its expansion process. This is a simulator that derives the flood water value in several-meter grid units by numerical analysis using input data such as precipitation, land use, building coverage, sewer pipes, and manholes. In addition to flood damage, many simulations have been developed to accurately reproduce various disaster phenomena such as tsunami [Makinoshima(2018)] and wildfire [Beloglazov(2016)]. In these simulations, each generation mechanism is modeled by a physical formula and then reproduced on a computer; these simulations are actually used for risk estimation and damage estimation in many regions.

Another approach to disaster simulation is social simulation, which models the behaviors of evacuees. These evacuation simulators reproduce human behavior in various disaster scenarios. Researchers have employed different methodologies for behavior modeling, including empirical and agent-based approaches [Ouyang(2014)]. The field has seen the development of numerous sophisticated models, each addressing specific aspects of evacuation dynamics. For instance, some models focus on dynamic destination selection [Pel(2012)], while others consider the complexities of indoor evacuations, including potential collisions between evacuees [Chen(2018)]. Researchers have also developed models that account for the influence of nearby evacuees on individual behavior [Li(2016)], as well as broader crowd evacuation models [Shendarkar(2008)]. In a notable application, Nguyen et al. [Nguyen(2013)] integrated smoke diffusion behavior into fire evacuation simulations, using the results to provide guidance to evacuees and inform efficient evacuation planning.

A new approach in the concept of cyber-physical systems is the simulation that models real-space physical elements in virtual space. Virtual Singapore exemplifies this approach, integrating terrain information, buildings, and social infrastructure data from across Singapore into a comprehensive virtual urban model [Soon(2017)][Ignatius(2019)]. This model is further enhanced by incorporating various real-time data, such as traffic information and location data for vehicles and people, creating a dynamic simulation environment. These advancements are underpinned by evolving IoT technologies developed for diverse applications. Cyber-physical systems expand upon the IoT concept, facilitating deeper interaction between smart cities' cyber and physical spaces. Researchers have applied these systems to various disaster-related scenarios, including landslide detection [Liu(2019)] and disaster response [Estrela(2017)]-[Nishiyama(2017)]. In the context of disaster prevention, the construction of detailed urban structure models enables highly accurate reproduction of disaster phenomena, enhancing the potential for effective feedback to physical spaces. This accuracy stems from the use of urban space model data to define parameters for physical disaster simulations. Furthermore, real-time data collection via IoT has the potential to improve the accuracy of both disaster phenomena and social simulations.

The integration of diverse models and technologies in disaster management has led to the development of comprehensive frameworks that incorporate multiple simulations and systems as a unified function. One such framework is the Integrated Emergency Response Framework (iERF) [Jain(2003)], which aims to integrate various emergency management tools, including simulation and visualization components. Another significant approach is the High Level Architecture (HLA) [Kirov(2015)], which standardizes different simulators and systems for distributed simulation. HLA facilitates the development of large-scale simulations by combining multiple smaller simulations, providing services such as data distribution and time synchronization through middleware. Dahmann et al. [Dahmann(1998)] have demonstrated the interoperability of various simulations by examining common technical architecture specifications using HLA. Practical applications of these integrated approaches have been implemented in disaster scenarios. For instance, a prototype architecture was developed to interoperate multiple simulators for evacuation, information provision, and emergency operations during an earthquake disaster [Fiedrich(2006)]. Similarly, a distributed simulation platform was constructed for evacuation simulations in the context of fire disasters caused by earthquakes [Hwang(2016)].

2.1 Limitations and Contributions

Despite advancements in disaster management simulations, challenges remain in system flexibility, scalability, real-time data integration, and interoperability. From the perspective of cyber-physical systems, examining these previous studies reveals that many existing simulations focus on single or limited factors. Individual simulations often fail to capture the complex interactions between different disaster factors, limiting their realism. The simplest solution to account for complex interactions would be to develop a single large system capable of reproducing various phenomena. However, this solution also has its problems. It is currently difficult to ensure scalability while reducing system modification costs for synchronizing with new simulations and systems. This becomes an obstacle when rapidly adopting new observation systems and prediction technologies that emerge from feedback in the virtual space of cyber-physical systems. When we aim to develop cyber-physical systems, we must be conscious of both reproducing complex phenomena and maintaining scalability. This becomes an essential consideration when incorporating disasters in our rapidly changing modern society into cyber-physical systems. When we can provide theoretical backing for the collaboration between different models to express complex real-world spaces, we will be able to bridge the gap between theoretical models and real-world scenarios.

To address these challenges, we propose a new orchestrator framework that enables federation of multiple different simulators and systems. This framework integrates systems and simulators via a federation platform, effectively combining the best components for each function while maintaining scalability and flexibility. The contributions of this paper are summarized as follows:

- Enhanced Flexibility and Interoperability: The proposed federation framework enables flexible expansion without the need to redevelop the entire sys-

tem when additional functions or new sensors are required. Moreover, it facilitates the federation of different systems and simulators, allowing for more comprehensive and realistic modeling and analysis of disaster scenarios. This increased flexibility and interoperability significantly improve the system's evolution and adaptability, promoting effective federation of diverse disaster management tools and technologies.
- Efficient Resource Allocation through a Federated Approach: This framework adopts a federated approach, enabling efficient resource allocation based on processing functions. This allows for maximum utilization of the capabilities of general-purpose computers across the federation.
- Improvement of Disaster Management Systems: The introduction of the orchestrator federation framework is expected to enhance the performance and flexibility of disaster management systems, serving as a more effective tool for disaster prevention, response, and recovery.

3 Orchestrator Framework

3.1 Overview

We have decided to develop a cyber-physical system by federating multiple simulators and systems. This approach aims to reproduce complex phenomena while ensuring scalability. In the proposed architecture, we develop an orchestrator framework that federates simulators and systems, enabling them to function as a single component through this framework. This configuration allows for the adoption of optimal systems and simulators for each function and component. Additionally, when new functionalities or sensors need to be added, the structure can be expanded without redeveloping the entire system. Furthermore, adopting this distributed form offers the advantage of allowing appropriate allocation of machine resources according to processing capabilities (those that can be handled by general-purpose computers or processors).

To federate not only simulators, which are a type of virtual system, but also real-time information systems, we apply the concept of CyReal to the development of our orchestrator framework. We then realize the orchestrator framework by developing two functions: a data exchange function and a timing control function.

In our previous research [Hiroi(2023)], we developed a prototype of the orchestrator framework. This paper provides a more detailed operational design of the orchestrator framework and evaluates its performance.

3.2 CyReal Approach for Orchestrator Framework

CyReal technology is designed to play a pivotal intermediary role in the concept of digital twins [Hiroi(2022)]. This innovative approach enables flexible replacement and integration of real and virtual entities, encompassing computer systems, people, and environments. By leveraging CyReal technology, the configuration strongly promotes digital twinning in disaster prevention IT systems. At its

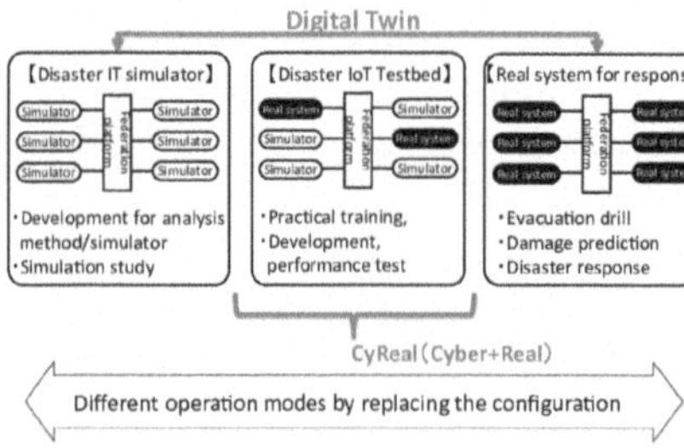

Fig. 1. CyReal Approach for Orchestrator Framework

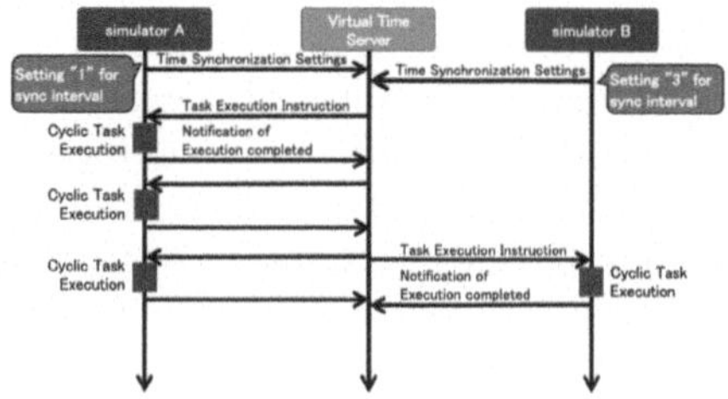

Fig. 2. Time Synchronized Function

core, a digital twin is a virtual representation of a real-world object that mirrors changes occurring in its physical counterpart within a computer system. This concept is particularly significant in the AI domain, as it allows for debugging various properties of the created twin. To illustrate, Fig. 1 presents a configuration where all subsystems are simulated and interconnected via a federation platform, exemplifying the digital twin concept in practice.

Conversely, the platform's simulations and systems can be entirely replaced with real-world counterparts. As illustrated on the right side of Fig. 1, this configuration represents a scenario where all subsystems are real and operational, including people, natural phenomena, and actual disaster prevention information systems. Taking this concept a step further, we propose an extension of the digital twin paradigm that integrates both real systems and simulators within a single subsystem, as depicted in the center of Fig. 1. This innovative approach, which we term"CyReal," represents a seamless fusion of cyber and real elements. By bridging the gap between virtual simulations and tangible, operational systems, CyReal offers a more comprehensive and adaptable framework for disaster prevention and management.

3.3 Orchestrator Framework Design

Main Purpose of This Paper. The Orchestrator Framework, following the CyReal approach, requires us to enable the three configurations shown in Fig. 1 and allow flexible changes between configuration modes. In other words, we must achieve complex federation and collaboration that includes not only simulators but also systems actually in operation. As this is a very large task in system development, we decided to implement it in stages. The aim of this paper is the federation and collaboration of multiple simulators as shown on the left side of Fig. 1. To develop a large-scale cyber-physical system, we decided to first build a mechanism for federating and collaborating simulators. Of course, after this development, we must consider the design of the cyber-physical system with the awareness of collaborating with information systems actually in operation.

To develop an orchestrator framework using the CyReal approach, several key aspects need to be addressed, including physical data exchange between simulators and systems, data interoperability, sequential processing of large-scale data, and timing control. We started with a design that is relatively easy to develop within our concept of federation and collaboration between simulators. In this paper, we design and implement a cyber-physical system to achieve federation and collaboration between simulators, and test its performance in terms of collaboration performance and scalability.

Our Federation Vision. The federation and collaboration we aim for is not merely about data sharing or exchange between simulations and systems. Rather, it is crucial to execute these in synchronization. Let's consider, for example, the case of reproducing the operation of information services during a flood disaster. This scenario includes a flood analysis simulator, a human behavior simulator, a communication and power failure simulator, and an information system. Each simulator performs calculations at regular time intervals (which we call a cycle). The flood analysis simulator calculates flood flow using continuity equations and equations of motion, while the human behavior simulator uses these results to calculate evacuation behaviors. Simultaneously, the failure simulator calculates the status of communication and power.

What's important is that these simulators exchange calculation results at each cycle and use the results from other simulators as input for the next cycle. For instance, the human behavior simulator adjusts information acquisition behavior based on the results from the failure simulator. The information system also operates in time synchronization with these simulators and uses the output from each simulator as its input.

Orchestrator Framework Structure. To achieve the operation described above, it is necessary to synchronize the time of multiple simulators and systems while exchanging data at each cycle. Regarding data exchange, when constructing a single large cyber-physical system, it was possible to share data between different calculation methods by registering results in a designated folder within the computer system or in a database. However, in the cyber-physical system we aim for, data exchange means sending and receiving data between simulators and systems assigned to different computer resources. In other words, it becomes necessary to realize data exchange over network access.

Concerning time synchronization, we must consider the time for as many simulators and systems as we are federating and collaborating. Each simulator and system's computational resource and content have their own time, according to which they execute calculations. By handling these times in a centralized manner, time synchronization becomes possible. To achieve this, we develop a function for data exchange at each cycle and a function to synchronize the time of multiple simulators and systems. Our orchestrator framework realizes federation and collaboration through these functions.

Data Exchange Function. First, we will explain the function of data exchange. The simulator and the system exchange data with each other every cycle. That is, they need to output their calculation results, transmit them over the network, and access the network to receive the calculation results of the other party. In other words, this is also the data transmission and reception of distributed simulations and systems. The federation bus mediates this transmission and reception (See Fig. 1). We prepare two methods for this transmission and reception: temporary files and network access.

The method using temporary files is a way for each simulator to record its calculation results as temporary files in the federation bus. This is very advantageous in that it allows for easy federation of existing simulators. In many cases, existing simulators have a write function. Therefore, federation becomes possible simply by specifying the federation bus as the destination for writing. For simulators that federate and coordinate, it is necessary to specify which temporary files to read. When strict time synchronization is not required for simulators, this Data Exchange Function, which enables simple federation and coordination, works effectively in simulation studies and develop and performance testing for component technologies such as analysis methods and simulators.

For network access, we use network protocols such as MQTT. The simulators and systems that operate collaboratively output their calculation results as MQTT messages and publish them. Simultaneously, they subscribe to MQTT messages from other simulators and systems. The federation bus acts as an MQTT server for this message publishing and subscribing, handling the sending and receiving of messages. The federation bus also plays a role in synchronizing the processing of simulators and systems. It constantly subscribes to MQTT messages from the connected simulators and systems. If a simulation starts and the federation bus receives messages from other simulators, it initiates synchronization.

In both methods, the federation bus knows in advance the information of the simulators and systems it is connected to. MQTT is used to manage the state and progress of all simulators. Once it receives connection completion messages from all simulators and systems, it publishes the start of the cycle as an MQTT message. The simulators and systems receive this cycle start message and proceed with their calculations while using data from other simulators and systems. When each simulator completes its calculation, it writes the results to a file or publishes them, and sends a completion message. After receiving completion messages from all simulators, the federation bus publishes the start of the next cycle as an MQTT message. This is how we implement the data exchange function. Of course, conventional simulators do not have such MQTT functionality built-in. Therefore, it is necessary to either add data input/output and data transmission/reception code to the simulator itself, or to provide such mechanisms to the simulator through an interface.

Time Synchronized Function. Next, we explain the time synchronization function. In our orchestrator framework, time synchronization controls the timing of different simulators and systems to synchronize them. In the federation of simulators and systems, several concepts of time exist. These include the time series of disaster damage data calculated by each simulator, the clock of the machine system running each simulator, the time series of information held by the systems, the clock of each system, and the processing time of each simulator's machine system and system. When realizing time synchronization, we must cover all these concepts of time. As the number of simulators and systems to be federated increases, time management becomes more complex. Special attention is needed for the system's processing time. For synchronization of simulators and systems, it's necessary to be aware of each other's cycles for data exchange. However, since each simulator and system requires different processing times for one cycle of calculation, a simple connection is insufficient to achieve this operation. The virtual clock server centrally manages these concepts of time. The virtual clock server is included as one of the functions within the federation bus.

Figure 2 shows the flow of time synchronization by the virtual clock server. The virtual clock server holds information about the simulators and systems in federation and collaboration. This server instructs the start of tasks to simulators and systems in a predetermined order. Following these instructions, the simulator or system executes its calculations. Upon completion, it outputs and sends the calculation results and notifies of task completion. When the virtual clock server receives the completion notification, it instructs the subsequent simulator or system to execute its task. By repeating these operations, one cycle of calculations for all connected simulators and systems is completed. After completing one cycle of calculations, the virtual clock server initiates the next cycle of calculations.

In this flow, different concepts of time are unified, allowing simulators and systems with varying execution times to effectively exchange data. The virtual clock server clarifies complex time processing, enabling the federated simulators and systems to function as one large cyber-physical system. It instructs each simulator to start its task, receives completion notifications, and instructs the execution of subsequent tasks. By repeating these operations, simulators and systems with different execution times can effectively exchange data. Overall, the orchestrator framework implemented through the CyReal approach enables seamless integration of systems and simulators, achieving efficient coordination and synchronization while promoting the digital twin concept in the field of disaster prevention.

4 Performance Evaluation and Discussion

We implement a prototype of the orchestrator framework proposed so far and perform performance tests to verify if the data exchange and time synchronization we envisioned are functioning. For this purpose, we address two evaluation tests: a load test and a scalability test. Then, we confirm that the data exchange and time synchronization we developed operate as intended.

4.1 Setup

For performance evaluation, we implement the orchestrator framework as a prototype and federate simple simulators implemented in Go language. In this paper, we use the temporary file method as the data exchange function. We configure the federated simulators to output and input data via temporary files, mediated by the federation bus. The time synchronization function operates by federating two or more independent simulators. The virtual clock consists of the VClock library for generating virtual time and a virtual clock server that synchronizes the execution of multiple simulators. By importing the VClock library into the simulators we want to federate and executing the necessary functions, the simulators notify the virtual clock server of their own execution status. The virtual clock server observes the execution status sent from each simulator and synchronizes the execution of the simulators.

We configure the federated simulators with a very simple structure. For the experiment, we prepare a physics simulator that calculates equations of motion and a human behavior simulator that moves in orthogonal plane coordinates. First, the physics simulator starts its calculations, and the human behavior simulator operates using those results. The physics simulator calculates the movement of objects, and the human behavior simulator receives information about the new position of the objects, then the humans in the simulator move to that position. While the calculation itself is very simple, this is the most simplified version of an evacuation behavior simulator during a disaster. Equations of motion are sometimes used in disaster phenomenon simulators. Therefore, the physics simulator uses a simple equation of motion. The position information calculated by the equation of motion is received by the human behavior simulator, and the agents move to that position. This is a minimally simplified configuration of the functions of an agent simulator related to evacuation. In evacuation simulators, the normal behavior is to avoid the calculated positions, but to simplify the interaction between the two, in this paper's experiment, we configure it to move to that position. All these simulators are federated to operate for cycles $c = 0, 1, ..., 20$.

We operate the prototype under two tests for performance testing, conducting experiments and discussions. The first test measures the overall processing time when this orchestrator framework is installed on a typical PC and simulators are federated. We set several data volumes for input and output in the simulators and examine the changes in processing time. This test investigates whether the orchestrator framework can achieve the expected federation and coordination even for simulators with high loads. Secondly, we increase the number of simulators federating and coordinating in the orchestrator framework and examine the state of federation and coordination. This is conducted as a scalability test to discuss whether the orchestrator framework has implemented the expected operations and to further consider future practical applications. Both the simulators and the orchestrator framework are executed on a computer running Windows 11 Pro 64-bit, equipped with a 2.3 GHz Intel Core i9 processor and 64 GB of RAM.

4.2 Performance Evaluation Tests

A) Load Test. The first test is a load test of the orchestrator framework. We gradually increase the amount of data handled by the simulators federating with the orchestrator framework and examine its performance. This test is to verify whether the orchestrator framework operates as expected even for simulators performing high-load calculations. The simulators federating in the orchestrator framework are the physics simulator and the human behavior simulator. The calculation in the physics simulator is performed using a single equation of motion. We incrementally increase this calculation by a factor of 2^n ($n = 0, 1, 2, ...$). Correspondingly, the calculation results written to temporary files and the amount of data received by the human behavior simulator also increase by a factor of 2^n. We examine the calculation time and the state of federation when the load is incrementally increased in this manner. If federation and coordination are achieved even for relatively large n, we can conclude that our orchestrator framework is capable of federating simulators that require large computational loads.

B) Scalability Test. The second test is a scalability test of the orchestrator framework. We gradually increase the number of simulators federating with the orchestrator framework and examine its performance. The goal of our orchestrator framework is to federate and coordinate simulators to operate as a cyber-physical system. This requires federating many simulators that mimic disaster phenomena, human behavior, infrastructure operations, information systems, and more. We anticipate that the number of federated simulators will likely be around 10. This test is to verify whether the orchestrator framework can federate 10 simulators and if it operates as expected in such conditions. The simulators federating in the orchestrator framework are the physics simulator and the human behavior simulator. We increase the number of these federating simulators to $k \times 2$ ($k = 1, 2, ...$). Then, at $k = 5$, we impose random delays of more than 10 s on the calculations of all simulators. We confirm that the virtual clock operates normally even if the order of calculations among the simulators changes. This is a delay tolerance test while ensuring scalability. If around $k = 5$ simulators can operate and exchange data without issues, we can conclude that our orchestrator framework is capable of federating simulators to constitute a cyber-physical system.

4.3 Result and Discussion

A) Load Test. The results of Test A) Load Test are shown in Fig. 3. The vertical axis shows the processing time from when the virtual clock instructs each simulator to start calculation until it receives completion reports from each simulator and ends one cycle. In other words, it shows the time from when the orchestra simulator starts a cycle's calculation until it finishes. When changing n from 0 to 100, most calculation times were around 0.050 s. At $n = 0, 20, 40$, the operation was stable, completing one cycle of calculation in about 0.050 s.

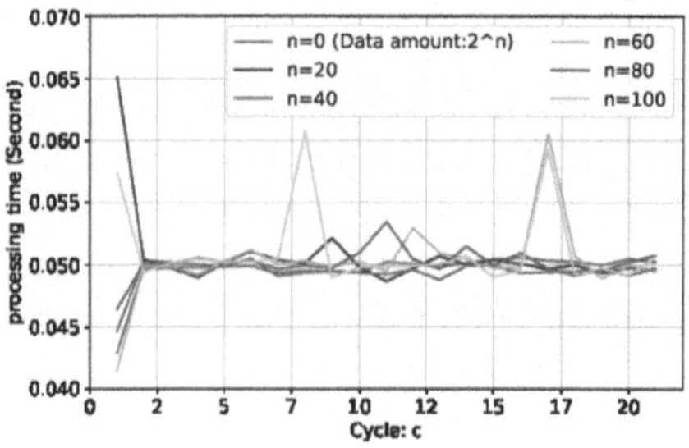

Fig. 3. A) Load Test Result

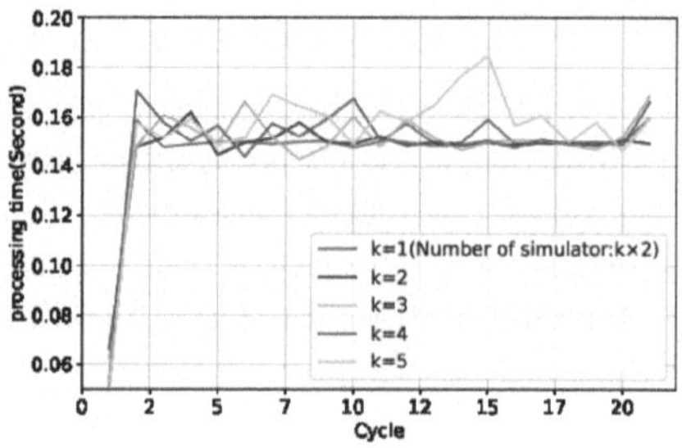

Fig. 4. B) Scalability Test Result

At $n = 60$ and above, there were occasional spikes to 0.060 s, indicating cycles with increased calculation time. However, even when increasing the data volume up to $n = 100$, the maximum calculation time was only 0.065 s, confirming that the increase in data volume had little impact on data exchange and time synchronization.

The prototype simulators used in this test were very simple: the physics simulator calculated positions using a simple equation of motion, and the human behavior simulator moved agents from their initial positions to locations derived by the equation of motion. Therefore, increasing the data volume did not increase the processing time of the calculations performed by each simulator. The aspect potentially affected by the increase in data volume was the data exchange between simulators. By conducting tests with increased data volumes, the amount of data recorded in temporary files also increased, leading to more read and write operations in the simulators. However, these results show that data exchange via temporary files is hardly affected by the increase in data volume.

B) Scalability Test. The results of B) Scalability Test are shown in Fig. 4. The vertical axis shows the processing time from when the virtual clock completes one cycle of operation, instructs each simulator to calculate, receives completion reports from each simulator, and ends one cycle. In other words, it shows the time for one cycle of operation of the orchestra simulator. When changing k in the number of collaborating simulators $k \times 2$ from 0 to 100, most calculation times were around 0.15 s. For $k = 1, 2$, the time for one cycle is stable at 0.14 to 0.15 s. At $k = 3$ and above, there were occasional spikes to 0.18 s, and especially at $k = 5$, there were cycles that took 0.18 s. However, even when increasing the number of collaborating simulators up to $k = 5$, the maximum calculation time was only 0.18 s, indicating no significant impact on the collaboration operation.

Table 1 shows the processing times for all simulators and the virtual clock. A random delay of up to 10 s was added to all simulators. In each cycle, the values in the table for physical simulators P_n and human behavior simulators H_n represent the processing time from receiving the start instruction to completion for each simulator. The value for the virtual clock is the processing time

Table 1. Delay Tolerance Test Result (P_n:physical simulators,H_n:human behavior simulators)

Cycle:c	P_1	H_1	P_2	H_2	P_3	H_3	P_4	H_4	P_5	H_5	VirtualClock
0	0.31	6.61	2.57	4.65	2.54	9.91	3.98	3.83	9.25	6.83	9.91
5	4.63	8.86	7.47	4.75	1.62	0.29	7.79	9.79	4.73	0.80	9.79
10	0.91	0.97	3.15	9.69	4.58	1.11	9.93	6.91	9.51	1.88	9.93
15	0.61	0.86	5.79	3.11	5.90	2.98	2.59	4.63	8.80	0.10	8.80
20	6.59	3.48	7.29	6.25	1.22	10.00	5.74	2.94	5.92	3.95	10.00

taken for one cycle. At cycle $c = 0$, due to randomly assigned delays, the simulator that took the longest calculation time was H_3 with a processing time of 9.91 s. Immediately after H_3 completed processing, the virtual clock received the completion message and ended the cycle in 9.91 s. Also, at cycle $c = 5$, the last simulator to finish calculation was H_4, taking 9.79 s, and immediately after that, the virtual clock ended the cycle. From Table 1, it was confirmed that even if the order of processing completion changed, the virtual clock waited for all simulators to complete processing before finishing one cycle. This indicates that even if significant delays occur in simulator calculations, the orchestrator framework operates one cycle according to the delay, demonstrating that the time synchronized function of the orchestrator framework is working as expected.

4.4 Discussion

The results of the load test revealed that even when the data volume increased 100-fold, the processing time was kept to about 0.065 s. This demonstrates that the orchestrator framework operates efficiently even for large-scale data processing. In the scalability test, even when the number of simulators was increased to 10, the processing time for one cycle was kept to about 0.18 s. This suggests the effectiveness of this framework when coordinating multiple simulators. The test results confirmed that the impact of increasing data volume and the number of simulators on processing time was relatively small, verifying the system's stability. Furthermore, in terms of scalability, the design allows for easy integration of different types of simulators, enabling response to various disaster scenarios.

Our goal was to build a single cyber-physical system by collaboratively implementing multiple simulators and systems. To achieve this, we developed a prototype of an orchestrator framework that collaboratively implements multiple simulators using the CyReal approach. In this paper, we designed and implemented a cyber-physical system for achieving coordination and collaboration between simulators, and tested its performance in terms of collaborative performance and scalability. Although the simulators used in the experiment were relatively simple, the experimental results confirmed that data exchange is possible even with large amounts of data, and that multiple simulators can be coordinated.

This demonstrates that we have achieved the coordination and collaboration between simulators that we aimed for.

However, since the simulators used in the experiment were relatively simple, to operate as a cyber-physical system during disasters, it is necessary to develop an orchestrator framework that coordinates more complex simulators and evaluate its performance. Actual disaster phenomenon simulators are composed of far more complex physical equations than the prototype simulators in this study, and will likely require more computation time. When the simulators themselves require a lot of computation time, ingenuity is needed to speed up the overall computation time. We are considering a method to skip some calculations within a range that does not compromise the overall accuracy of the calculation. Also, while this paper does not consider the order of processing between simulators, for some phenomena, it may be necessary to strictly adhere to the processing order. We need to consider such relationships that should exist between simulators. Furthermore, while this paper used temporary files for data exchange, we believe that by incorporating network access, we can aim for applications and service developments such as operator training and evacuation drills.

5 Conclusion

This paper presented an orchestrator framework designed to address the complex challenges of disaster management through the integration of multiple simulators and systems. Our approach, based on the CyReal concept, aims to bridge the gap between virtual simulations and real-world operational systems, offering a more comprehensive and adaptable framework for disaster prevention and management.

The key contributions of this research include the development of an integrated federation framework that effectively combines multiple simulators and systems through a federation platform, the implementation of a data exchange function and a time synchronization mechanism that allow for efficient coordination between diverse simulators, and the demonstration of the framework's scalability and performance through load and scalability tests, showing its capability to handle increased data volumes and multiple simulators with minimal impact on processing time.

Our experimental results, using simplified physics and human behavior simulators, confirmed the framework's ability to maintain stable performance even with a 100-fold increase in data volume and coordination of up to 10 simulators. The framework demonstrated resilience to random delays, validating the effectiveness of our time synchronization approach.

However, we acknowledge the limitations of our current work, particularly the use of simplified simulators in our experiments. Future research directions include integration and testing with more complex, realistic disaster simulators to evaluate performance under more demanding computational loads, exploration of optimization techniques, such as selective calculation skipping, to enhance overall computational efficiency without compromising accuracy, investigation of strict processing order requirements for certain phenomena and how to incorporate these into the framework, and expansion of the data exchange mechanism to include network access, facilitating applications such as operator training and evacuation drills.

In conclusion, while our orchestrator framework shows promise in addressing the challenges of integrating multiple simulators for disaster management, further development and testing are needed to fully realize its potential in real-world disaster scenarios. This research represents a significant step towards creating more robust, flexible, and comprehensive cyber-physical systems for disaster prevention and management.

Acknowledgement. This work was supported by JST FOREST Program, Grant Number JPMJFR226Z, and the commissioned research(No. 0820103) by National Institute of Information and Communications Technology (NICT), Japan.

References

Yamagata, Y., Maruyama, H.: Urban Resilience -A Transformative Approach. Springer International Publishing (2016)

Makinoshima, F., Imamura, I., Abe, Y.: Enhancing a tsunami evacuation simulation for a multi-scenario analysis using parallel computing. Simul. Model. Pract. Theory **83**, 36–50 (2018)

Beloglazov, A., Almashor, M., Abebe, E., Richter, J., Charles, B.: Simulation of wildfire evacuation with dynamic factors and model composition. Simul. Model. Pract. Theory **60**, 144–159 (2016)

Ouyang, M.: Review on modeling and simulation of interdependent critical infrastructure systems, reliability engineering & system safety, vol. 121, pp.43–60. Elsevier (2014)

Pel, A.J., Bliemer, M.C.J., Hoogendoorn, S.P.: A review on travel behaviour modelling in dynamic traffic simulation models for evacuations, transportation, vol. 39, no.1, pp.97–123, Springer (2012)

Chen, L., Tang, T.Q., Huang, H.J., Wu, J.J., Song, Z.: Modeling pedestrian flow accounting for collision avoidance during evacuation. Simul. Model. Pract. Theory **82**, 1–11 (2018)

Li, W., Li, Y., Yu. P., Gong. J., Shen, S.: The trace model: a model for simulation of the tracing process during evacuations in complex route environments, simulation modelling practice and theory. vol. 60, pp. 108–121 (2016)

Shendarkar, A., Vasudevan, K., Lee, S., Son, Y.J.: Crowd simulation for emergency response using bdi agents based on immersive virtual reality, simulation modelling practice and theory, vol. 16, no. 9, pp. 1415–1429. Elsevier (2008)

Nguyen, M.H., Ho, T.V., Zucker, J.D.: Integration of smoke effect and blind evacuation strategy (SEBES) within fire evacuation simulation, simulation modelling practice and theory, vol. 36, pp. 44–59. Elsevier (2013)

Soon, K.H., Khoo, V.H.S.: CityGML modelling for singapore 3D national mapping. In: Proceedings og The International Archives of Photogrammetry, Remote Sensing and Spatial Information Sciences, vol. 42, p. 37 (2017)

Ignatius, M., Wong, N.H., Martin, M., Chen, S.: Virtual singapore integration with energy simulation and canopy modelling for climate assessment. In: IOP Conference Series: Earth and Environmental Science, vol. 294, no. 1, p. 012018. IOP Publishing (2019)

Liu, Z., Tsuda, T., Watanabe, H., Ryuo, S., Iwasawa, N.: Data driven cyber-physical system for landslide detection. Mob. Netw. Appl. **24**(3), 991–1002 (2019)

Estrela, V.V., Hemanth, J., Saotome, O., Grata, E.G., Izario, D.R.: Emergency Response Cyber-physical System for Flood Prevention with Sustainable Electronics, pp. 319–328. In Brazilian Technology Symposium, Springer (2017)

Mariappan, R., Reddy, P.N., Wu, C.: Cyber physical system using intelligent wireless sensor actuator networks for disaster recovery. In: Proceedings of 2015 International Conference on Computational Intelligence and Communication Networks (CICN), pp. 95–99. IEEE (2015)

Nishiyama, H., Suto, K., Kuribayashi, H.: Cyber physical systems for intelligent disaster response networks: conceptual proposal and field experiment. IEEE Netw. **31**(4), 120–128 (2017)

Hiroi, k., Kohiga, A., Fukaya, S., Shinoda, Y., An orchestrator framework for IoT-based disaster prevention simulation. In: Proceedings of IEEE Sensors 2023 Conference (SENSORS2024), pp. 1–4 (2023)

Hiroi, k., Nakagawa, S., Takahashi, R., Kohiga, A., Fukaya, S., Shinoda, Y.: Demo: flood damage cyrealization with an orchestrator framework. In: Proceedings of the 22nd International Conference on Pervasive Computing and Communications (PerCom 2024) [Demo session] , pp. 1–3 (2024)

Hiroi, k., Kohiga, A., Shinoda, Y.: Performance evaluation of a cyreal sensor system. Int. J. Inf. Soc. (IJIS) **14**(2), 75–84 (2022)

Jain S.: McLean, a framework for modeling and simulation for emergency response. In: Proceedings of the 2003 Winter Simulation Conference, vol. 1, pp. 1068–1076 (2003)

Kirov, G., Zlateva, P., Velev, D.: Software architecture for rapid development of hla-integrated simulations for critical infrastructure elements under natural disasters. Int. J. Innov. Manage. Technol. 6.4, 244 (2015)

Dahmann J.S., Morse K.L.: High level architecture for simulation: an update. In: Proceedings of 2nd International Workshop on Distributed Interactive Simulation and Real-Time Applications, pp. 32–40 (1998)

Fiedrich, F.: An HLA-based multiagent system for optimized resource allocation after strong earthquakes. In: Proceedings of the 38th Conference on Winter Simulation Winter Simulation Conference, pp. 486–492. IEEE (2006)

Hwang, S., Starbuck, R., Lee, S., Choi, M., Lee, S., Park, M.: High level architecture (HLA) compliant distributed simulation platform for disaster preparedness and response in facility management. In: Proceedings of the 2016 Winter Simulation Conference, pp. 3365–3374. IEEE (2016)

Towards Maintaining Awareness Data in Emergencies Involving Critical Infrastructure - A Framework for Process and Actions

Jacimar F. Tavares(✉) and Marcos R. S. Borges(✉)

Programa de Pós Graduação em Informática, Departamento de Ciência da Computação, Instituto de Matemática, Universidade Federal do Rio de Janeiro, Rio de Janeiro, Brazil
jacimar.tavares@gmail.com, mborges@ppgi.ufrj.br

Abstract. The consequences of a disaster are multifaceted, especially with regard to its adverse effects. It is well known that negative effects are intensified when the disaster is unexpected and response measures are not properly prepared, which can result in inestimable consequences, such as loss of human lives. It is known that negative effects are also multiplied when the catastrophe affects critical infrastructures (CIs) such as transportation, health services and energy, among others, as these are complex systems with their own characteristics. This paper presents the path that is being taken towards a more in-depth solution that enables the collection and storage of awareness data, generated through the interaction between command and control agents (decision makers) combined with awareness elements in the communication, coordination and communication of actions to analyze disaster data involving CIs. The idea is that, by analyzing data from disasters in CIs, it is possible to generate insights that, when maintained, will assist future disasters involving CIs. A framework is presented, developed by analyzing several sources of information, from newspapers to government reports, about the biggest disaster in the history of the Petrópolis city, located in the Rio de Janeiro, Brazil.

Keywords: Critical Infrastructures · awareness · disasters

1 Introduction

In various aspects of everyday life—whether it's accessing clean water, powering homes, managing finances through digital platforms, or commuting via public transport—people rely on what are known as critical infrastructures (CIs). These systems, which can range from individual components to large-scale networks that span neighborhoods, cities, states, or entire nations, play an indispensable role in maintaining societal stability. They support essential services tied to health, safety, security, and economic continuity. Any disruption or damage to these infrastructures could significantly impair or even disable the systems that communities depend on.[4]. In Spain, as in other countries, certain infrastructures are officially classified as critical due to their strategic role in delivering essential services. These systems must remain continuously operational, as there are no effective alternatives. Any disruption or damage could seriously affect vital services and have a substantial impact on the population's daily life.

Published by Springer Nature Switzerland AG 2026
W. Seböck et al. (Eds.): ITDRR 2024, IFIP AICT 752, pp. 35–46, 2026.
https://doi.org/10.1007/978-3-031-97115-0_3

When examining the factors that can lead to the disruption of critical infrastructures, it's important to account for what are commonly referred to as natural hazards. These include a wide range of events—whether natural phenomena, physical occurrences, or human actions—that have the potential to cause harm to people, damage to property, disruption of economic and social systems, or environmental degradation. Such threats may not always be immediate; some exist as underlying risks with the potential to manifest in the future. Their origins can stem from natural causes like geological or meteorological activity, as well as from human-related sources such as environmental damage or technological failures [5]. Natural hazards will remain as sources of threat to CIs, human activities, and society as a whole, and this is partly influenced by climate change and factors associated with rapid development, urbanization, and population and economic growth, which contribute to environmental degradation [6].

Another aspect relevant to this research is awareness, which is the process by which individuals interpret and attribute meanings to the sensory stimuli they receive from the environment. It involves the organization and interpretation of these stimuli, allowing humans to understand and respond to the world around them [2]. In the context of critical infrastructures, awareness plays a fundamental role in identifying and assessing risks related to adverse events, such as natural disasters and cyberattacks. The ability to detect and anticipate potential threats is vital for adopting preventive measures and executing effective responses. Furthermore, awareness directly impacts how people react to disasters, influencing both decision-making and behavior during and after catastrophic situations. Therefore, a deep understanding of the role of awareness is essential for effective risk management and critical infrastructure security [17].

Finally, Situational Awareness stands out. It is essential for making decisions quickly and efficiently. It is based on how a person perceives the environment around them, which helps them decide and act. However, this awareness depends on several individual factors, such as the way we process information, the ability to do things automatically, experience, goals and training we have had. Other elements such as the functioning of systems, interface design, stress level, workload, complexity of tasks and the use of automation also influence this process [18]. In this work, the term awareness will be used to refer to situational awareness in an emergency management scenario, but not ignoring the psychological/social/medical awareness that each decision-maker involved may have. This implies focusing on obtaining awareness of the impacts of disasters on CIs and their relationships. For example, if a hospital network is impacted by a disaster, it may restrict the response to referring affected people to receive emergency medical care. The awareness we are trying to raise at this point is: what impact will the unavailability of the health CI have on the response and flow of care to victims? The infrastructure itself does not represent the disaster, in this example, but its unavailability can lead to different insights that can be used in future disasters involving CIs. Questions such as: what is the impact of one CI on another? If there is no power distribution, then there may be no distribution of pumped water. If there are no roads, how will unpumped drinking water reach those in need? This type of final and non-obvious awareness is what we intend to capture for future use.

Sensors are essential devices for data collection in various areas, from meteorology to agriculture, and play a crucial role in the context of natural disaster management.

In disaster scenarios, information is vital for effective decision-making, and drones are emerging as an innovative tool for capturing data in difficult-to-reach or dangerous areas. Drones, equipped with different types of sensors, are capable of flying over disaster-affected areas, capturing high-resolution images, videos and data in real time. Sensors such as high-definition cameras and thermal imaging can be used to map damaged areas, identify victims, assess damage to critical infrastructure and monitor changes in the environment. Sensor data plays a vital role in enhancing the situational awareness of command and control teams. By offering a detailed and real-time picture of ongoing events, it enables these teams to detect critical issues quickly, deploy resources where they are most needed, and effectively manage both emergency response and recovery efforts. [1]. In short, the combination of sensors in a network represents a powerful tool for disaster management, providing valuable information that can save lives, minimize damage and accelerate crisis response. In this research, it is believed that a network of sensors useful for capturing information about disasters, often combined with equipment such as drones, can contribute to making data available to command and control teams (decision makers) for later analysis.

This paper aims to show the path that research is following and to present the solution that is being developed for capturing, storing, and making available data on the awareness that command and control teams can generate when acting in the analysis of disaster data involving CIs. It is known that what transforms natural hazards into a disaster or catastrophe is linked to a set of factors. The threat of a storm, for example, can trigger varied effects in different regions and nations, so it is crucial to examine the specific context in which the disaster occurs in order to carry out a comprehensive analysis of its repercussions. One must also consider the negative impacts that disasters cause (such as loss of life with impact on family structures, destruction of intangible cultural heritage, etc.). It's important to emphasize that this paper does not intend to show what can be done with the awareness data obtained. We are limiting ourselves to the capture, storage and provision of these data. Therefore, the motivation for this work is the fact that CIs can be affected by emergencies and emergencies require actions to mitigate the damage, but such actions are performed by different types and profiles of professionals, with different awareness levels. The use of sensors and technologies to assess affected areas can be an ally, but collaborative resources are needed to enable the collection of shared information, both on the effects and impacts on CIs and, in the context of this work, on the awareness obtained when analyzing the disaster. Sensors combined with information capture software, with awareness elements, can allow the formalization of useful knowledge for command and control teams [1]. The problem that this ongoing research aims to address is the lack of a solution that allows maintaining awareness data, including non-obvious awareness (as exemplified), obtained through communication, coordination and communication between stakeholders. In this sense, it is being proposed that a network of sensors of various purposes (this work lists the categories of sensors relevant to this research), can be used to collect preliminary data on disasters involving CIs. It is worth noting that the CIs presented in the developed framework are those affected by the largest disaster in the history of the Petrópolis city, located in Rio de Janeiro, Brazil and sensors types also present in the framework are the result of the analysis of what would have been useful to capture relevant data from this same disaster, considering the current information on the impacts caused. The hypothesis raised is: Is it possible to capture, store and distribute awareness data collected in emergencies involving CIs, with the aim of helping stakeholders (command and control agents) in the future? In short, the focus of the solution being developed is mainly on awareness, which is the basis for obtaining data (capture, storage and provision), generated from the cooperation, communication and coordination of stakeholders, in the analysis of emergency data, in critical infrastructures. To make this possible, the following methodology is being followed:

- Study of the themes related to this research;
- Bibliographical survey of literature, with study of technologies already existing in research.
- Study of the different types of sensors and awareness elements available in the literature, which may be useful in the scope of the disaster analyzed.
- Creation of the framework that will encompass the awareness criteria and the processes with actions that will enable the data to be stored to be explored by command and control teams in the future.
- Conducting the evaluation (Proof of Concept) of the framework proposal and recording the results.

The paper is structured as follows: following the introduction, we present the theoretical foundations that underpin this research. Next, we describe the development of the ongoing research. Finally, the paper concludes with a section dedicated to evaluation and future work.

2 Background

This section aims to provide an overview of existing theories and concepts that are relevant to the topic of this research. This section is essential to situate the reader within the academic context, showing how the study fits into the existing knowledge of the area.

2.1 Disasters and Critical Infrastructure

A disaster is characterized as a situation triggered by a natural hazard, resulting in damage, disruption to livelihoods or the economy, and/or loss of life, to an extent that exceeds the capacity of the affected population to cope [7]. Although only a small fraction of hazards result in disasters, the presence of a hazard is generally a necessary condition for a disaster to occur [8].

According to the European Council, Critical Infrastructures (CIs) are defined as an asset, system or part thereof that is essential for the maintenance of vital societal functions, health, safety, economic or social well-being of people, and whose disruption or destruction would have a significant impact as a result of the inability to maintain these functions. Due to the increase in the number of disasters, both natural and otherwise, it is crucial to understand the effects caused by these disasters on CI, in order to prevent, mitigate and quickly recover from the negative impacts they cause. This paper presents the results of the study of these relationships and displays the conceptual map that was produced by researchers from the research group. The map is intended to support a comprehensive understanding of how critical infrastructures are impacted by the disaster. Although the conceptual map presented maps a general view, it will also be considered within the scope of the analysis of the disaster that is mentioned in this work, which occurred in 2022, in a more reduced form. It is expected that it will be useful in preparing governments and society for future disasters, being ready to understand their effects on CI.

There are several types of disasters. A basic classification divides disasters into two categories: natural and non-natural, affecting different types of CIs, or affecting the relationships between them. For example, the interruption of the power supply can affect an entire telecommunications system, leaving areas completely isolated and without communication with other locations.

Critical Infrastructure and disasters do not have a direct relationship. In our view of an indirect relationship, disasters generate some effects, and these effects affect infrastructure both directly and indirectly. Furthermore, when one infrastructure is affected, it can indirectly affect other infrastructures. It is important to represent this indirect relationship to understand why disasters of the same type affect the same critical infrastructure differently. For example, a snowstorm may block roads (effect) which affects critical transportation infrastructure, which indirectly affects food supplies. The same snowstorm may freeze agricultural fields (effect), which causes a reduction in food production which will indirectly affect food supplies. This, however, is not a predetermined relationship; it depends on the specific disasters and their effects.

2.2 Awareness

Awareness, or consciousness, is a fundamental concept that permeates several areas of knowledge, including psychology, neuroscience and philosophy. The definition of awareness encompasses the ability to perceive and understand not only the external environment, but also internal states, such as emotions and thoughts. In psychological terms, consciousness is often described as a subjective experience that allows the individual to interact adaptively with the world. According to [14], consciousness is a multidimensional phenomenon that involves cognitive, emotional and social processes, and is essential for decision-making and learning.

In the field of neuroscience, studies have shown that consciousness is closely linked to patterns of brain activity. Using techniques such as functional magnetic resonance imaging (fMRI), researchers such as [15] have identified specific brain regions associated with states of consciousness, highlighting the importance of integrating information to form a conscious experience. These findings suggest that consciousness is not an isolated characteristic, but rather a dynamic process that emerges from the interaction between different neural systems.

Awareness also plays a fundamental role in fostering empathy and shaping social dynamics. The ability to put oneself in another person's shoes is intrinsically linked to emotional awareness, which allows individuals to understand and respond appropriately to the emotions of others. According to [16], emotional intelligence, which includes awareness of oneself and others, is a vital component for building healthy and effective relationships. A lack of awareness can lead to misunderstandings and interpersonal conflicts, highlighting the need to cultivate this skill in social contexts. In short, awareness is a multidimensional concept with significant implications in various spheres of human life. Promoting awareness, both in personal and social contexts, can lead to positive results in terms of mental health, interpersonal relationships, and learning. Therefore, investing in practices that stimulate awareness is essential for the integral development of the individual and for building a more empathetic and reflective society.

Situational awareness (SA) [18] can be understood as the capacity to perceive and comprehend elements within a given environment, along with the ability to anticipate how these conditions may evolve. This understanding serves as a foundation for more informed and effective decision-making, particularly in dynamic contexts. One widely accepted model conceptualizes SA in three levels. At the initial level, individuals focus on detecting and recognizing key aspects of their surroundings by identifying information that is most relevant to the situation at hand. The second level is comprehension, where this information is processed and its meaning is interpreted. The third level is projection, where the individual anticipates future events based on prior understanding. This model highlights that SA depends on factors such as experience, workload, and human-machine interface. As mentioned in the introduction, situational awareness is also an important aspect of this research, as it enables the final capture of useful data for future emergencies.

2.3 Sensors and Others Technologies

There is research that supports the idea that human sensors can contribute to the context of data analysis, as can be seen in [9] and [10], which can be brought to the scope of disasters involving CIs. Human sensors can be defined as the possibility of replicating the ability to analyze data and provide analysis results using the human intellect and cognitive abilities of each individual. The place where such analyses are shared can often be on social networks, TV channels and other available media, with different formats (text, audio files, video, etc.).

The human influence is undeniable and deeply significant in the technology landscape. While digital algorithms are powerful, their ability to understand and interpret data is incomparable to the human mind. Humans have the ability to add value to the analysis process, especially when dealing with scattered or incomplete information. Furthermore, human decision-making often transcends the capabilities of digital systems. Our intuition, experience, and contextual understanding enable us to act in ways that algorithms simply cannot replicate. In the context of this work, human sensors can provide data from the analysis of disasters involving CIs, in addition to imprinting their personal awareness on everything they analyze, based on their know-how. Looking at past disasters, such as the disaster in Petrópolis and the region, it is possible to collect information generated by human sensors in different media, such as publications from the time, newspaper, and posts from social networks and public agencies.

In [11] it is said that a sensor is an electronic component that has the function of detecting and recording events or changes in the environment around it. These devices, which can take different forms, from simple modules to complex systems, are responsible for capturing physical phenomena, such as light, temperature, movement, among others, and converting this information into measurable digital signals. These digital signals are then forwarded to other electronic components, usually a computer processor, which interprets them and uses them for different purposes. The ability of a sensor to transform physical phenomena into digital data enables their display on screens, their reading by other electronic devices and their processing by means of specific software, opening up a wide range of possibilities in the area of technology. Analyzing the work in [11] it was possible to see a categorization of the different types of sensors that apply to the context of the framework of this work and to the context of the disaster of Petrópolis. They are:

- Level Sensors: Measure the volume or quantity of fluids or substances in systems, both open and closed.
- Temperature Sensors: Measure and monitor temperature in various environments, from household to industrial systems. They use technologies like infrared to detect thermal radiation, crucial for process control, environmental monitoring, and electronics.
- Proximity Sensor: Detect the presence or proximity of objects without physical contact, using methods like light reflection or capacitance detection. Useful in applications requiring remote sensing.
- Pressure and water quality sensors: Pressure sensors monitor system pressure variations, alerting to problems. Water quality sensors detect contamination, ensuring safety in industries and distribution systems.
- Chemical sensors: Detect chemical variations in air or liquids. They are used in urban safety, industrial monitoring, detecting harmful agents, and even space station recycling operations.
- Gas sensors: Monitor air quality by detecting toxic or flammable gases, especially useful in industrial environments and disaster scenarios.
- Smoke sensors: Emit or detect infrared radiation, identifying environmental characteristics and heat leaks, with applications in electronics and chemical detection.
- Image sensors: Convert optical signals to electrical signals for display or storage, used in cameras, night vision, radar, thermal imaging, and sonar systems.
- Motion sensor: Detect and convert movement into electrical signals, useful in detecting human presence in areas where motion is not expected.

Drones have already proven useful for this role, enabling the collection of disaster information. Among all the categories mentioned above and included in the framework, different sensor equipment and technologies can be selected to be used in CIs. In the future, some sensor models will be tested in disasters with CIs, following this research.

3 Work Development

To achieve the objectives presented in this article, the path to developing a solution for capturing, storing, and making data available is being shown based on the insights that command and control teams can generate when acting in the analysis of disaster data involving CIs. To this end, Fig. 1 is considered, which presents a conceptual map with the effects of disasters on critical infrastructures.

On the left side of the map, the different types of disasters are listed, while on the right side, the critical infrastructures affected are shown. In the center, the relationships between disasters and infrastructures are highlighted, represented by the terms "affect"

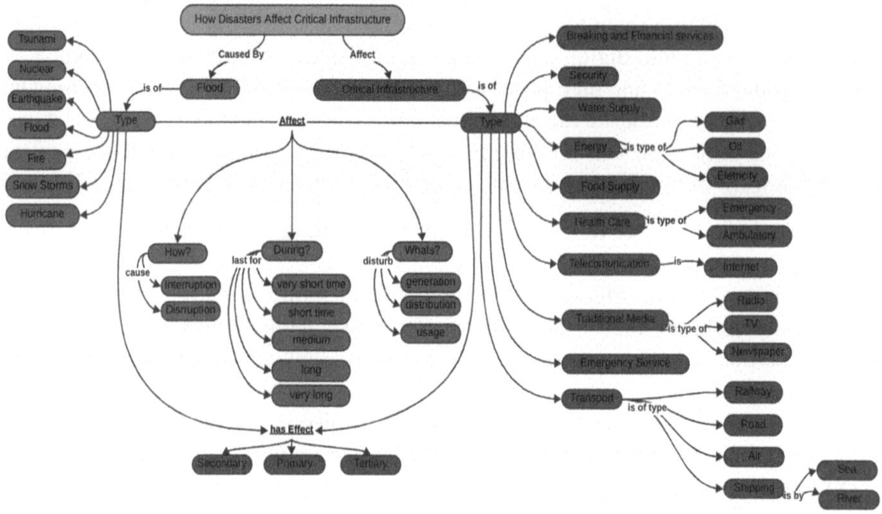

Fig. 1. Conceptual Map of the relationships between disasters and CIs.

and "have effects". For the "affect" relationship, attributes were added that specify what was affected (generation, distribution or consumption), how it was affected (interruption or rupture) and the duration of the impact (from a very short time to a very long time). These attributes can be expanded as needed to represent the affectation relationship. Furthermore, it is important to emphasize that infrastructures are interrelated [12], and therefore, we sought to demonstrate these interrelationships by classifying the effects into three basic categories: direct (primary effect) or indirect (secondary or tertiary). In the latter case, the effect is considered indirect when it is generated by problems in an infrastructure that was directly affected [13]. To enhance the scope of the analysis, the research group intends to incorporate additional interrelationships in future developments.

By comparing the conceptual mapping in Fig. 1 with the data from the disaster that occurred in 2022 in Petrópolis, extracted from various journalistic sources after the tragedy, it was possible to determine that CIs such as water supply, energy, health system, transportation, and telecommunications were individually affected and impacted in their relationships. The conceptual framework proposed and presented in Fig. 2 shows that such CIs are now part of the monitoring flow in question (layer of monitored CIs).

The sensor network layer was created with the objective of synthesizing all the possibilities of using these technologies in disasters involving CIs. To arrive at these types of sensors, the categories raised in the literature in the area were analyzed and their objectives were crossed with the contribution they can make to emergency management involving CIs. All sensors that can be used to collect data from CIs affected by the disaster generate outputs in formats such as photos, videos, textual information, and audio files, which are stored in a database and accessible by the Drone To Rescue software, which was developed in previous research by this same research group. This software already exists and is presented in detail in [1].

With the data in storage, the core business layer comes into action. It is called core business because all the business logic that involves analysis, classification (creating, for example, timelines with events) and elimination of irrelevant data is enhanced by coordination, cooperation and communication [3] between command and control agents, responsible for making decisions in a disaster. Once the team of agents is formed, they can analyze, classify and eliminate data by communicating with each other with the help of awareness elements and processes with actions.

At this point in the research, the focus is on deepening, within the Core Business Layer, the awareness criteria supported. It is important to emphasize that the idea of the framework is to also allow the insertion or replacement of CIs or sensors and their types, for monitoring different disasters, adapting them to different realities.

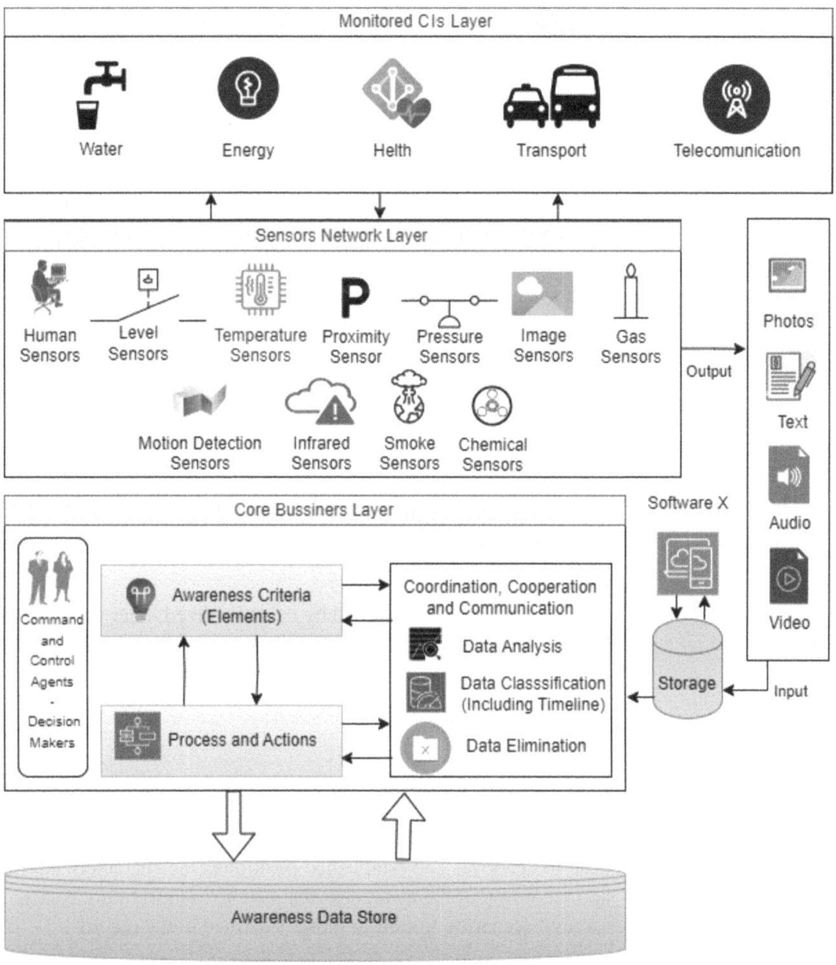

Fig. 2. Created Framework.

The processes and actions are the set of agreements that are established by the command and control team, in order to organize themselves (following, for example, their hierarchical relationships of ranks and responsibilities) to perform the analysis, classification and elimination of data, through their own coordinated organizations, in a collaborative manner and with active and intense communication, combined with the awareness elements contextualized in this work. In this research, it is argued that the result of all this interaction will generate new data that can be recorded and maintained. Therefore, it is necessary that the awareness data on facts, hypotheses, conclusions and inconclusions be structured in a way that allows them to be registered in what we call the Awareness Data Store. Below (Table 1), we present the form that illustrates the proposed structure for recording each of the captured awareness.

Table 1. Awareness Registration

Label	Description
Awareness Identification	ID created to awareness identify obtained
Title	Title that summarizes awareness obtained
Involved parties and their profiles	List containing: name of the party involved in the process and discovery of the awareness + description of the profile party involved. Exemple: Firefighter João Silva. Lieutenant of the fire department of the fourth battalion. Specialty: rope rescue in aerial access locations
Analyzed Scenario	Textual and detailed description of the scenario being analyzed. Contains information about the disaster and all details obtained by network sensors. Example: Flooding of Coronel Veiga Street, due to the overflow of the Quitandinha River
Involved Artifacts	List of stored artifacts and their identifications. Includes videos, photos, reports and all captured material involved in the damage caused to the analyzed area, which are supporting the awareness being reported
Considered Thesis	Report of the thesis generated by those involved, after the execution of all the analysis, coordination, collaboration and coordination processes. Here, the thesis created based on the awareness obtained is recorded
Position Status	() Preliminary () Inconclusive () Conclusive
Firmed position (Final Awareness)	Formalization of the established position after defining the thesis described above. The established position is the characterization and recording of the awareness that can be used in future disasters, through scenarios similar to those described in the record

4 Evaluation and Future Works

Much of the data that can be stored in the Awareness Data Store is being collected in this research and will be included in future publications. It is already understood that awareness can allow for different interpretations of a given disaster event, as shown by this research group in [1]. In the "authority impact" criterion, the question "Who are the individuals or entities present and actively involved in the actions being carried out?" was asked in a questionnaire, conducted with a real team of command and control agents. It was followed by the scenario reproduced below:

- Consider that the role of each professional involved in the analysis of the disaster images is defined, and that each participant is marked with a symbol (icon) that clearly represents their function (e.g., risk analyst, etc.).

And followed by the question:

- Do you think that visualizing the representation of each participant can influence your awareness of the facts they report?

The results showed that having a clear understanding of the profile of the professional giving their opinion on a disaster event is essential for 40% of respondents, but very important for the other 30%. The Awareness Data Store would store data on the awareness of those involved in a given event, as well as information on its impacts as an authority to give such an opinion. In the future, this data could be analyzed taking into account this combination of information for future disasters. The same principle applies to the processes and actions introduced in the framework. What processes were followed and what actions were taken during the analysis of data from the sensor network?

As previously mentioned, the framework introduced in this paper is part of a series of research projects that have been developed by this group in the area of CIs. At this point, our goal in presenting it is to show the general and conceptual vision we are working on towards a solution that allows the storage of awareness data in disasters involving CIs. We hope that future publications will delve deeper into the issues that remain open in this work, providing more details on how the framework can be used in practice. In this sense, one of the steps to be taken is to search for groups of command and control agents so that we can validate our proposal and, mainly, enrich the framework with more details about the elements (criteria) of awareness, as well as the processes and actions that can be taken.

Acknowledgement. Part of the work of Marcos Borges in this article was carried out while he was affiliated with TECNUN/University of Navarra. Marcos Borges was partially supported by FAPERJ under Grant # E-26/202.876/2018.

References

1. França., J., Tavares, J., Dias, A., Borges, M.: Providing situational awareness to emergency responders using drones. https://doi.org/10.1007/978-3-031-34207-3_5 (2023)

2. Frazão, L.M., oKajiMa FuKuMitsu, K.: Gestalt-terapia: fundamentos epistemológicos e influências filosóficas. 2014 v. São Paulo: Summus, **224** (2014)
3. Pimentel, M., Gerosa, M.A., Filippo, D., Raposo, A., Fuks, H., Lucena, C.J.P.: Modelo 3C de colaboração no desenvolvimento de sistemas colaborativos. Anais do III Simposio Brasileiro de Sistemas Colaborativos, Natal - RN, 20 a 22 de Novembro de 2006. ISBN 85–7669–097–7. Porto Alegre: SBC (2006)
4. BOE.es - BOE-A-2011–7630 Ley 8/2011, de 28 de abril, por la que se establecen medidas para la protección de las infraestructuras críticas. (no date). https://www.boe.es/buscar/act.php?id=BOE-A-2011-7630 Accessed 16 Sept 2021
5. UNISDR (no date) 'Building the resilience of nations and communities to disasters'. www.unisdr.org/wcdr Accessed 16 Sept 2021
6. Nyman, M.R.: Organizational Lessons Learned Learned: Natural Hazards Affecting Critical Infrastructure. Karlstad University (2018)
7. Wisner, B., Gaillard, J., Kelman, I.: Framing disaster. Handbook Hazards Disaster Risk Red. (2015). https://doi.org/10.4324/9780203844236.ch3
8. Quarantelli, E.L, Lagadec, P., Boin, A.: 'A Heuristic Approach to Future Disasters and Crises: New, Old, and In-Between Types', in Rodríguez, H., Quarantelli, Enrico L., and Dynes, R. (eds) Handbook of Disaster Research (2007). http://www.unisdr.org Accessed 20 Sept 2021
9. Erickson, T.: Geocentric crowdsourcing and smarter cities: enabling urban intelligence in cities and regions. In: 1st Ubiquitous Crowdsourcing Workshop at UbiComp (2010)
10. Falcão, A.G.R., de Souza Baptista, C., de Menezes, L.C.: Crowd4City: Utilizando Sensores Humanos como fonte de dados em cidades inteligentes. In: SIMPÓSIO Brasileiro De Sistemas De Informação (SBSI), **8** 2012, Porto Alegre: Sociedade Brasileira de Computação, pp. 489–494 (2012)
11. Javaid, M., Haleem, A., Shanay Rab, S.R., Pratap Singh, R., Suman, R.: Sensors for daily life: a review. Sens. Int. (2021)
12. Laugé, A., Hernantes, J., Sarriegi, J.M.: Critical infrastructure dependencies: a holistic, dynamic and quantitative approach. Int. J. Crit. Infrastruct. Prot. **8**, 16–23 (2015)
13. Laugé Eizaguirre, A.: Crisis Management Toolbox: the Relevant Role of Critical Infrastructures and their Dependencies (2014)
14. Dienes, Z., Seth, A.K.: Measuring consciousness. Psychol. Sci. **21**(1), 16–24 (2010)
15. Dehaene, S., Changeux, J.P., Naccache, L., Sackur, J., Sergent, C.: Conscious, preconscious, and unconscious processing: a multi-level analysis. Nat. Rev. Neurosci. **7**(3), 200–210.9 (2006)
16. Goleman, D.: Emotional Intelligence: Why It Can Matter More Than IQ. Bantam Books (1995)
17. Brassett, J., Vaughan-Williams, N.: Security and the performative politics of resilience : critical infrastructure protection and humanitarian emergency preparedness. Secur. Dialogue **46**(1), 32–50 (2015)
18. Endsley, M.R.: Toward a theory of situation awareness in dynamic systems. Hum. Factors **37**(1), 32–64 (1995)

Training

Digitalization of Table-Top Exercises: An Emergency Response Training Showcase

Anna Sumereder[1(✉)], Bernhard Bürger[2], and Robert Woitsch[1]

[1] BOC Group, Vienna, Austria
{anna.sumereder,robert.woitsch}@boc-group.com
[2] Austrian Institute of Technology, Vienna, Austria
bernhard.buerger@ait.ac.at
https://www.boc-group.com/en/, https://www.ait.ac.at/

Abstract. Table-top exercises are widely used to train complex scenarios while representing real world events. However, structured data collection and evaluation are usually limited in such exercises. To foster decision support based on the findings, this paper describes the relevant components advancing conventional towards digitalized table-top exercises by introducing a hybrid model-based approach. The underlying conceptualizations and the physical components to digitalize such exercises are presented in conjunction with a proof-of-concept – the Scenario Scanner. Project MEASURE is introduced to reflect on the model-based digitalization of table-top exercises. It transfers the approach to the emergency management domain, where table-top exercises are a commonly used tool to simulate the response to potential hazards. The Scenario Scanner is configured for an emergency scenario and selected application samples are presented. The discussion presents how results derived from table-top exercises could be linked to functional or full-scale emergency exercises and covers further potential use cases.

Keywords: Modelling · Digitalization · Scenario Scanner · Table-Top Exercise · Emergency

1 Introduction

Table-top exercises (TTX) refer to role-playing activities in which moderators present a scenario and participants respond by playing a role. Usually, the goal of such exercises is to work on realistic critical scenarios in a safe environment [10], contributing to establishing a positive failure culture. Also, TTX offer the advantage of requiring less resources compared to real world exercises. Theodoridis et al. [39] stress the importance of such exercises including cooperation among diverse participants to continue education for national and transnational decision makers, policy experts and specialists. In a broader context, international cooperation and information sharing are relevant for learning - like players from multiple countries participating in a computer security exercise [28].

Published by Springer Nature Switzerland AG 2026
W. Seböck et al. (Eds.): ITDRR 2024, IFIP AICT 752, pp. 49–65, 2026.
https://doi.org/10.1007/978-3-031-97115-0_4

In particular, crisis resilience can be improved through TTX [35,42]. This especially applies to emergency response organizations, such as fire and rescue services, which need to excel in volatile high-risk environments. To be ready when crises occur, conducting exercises supports preparedness before these services are requested to assist. Exercises enable shared mental models [13] by testing emergency responders' capabilities within a fictional and non-critical environment. This promotes learning on two levels [5] - individual and organizational. On an individual level, personnel practice critical skills and understand their role within a response team [15,31] while participating in a fictional scenario. Those skills developed in exercises can be applied during real-life events. On an organizational level, exercises help to identify the capabilities required to perform a similar real-life scenario and to draw conclusions for necessary improvements, such as adapted operating procedures, equipment, training and the like. Besides the learning effects, exercises ensure accountability [4] and give an indication on organizations' current state of preparedness.

As described above, conventional TTX are a key asset for learning - especially for exercising in critical domains. The following key research questions are addressed in this paper: *RQ1* - What added value can be achieved by digital transformation applied on TTX? *RQ2* - What is needed to digitalize TTX?

This paper aims at examining TTX by means of digitalization to enable an immediate and more transparent exercise evaluation. This allows organizations, such as emergency services, to train and prepare in a secure environment. The motivation and the research questions for digitalizing TTX are outlined above. In the next section, a brief overview of related work is given. The third section covers the conceptualization of digitalized TTX and the related methodology. Hereinafter, the proof-of-concept (referred to as Scenario Scanner) is presented. An emergency TTX showcase from project MEASURE [25] follows. Section six discusses findings from the emergency domain showcase, as well as digitalized TTX in a broader context. A conclusion including an outlook closes the paper.

2 Related Work

The related work section covers a selection of literature on TTX, hybrid modelling and digital transformation.

In general, exercises may be conducted in various formats differing in the level of realism and focusing more on theoretical discussion or on practical action. While functional (FX) and full-scale exercises (FSX) simulate fictional emergency events in the physical world, TTX concentrate on discussion-based walkthroughs of a theoretical but realistic scenario [42]. According to [12,44], TTX are utilized for personnel training aiming at coordination, efficient mitigation and incident resolution, as well as supporting the preparedness of organizations and highlighting inefficient processes. Mostly a linear format is followed and there is no systematic data collection about participants' learning. Typically, active and passive roles in a TTX can be differentiated [10]. Participants (or players) are actively discussing, performing roles including responsibilities as well as initiating response actions during the exercise. Moderators (or facilitators) provide situation updates, additional information and active guidance for the participants. Observers are not directly participating but may provide domain expertise or ask questions. Note takers document any exercise activities such as the players' discussions and compliance with plans, policies or procedures.

Addressing sophisticated attacks and accelerating automation introduced by new technologies, digital organizations and societies require advanced learning and training environments. Cyber ranges simulating diverse infrastructures are utilized for security exercises to prepare and train organizations or individuals (e.g. for building awareness) [22,23,34]. Such cyber ranges consider design principles like scalability, flexibility and the utilization of open-source technologies. These result in the following building blocks: a computing platform, infrastructure provisioning, software provisioning and a scenario engine. Following aspects can be considered as highlights in cyber exercises [14]: (a) trust among exercise stakeholders, (b) people and culture, (c) realistic exercises to realize exercise goals, (d) complementary findings from various stakeholders, and (e) coordination between exercises. Specifically relevant attributes [8] for TTX are easy implementation, engagement and motivation, tailoring to target groups (including their objectives, requirements and preferences), flexibility and adaptability to changes, as well as accessibility for both remote and physical stakeholders. Besides, [21] state that acquiring competences such as communication and organizational skills can be supported by information technology. In addition, they stress the relevance of online table-top environments including gamification capabilities, assessment of and agile adaptation to participants' competencies. In cyber security trainings, [9] considers following aspects relevant: suitability, real-life experience, scalability and adaptability, accessibility, training frequency and regular updates, cost efficiency and humans' perspective.

In terms of achieving successful exercises, a suitable assessment consists of monitoring (referring to data collection) and evaluation (referring to data interpretation) [35]. Throughout the evaluation, observations from the exercise are contrasted with pre-defined expectations [2]. Such expectations are reflected in the assessment and commonly formulated as objectives, goals or targets. A common way of monitoring (emergency) exercises is by deploying human observers [7,11]. However, due to human nature, this method is prone to bias and inconsistent data quality. Additionally, data analysis and compilation are laborious and time-consuming. Dependent on the exercise size and complexity, it can take months until an evaluation report is completed and published.

This is where (digital) models promise to provide a way of more swift and reliable exercise evaluation results. Hybrid models [19] bridge the need for human interpretation including intuitive usage and graphical representations as well as the need for digital device interpretation, like formal correctness, completeness or expressiveness. Combined with meta modelling [18] hybrid models allow for applying algorithms like simulations or optimizations in a human- and technology-oriented way. By this, complexity of real-world scenarios can be reduced. Various model types with different formalization and digitalization levels such as strict formalized technology models, semi-formal digitalized models or less formalized haptic table-top models may be differentiated.

Not only digital models, but digital technologies overall hold the potential to boost organizational learning. This is true in emergency management, as it is in other application areas. Speed and depth of learning and teaching [16] can be improved, provided that digital capacities evolve with increasing digitalization levels [40]. For instance, in the context of product-service systems [32], companies are encouraged to accelerate service orientation, which results in new value and growing customer relationships. Wang et al. [45] explore the need of digital technologies in green supply chains and differentiate five technologies, which are the Internet of Things, big data, cloud computing, blockchain, and artificial intelligence (AI). Economic, social and environmental achievements [1] can be reached, for instance by reducing resources or improving operational efficiency.

Summing up the literature findings, TTX seem to be predominantly used in an emergency, security and military context. An objective data collection and evaluation is often not given, as documentation is usually done by human observers and note-takers. By gathering data through technology, it is expected that more comparable and reliable results can be obtained. Easier monitoring over time enables to see whether certain teams or scenarios lead to different results after putting improvement measures into place. Overall, research on hybrid exercise approaches, considering a combination of digital and physical aspects, is limited. In this paper models are expected to bridge humans and technology by serving as a means of documentation and at the same time as a foundation for advanced processing. Based on the literature findings, it is expected that additional benefits (like facilitating the exercise assessment) are achieved by digital transformation applied on conventional TTX (RQ1).

3 Digitalized Table-Top Exercises

The challenge is to introduce digital technologies on top of TTX, while still being flexible enough to incorporate relevant exercise characteristics, being able to adapt to domain-specific purposes, and being comprehensible by devices and human experts. Hence, TTX are interpreted as hybrid models taking into account physical and digital aspects. Physical models created on the table by human exercise participants are the starting point. On top of this, digitalized models, interpreted by machines, serve as a foundation for more advanced operations. Therefore, haptic modelling elements shifted on a table-top are digitally captured and stored in form of concept data. The following subsections cover what is needed to digitalize a TTX (RQ2). This includes the relevant concepts presented in form of a meta model and the underlying methodology.

3.1 Conceptualizing Digitalized Table-Top Exercises

Digitalization environments (Fig. 1) consist of: digital models, digital-physical interactions and physical realizations. In contrast to comprehensive digitalization environments described by [37], digitalized TTX mainly aim at models and interactions defining and realizing a digital shadow. The conceptualization was designed with the meta modelling toolkit CoChaCo (referring to Concept, Characteristic and Connector) [17]. In the following, TTX-specific instantiations for each building block are described in more detail. This work does not cover concepts realizing a digital twin (e.g. actuators or robotic platforms) and omits common aspects (e.g. power supply or extension cables) for a better readability.

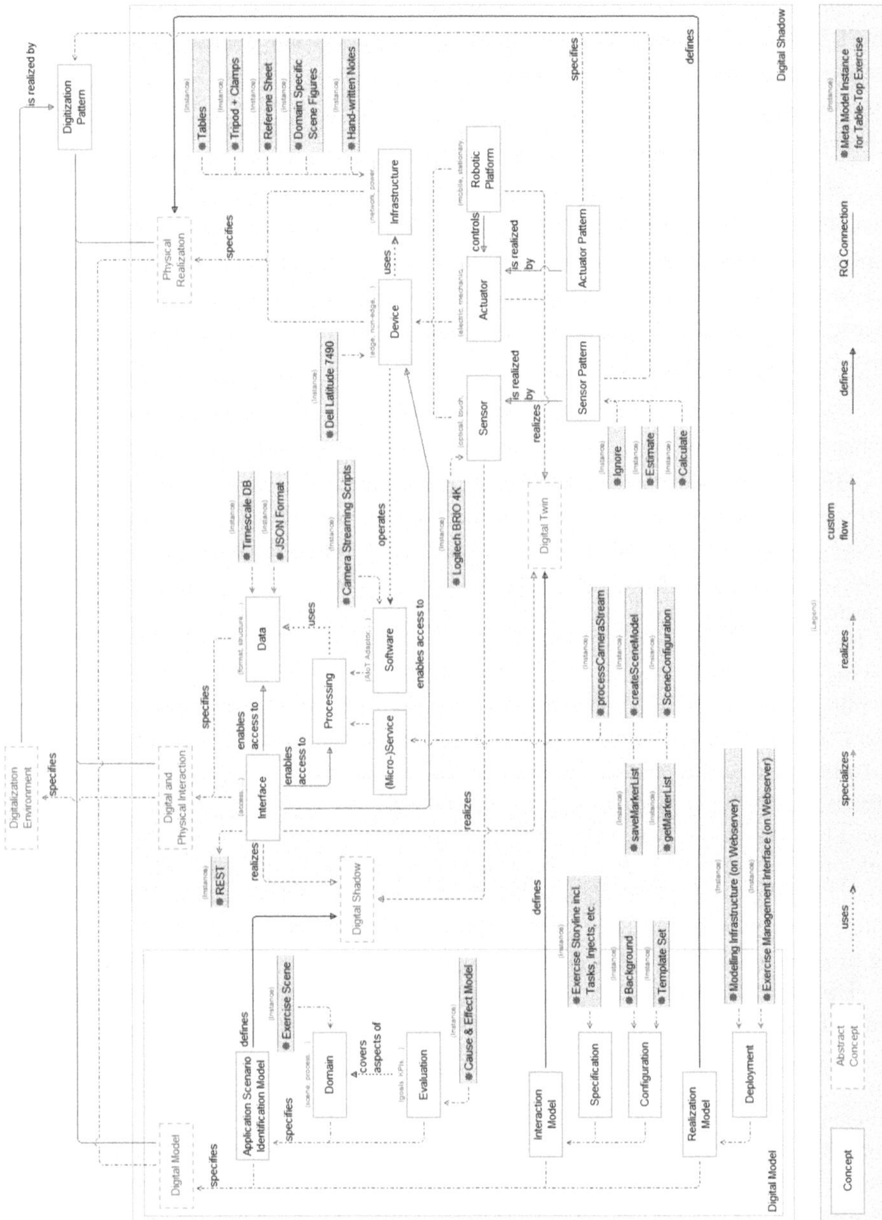

Fig. 1. Conceptualization of digitalization environments (based on [37]), where instances of digitalized table-top exercises are highlighted.

Digital Models (left block Fig. 1) - Digital models are used as a means of documenting and monitoring TTX. Scene models capture the TTX itself. In addition to the physical models on the table, the more formal digital models serve as a foundation for advanced operations, such as simulation, analysis or optimization. Complementary models tracing the participants' actions, manifesting causes and effects are used for monitoring and evaluation. Supplementary to the TTX documentation and monitoring, models are considered to contribute to transparently managing digitalized TTX by serving as an intermediary between digital and physical assets. To specify the interaction between physical and digital building blocks, a description of the exercise, including for instance a storyline, tasks and injects, is needed. Here, configurations with respect to the domain and selected templates are required. Mapping models based on unique IDs describe the relationship between haptic figures and their digital representations. The mapping models function as a foundation for the digitalized TTX configuration. Furthermore, to realize the digitalization of TTX, two main deployment aspects are covered: the deployment of the modelling infrastructure (digitalizing the physical models on the table) and the deployment of the TTX management interface (for technical monitoring, operation and settings). A model-based description of the deployment model encapsulates the benefits of hybrid models being interpretable by humans and machines.

Digital-Physical Interactions (middle block Fig. 1) - The digital-physical interaction ensures the accessibility for both remote and physical stakeholders. REST interfaces are utilized for accessing relevant components and services. The camera streaming scripts are the major software for digitalizing and processing the data, enabling objective TTX monitoring. The data (e.g. position of the haptic figures) is stored in JSON format in a Timescale database. Following services are relevant to handle the digitalization of the physical elements (equipped with markers) on the table and their transformation into digital models: *ProcessCameraStream* processes the video stream from the cameras, converts it to pictures and identifies the markers and their position. *SaveMarkerList* creates a JSON file based on the processed camera stream data and saves it in the Timescale database. *GetMarkerList* provides the marker list entry from the database. *CreateSceneModel* uses the marker list and automatically triggers the model creation in the modelling tool. *SceneConfiguration* allows for additional configuration enabling tailoring to target groups and flexible scenarios (e.g. table figures and model background configuration).

Physical Realizations (right block Fig. 1) - To realize TTX, obviously physical infrastructure is needed, such as tables and a suitable space. In addition to that, digitalized TTX require digitalization specific infrastructure on top. Easy implementation and transportation as well as suitability, adaptability and cost efficiency were chosen as selection criteria for the digitalization hardware. Components are: a tripod and clamps for mounting the monitoring sensors, a reference sheet for framing the table-top playground, paper-based domain-specific figures and handwritten notes. Currently, printed marker tags on the figures refer to unique IDs (easing the physical-digital interaction). The haptic figures associated with a graphical notation come with some domain semantics. A laptop serves as an edge device that is connected to the cameras (corresponding to sensors). The edge device is connected to WIFI and operates the camera scripts.

Digitalization Patterns - The following digitalization patterns - facilitating digital transformation by means of structuring relevant efforts - described by [36] are applied for monitoring TTX. First, the *ignore* pattern refers to focusing on aspects that are relevant for the TTX. The aim is not to produce a completely realistic duplication of the real world, but rather to practice specifically challenging situations. Hence, details irrelevant in the context of the TTX goals are ignored. Second, the *estimate* pattern is applied when scaling the real world down to a TTX, as well as when introducing specific digitalization devices or algorithms, such as image recognition. The *calculate* pattern is utilized for capturing the position of haptic modelling elements on the table-top and their changes over time in a TTX.

3.2 Methodology Supporting Digitalized Table-Top Exercises

Initially, the basic digitalization hardware must be calibrated. This is independent from the methodology and includes the positioning of the cameras while utilizing the calibration sheet shown in Fig. 2a.

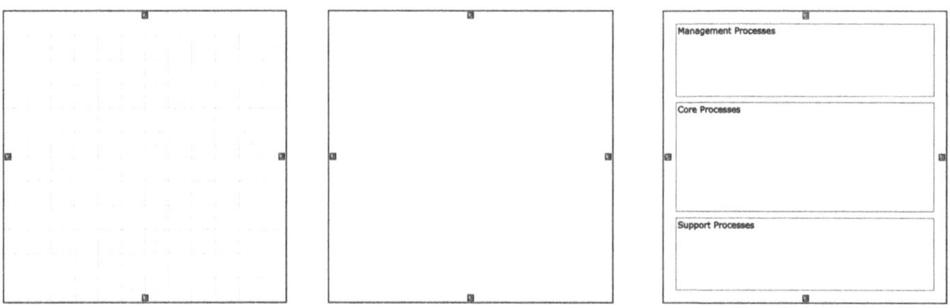

(a) Camera calibration (b) Free modelling (c) BPMN template

Fig. 2. Calibration and pre-configuration of templates for hybrid modelling.

Hereinafter, two different methodologies for hybrid modelling are differentiated: either template-based or free (Fig. 2b). Following a template-based methodology builds upon sets of templates providing guidance. For this, a set of haptic figures and a corresponding table canvas in line with the domain and context of the TTX are pre-configured. Templates can either be aligned with the domain such as emergency management or be domain-agnostic following more generic standards, languages or methods such a business process modelling [38] (Fig. 2c). A limitation of this approach is that upfront preparation is required, which might be time-consuming and challenging, in case the domain stakeholders are not sure on the template scope. Also, the templates must be generic enough so that exercise participants can engage in TTX without lengthy instructions. In contrast, working freely poses additional requirements on the system and the digitalization technology. For instance, new haptic figures must be recognized by the digitalization technology and added to the digital modelling tool instantly.

In general, following the free approach is considered suitable for modelling, like in the context of (digital) design thinking [26] supporting innovation and problem solving utilizing the Scene2Model tool [29]. However, for TTX requiring preparation - including an exercise storyline and related tasks - the template-based approach is considered more appropriate. As a generic structure for establishing templates (tested on production, construction and emergency scenarios), haptic figures for following categories are provided: indicator (e.g. goal, KPI), input (e.g. regulation, context), organizational structure (e.g. personnel, stakeholder), output (e.g. solution, optimization), resource (e.g. material, machine), transformation (e.g. algorithm, digital technology) and flexible note elements.

4 The Scenario Scanner

The Scenario Scanner uses hybrid models to bridge the human and the digital perspective. Here, hybrid modelling - including physical models constituting a step towards gamification - is expected to speed up human-driven understanding, as well as to foster engagement and motivation. An improved management of complex systems, starting from exercises and ranging to drawing conclusions about causal relations in a broader context, is anticipated. The Scenario Scanner - supporting the digitalization of TTX (RQ2) - is a combination of physical and digital infrastructure, complemented with human operations (Fig. 3). In the following subsections, the main building blocks - scanner, models and operator - are outlined. Thereafter, the showcase in Sect. 5 serves as an application case.

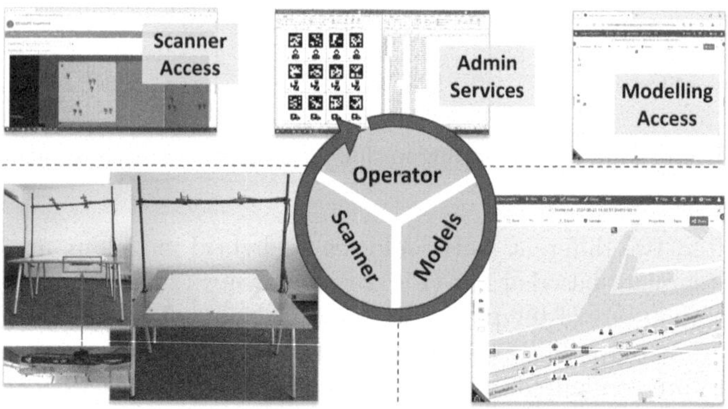

Fig. 3. The Scenario Scanner - proof-of-concept for digitalized table-top exercises.

4.1 Scanner

From an infrastructure perspective the Scenario Scanner consists of following components: a table (or two combined tables) at least 140*140 cm, standing free so that TTX participants can walk around, four cameras from type Logitech BRIO 4K-Webcam with 4096*2160 pixel and 30 fps, a tripod and clamps to mount the cameras approximately 95 cm above the table, a table reference sheet sized 120*120 cm with a grid layout (Fig. 2a) for configuring the camera positioning, and an edge device - Dell Latitude 7490 with Intel Core i7 processor and 16 GB RAM - connected to power below the table operating the cameras. So-called snapshots capture digital scenes of the haptic figures using the infrastructure.

4.2 Models

From a modelling perspective, a process management modelling suite [6] serves as a foundation. In addition to process modelling features, it is configured with an additional model type for digitizing the physical models including a domain-specific set of haptic modelling figures and a suitable model background. The selection of haptic modelling elements can benefit from existing standard operating procedures (SOPs), training materials and the like. The model creation pipeline is partially automated and triggered by the operator.

4.3 Technical Operator

Conventional TTX are handled by a moderator holding appropriate domain expertise. In addition, digitalized TTX need an operator that brings together the physical scanner and the digital models. Thus far, the technical operator covers infrastructure and functionality of digitalized TTX. He/She ensures that the cameras are configured and streaming, as well as that the digital models are created based on the physical figures on the table. Therefore, the operator requires access to the scanner and the modelling tool as well as additional services for administration. First, access to the scanner covers aspects such as the camera selection, the camera preview, the table background configuration and starting/stopping the recording of the haptic figures in defined intervals. Currently one snapshot per minute is set as default. Second, access to the modelling tool is needed to manually adapt and extend the models deeming from the scanner recording. Third, administration services are utilized to deploy the underlying meta model and the configuration of the haptic figures ensuring adaptability.

5 The MEASURE Project Showcase

Exercises are a cornerstone for first responders, to train for potential crisis scenarios, to be prepared for them and to discover optimization potential in their operations. Analysis and evaluation capabilities can highly influence the quality of the exercise learning - respectively the outcome of an exercise [3,35]. Project

MEASURE integrates digital technologies, like sensors and AI, to create transparent and instant evaluation outcomes for emergency response exercises. The goal is to provide insights on the most effective response strategies, leading to the revision of existing SOPs. In advance to applying the technologies in a field exercise, the project makes use of TTX that are supported by a system of performance indicators and objectives. Data, such as time stamps or geo-locations of personnel, captures actions and decisions over the course of an exercise, which can be used to assess the quality of the emergency response. This allows for the identification of areas needing improvement and tracing issues back to their root causes. To accomplish this, the complexity of real-world activities is broken down into digital models. Such models represent a simulated version of the exercise, which then can be compared with real-world data. To digitalize such TTX for handling emergency scenarios, the use case specific configuration of the Scenario Scanner and insights from the MEASURE showcase are described below.

5.1 Table-Top Exercises in Emergency Management

TTX are designed to stimulate discussion, to enable crisis managers and first responders to apply existing plans or procedures, and to test alternative decisions based on potential emergencies - [41] also refers to simulation exercises. A simulation of an emergency scenario is presented to participants, so that they can discuss and play through the scenario to establish appropriate responses. The focus is on coordinating, integrating and merging existing plans, strategies, procedures, roles and responsibilities before, during or after the simulated event. Emphasis is put on communication among all participants within and beyond organizations. Typically, TTX do not make use of simulation going beyond scenario descriptions and pre-formulated injects. MEASURE goes one step further and digitalizes the TTX for advanced processing. The duration of a TTX depends on the target audience, the subject matter to be practiced, and the exercise objectives. In MEASURE, domain experts approximated that an hour is appropriate to discuss emergency plans and procedures for the pre-defined scenario. TTX are guided by a moderator and conducted prior to a FSX as a preparation. In contrast to the technical operator (Sect. 4.3), the role of the domain moderator is quite flexible and can vary depending on the phase of the exercise and the scenario (e.g. alternating between an observational or an instructive role).

To test the Scenario Scanner's potential a road traffic collision scenario was chosen. Traffic accidents are routine tasks for fire and ambulance services. They occur several times a year and their extent can be modified easily by changing the number of vehicles and casualties involved. By altering elements like the type of vehicles or additional hazards, the complexity can be increased or decreased, according to the participants' skills. This allows testing specific features of the Scenario Scanner, for instance by evolving the scenario from a single car with one passenger to a fully loaded bus or a truck with hazardous materials. In line with the highlights of exercises described in the related work, the Scenario Scanner is developed to meet flexibility, adaptability and scalability requirements. During six technology trial runs, the scenario entailed a car that collided with a bus on a motorway leading to 20 casualties. The scanner was used to facilitate an immersive play-like TTX. By taking the role of the first team arriving on the scene, participants from fire and ambulance services were asked to discuss and decide which actions to take in order to provide aid, in line with the SOPs of their organization. In the first phase, this entailed situational reconnaissance and communicating crucial information to other (fictional) approaching response teams and the control room, while considering their own safety. As further resources arrived (through moderator placing paper-based haptic modelling elements on the table), they had to assign tasks to those teams, set operational priorities and align with other services (e.g. police impersonated by the moderator).

5.2 Scenario Scanner Configuration for Emergency Exercises

A use case specific configuration of the Scenario Scanner aiming at emergency exercises is composed of two Scenario Scanners, a targeted modelling table template and a set of domain-specific haptic modelling figures, as well as related emergency specific service configurations. Individual Scenario Scanners are built up for each organization involved in the TTX - in MEASURE, essential users are rescue and fire services staff. During the trial sequences in the project, the Scenario Scanner was tested and improved. A team of three people haptically modelling worked well. As a team of first responders usually consists of three people in Vienna (rescue services) and a crew for a fire engine consists of six people, two Scenario Scanners are used. This allows on the one hand that every organization can focus on their own procedures (if needed also physically distributed) and on the other hand that the physical scanner is not too crowded so that the TTX participants are still able to walk around. As a targeted physical modelling table template, MEASURE experiments with different types of maps such as satellite or street map views (Fig. 4a) corresponding with the accident storyline of the TTX. Reference tags are added at the borders of the table template. This ensures that the positioning of the haptic modelling elements on the table (Fig. 4b) is also correct for the digitalized model (Fig. 4c).

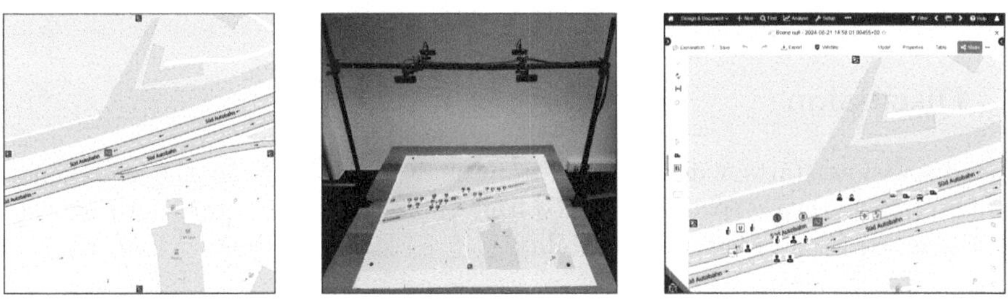

(a) Map data from OpenStreetMap [30] (b) Physical scanner and haptic modelling area (c) Digitalized model of a table-top exercise scene

Fig. 4. Scenario Scanner for digitalized emergency table-top exercises.

In collaboration with domain experts from rescue and fire services, a set of haptic modelling figures was developed and configured (Fig. 5). The figure markers include their IDs and a graphical representation. Both are digitally deposited in the modelling toolkit. As a print out, the same figures are used as haptic modelling elements directly in the TTX. Figures can be categorized in accordance with the methodology presented in Sect. 3.2. For instance, the emergency operations manager (see "EL" sign in Fig. 5b) is part of the organizational structure. The visualizations range from generic icons, over icons specified with domain-specific abbreviations, to tactical symbols from the emergency domain. The table template is not only physically plotted as a background for the table-top (Fig. 4), but also set as an backdrop for the digitalized models. Advanced service configurations allow the collaboration of two or more Scenario Scanners - in MEASURE one for the rescue service (scanner A) and one for the fire service (scanner B). To enable the interaction of the individual organizations A and B, an online view is enabled that visualizes the figures that are not congruent in both scanners. This allows organization A to react to activities conducted by organization B and vice versa. All organizations can be at one location for the TTX. However, due to the scanner collaboration feature, exercises of individual organizations can be coordinated and they can also exercise from remote locations. Supporting a hybrid approach, expert advisors or evaluators can participate remotely.

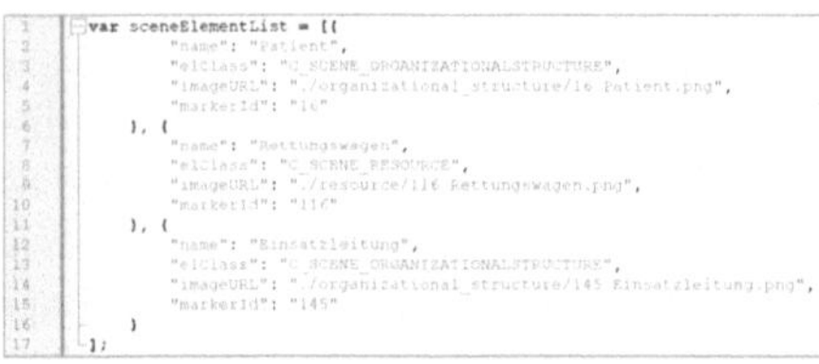

(a) JavaScript code to configure modelling infrastructure to domain-specific elements

(b) Selection of domain-specific haptic modelling elements

Fig. 5. Template configuration using domain-specific modelling elements.

6 Discussion

The discussion starts with insights from digitalized TTX in the emergency domain (see showcase Sect. 5). Derived from those findings, more generic aspects are discussed for a broader applicability.

6.1 Insights from Digitalized Table-Top Exercises in Emergency Management

A series of six iterative test events evolving around similar traffic accident scenarios was conducted with emergency experts to validate the scanner. Debriefing was conducted after each session and participants were asked to fill out a standardized questionnaire (TAM2 [43]) to evaluate the solution. Most participants considered the scanner effective (addressing RQ1) for their training purposes and stated that the interaction with the technology was clear. An application for a broad range of scenarios is yet to be tested. It is worth noting that there are few defined criteria or KPIs regarding the successful management of emergency response scenarios. The exercise participants made their decisions based on the overall mandate of their organization, meaning for instance that casualties had to be treated and transported to a hospital as swiftly as possible. Pre-defined absolute criteria, such as a minimum or maximum time frame were not considered by them. Due to the complexity, dynamics and variety of tasks during crisis situations [20,33], this is not unusual in emergency response organizations. As observed and also stated by [24], time-related criteria are the primary metric for judging performance of ambulance services, rather than patient-outcome for example. Additional complexity is added when considering the perspective of diverse stakeholders. When observing an emergency from the perspective of individual casualties, emergency responders have the difficult position of never responding too fast or providing too much aid. When taking the perspective of responders, only limited resources (e.g. staff, vehicles or material) are available. Allocating more resources than necessary to one distress call can mean not having enough for the next. Even though defining KPIs for emergency responders is a challenge, there is an undeniable benefit of monitoring and transferring the results using digital models. Especially, the documentation process of TTX can be accelerated and the reasonability of proposed KPIs can be confirmed or contradicted. In addition to collecting and analysing data, reality can be evaluated against ideal values - considering both exercises and real emergency events.

6.2 Extended Insights for Digitalized Table-Top Exercises

Going beyond TTX in the emergency domain, it is considered that also stakeholders from various other domains may benefit, like in the European project MODAPTO [27], where TTX have been explored in the context of simulating to-be production scenarios and supporting documentation of industrial production units. Literature shows that TTX are already heavily used in the cybersecurity field. Based on the showcase findings, it is anticipated that TTX promise insights when testing performance and checking the validity of KPIs. This could be spread to diverse domains by applying performance indicators to make sure an organization is on track. In contrast to conventional TTX, the Scenario Scanner and the digitalization facilitate hybrid participation of two or more organizations, from distributed locations as well as remotely (addressing RQ1). Individual organizations can exercise with their own Scenario Scanner, running and maintained by an operator at their preferred location. This poses advanced considerations for conducting digitalized TTX. Here, the Scenario Scanner enables scalable and adaptable scenarios tailored to the TTX participants in a cost-efficient way. Particularly, communication and organizational skills among distributed heterogeneous participants are trained. Related status dashboards, including combined views, are required and may be supported by digital technologies.

7 Conclusion

TTX can be interpreted as models differentiating physical models on the table-top and digital models serving as a foundation for simulation, analysis or optimization. The Scenario Scanner - consisting of scanner, models and operator (compare RQ2) - is used to digitalize TTX for an emergency exercise showcase. The haptic modelling elements shifted on the table-top are digitally documented in form of concept data. This allows for comparison among distributed teams conducting such exercises or different alternatives on how to handle such an exercise. The models showing domain-specific scenes from emergency exercises can further on be linked to processes specifying procedures. For measuring performance related aspects, the scenes can be concretized with targeted KPI models.

A plethora of digital technologies and services like ChatGPT or AI open up a huge potential to extend the hybrid TTX modelling approach. Further experimentation including additional services, such as recognizing hand-written notes, speech recognition during physical TTX, or aggregations based on image recognition will be considered. For instance parts of a domain template (e.g. specific areas symbolizing wood in Fig. 4a) can be recognized on a map and semantically annotated. Placing elements in such selected areas can for instance serve as a performance indicator and may result in better/worse TTX ratings.

Taking a step back, it is planned to evaluate the Scenario Scanner also as an exercise planning tool for FX or FSX. In this case a team of exercise designers may create a digital model of the scenario and discuss the ideal course of the exercise. Data is collected by utilizing sensors (adapted to the exercise type). Depending on the exercise goals, such sensors can range from geo-positioning of staff to voice recordings from radio communication. Prior to conducting a sensorized FSX, the digitalized TTX simulates the real field exercise using the Scenario Scanner. Several insights from the TTX may be included in the real exercise (addressing RQ1). When the exercise in the physical world has been performed, it can be compared with the "ideal" version from the digital model.

Acknowledgments. The project "MEASURE" has received funding within the Austrian security research program KIRAS of the Austrian Federal Ministry of Finance and managed by the Austrian Research Promotion Agency.

References

1. Arenkov, I., Tsenzharik, M., Vetrova, M.: Digital technologies in supply chain management. In: Proceedings of the International Conference on Digital Technologies in Logistics and Infrastructure (ICDTLI 2019). Atlantis Press (2019)
2. Bearman, C., Rainbird, S., Brooks, B., Owen, C., Curnin, S.: A literature review of methods for providing enhanced operational oversight of teams in emergency management enhanced operational oversight of teams in emergency management. Int. J. Emergency Manage. **14**, 254–274 (2018)
3. Beerens, R., Tehler, H.: Scoping the field of disaster exercise evaluation - a literature overview and analysis. Int. J. Disaster Risk Red. **19**, 413–446 (2016)

4. Beerens, R., Tehler, H., Pelzer, B.: How can we make disaster management evaluations more useful? an empirical study of dutch exercise evaluations. Int. J. Disaster Risk Sci. **11**(5), 578–591 (2020)
5. Biddinger, P.D., et al.: On linkages: using exercises to identify systems-level preparedness challenges. Pub. Health Rep. **123**(1), 96–101 (2008)
6. BOC Group: ADONIS - Business Process Modelling. boc-group.com/en/adonis/
7. Borodzicz, E., Van Haperen, K.: Individual and group learning in crisis simulations. J. Contingencies Crisis Manage. **10**(3), 139–147 (2002)
8. Chowdhury, N., Gkioulos, V.: A framework for developing tabletop cybersecurity exercises, pp. 116–133. Springer. Cham (2023)
9. Chowdhury, N., Katsikas, S., Gkioulos, V.: Modeling effective cybersecurity training frameworks: a delphi method-based study. Comput. Secur. **113** (2022)
10. CISA.gov: Cybersecurity tabletop exercise tips. www.cisa.gov/sites/default/files/publications/Cybersecurity-Tabletop-Exercise-Tips_508c.pdf
11. Dillon, B.: Emergency Planning, 2nd edn. Crisis and Disaster Management. Oxford University Press, Oxford (2014)
12. Edzén, S., Sein, M.: Designing theme-based tabletop exercise for identifying and dealing with coordination problems in emergencies. IJEM 12 (2016)
13. Endsley, M.R.: Situation awareness in dynamic human decision-making: theory. In: Gilson, R.D., Garland, D.J., Koonce, J.M. (eds.) Situational Awareness in Complex Systems: Proceedings of a Cahfa Conference. pp. 27–58. Embry-Riddle Aeronautical University Press (1994)
14. Ertan, A., Kuprys, A., Lillemets, P., Nordli, G.M.: Cyber exercises: a vision for nato. a cycon 2021 workshop summary report (2021). https://ccdcoe.org/uploads/2022/07/Cyber-Exercises-A-Vision-for-NATO-Summary-Doc-August-2021.pdf
15. Flin, R.H.: Sitting in the hot seat : leaders and teams for critical incident management. John Wiley & Sons Ltd (1996)
16. ICF Consulting Services Ltd: Literature review on the impact of digital technology on learning and teaching (2015)
17. Karagiannis, D., Burzynski, P., Utz, W., Buchmann, R.A.: A metamodeling approach to support the engineering of modeling method requirements. In: 2019 IEEE 27th International Requirements Engineering Conference (RE). pp. 199–210 (2019)
18. Karagiannis, D., Kühn, H.: Metamodelling Platforms. In: Bauknecht, K., Tjoa, A.M., Quirchmayr, G. (eds.) EC-Web 2002. LNCS, vol. 2455, pp. 182–182. Springer, Heidelberg (2002). https://doi.org/10.1007/3-540-45705-4_19
19. Karagiannis, D., Woitsch, R.: Knowledge engineering in business process management. In: vom Brocke, J., Rosemann, M. (eds.) Handbook on Business Process Management, vol. 2. Springer (2010)
20. Kern, E.M., Hartung, T.: Zielorientiertes risikomanagement bei einsatzorganisationen. In: Kersten, W., Wittmann, J. (eds.) Kompetenz. Interdisziplinarität und Komplexität in der Betriebswirtschaftslehre. Springer Gabler, Wiesbaden (2013)
21. Kvietinskaitė, G., Bukauskas, L., Krinickij, V.: Cyber security table-top exercise gamification with dynamic scenario for qualification assessment. In: Stephanidis, C., Antona, M., Ntoa, S., Salvendy, G. (eds.) HCI International 2022 - Late Breaking Posters, pp. 54–62. Springer Nature Switzerland, Cham (2022)
22. Leitner, M., et al.: Enabling exercises, education and research with a comprehensive cyber range. J. Wirel. Mob. Netw. Ubiquitous Comput. Depend. Appl. 12 (2021)
23. Leitner, M., et al.: Ait cyber range: Flexible cyber security environment for exercises, training and research. In: Proceedings of the 2020 European Interdisciplinary Cybersecurity Conference. EICC '20, Association for Computing Machinery, New York, NY, USA (2021)

24. MacFarlane, C., Benn, C.A.: Evaluation of emergency medical services systems: a classification to assist in determination of indicators. Emerg. Med. J. **20**(2), 188–191 (2003)
25. MEASURE Consortium: MEASURE Project. projekte.ffg.at/projekt/4491912
26. Micheli, P., Wilner, S., Bhatti, S.H., Mura, M., Beverland, M.B.: Doing design thinking: conceptual review, synthesis, and research agenda. J. Prod. Innov. Manag. **36**(2), 124–148 (2019)
27. MODAPTO Consortium: MODAPTO Project. modapto.eu/
28. Moutenot, L., Berman, G., Marques, R.P., Smith, P., Busquim e Silva, R.: Building capacity for computer security assurance activities through international cooperation (2022). psmth.github.io/papers/CN313-127-Akhras-et-al.pdf
29. OMiLAB: Digital Design Thinking using S2M. omilab.org/activities/scene2model/
30. OpenStreetMap Foundation: OpenStreetMap. openstreetmap.org/copyright
31. Paton, D., Jackson, D.: Developing disaster management capability: an assessment centre approach. Disaster Prev. Manag. **11**, 115–122 (2002)
32. Pirola, F., Boucher, X., Wiesner, S., Pezzotta, G.: Digital technologies in product-service systems: a literature review and a research agenda. Comput. Industry **123** (2020)
33. Pruchnicki, S., Dekker, S.: Resilience engineering in prehospital emergency medical services. In: Keebler, J.R., Lazzara, E.H., Misasi, P. (eds.) Human Factors and Ergonomics of Prehospital Emergency Care. CRC Press, Boca Raton, FL (2017)
34. Reuter, L., et al.: Supporting flexible and engaging computer security training courses with the online learners platform and hands-on exercises. IAEA International Conference on Computer Security in the Nuclear World: Security for Safety (2023)
35. Sinclair, H., Doyle, E.E., Johnston, D.M., Paton, D.: Assessing emergency management training and exercises. Disaster Prevent. Manage. Int. J. **21**(4), 507–521 (2012)
36. Sumereder, A., Woitsch, R.: igitization principles for application scenarios towards digital twins of organizations. Eccomas (2022)
37. Sumereder, A., Woitsch, R., Bürger, B.: Requirements derived from digitalization patterns. In: Navigating Unpredictability: Collaborative Networks in Non-linear Worlds. pp. 99–114. IFIP Advances in Information and Communication Technology. Springer (2024)
38. The Object Management Group: Graphical notation for specifying business processes in a business process diagram. omg.org/bpmn/
39. Theodoridis, G., Georgescu, A., Garban, H.N.: Lessons from a didactic table-top exercise during a european training course. Int. J. Cyber Diplomacy 22 (2021). https://ijcd.ici.ro/documents/18/2021_article_7.pdf
40. Timotheou, S., et al.: Impacts of digital technologies on education and factors influencing schools' digital capacity and transformation: a literature review. Educ. Inf. Technol. **28** (2022)
41. UN Office for Disaster Risk Reduction: Design and conduct of simulation exercises - simex: a companion for implementing sendai framework priority 4 on enhancing disaster. Sendai Framework for Disaster Risk Reduction 2015-2030 (2020)
42. US Homeland Security: Homeland Security Exercise and Evaluation Program (HSEEP). US Department of Homeland Security, Washington, D.C. (2020)
43. Venkatesh, V., Davis, F.: A theoretical extension of the technology acceptance model: Four longitudinal field studies. Manage. Sci. **46**, 186–204 (2000)

44. Vykopal, J., Čeleda, P., Švábenský, V., Hofbauer, M., Horák, M.: Research and practice of delivering tabletop exercises. In: Proceedings of the 2024 on Innovation and Technology in Computer Science Education V. 1. p. 220–226. ITiCSE 2024, Association for Computing Machinery, New York, NY, USA (2024)
45. Wang, Y., Yang, Y., Qin, Z., Yang, Y., Li, J.: A literature review on the application of digital technology in achieving green supply chain management. Sustainability **15**(11) (2023). www.mdpi.com/2071-1050/15/11/8564

Modeling the Case of Cyber Espionage for Executive Game Simulations

Jennifer-Marieclaire Sturlese(✉) and Ronald Hochreiter

University of Applied Sciences Wiener Neustadt, Johannes-Gutenberg Str. 2, 2700 Wiener Neustadt, Austria

jmc.sturlese@fhwn.ac.at

Abstract. We model the use-case of cyber espionage for the purpose of game simulations for training executives that lack technical proficiency preparing for the implementation of the NIS2 directive in EU member states. In the first part of the paper, we lay out the common practices of classifying cyber attacks and cyber defense measures suggested by a strong body of literature in the field of cyber security. We formally validate the requirements of a use-case for game simulations and argue for cyber espionage being a purposeful use-case for executive training. In the second part, we explain our two models that demonstrate the functionality, behavior and activity sequence of our proposed executive game simulation for the use-case of cyber espionage. Finally, we discuss avenues for game development and testing.

Keywords: cyber security · cyber espionage · gamification

1 Introduction

The knowledge gap between executives with generic business and economics backgrounds who hold managerial responsibilities and the personnel whose profession is technical expertise is not a novel topic in literature. With digitalization affecting heavily the global service industry and given the upsurge to the technology sector, many tend to actually forget that there is still a major proportion of organizations embedded in any national economy that would most definitely not consider themselves as digital businesses, tech giants or tech start-ups. The EU introducing the NIS2 directive marks a significant advancement in the union's approach to cyber security as new regulations oblige organizations of almost any size and operation field to adhere to strict cyber security practices and being held accountable for if a cyber attack damages the organization by exploiting vulnerabilities due to negligent cyber security practices[1]. The union's prioritization of cyber security posits a new challenge for many executives: While

[1] Directive (EU) 2022/2555 of the European Parliament and the Council, dated 14 December 2022, on measures for a high common level of cyber security across the Union (NIS2 directive) will take full effect on 17 October 2024. For details see: https://www.enisa.europa.eu/topics/cybersecurity-policy/nis-directive-new.

Published by Springer Nature Switzerland AG 2026
W. Seböck et al. (Eds.): ITDRR 2024, IFIP AICT 752, pp. 66–81, 2026.
https://doi.org/10.1007/978-3-031-97115-0_5

NIS2 applies to all sectors regardless of the degree of the executive technical affluence, all organizations need to apply the implications for compliance, risk management, and operational continuity [1]. Essentially, the implementation of the NIS2 directive is particularly challenging for executives who do not possess a technical background. This is the core why this paper becomes relevant: The knowledge gap of non-technical executives can hinder proper implementation and lead to vulnerabilities for which they will be held accountable for. Therefore, it is essential to provide simulation training for executives on persisting threats to cyber security. Here, the focus must lie on the awareness of the scope, mechanisms of attack and defense, and overall impact severity. Ultimately, we propose a game simulation dedicated to executives with a non-technical background to help making informed decisions. This approach is, to our knowledge, novel to the extent that existing game simulations in the field of cyber security continue to address domain experts and students in technological degrees. We aim to contribute to narrowing the knowledge gap on cyber security of executives with business and economics expertise lacking technical proficiency.

Cyber security is a broad field with many sub-domains, making it impossible to capture them all in a single game simulation. Henceforth, we need to concentrate on one particular scenario that must serve to great extent our aim of facilitating knowledge on cyber attack and defense mechanisms for non-domain experts, such as executives without technical proficiency. To select one use-case out of many is not an easy task to achieve. This is why we ask ourselves the following research question: *To which extent is cyber espionage a suitable use-case for modeling an executive game simulation?* In attempting to answer this, we formally validate the selected use-case by making use of the SMART acronym, a tool to formulate abstract strategies into actionable goals [2]. This seems appropriate for two main reasons. First, it is a management tool commonly applied in the (public) management domain and for two, it is generally useful for concretizing abstract phenomena, such as cyber security ought to be, especially for non-technical executives [3]. After arguing for cyber espionage being a purpose-fit use-case for an executive game simulation, what follows are two UML models that capture for (a) the use-case of a game simulation and (b) the sequence of activities in which the simulation is followed through. Lastly, we discuss the avenues of implementing the proposed models in concrete game development and testing.

2 Gamification, Cyber Attacks and Cyber Security

In the past decade, there has been recognized an upsurge in the topic of *gamification* for cyber security, as the nature of this topic appears to be quite suitable for employing game simulations [4–7]. In like manner, there has been a growing interest in employing a game-theoretic approaches to address both cyber and physical security problems [8,9]. Typically, the attacker's goal revolves around inflicting maximum harm to cyberspace, while the defender endeavors to mitigate the impact. This inherent conflict between the objectives of the attacker and defender underscores the relevance of employing a game-theoretic perspective to analyze issues concerning cyber security [8]. In particular, the utilization of the Stackelberg game model has gained recently notable attention [10]. Stackelberg security game (SSG) models have been implemented in various high-stakes security contexts as these models predominantly target systems where a single defender operates, despite being integrated into a more intricate system involving multiple stakeholders [11]. Within the class of SSG, there exists a scenario where the leader is required to commit to a strategy observable by the follower, prior to the latter choosing its own strategy [12]. Game theory offers mathematical models for examining strategic decision-making among multiple participants, where players compete for limited and shared resources [13]. Essentially, it enables the modeling of conflict situations and the prediction of participant behavior [13].

The rapid progression of ICT has been met with an alarming rate of cyber attacks conducted by malevolent hackers exploiting critical vulnerabilities. Many organizations have aimed to develop timely, relevant, and actionable cyber threat knowledge about emerging threats and key threat actors to enable effective cyber security decisions [14]. Cyber Threat Intelligence (CTI) is defined by Serketzis (2019) [15] as "analysis of information on the intention, opportunity and capacity of malicious actors, concerning potential or current attacks which threaten an organization". As a result, CTI has the potential to deliver actionable knowledge, facilitating the development of a more robust cyber defense strategy against both present and upcoming threats through early detection and collaborative sharing of CTI data [16]. Large amounts of data present in the field of cyber security consist of textual format including data from internal network devices such as databases, workstations, routers, switches, gateways, et cetera [14].

Additionally, emerging sources of valuable data include various hacker community platforms, e.g. hacker forums. Moreover, open source Intelligence (OSINT) sources also offer substantial information, which can greatly assist organizations in crafting comprehensive and integrated cyber defenses [14]. OSINT is an interesting subject of research as it is typically the legal form of information sharing, illustrating the opposite of cyber espionage, which is illegal information attainment [17]. Common approaches to building CTI involve natural language processing (NLP) and text mining [14]. Such methodologies hold substantial promise in traditional CTI analytics, encompassing various threats like malware analysis, phishing detection (such as identifying fake emails and websites), anomaly detection, and more [14,18]. CTI aids defenders in pinpointing vulnerabilities, comprehending malware behavior, and contextualizing attack patterns [15,19] with a range of countermeasures in a cyber security sense including semantic matching, coreference resolution, distant supervision, tagging, parsing, entity resolution, feature selection/reduction, ontology development, among others [14]. Particular attention is dedicated to the last mentioned, as computer science has coined Ontology, originating from philosophy, as a method for knowledge sharing, offering syntactic, semantic, and conceptual perspectives on information [20]. According to Noy (2001), an ontology creates a shared vocabulary for researchers requiring information exchange within a specific domain. This encompasses machine-interpretable definitions of fundamental concepts within the domain, along with the relationships among them [21]. Merah and Kenaza (2021) propose a domain ontology to monitor cyber risk, drawing upon internal and external data sources. They followed the Ontology 101 principles [21] and used the open-source Protégé (Stanford University 22). This ontology is implemented using OWL, and its effectiveness is demonstrated through an application within a cyber risk monitoring framework and SWRL to define reasoning rules. This application gives an overview of cyber risks reported by analyzers given by CTI sources to get new knowledge, that can contribute to the cyber security decision-making process [16].

The ATT&CK ICS[2] framework has a comprehensive coverage of contemporary global cyber threats [22]. The ATT&CK framework is a renowned source of such intelligence, offering a taxonomy and detailed information on adversary tactics and techniques derived from real-world observations [19] and therefore encompasses 300 attack tactics, systematically organized in a knowledge base and categorized by threat actors' processes from initial access to impact, in chronological order. This framework addresses cyber attacks targeting both information technology networks and operational technology networks, making it highly suitable for use by facilities' network personnel. ATT&CK supports various security applications from both adversary and defender perspectives, including adversary emulation, red teaming, defensive gap assessment, and the identification and modeling of adversary behavior [23].

By contrast, the National Institute of Standards and Technology (NIST) has developed a framework of cyber security measures in fighting cyber threats [24] widely applied in the cyber security research community (see [25–29]). For the present article, we focus on the *framework core* [24, p. 7] where the essential activities of the cyber security framework are mentioned: Identify, protect, detect, respond, recover.

3 Modeling Cyber Espionage as SMART Cyber Attack

Selecting a proper cyber attack as a use-case for executive game simulations necessitates meeting requirements of a purpose-fit use-case. Therefore, we formally validate *Cyber Espionage* by employing the SMART acronym, a common practice in management, thus highly effective when selecting a use-case targeted for a managerial executive audience.

3.1 Use-Case Requirements

The user group that will engage with a game simulation in the scenario of cyber espionage will be of public executive nature. This entails non-exhaustively police officials with managing purposes, executives in public organizations, such as

[2] https://attack.mitre.org/matrices/ics/.

public administration and public universities with and without technical background. Essentially, a public management perspective must therefore be integrated into selected and operating with a suitable use-case of a smart cyber attack scenario. For the requirements listed above, we found the multi-faceted, thus *wicked* problem of cyber espionage to be a suitable use-case as a smart cyber attack for our executive game simulation. The reasoning is as follows: Cyber espionage is a sub terrain of cyber security, involving different kinds of technical operations as well as social manipulations to work. It is relevant for the industry as well as for national protection [30,31].

Committing to one clear use-case when developing a game simulation requires thorough analysis of potential use-cases along with the spectrum that the use-case is embedded in. Therefore, we employed the acronym SMART [2] to narrow down potential use-case scenarios in the domain of cyber security for national defense. In our case, this means defining a use-case that is specific, measurable, attractive[3], realistic, and timely [2,32] (Table 1).

Table 1. Cyber Espionage as SMART Use-Case for Cyber Attacks

Specific	Cyber Espionage: EaaS targeting National Security
Measurable	Costs of Information Leak EaaS transaction fees
Attractive	High stakes, high risk Wicked Problem
Realistic	SolarWinds, Anthem hack
Timely	National Security Paradigm of 21st century

Ad Specific. Under the umbrella term of cyber espionage fall certain operation technology attacks. The ATT&CK Matrix gives an overview of techniques used to attack system vulnerabilities yet does not mention specifically cyber espionage. Yet several technical operations can be used for cyber espionage reasons. These include (non-exhaustively): identity theft, malware infection, spear phishing [18], insider threat [33,34], ransomware attacks. The internet has given rise to *Espionage as a Service* (EaaS), now a major threat [35,36]. Cyber criminals have come to the realization that obtaining sensitive information can be vastly profitable, as data can be sold anonymously online [35,36]. EaaS providers range from low-level hackers to organized criminal gangs that infiltrate both corporate and governmental websites through plugins, using advanced techniques targeting major industries and entire nations [35].

[3] in line with Locke (1981) *achievable* has been replaced with *attractive* for improved context-fit.

Ad Measurable. In 2012, the director of MI5 disclosed an incident where a UK company experienced an £800 million loss due to a cyber attack sponsored by a state, resulting in intellectual property losses and disadvantages in contract negotiations [17]. According to the US Intellectual Property Commission (2017), trade secret theft is estimated to cost 13% of GDP, translating to a financial impact of between $180 billion and $540 billion on the $18 trillion U.S. economy [17]. In the UK, estimates indicate that out of £27 billion lost to cyber crime, £7.6 billion is attributed to industrial espionage, including £2 billion in financial services, £1.2 billion in aerospace and defense, and £1.6 billion in mining (Cabinet Office/Detica 2011) [17].

Ad Attractive. Executive game simulations on cyber security build upon the ability of the decision-maker to picture the persistent cyber attack in accurate terms. We chose cyber espionage as a smart cyber attack because espionage itself is a topic that both decision-makers with and without technical expertise can grasp sufficiently and is relevant in both the industry and national concerns [31,37]. Cyber espionage can be regarded as a wicked problem due to its multifaceted nature, presenting numerous challenges at once [38,39]. Unlike conventional problems with clear boundaries and known solutions, cyber espionage involves multiple layers of technological superlative, diplomatic relations, international affairs, legal ambiguities, and evolving tactics employed by adversaries [17,40,41]. Its impact spans across national security, economic stability, intellectual property rights, and individual privacy, posing dilemmas that are interconnected and difficult to isolate [17,31,39–41].

Ad Realistic. The SolarWinds cyber espionage attack, attributed to a threat actor group known as CozyBear and discovered in late 2020, involved compromising SolarWinds' Orion software updates with a backdoor, allowing threat actors to access numerous organizations worldwide, including government agencies and major corporations [42–46]. This supply chain attack exploited trusted software updates to infiltrate networks and conduct espionage, underscoring vulnerabilities in software supply chains and the sophisticated nature of modern cyber espionage tactics [42–46]. The incident highlighted the importance of supply chain security and raised concerns about the broader implications for global cyber security [42–46]. Another instance is the Anthem hack, attributed to a threat actor group known as Deep Panda, occurred in 2014 and was a significant cyber espionage incident targeting Anthem Inc., one of the largest health insurance companies in the United States [47]. The attackers gained unauthorized access to Anthem's computer network, compromising sensitive personal information of approximately 78.8 million individuals, including names, social security numbers, dates of birth, and other sensitive data [48,49]. The breach was believed to be aimed at gathering sensitive data rather than financial gain, demonstrating the vulnerability of personal data and the potential impact on affected individuals [48,49].

Ad Timely. Espionage, historically a global criminal act against national security, has evolved significantly with technological advancements and the rise of terrorism and involved countermeasures [50]. Contemporary technology has expanded the tactics designated to espionage, making it harder to detect and defend compared to conventional espionage [50]. Recently, the handling of cyber espionage has sparked numerous international disputes [50–52]. In particular, the upsurge of information technology accessibility has democratized espionage, altering its nature [50,52,53]. This democratic accessibility, combined with the anonymity provided by the internet, the identification and prosecution of cyber spies becomes more and more difficult [52,54]. Unlike conventional espionage, cyber espionage presents unique challenges to the international legal system due to its distinct characteristics [52]. The current state of international law is ill-equipped to handle these new problems, urging for an updated framework that includes a clear definition of digital sovereignty and holds states accountable for cyber espionage [54] for which the Tallinn Manual has been a cornerstone towards this direction [55]. Essentially, it seems fair to say that cyber espionage is the new national security paradigm of the 21st century [50].

3.2 Use-Case Modeling Using UML

In the following we display and describe the two models we created for modeling our validated use-case of cyber espionage for our game simulation aimed at executive decision-makers. For this, we made use of the UML modeling notation to model two diagrams, a UML use-case diagram and a UML activity diagram [56,57]. In both of the diagrams (see Fig. 1 and Fig. 2) there are two main actors. The actor type `User` and `SpyBot`. While the former represents the human, in our case, an executive decision-maker, the latter is a system-internal actor, in our case, an enemy character controlled by the system. The goal of the former is to secure and defend his or her organization that is being under cyber attack by the latter. Thus, the goal of the adversary is to find vulnerabilities in the user's defend tactics to espionage on them. See table 2 for an overview.

Table 2. Actor Types

	Defense	Attack
Actor	User	SpyBot
Description	Executive decision-maker human	Enemy character controlled by the system
Main Goal	Defense	Espionage attack

The classifier represents the decision support system (DSS) in which the game simulation is being executed. It is depicted as a rectangle with its name in the top left corner. There are two sub-systems (illustrated by the `sub-system` name in the top right corner) which is for one the graphical user interface (GUI) in which the actor 'user' can actively select actions (i.e. use-cases) and for two the

EXE environment, where the SpyBot algorithms take place and is isolated from the GUI. Actors of type 'user' are located outside the classifier boundary, while two subsystems are located within the classifier [58,59]. The software agent (in our case, the SpyBot), being part of the system under consideration, is placed within the system boundary [58,59]. See table 3 for a summary.

Table 3. System Boundaries

Classifier	DSS	Decision Support System
Subsystem 1	GUI	Graphical User Interface
Subsystem 2	EXE	Executable Environment of SpyBot

A use-case depicts system functionality or behavior in traditional UML use-case diagrams. Our approach encompasses diverse game-simulation related behaviors, such as loading the attack scene (illustrated by the `LoadScene` use case) to start the simulation with the SpyBot along with system functionalities, such as attacks being displayed at a dashboard (illustrated by the `DisplayDashboard` use case). While the latter mentioned is a static function that does not necessarily trigger behavior of the SpyBot located in the sub-system EXE, the former behavioral use-case triggers the activation of the software agent Spybot and forces to start which is demonstrated with an include-relation. Once the simulation has started (function `RunScript` loads all necessary items into the simulation), the user can choose to take several actions. These are grouped within the use- case `SelectDefense` which is an extension point. Hence, the user can opt between five major categories of defense tactics which are taken from the NIST Cybersecurity Framework [24, p. 7]: *Identify, Protect, Detect, Respond, and Recover* [28]. For exemplary reasons, in our UML use-case model we visualized the scenario of the user selecting `Protect`. In detail, this selection is made as a first defense measure, before an actual attack by the SpyBot has been initialized. Hence, it is a precautionary action. Here, the user selects the use-case `activate spam filter`. On the adversary side, the SpyBot has the extension point `SelectEspionageAttack` with a range of malevolent tactics aimed at harming the defendant. Here, the five major categories of attack patterns are taken from the ATT&CK Matrix discussed in Sect. 2. In our use-case, there are: Credential Access, Lateral Movement, Collection, Command-and-Control, and Exfiltration. For exemplary reasons, in Fig. 1 the SpyBot chooses to launch a spear phishing attack, which falls under the category of credential access, and thus the use-case is called `send phishing email` with an infected attachment. Ultimately, the defendant is protected against this phishing attack because of the prior activated spam filter that now detects the incoming malevolent email with infected attachment and signals an intrusion attempt and will be displayed at the GUI Dashboard which can be viewed if the use-case `VisitDashboard` is once more taken. Table 4 gives an overview of all use-cases, their functionality or behavior. Figure 1 shows the UML use-case diagram.

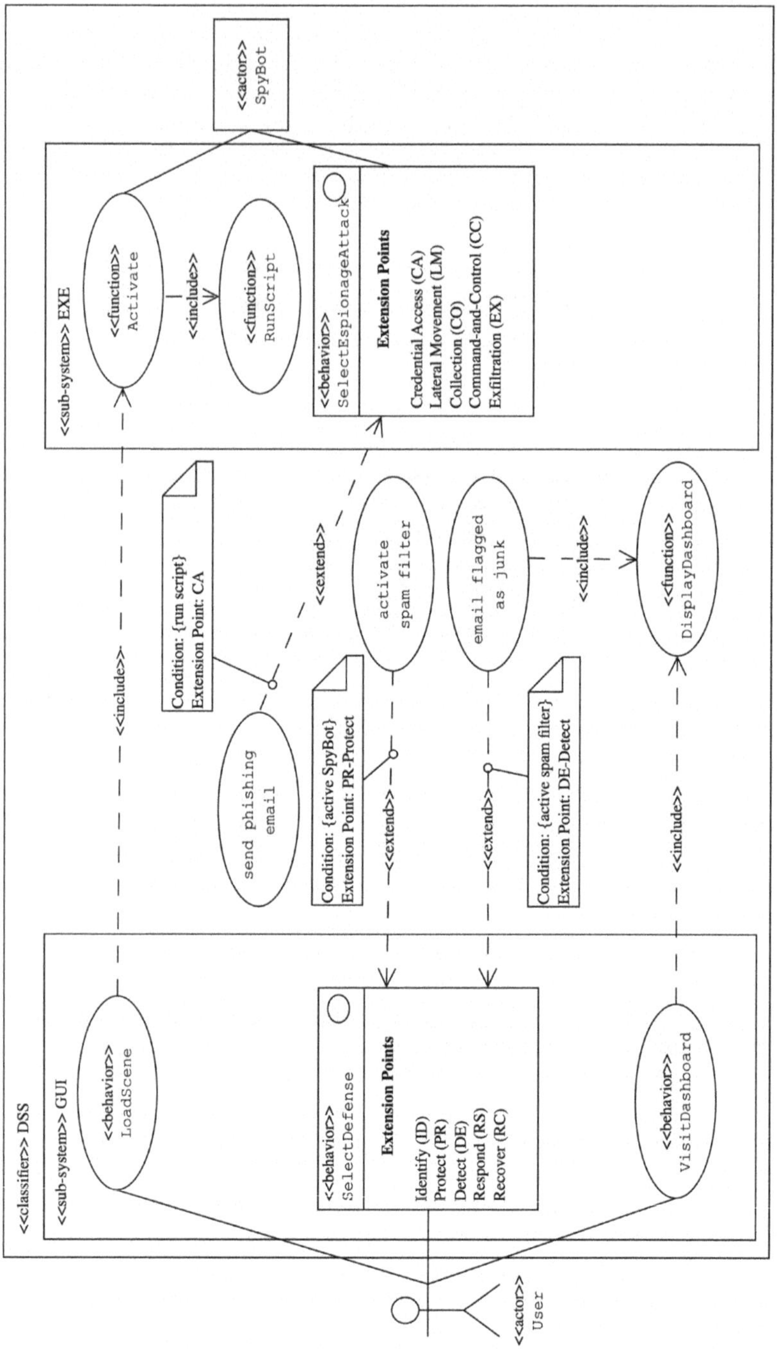

Fig. 1. UML Use-Case Model

Table 4. Use-Cases

No.	Use-Case	Utility	Detail	Relation
[1]	`LoadScene`	Behavior	User initializes simulation	include [2]
[2]	`Activate`	Function	Spybot gets triggered to init	include [1, 3]
[3]	`RunScript`	Function	Loading the simulation's script	include [2]
[4]	`SelectDefense`	Behavior	Exension Points	extend to [5, 9]
[5]	`SelectDefense.Protect`	Behavior	User activates spam filter	extend of [4]
[6]	`SelectEspionageAttack`	Behavior	Exension Points	extend to [7]
[7]	`SelectEspionageAttack.CredentialAccess`	Behavior	SpyBot sends phishing email	extend of [5]
[8]	`SelectDefense.Detect`	Behavior	Email flagged as junk	extend of [4]
[9]	`DisplayDashboard`	Function	Dashboard logs detected junk mail	include [8, 10]
[10]	`VisitDashboard`	Behavior	User views dashboard	include [9]

Ultimately, the UML use-case diagram highlights the possible options of actors to interact with a system [56–58]. To demonstrate the sequential process of the use-case actions, a UML activity diagram fits better the purpose [56,57]. This is why, we modeled the sequence of the simulated espionage attack, placing pronounced emphasis on the order of executable steps. Figure 2 shows the UML activity diagram of the same use-case that we modeled in Fig. 1 yet with a differentiated focus. This model shows that there are two spheres within the process of that specific use-case and highlights that the starting point is initialized by the user (see Table 2 for details). While the simulation is started by the trigger of the user's behavior of `LoadScene`, see Table 4 for details, the activity of `RunsScript` is a function follows after initializing the Spybot. Now, the user may begin to take precautionary measures to defend himself or herself before a sudden attack occurs. The user can choose between five categories (see NIST framework for reference), for exemplary reasons, in the UML activity diagram in Fig. 2 the scenario of the phishing attack is visualized in depth. The first round is completed when the espionage attack has been mitigated successfully. The activity diagram highlights the sequence of the actions to happen in order.

4 Game Development and Testing

The diagrams provided demonstrate the models of potential game simulation for an executive audience. What is of particular interest now is how this would be implemented into the actual game development. Following the lifecycle approach to game development by Babu and Maruthi (2013) [60], after having conceptualized the model, the coding with an game engine would follow. Here, we are keen to use *Godot*[4] which is an open source game engine (MIT licensed), popular for simple 2D game simulations. The game engine employs its own programming

[4] https://godotengine.org.

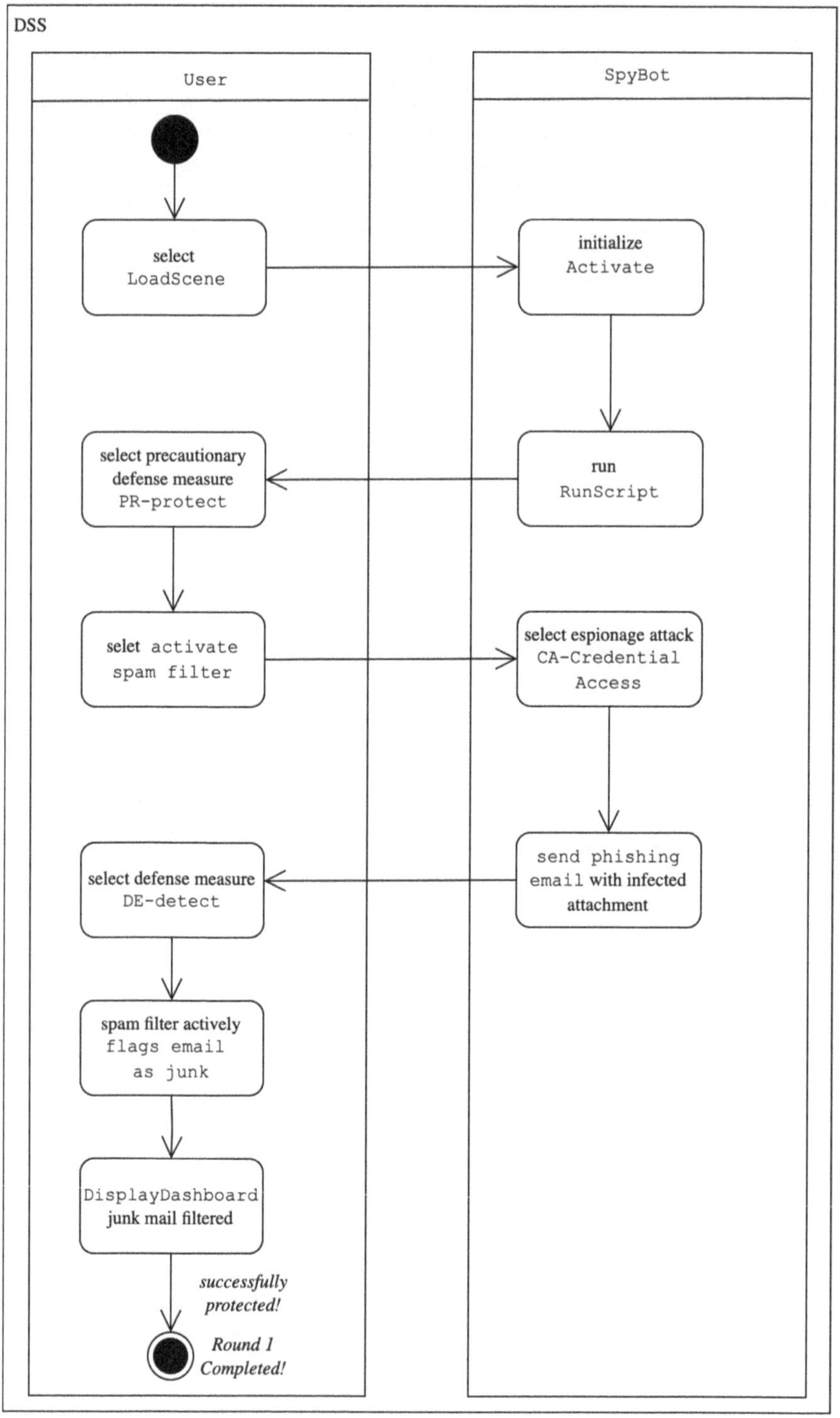

Fig. 2. UML Activity Model

language, *GD Script*, that is similar to Python (see footnote 4 for details). Our reasoning of opting for this game engine follows the subsequent logic: Our game simulation for an executive audience requires a straight-forward 2D interface, putting the decisions of the executive player at center stage. Regarding operationality, it is henceforth equally important to create a game simulation that can run on any desktop platform and is deployed to web.

After having developed a low-fidelity mock-up with Godot, in line with the lifecycle of game development, a group ranging between 5-10 persons stemming from the target user audience will be invited to test the prototype under experimental settings. In contrast to testing with human subjects stands automated game testing as demonstrated by Ariyurek, Betin-Can, and Surer in their works of 2019 and 2020 [61,62]. Automated game testing would eventually be more effective in identifying technical bugs, yet the critical human, more precisely, executive non-technical viewpoint, would be missed out on. Therefore, depending on the resources available for testing, whether to include automated game testing or not may be a decision to take later on in the development process. At this stage, further conclusions will be drawn to improve and debug the game model.

Our endeavour of creating a prototype for executive game simulations are particular relevant in light of the substantial lack both open source and commercial training solutions for executives without strong technical proficiency. Henceforth, the results of our conceptual models aim to serve as an accessible instrument for bridging this gap. Ultimately, the prototype aims to simulate realistic cyber espionage attack scenarios in a controlled environment, allowing participants to experience the pressures of decision-making in the situation of persisting cyber threats, which conventional training cannot replicate. Our model is specifically designed for executives, translating technical cyber security concepts into managerial decisions without the need for technical expertise, making it essential for strategic leadership with regards to the approaching NIS2 implementation.

5 Conclusion

In the present article we asked ourselves the question whether cyber espionage posits a suitable use-case for modeling an executive game simulation. With theoretical backgrounds of gamification, we know that learning is facilitated through game approaches. Moreover, the subject of cyber security is by nature bound to be very fitting to model into game simulations, as there is an existing large body of literature dealing with game-theoretic approaches to cyber security. In general, cyber attacks have been categorized in the MITRE ATT&CK Matrix and hold strong presence in literature dealing with cyber threat intelligence altogether. Correspondingly, the NIST cybersecurity framework fortifies five high-level actions to take when being confronted with cyber attacks. Ultimately, we have implemented these two frameworks into our game simulation that is aimed at enabling understanding the cyber attack and defense interplay specifically for executive decision-makers. For this, we formally validated the use-case of cyber espionage and argued following the SMART acronym, a commonly applied management tool. We then modeled two UML diagrams, a use-case diagram for demonstrating the functionalities of our game simulation and a activity diagram that highlights the sequence of actions. While our examples are straight-forward and intuitive to understand, we urged to outlay the attack and defense mechanisms. With these results of a conceptual model of an executive game simulation on cyber espionage, what naturally would follow is the development of a low-fidelity prototype using an open source game engine and then to test with humans and eventually making use of automated game testing algorithms.

References

1. Schmitz-Berndt, S.: Defining the reporting threshold for a cybersecurity incident under the nis directive and the nis 2 directive. J. Cybersecur. **9**(1), tyad009 (2023)
2. Doran, G.T.: There's a smart way to write managements's goals and objectives. Manage. Rev.**70**(11) (1981)
3. Burrell, D.N., Aridi, A.S., Nobles, C.: The critical need for formal leadership development programs for cybersecurity and information technology professionals. In: International Conference on Cyber Warfare and Security, pp. 82–91. Academic Conferences International Limited (2018)
4. Malone, M., Wang, Y., James, K., Anderegg, M., Werner, J., Monrose, F.: To gamify or not? on leaderboard effects, student engagement and learning outcomes in a cybersecurity intervention. In: Proceedings of the 52nd ACM Technical Symposium on Computer Science Education, pp. 1135–1141 (2021)
5. Ashley, T.D., Kwon, R., Gourisetti, S.N.G., Katsis, C., Bonebrake, C.A., Boyd, P.A.: Gamification of cybersecurity for workforce development in critical infrastructure. IEEE Access **10**, 112487–112501 (2022)
6. Jelo, M., Helebrandt, P.: Gamification of cyber ranges in cybersecurity education. In: 2022 20th International Conference on Emerging eLearning Technologies and Applications (ICETA), pp. 280–285. IEEE (2022)
7. van Steen, T., Deeleman, J.: Successful gamification of cybersecurity training. Cyberpsychol. Behav. Soc. Netw. **24**(9), 593–598 (2021)
8. Do, C.T., et al.: Game theory for cyber security and privacy. ACM Comput. Surv. (CSUR) **50**(2), 1–37 (2017)
9. Liang, X., Xiao, Y.: Game theory for network security. IEEE Commun. Surv. Tutor. **15**(1), 472–486 (2012)
10. Korzhyk, D., Yin, Z., Kiekintveld, C., Conitzer, V., Tambe, M.: Stackelberg vs. nash in security games: an extended investigation of interchangeability, equivalence, and uniqueness. J. Artif. Intell. Res. **41**, 297–327 (2011)
11. Lou, J., Smith, A.M., Yevgeniy, V.: Multidefender security games. IEEE Intell. Syst. **32**(1), 50–60 (2017)
12. Paruchuri, P., Pearce, J.P., Marecki, J., Tambe, M., Ordonez, F., Kraus, S.: Playing games for security: an efficient exact algorithm for solving bayesian stackelberg games. In: Proceedings of the 7th international joint conference on Autonomous agents and multiagent systems-vol. 2, pp. 895–902 (2008)
13. Manshaei, M.H., Zhu, Q., Alpcan, T., Bacşar, T., Hubaux, J.P.: Game theory meets network security and privacy. ACM Comput. Sur. (CSUR) **45**(3), 1–39 (2013)

14. Samtani, S., Abate, M., Benjamin, V., Li, W.: Cybersecurity as an industry: a cyber threat intelligence perspective. The Palgrave Handbook of International Cybercrime and Cyberdeviance, pp. 135–154 (2020)
15. Serketzis, N., Katos, V., Ilioudis, C., Baltatzis, D., Pangalos, G.J.: Actionable threat intelligence for digital forensics readiness. Inf. Comput. Secur. **27**(2), 273–291 (2019)
16. Merah, Y., Kenaza, T.: Ontology-based cyber risk monitoring using cyber threat intelligence. In: Proceedings of the 16th International Conference on Availability, Reliability and Security, pp. 1–8 (2021)
17. Mark Button. Economic and industrial espionage (2020)
18. Goel, S., Williams, K., Dincelli, E.: Got phished? internet security and human vulnerability. J. Assoc. Inf. Syst. **18**(1), 2 (2017)
19. Ekelhart, A., Kiesling, E., Kurniawan, K.: An att&ck-kg for linking cybersecurity attacks to adversary tactics and techniques (2021)
20. Raffat, S.K., Siddiqui, M.S., Shaikh, Z.A., Memon, A.R.: Ontology: a scientific classification technique. Sindh Univ. Res. J. **44**(2AB), 63–68 (2012)
21. Noy, N.F., McGuinness, D.L., et al.: Ontology development 101: a guide to creating your first ontology (2001)
22. Kwon, R., Ashley, T., Castleberry, J., Mckenzie, P., Gourisetti, S.N.G.: Cyber threat dictionary using mitre att&ck matrix and nist cybersecurity framework mapping. In: 2020 Resilience Week (RWS), pp. 106–112. IEEE (2020)
23. Strom, B.E., Applebaum, A., Miller, D.P., Nickels, K.C., Pennington, A.G., Thomas, C.B.: Mitre att&ck: Design and philosophy. In: Technical report. The MITRE Corporation (2018)
24. National Institute of Standards and Technology: Framework for improving critical infrastructure cybersecurity. Technical report, NIST (2018)
25. Teodoro, N., Gonçalves, L., Serrão, C.: Nist cybersecurity framework compliance: a generic model for dynamic assessment and predictive requirements. In: 2015 IEEE Trustcom/BigDataSE/ISPA vol. 1, pp. 418–425. IEEE (2015)
26. PF Möller, D.: Nist cybersecurity framework and mitre cybersecurity criteria. In: Guide to Cybersecurity in Digital Transformation: Trends, Methods, Technologies, Applications and Best Practices, pp. 231–271. Springer (2023)
27. Alshar'e, M.: Cyber security framework selection: comparision of nist and iso27001. Appl. Comput. J. 245–255 (2023)
28. Mylrea, M., Gourisetti, S.N.G., Nicholls, A.: An introduction to buildings cybersecurity framework. In: 2017 IEEE Symposium Series on Computational Intelligence (SSCI), pp. 1–7. IEEE (2017)
29. Saritac, U., Liu, X., Wang, R.: Assessment of cybersecurity framework in critical infrastructures. In: 2022 IEEE Delhi Section Conference (DELCON), pp. 1–4. IEEE (2022)
30. Miller, S.: Espionage: ends and means. In: The Ethics of National Security Intelligence Institutions, pp. 89–104. Routledge (2024)
31. Bottom, N.R., RJ Gallati, R.: Industrial espionage: Intelligence techniques and countermeasures. Butterworth Oxford (1984)
32. Locke, E.A., Shaw, K.N., Saari, L.M., Latham, G.P.: Goal setting and task performance: 1969–1980. Psychol. Bull. **90**(1), 125 (1981)
33. RC Nurse, J., et al.: Understanding insider threat: a framework for characterising attacks. In: 2014 IEEE Security and Privacy Workshops, pp. 214–228. IEEE (2014)
34. Gheyas, I.A., Abdallah, A.E.: Detection and prediction of insider threats to cyber security: a systematic literature review and meta-analysis. Big Data Anal. **1**(1), 6 (2016)

35. Ms Snigdha Bishwal and Ms Sivashrita Bharadwaj: Stealing the edge: how corporate espionage threatens india's growth. Educ. Administr. Theory Pract. **30**(6), 548–552 (2024)
36. Rivera, R., Pazmiño, L., Becerra, F., Barriga, J.: An analysis of cyber espionage process. In: Developments and Advances in Defense and Security: Proceedings of MICRADS 2021, pp. 3–14. Springer (2022)
37. Pun, D.: Rethinking espionage in the modern era. Chi. J. Int'l L. **18**, 353 (2017)
38. Chawla, A.: Cyber-terrorism a wicked problem. J. Criminol. Forensic Stud. **5**(1), 180058 (2023)
39. Carr, M., Lesniewska, F.: Internet of things, cybersecurity and governing wicked problems: learning from climate change governance. Int. Relations **34**(3), 391–412 (2020)
40. F Malone, E., J Malone, M.: The "wicked problem" of cybersecurity policy: analysis of united states and canadian policy response. Canadian Foreign Policy J. **19**(2), 158–177 (2013)
41. A Sipper, J.: Hypergaming for cyber: strategy for gaming a wicked problem. Military Cyber Affairs **5**(1), 5 (2022)
42. Alkhadra, R., Abuzaid, J., AlShammari, M., Mohammad, N.: Solar winds hack: in-depth analysis and countermeasures. In: 2021 12th International Conference on Computing Communication and Networking Technologies (ICCCNT), pp. 1–7. IEEE (2021)
43. Martínez, J., M Durán, J.: Software supply chain attacks, a threat to global cybersecurity: solarwinds' case study. Int. J. Safety Secur. Eng. **11**(5), 537–545 (2021)
44. Huddleston, J., Ji, P., Bhunia, S., Cogan, J.: How vmware exploits contributed to solarwinds supply-chain attack. In: 2021 International Conference on Computational Science and Computational Intelligence (CSCI), pp. 760–765. IEEE (2021)
45. Sterle, L., Bhunia, S.: On solarwinds orion platform security breach. In: 2021 IEEE SmartWorld, Ubiquitous Intelligence & Computing, Advanced & Trusted Computing, Scalable Computing & Communications, Internet of People and Smart City Innovation (SmartWorld/SCALCOM/UIC/ATC/IOP/SCI), pp. 636–641. IEEE (2021)
46. Akhtar, N., Aziz, O., Hussain, T.: Latest trends in the cybersecurity after the solar wind hacking attack. Foundation University Journal of Engineering and Applied Sciences (HEC Recognized Y Category, ISSN 2706-7351), **1**(2), 14–24 (2020)
47. Smyth, V.: Cyber-security fortresses built on quicksand. Netw. Secur. **2015**(8), 5–8 (2015)
48. Koch, D.D., et al. Is the hipaa security rule enough to protect electronic personal health information (phi) in the cyber age? J. Health Care Finance **43**(3) (2016)
49. Floyd, T., Grieco, M., Reid, E.F.: Mining hospital data breach records: cyber threats to us hospitals. In: 2016 IEEE Conference on Intelligence and Security Informatics (ISI), pp. 43–48. IEEE (2016)
50. Dmytrenko, S.: Espionage counteraction as national security paradigm of 21st century. *3C*, 34(1), 57
51. Ovidiu Horia Maican: Legal aspects of economic espionage. Perspect. Law Pub. Administr. **8**(2), 385–392 (2019)
52. R Early, B., Gartzke, E.: Spying from space: reconnaissance satellites and interstate disputes. J. Conflict Resol. **65**(9), 1551–1575 (2021)
53. Bederna, Z., Szadeczky, T.: Cyber espionage through botnets. Secur. J. **33**(1), 43–62 (2020)
54. Eldem, T.: The governance of turkey's cyberspace: between cyber security and information security. Int. J. Public Adm. **43**(5), 452–465 (2020)

55. N Schmitt, M.: Tallinn manual 2.0 on the international law applicable to cyber operations. Cambridge University Press (2017)
56. Booch, G.: The unified modeling language user guide. Pearson Education India (2005)
57. Rumbaugh, J.: The unified modeling language reference manual. Pearson Education India (2005)
58. Bauer, B., Odell, J.: Uml 2.0 and agents: how to build agent-based systems with the new uml standard. Eng. Appl. Artif.l intell. **18**(2), 141–157 (2005)
59. Guedes, G.T.A., Vicari, R.M.: Applying auml and uml 2 in the multi-agent systems project. In: Advances in Conceptual Modeling-Challenging Perspectives: ER 2009 Workshops CoMoL, ETheCoM, FP-UML, MOST-ONISW, QoIS, RIGiM, SeCoGIS, Gramado, Brazil, November 9-12, 2009. Proceedings 28, pages 106–115. Springer (2009)
60. Babu, K.S., Maruthi, R.: Lifecycle for game development to ensure enhanced productivity. Int. J. Innov. Res. Comput. Commun. Eng. **1**(8), 1490–1503 (2013)
61. Ariyurek, S., Betin-Can, A., Surer, E.: Automated video game testing using synthetic and humanlike agents. IEEE Trans. Games **13**(1), 50–67 (2019)
62. Ariyurek, S., Betin-Can, A., Surer, E.: Enhancing the monte carlo tree search algorithm for video game testing. In: 2020 IEEE Conference on Games (CoG), pp. 25–32. IEEE (2020)

From Dynamic Decision-Making Assessments Using Virtual Simulation-Based Training to Targeted Training of Incident Commanders

Stella Polikarpus[1](✉), Reet Kasepalu[1,2], and Edna Milena Sarmiento-Márquez[2]

[1] Estonian Academy of Security Sciences, Tallinn, Estonia
stella.polikarpus@sisekaitse.ee
[2] Tallinn University, Tallinn, Estonia

Abstract. The dynamic decision-making (DDM) competence of first level rescue incident commanders have been assessed using Virtual Simulation-based Training (VSBT) and Effective Command (EC) behavioral marking framework for more than seven years in Estonia. VSBT is well studied and a very promising training method for first responders' DDM. Although the EC has been used, there has been no longitudinal study about incident commanders' DDM using VSBT. Therefore, there are no training suggestions provided to organizations that take into account the commanders' individual development paths. We explored how the commanders' DDM competence has changed from 2017 to June 2024. An analysis of 1133 certificates explored performance variations and commander profiles, serving as a foundation for tailoring suggestions for training methods according to the strengths and weaknesses of DDM behaviors. First, we found that incident commanders perform better in the first two levels of situational awareness: perception and comprehension; and planning. The lower scores concern the third phase of situational awareness: prediction, as well as communication, and review behaviors. We identified three groups of commanders: first, the "progressors", are commanders whose overall assessment results have been excellent, or have improved over time. The second group is the "stagnants", whose overall results have remained constant over the different assessments. The final one refers to the "regressors", who are commanders whose competences have decreased over the years. We provide training suggestions that could play a role in the development of DDM behaviors.

Keywords: dynamic decision-making (DDM) · virtual simulation-based training (VSBT) · Effective Command behavioral marking framework (EC) · Collaborative Authoring Process Model for Virtual Simulations (CAPM)

1 Introduction

Currently, there are less operational incidents responded to by rescue incident commanders than a decade ago, therefore the possibility to practice dynamic decision-making (DDM) in real incidents over the years to gain DDM competence has decreased [1]. A

Published by Springer Nature Switzerland AG 2026
W. Seböck et al. (Eds.): ITDRR 2024, IFIP AICT 752, pp. 82–97, 2026.
https://doi.org/10.1007/978-3-031-97115-0_6

longitudinal review of disaster-related literature, published a decade ago, emphasized the critical importance of training and advanced preparation for effective emergency responses [2]. However, it noted that much of the training proposed following official disaster investigations had been developed in an ad hoc fashion, lacking systematic organization and coordination. They also noted that skills are most powerfully developed through simulations and role-plays [2]. Therefore it is argued that virtual simulation-based training (VSBT) is the way to improve or at least maintain the needed DDM competence level of rescue officers [1, 3]. Most research focusing on first responders using VSBT has used a cross-sectional study approach where each participant's DDM competence has only been measured once [3–5]. In a previous study we also followed this approach when inspecting how incident commanders' situation awareness (SA) levels should be measured using VSBT and Effective Command behavioral marking framework (EC) [6]. A one-time assessment or analysis of DDM among first-level rescue commanders yields valuable insights into the use of IT for disaster risk reduction and DDM training. However, it does not account for the long-term impact of IT utilization, particularly in crisis management training.

The EC behavioral marking framework [3] has been used in Estonia since 2016 to assess rescue incident commanders' DDM competence [7]. The named framework measures with nine criteria eight DDM behaviors using VSBT. The first three behaviors in the framework are connected to SA. A study evaluating the effectiveness of incorporating the new concept of SA into a curriculum for commanders proved that the training program called "Training and Assessment Day" is effective to learn SA levels [7]. In the aforementioned study the two assessment results of the same commanders were compared. However, the study focused on the effectiveness of training SA only, not the whole DDM competence, additionally it did not look how individual commanders' DDM behaviors have developed over time.

EC has also been used and studied in other countries such as Portugal. An action research study about developing virtual simulation scenarios demonstrated the adequacy of the training program using EC together with a virtual reality simulation, offering a set of methodological and practical guidelines that can be considered in identical training contexts [8]. Additionally, a study assessing DDM competences of two groups, one year apart from each other, reported that the training course promoted the development of decision-making competence in the management of emergency operations using virtual reality simulations [5]. The developer of EC, Dr. Katherine Lamb and her colleagues also performed a single time overview of the use of EC to assess DDM competence at four different command levels. The study found out strengths and weaknesses based on average scores of DDM behaviors for the first two incident command levels [3].

Although a structured analysis of incident command assessments should inform subsequent training cycles for both individuals and organizations [3] it is still unclear how commanders have performed during DDM assessments over the years in Estonia. The studies cited above are a snapshot of cross-sectional design to get an organizational overview of DDM training and assessment results. To the best of our knowledge, there is no study that has looked at the individual evolution of incident commanders' DDM competence over time when VSBT is implemented. Furthermore, there are now three doctoral studies defended that have all focused on different aspects of VSBT implementation in rescue organizations [9–11], however none of these studies looked at the individual commanders' DDM competences over time.

Evolving global and local contexts demand a rapid adaptation in terms of the training of incident commanders. For instance, there are security concerns in Estonia following Russia's full-scale attack on Ukraine in 2022. The DDM competences of Ukraine's rescue incident commanders is being tested under challenging conditions, and they confront unprecedented demands while responding to such type of aggressions. Additionally, climate crises bring about extra challenges for decision-makers as floods or forest fires become more frequent. These pressing changes in the world demand evidence for the effectiveness of VSBT interventions in the long term for all first responders. Therefore, there is an urgent need to build on the strengths of the existing training of incident commanders so they can respond effectively to current and future challenges.

In this study we seek to understand the changes in rescue incident commanders' DDM competence and behaviors over time to effectively face future challenges and identify specific training needs. We propose two research questions (RQ):

1. How have the strengths and weaknesses of rescue incident commanders' DDM behaviors changed over time?
2. How could the commanders be grouped to offer training for different groups of Estonian incident commanders to better prepare them for future risks while improving their DDM competence?

2 Dynamic Decision-Making Competence

While a decision involves committing to actions intended to produce satisfactory results for certain individuals [12], DDM entails making a series of interdependent decisions in a dynamic environment influenced by previous decisions and autonomous changes [13]. Different types of decisions can be assessed: a) selecting a subset from multiple alternatives, b) binary accept/reject choices, c) evaluations backed by action commitments, and d) constructing ideal solutions with available resources [12].

The EC assessment platform is structured around the DDM model known as SPAR, which stands for Situation Awareness, Planning, Action, and Review [3, 14]. All eight DDM behaviors assessed using VSBT are directly connected to this DDM model. The first three behaviors assessed using EC are the three levels of SA. We use Endsley's definition referring to SA as a person's perception of environmental elements over time and space, comprehension of their meaning, and projection of their near-future status [15]. According to this concept, three SA levels are measured: SA level 1 perception (SA1); SA level 2 comprehension (SA2) and SA level 3 prediction (SA3) [16]. The fourth assessed behavior is decision-making, followed by plan, command, communication, and the last behavior is review [3].

To create reliable and valid virtual simulation scenarios for the assessment of SA and DDM, we developed and tested the Collaborative Authoring Process Model for Virtual Simulation Scenarios (CAPM) [17]. It is a five-step model, where in first step authors write the virtual scenario map, in second step they author the virtual simulation user guide and VR file. Thirdly, they test the scenario with other experts on the field and agree threshold level of possible solutions, then they make changes in user guide and VR file and in last step the scenario is modelled to all assessors. Afterward, we reflected on the use of CAPM for SA assessments and it was found to be a good process model to generate virtual simulation scenarios that allow assessing three distinct levels of SA [6].

Due to the high risk and time-critical character of DDM competence, commanders tend to use three different decision-making strategies within the first minute of response on the scene: recognition-primed decision (RPD) [18], procedural decision-making or value-based decision-making [14]. After the first actions are executed, but still during the response phase of the incident, the commanders have more time to formalize the initial plan and use formal decision-making while reviewing their plan to solve the incident.

While recognition-primed decision (RPD) is an example of a naturalistic approach to decision-making, procedural decision-making is a normative approach to decision-making [19]. The Estonian Rescue Board documentation, which regulates the response to disasters, utilizes the normative decision-making model 'Observe, Decide, Command and Control' [20]. Unfortunately, the normative decision-making model does not reflect how people make decisions in time-critical high-risk situations. Normative decision-making models can be viewed as sequential steps for successful decision making [19]. It is anticipated that the commander will select the optimal solution to address the incident. Normative decision-making models can serve as effective tools for training novices, as the rational choice approach aligns better with their decision-making process compared to RPD [19]. Novices lack diverse mental models for RPD; therefore, VSBT can be utilized to develop these patterns for them. In academic research in Estonia, the DDM behaviors of working incident commanders across country are assessed using VSBT. Evaluating the behavior of in-service commanders in time-critical and high-risk situations necessitates the application of EC and SPAR DDM model. It should be noted that knowledge of standard operational procedures is also assessed as part of EC utilization using VSBT.

War probably would present a significant and currently relevant challenge for Estonian rescue commanders, for which they might be inadequately prepared. Dynamic risk assessment is an important part of DDM competence, especially SA level 3 from the SPAR model [14]. Even if we developed plans and procedures to manage incidents during wartime, they would become outdated as soon as actual war activities commenced in the country. Therefore, it is crucial to incorporate the review behavior as part of the evaluation process. Furthermore, we need to train our commanders using VSBT to solve a diversity of scenarios to provide them with general DDM competence [6], instead of relying on a mechanical repetition of certain procedures.

3 Methodology

3.1 Data Collection

In Estonia, the EC behavioral marking framework implementation involves two assessors completing an assessment certificate for each in-service incident commander [7]. We analyzed the results of first level incident commanders' assessment from the EC platform from 2017 until the 24th of June 2024. We filtered and discarded irrelevant certificates for the purposes of this study as they were not part of formal assessment (e.g., training, incident attending, etc.). The final dataset included data from 1133 formal assessments. The details of the assessment methodology and the training of assessors have been described in earlier publications [3, 6]. Eight behaviors (perception (SA1); comprehension (SA2); prediction (SA3); decision-making; plan; communication; command; review) are assessed through nine assessment criteria on a Likert Scale from 1 to 5. We used the overall assessment color (green, amber or red) and the average score of each behavior in our study. Since 2019, green indicates that the incident commander possesses excellent DDM competence. Amber signifies that the DDM competence meets the occupational qualification standard threshold, while red indicates that DDM competencies fall below the threshold [7]. Based on the overall assessment result, commanders need to be reassessed at specific intervals. If the overall assessment result is red, the next assessment occurs within six months to one year. For amber, the reassessment interval was two years, while green results warrant a three-year interval.

3.2 Data Analysis

Although in Estonia, the first level incident commanders have been assessed from 2016, during the first year the tool only allowed to record binary results (pass/fail) instead of using a 5-Point Likert scale. Because of this, we discarded the 2016 assessments and analyzed a total of 1133 assessments. For RQ2, we analyzed only the incident commanders who had been assessed three or more times (228 commanders, see Table 1).

Regarding RQ1, we report descriptive statistics (mean scores, standard deviation, max and min results). We present the mean scores for eight assessed behaviors, as well as the overall scores calculated as the sum of these eight behaviors. Furthermore, we used a repeated-measures ANOVA to distinguish statistically significant differences in the commanders' behaviors. The first within the subject factor was the average score of each DDM behavior and the second between the subject factor was the overall assessment color. For RQ2, we considered only the last three assessment rounds from commanders who had been assessed more than three times (see Table 1). RStudio 2024.04.1 was utilized to calculate percentages and category averages for each development path, perform a repeated-measures ANOVA and post-hoc tests, and visualize the results.

3.3 Participants

The dataset with 1133 assessments included a total of 489 male incident commanders (see Table 1). There were 125 commanders assessed once, and 136 commanders assessed twice. The biggest group was the commanders who had been assessed three times (181), and 47 commanders had been assessed more than three times.

Table 1. Number of incident commanders in the dataset and how many rounds their DDM had been assessed (n = 1133)

Assessment rounds	Commanders assessed from 2017 to June 2024
Assessed one times	125
Assessed two times	136
Assessed three times	181
Assessed four times	42
Assessed five times	5
Total number	489

4 Results

4.1 Incident Commanders' Strengths and Weaknesses of DDM Behaviors

Table 2 presents the mean (M) scores and standard deviations (SD) for all eight DDM behaviors assessed using EC with VSBT. When ranking the mean scores from high to low (see column Rank in Table 2), we observe the top three behaviors (perception SA1, comprehension SA2, plan) and the lowest three behaviors (review, prediction SA3, communication). The differences between the mean scores of the eight behaviors are rather small. The top three DDM behaviors were perception SA1 ($M = 3.369$, $SD = 0.380$), comprehension SA2 ($M = 3.330$, $SD = 0.398$) and plan ($M = 3.303$; $SD = 0.399$). These three behaviors also had the smallest standard deviation. Moving on, the three weakest behaviors, though still above the threshold, are review ($M = 3.212$), SA3 - prediction (SA3) ($M = 3.230$), and communication ($M = 3.231$).

We analyzed whether the mean scores of the strongest DDM behaviors are statistically significantly higher than the mean scores of the weakest behaviors. When applying a Greenhouse-Geisser correction, the mean scores for the eight behaviors were statistically significant ($F = 23.083$, $df = 6.365$, $p < .001$). A post hoc T-test showed that SA1 is statistically significantly different from all other seven behaviors (t values from 4.085 to 10.895, $p < .001$); SA2 is different from SA3 ($t = 5.761$, $p < .001$), communication ($t = 3.516$, $p = 0{,}006$) and review ($t = 6.810$, $p < .001$); SA3 is different from decision-making ($t = -4.253$, $p < .001$), plan ($t = -3.944$, $p = 0{,}001$) and command ($t = -3.998$, $p = < .001$); Decision-making is different from review ($t = 5.302$, $p < .001$) and Plan is different from review ($t = 4.993$, $p < .001$); as well communication differences from review ($t = 3.293$, $p = 0{,}012$). And lastly, command behavior is statistically different from review ($t = 5.047$, $p < .001$). Additionally, it became clear that the two weakest behaviors prediction (SA3) and review are not statistically significantly different from each other.

4.2 Commanders Long-Term Training Needs Analysis

Our RQ2 focuses on identifying the types of training required for various groups of Estonian incident commanders to enhance their preparedness for future risks while simultaneously improving their DDM capabilities. When visualizing the individual development

Table 2. Descriptive statistics for DDM eight behaviors years 2017- June 2024 (n = 1133)

DDM behaviors	Rank	Mean	SD	Min	Max
Perception (SA1)	I	3.369	0.380	2.100	5.000
Comprehension (SA2)	II	3.330	0.398	1.550	5.000
Prediction (SA3)	VII	3.230	0.408	2.000	5.000
Decision-making	IV	3.279	0.415	2.000	5.000
Plan	III	3.303	0.399	1.750	5.000
Communication	VI	3.231	0.412	1.850	5.000
Command	V	3.277	0.408	2.000	5.000
Review	VIII	3.212	0.407	1.650	5.000
Overall score		26.231	2.734	15.000	40.000

paths taking into account the commanders' overall assessment results, we found that many different trajectories had been taken by the commanders, altogether 15 different paths. Figure 1 indicates that no commander had scored a red result in the first two results. It should be mentioned that if commanders have two red overall assessment results in a row, he could no longer work as commander due to the Estonian Rescue Board internal regulations. Neither had it been possible to achieve a green result after getting a red result in the second assessment round, however one person managed to get a green result after being assessed with red in the first round. Commanders with red results were signed mentors by the Rescue Board to help them individually. Unfortunately, it occurred (for one commander) that after scoring a green result, the commander indeed was given a red result in the next assessment round. Nevertheless, these trajectories are an exception.

Deriving from the 15 development paths, three groups were identified:

1. **Progressors**: commanders whose assessment results have been always green and commanders whose results improved over time, from either red to amber or from amber to green.
2. **Stagnants**: commanders, whose assessment results have stayed the same over time on the threshold level.
3. **Regressors**: commanders whose assessment results have dropped over time, from either amber to red, or green to amber.

Altogether there were 228 commanders who had been assessed three times and out of these, 109 commanders (47,8%) belonged to the Stagnants. 63 (27,6%) of the commanders were labelled as the Progressors, and 56 commanders (24,6%) belonged to the Regressors.

We assumed that the Progressors' overall scores would be higher than the results from the Stagnants and the Regressors. Additionally, we thought that the Regressors would have the lowest overall score on average. An ANOVA test was conducted to examine the differences in scores between the groups: Progressors, Stagnants, and Regressors. The results of the ANOVA were significant, $F(2,21) = 33.14$, $p < 0.001$, indicating that there are significant differences in scores between the groups. To further investigate these

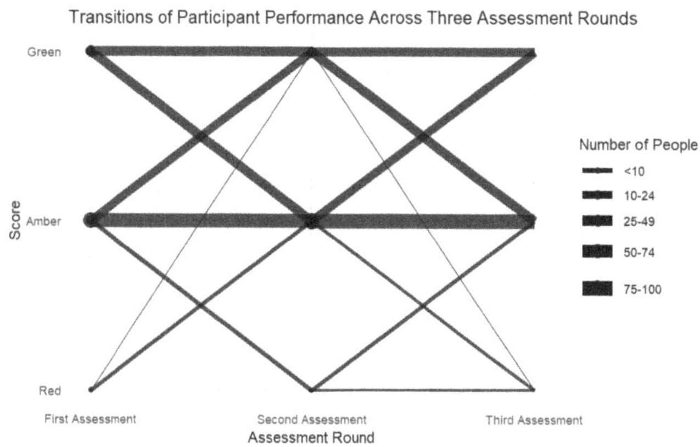

Fig. 1. First level rescue commanders' development paths throughout three assessment rounds. The line width represents the number of commanders per trajectory. For instance, the thicker line represents the path most frequently evidenced ($n = 684$ assessments and 228 commanders).

differences, Tukey's Honest Significant Difference (HSD) post-hoc test was performed. The results of the Tukey HSD stated that the Regressors had significantly higher scores than the Stagnants ($df = 0.09$, $p = 0.0206$), the Progressors also had significantly higher average scores than the Stagnants ($df = 0.25$, $p < 0.001$), and the Progressors had significantly higher scores than the Regressors ($df = 0.16$, $p < 0.001$). This means that our first assumption was confirmed, the Progressors scored the highest, however it was the Stagnants who scored the lowest instead of the predicted Regressors.

The same trend as in the average scores was also perceivable in all eight DDM behaviors. The Progressors had the highest average scores in all DDM behaviors, followed by the Regressors, leaving the Stagnants at the bottom (see Fig. 2). The biggest differences in the eight DDM behaviors are in communication, decision-making, command, and plan. The three groups are most similar in the categories: SA1 prediction, SA2 comprehension and review. This means they share two strengths and one weak DDM behavior.

Progressors are commanders whose assessment results have been always green, improved over time, from either red to amber or from amber to green (see Fig. 3). The Progressors comprise of commanders who have had an excellent result throughout the three rounds (10%), commanders who have attained a green result after receiving an amber result once (11%) or twice (10%). One person who had started with a red result, received a green result in the second round, and an amber result in the third round. 2% of the commanders started with a red result and managed to increase their result in the following two rounds to amber. When examining the average scores of the DDM behaviors, it is evident that the average results for everyone have declined, even within the Progressors group (see Fig. 4). The highest drop is present in the command behavior, followed by the communication and review behavior.

The most prominent commanders in the Stagnants are also the biggest group in the overall sample. 31% of the commanders have attained an amber result in all three assessment rounds (see Fig. 5). Additionally, commanders who have scored an amber

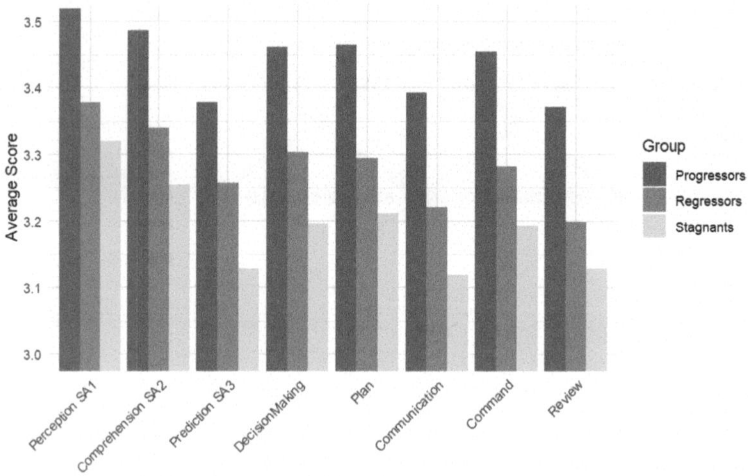

Fig. 2. Group Performance Disparities in Eight DDM Behaviors: Progressors, Regressors, and Stagnants (n = 684 assessments and 228 commanders)

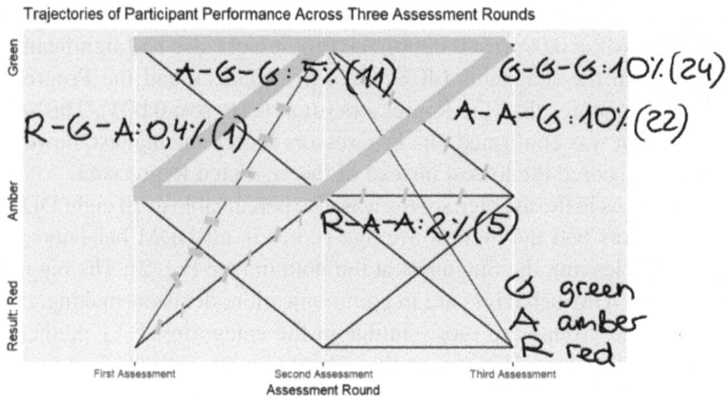

Fig. 3. The Progressors comprise of commanders who had increased their assessment result or had provided excellent results throughout three assessments, the number in brackets indicates the number of commanders taking the development path (n = 6).

result in the first and the last assessment round even though they had decreased their result to red in the second round (3%) or increased their result to green (9%), have been included in the Stagnants group. 14 commanders who attained a green result in the first and third round, but an amber one in the second round, have also been appended to the Stagnants group.

Diving into the distinct DDM behaviors, a trend for decline in all categories is perceivable (Fig. 6). When comparing with the group Progressors, the results are lower overall (the highest average result for the Stagnants is 3,49, for Progressors it is 3,64) and the decrease from round 3 to round 1 higher (compare –0,31, and –0,24 for the Stagnants and –0,23, and –0,18 for the Progressors). The behaviors that had decreased over 0,20

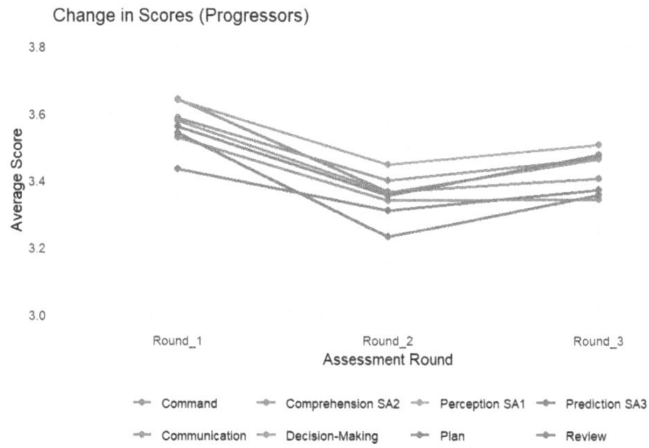

Fig. 4. The Progressors showcased a decline in all DDM behaviors, especially in command, communication, and review (63 commanders).

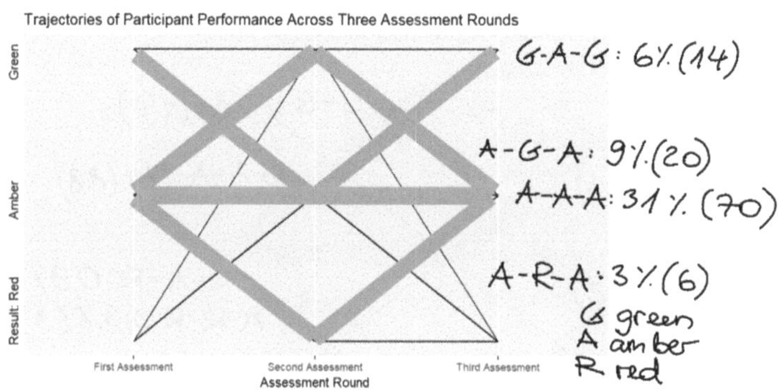

Fig. 5. The Stagnants are the biggest group, 70 commanders out of 228 have not changed their threshold level result within six to seven years.

on average for the Stagnants were: decision-making, SA1 perception, command, review, and communication.

The last group is called the Regressors: commanders whose assessment results have dropped over time, from either amber to red, or green to amber (see Fig. 7). Commanders have mostly decreased their result from green to amber after scoring green once (12%) or after scoring a green result twice (8%). Very problematic are three commanders who have received a red overall assessment result twice after scoring an amber result at first. There was one commander (0,4%) who scored a green result after first scoring an amber one, only to end up scoring a red result in the third round.

Looking into the eight DDM behaviors, the results have plummeted when comparing the first result with the third one (see Fig. 8). The decrease in the results is the highest when comparing the group to the Stagnants and the Progressors, however, the results from the first round were much higher than the results for the Stagnants. This group

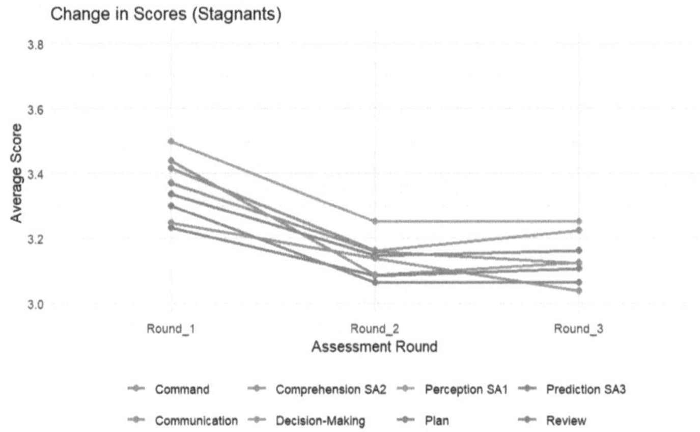

Fig. 6. The Stagnants show a decrease in DDM behaviors: decision-making, SA1 perception, command, review, and communication (109 commanders).

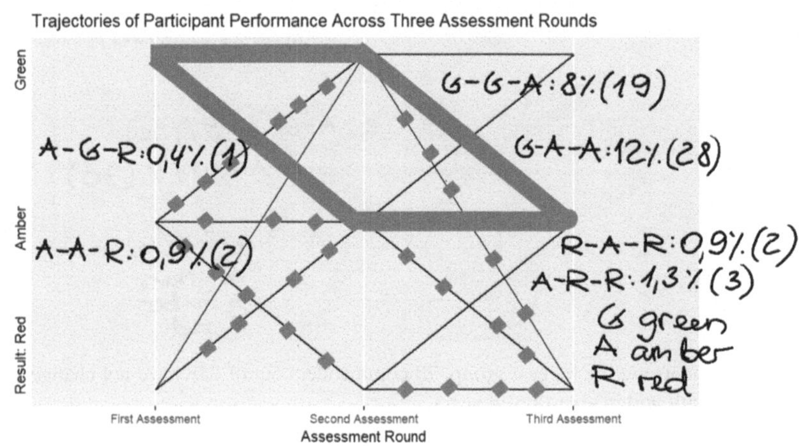

Fig. 7. Regressors: commanders who are showing decreased DDM performance over time.

has decreased the most in the categories: command, decision-making, SA1 - prediction, review and communication.

5 Discussions

RQ1 identified the strengths and weaknesses of incident commanders' DDM behaviors. We found out that the average scores of all eight DDM behaviors were above threshold. The top three strengths of Estonian commanders DDM behaviors relate to: perception SA1, comprehension SA2 and planning. Interestingly, these three behaviors also had the smallest SD (see Table 2), indicating that individual differences in behaviors regarded as strengths are less pronounced than those considered as weaknesses. This approach is likely sufficient if DDM competence is applied in routine, day-to-day incidents such as

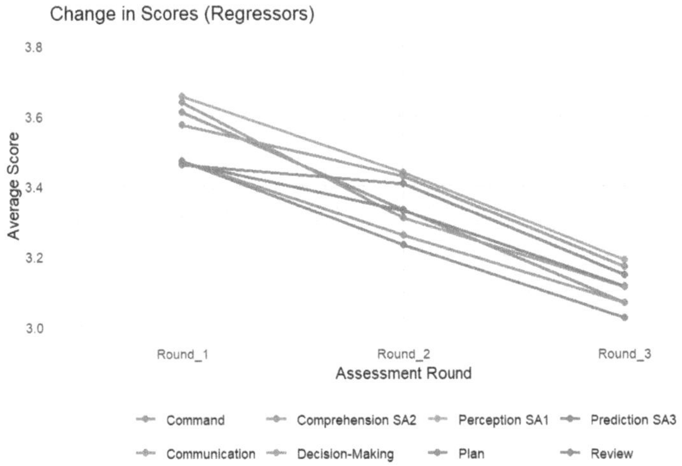

Fig. 8. The Regressors plummeted in command, decision-making, prediction (SA1), review and communication (56 commanders).

apartment fires or car accidents that do not involve additional unpredictable risks. The weakest three behaviors were communication, prediction SA3, and review. Same results have been found earlier in Estonia [6] that DDM behavior strengths and weaknesses are statistically significantly different from each other. However, the study from UK does not seem to confirm it [3], indicating the importance of competences assessment context. These behaviours require specialized training to effectively respond to new types of incidents, such as fires resulting from bomb attacks during wartime.

Upon grouping commanders to address RQ2, we identified three distinct groups: Progressors, Stagnants, and Regressors (see Fig. 2). However, it was observed that the assessment results have declined across all groups. The biggest decline for the Regressors group was command, decision-making, SA3 prediction, review and communication (Fig. 8). These behaviors could not be easily trained using standard operational procedures. The Stagnants declined in decision-making, SA1 perception, command, review, and communication (Fig. 6) while in the case of the Progressors it was command, communication, and review (Fig. 4). Given that the assessment results for even the Progressors had declined over time, it is evident that maintaining excellence in all DDM behaviors is challenging. Therefore, additional training methods should be implemented to prevent further decline. From the results of the DDM behavior analysis of commander groups, we could suggest that the training priority of the organization should be improving review, command and communication behaviors as these trainings are needed by all incident commanders. Review shares many similarities with the skill of reflection, which is why incident commanders should be encouraged to engage in reflective practices during debriefings of their own incidents. Decision-making training is needed by the groups the Regressors and the Stagnants. Interestingly, the Regressors are weaker in prediction SA3, while Stagnants in SA1 perception. To train SA1 perception, a tool named FireFront could be used, as this tool is specially designed to improve the information collection skills of the commanders [21]. We further suggest that the current reassessment intervals for overall green and amber results are excessively long, as even the competence of the Progressors tends to decline during the two- to three-year interval period.

Additionally, more VSBT that supports the entire DDM competence and eight behaviours is necessary for all groups, as effective training in review and prediction (both weaknesses for all groups) can only occur if scenarios dynamically change based on the commanders' decisions. Scenarios should be created using CAPM and they should aim to train future risks [17]. Communication exercises can also be conducted without VSBT by using radio sets, for example, to communicate and clarify plans.

5.1 Practical Implications and Limitations

Given that the review of DDM behavior has been identified as the primary weakness among Estonian rescue incident commanders, training focused on behavior review should be prioritized by the organization to sustain and enhance the commanders' DDM competence. To train the review behavior, the EC platform should be used by the commanders and their mentors to reflect on the DDM of real incidents, not only in VSBT. The platform facilitates self-rating and incident monitoring; however, its usage in Estonia is minimal. A systematic self-reflection would improve reviewing behavior in future DDM situations. In addition to this, the EC platform dashboard should provide a better overview of the distinct DDM behaviors for the planners of trainings. As indicated earlier, the rate of incidents is dropping and therefore suitable tools ought to be used to train and study DDM competences using VSBT [17], and augmented reality (AR) [22, 23]. Assessment rounds using VSBT should be conducted more frequently than the current interval of every three years, as research has shown that VSBT is suitable for DDM training [9–11].

The commanders belonging to the group Stagnants lack perception SA1 skills, which could be effectively trained using FireFront to distinguish relevant information from irrelevant [21]. With this, they would also prevent cognitive overload which in turn could put them in an advantageous position for effective decision-making. The Regressors are in urgent need of a training solution where the scenarios dynamically change based on the commanders' decisions as improving review and prediction behaviors can only occur then. Training the review behavior should be taken up as a priority for everyone, but this is of pivotal importance for the Regressor group.

The major limitation comes from the methodology used to assess incident commanders in Estonia. So far, DDM competence has been assessed only using VSBT. In Estonia we use virtual reality software XVR On-Scene and CAPM, and it is not clear whether the use of other software and scenario construction models to assess DDM competences would provide similar results. Another methodological limitation relates to the unequal distribution of individuals in each group as it might influence some of the statistical analyses. To mitigate the issue, we considered correction coefficients. Additional limitations originate from the sample used for this study as it included only one European country from a single organization, which impedes the generalization of results. Furthermore, all the participants were male as all commanders in Estonia are male.

In future studies it should be considered what the potential confounding factors are that might influence the development of DDM competence over time (e.g., organizational changes, training program modifications). This analysis relies on quantitative assessment scores, therefore future studies should incorporate qualitative insights from commanders themselves and their trainers to provide richer context for the observed trend of competence decline.

6 Conclusion

This study examined the DDM competence of first level rescue incident commanders using VSBT and the EC framework at a national level in Estonia. Analysis of 1133 certificates of in-service commanders revealed three commander profiles—Progressors, Stagnants, and Regressors. Commanders performed well in the two phases of situational awareness: perception, comprehension, and DDM behavior planning but struggled with prediction, communication, and review. Even if it has been argued that the systematic assessment of commanders DDM competence should improve individual and organizational learning [3], the results have proved otherwise in Estonia. VSBT using EC and CAPM indeed allows to assess eight DDM behaviors as indicated earlier [6], however the current system is not efficient enough to keep the commanders' DDM competence up to date and improving. Unfortunately, the managers of the Estonian Rescue Board only receive a non-transparent overall result of the DDM competence assessment. The provided dashboard in the EC platform does not allow a good overview of the change in the commanders' DDM behaviors. However, if transparent analytics [24] were introduced, the increased understanding of the state-of-the-art skills could help develop professional skills [25] and could thus improve DDM behaviors of the commanders. More training possibilities are needed to prepare Estonian rescue incident commanders for future challenges.

References

1. Lamb, K., Boosman, M., Davies, J.: Introspect model: Competency assessment in the virtual world. In: ISCRAM 2015 Conference Proceedings - 12th International Conference on Information System Crisis Response Management, no. August 2005, pp. 235–243 (2015). https://www.idl.iscram.org/files/katherinelamb/2015/1281_KatherineLamb_etal2015.pdf
2. Wilson, J.P., Gosiewska, S.: Multi-agency gold incident command training for civil emergencies. Disaster Prev. Manag. **23**(5), 632–648 (2014). https://doi.org/10.1108/DPM-11-2013-0212
3. Lamb, K., Farrow, M., Olymbios, C., Launder, D., Greatbatch, I.: Systematic incident command training and organisational competence. Int. J. Emerg. Serv. **10**(2), 222–234 (2021). https://doi.org/10.1108/IJES-05-2020-0029
4. Wijkmark, C.H., Heldal, I., Metallinou, M.-M.: Experiencing immersive VR simulation for firefighter skills training. In: Adrot, A., Grace, R., Kathleen, M., Zobel, C. (eds.) Proceedings of the 18th ISCRAM Conference, Blacksburg, pp. 913–921 (2021). http://idl.iscram.org/files/ceciliahammarwijkmark/2021/2383_CeciliaHammarWijkmark_etal2021.pdf
5. Reis, V., Neves, C.: Simulations in virtual reality: assessment of firefighters' decision-making competence. IE Comun. **31**, 28–39 (2020)

6. Polikarpus, S., Sarmiento-Márquez, E.M., Ley, T.: Creation and use of virtual simulations for measuring situation awareness of incident commanders. In: Gjøsæter, T., Radianti, J., Murayama, Y. (eds.) ITDRR2022, Informatio, pp. 23–38. Springer, Cham (2023). https://doi.org/10.1007/978-3-031-34207-3_2
7. Polikarpus, S., Ley, T., Poom-Valickis, K.: Developing the situational awareness of incident commanders: evaluating a training programme using a virtual simulation. Proc. Est. Acad. Secur. Sci. **19**, 195–226 (2020). https://doi.org/10.15158/fe4h-ch75
8. Reis, V., Neves, C.: Application of virtual reality simulation in firefighter training for the development of decision-making competences. In: 2019 International Symposium on Computers in Education (SIIE), pp. 1–6. IEEE (2019). https://doi.org/10.1109/SIIE48397.2019.8970143
9. Polikarpus, S.: The Role of Trainers in Designing and Implementing Virtual Simulation-Based Training in Rescue Organisations. Tallinn University (2024). https://www.etera.ee/zoom/202339/view
10. Wijkmark, C.H.: Virtual Reality for Fire and Rescue Service professionals' training. Western Norway University of Applied Sciences (2024). https://hvlopen.brage.unit.no/hvlopen-xmlui/handle/11250/3134389
11. Reis, V.M.: Formação profissional de bombeiros portugueses: aplicação da simulação virtual ao desenvolvimento das competências de tomada de decisão. Universidade Aberta Formação (2018). https://doi.org/10.13140/RG.2.2.33677.55523
12. Yates, J.F., Tschirhart, M.D.: Decision making expertise. In: Ericsson, K.A., Charness, P.J., Feltovich, P.J., Hoffman, R. (eds.) The Cambridge Handbook of Expertise and Expert Performance, pp. 421–438. Cambridge University Press, New York (2006). https://doi.org/10.1017/cbo9780511816796.024
13. Donovan, S.J., Güss, C.D., Naslund, D.: Improving dynamic decision making through training and self-reflection. Judgm. Decis. Mak. **10**(4), 284–295 (2015). Accessed 07 June 2020. https://doi.org/10.1017/S1930297500005118
14. Launder, D., Perry, C.: A study identifying factors influencing decision making in dynamic emergencies like urban fire and rescue settings. Int. J. Emerg. Serv. **3**(2), 144–161 (2014). https://doi.org/10.1108/IJES-06-2013-0016
15. Endsley, M.R.: Measurement of situation awareness in dynamic systems. Hum. Factors J. Hum. Factors Ergon. Soc. **37**(1), 65–84 (1995). https://doi.org/10.1518/001872095779049499
16. Endsley, M.R.: Toward a theory of situation awareness in dynamic systems. Hum. Factors J. Hum. Factors Ergon. Soc. **37**(1), 32–64 (1995). https://doi.org/10.1518/001872095779049543
17. Polikarpus, S., Ley, T., Poom-Valickis, K.: Collaborative authoring of virtual simulation scenarios for assessing situational awareness. In: Adrot, A., Grace, R., Moore, K., Zobel, C. (eds.) Proceedings of the 18th ISCRAM Conference, Blacksburg Blacksburg, VA, USA, pp. 229–237 (2021). https://www.idl.iscram.org/files/stellapolikarpus/2021/2328_StellaPolikarpus_etal2021.pdf
18. Klein, G.: Naturalistic decision making. Hum. Factors **50**(3), 456–460 (2008). https://doi.org/10.1518/001872008X288385
19. Jonassen, D.H.: Designing for decision making. Educ. Technol. Res. Dev. **60**(2), 341–359 (2012). https://doi.org/10.1007/s11423-011-9230-5
20. Päästeamet. Sündmuskoha tasandi päästetöö korraldamise juhend. Käskkiri nr 1.1–3.1/61 (2022)
21. Thoelen, F., et al.: FireFront: a new tool to support training in fireground situation awareness, situation understanding and bias. Int. Fire Prof. **34**, 34–39 (2020)

22. Hofmann, J., Polikarpus, S.: Application of Augmented Reality in firefighters training: from safe to SafAR. In: Wechner, R., Bues, M., Kloos, U. (eds.) GI VR/AR Workshop 2022, pp. 1–9. Gesellschaft für Informatik (2022). https://doi.org/10.18420/vrar2022_184
23. Polikarpus, S., Terep, T., Reitel, K.: Liitreaalsuse kasutamine väljaõppes: pääste tulevik? Turvalisuskompass **5**(2), 235–267 (2023). https://doi.org/10.15158/W11G-MP89
24. Ley, T., et al.: Towards a partnership of teachers and intelligent learning technology: a systematic literature review of model-based learning analytics. J. Comput. Assist. Learn. **39**(5), 1397–1417 (2023). https://doi.org/10.1111/jcal.12844
25. Tammets, K., Ley, T.: Integrating AI tools in teacher professional learning: a conceptual model and illustrative case. Front. Artif. Intell. **6**(2022) (2023). https://doi.org/10.3389/frai.2023.1255089

Interactive Disaster Training Scenario Generation System with Large Language Models

Koki Asami(✉), Kei Hiroi, and Michinori Hatayama

Kyoto University, Gokasho, Uji, Kyoto 611-0011, Japan
asami@dimsis.dpri.kyoto-u.ac.jp, {hiroi,hatayama}@imdr.dpri.kyoto-u.ac.jp

Abstract. This paper introduces an advanced interactive disaster training scenario generation system powered by Large Language Models (LLMs) to address the critical issues in scenario-based disaster training such as the need for expert knowledge, formalization of the scenario and time consumption. By adopting Retrieval-Augmented Generation (RAG) and the chatbot-based interface as a Human-in-the-Loop (HITL) enables the generation of customised scenarios for different types of disasters and regional characteristics while ensuring the quality. The feasibility of the proposed method is tested by analysing the generated scenarios and interviewing users. We have confirmed that it is possible to generate scenarios tailored to specific disaster and regional characteristics by referring to actual training scenarios and geographical information, using RAG methods to provide domain knowledge specific to disaster response, which vanilla LLMs do not have. Future enhancements will incorporate dynamic real-time data and detailed user feedback to further optimize system performance and applicability in disaster response training.

Keywords: Disaster training · Generative AI · Large Language Model

1 Introduction

In recent years, the frequency and severity of natural disasters have underscored the need for robust disaster management strategies [1]. Events such as the Noto Peninsula Earthquake of 2024 have exposed critical deficiencies in the case of unexpected situations. In light of these challenges, comprehensive and wide-ranging disaster training programs have emerged as a pivotal element in enhancing the preparedness and operational capabilities of emergency management agencies. These training programs are essential not only for fostering clear communication and seamless coordination among various stakeholders but also for equipping responders with the skills necessary to make rapid, informed decisions under pressure.

Disaster training methods have evolved significantly, with several approaches being proposed to enhance the effectiveness of disaster response. One of the

Published by Springer Nature Switzerland AG 2026
W. Seböck et al. (Eds.): ITDRR 2024, IFIP AICT 752, pp. 98–114, 2026.
https://doi.org/10.1007/978-3-031-97115-0_7

Fig. 1. Disaster training at Kumamoto Prefectural Office

methods gaining attention in recent years is the scenario-based training approach, as illustrated in Fig. 1 and 2. This method involves pre-designed disaster scenarios and scripts to assess and train responders' abilities to handle various situations that may arise during an actual disaster. The training process is divided into two roles: controllers and players. Controllers are responsible for presenting the challenges (scenario injections) according to the disaster scenario, while players collaborate as an organization to address and solve the issues presented [2]. The advantage of this method over traditional, more passive disaster drills is that it actively engages participants, requiring them to think and act as they would in a real emergency. Additionally, the complexity and difficulty of the training can be adjusted based on the scenario, allowing both beginners and experienced personnel to participate effectively [3], thus the scenario creation is the most important step of the scenario-based training.

The purpose of disaster training in local governments is to train people who are able to handle manage disaster response. However, it is questionable whether current disaster training in Japan achieves this goal.

These are the challenges associated with conventional training:

1. **Specialized Knowledge Requirement**: Developing realistic and relevant training scenarios necessitates a high level of expertise in disaster response. Scenario designers must understand the critical points that could become problematic during an actual disaster, knowledge that general staff members may not possess. Although some regions employ dedicated crisis management officers, not all municipalities have such resources, leading to disparities in the quality of training scenarios across different areas.
2. **Formalization of scenarios**: It is important to tailor training scenarios to the specific characteristics of the region in which the training will take place.

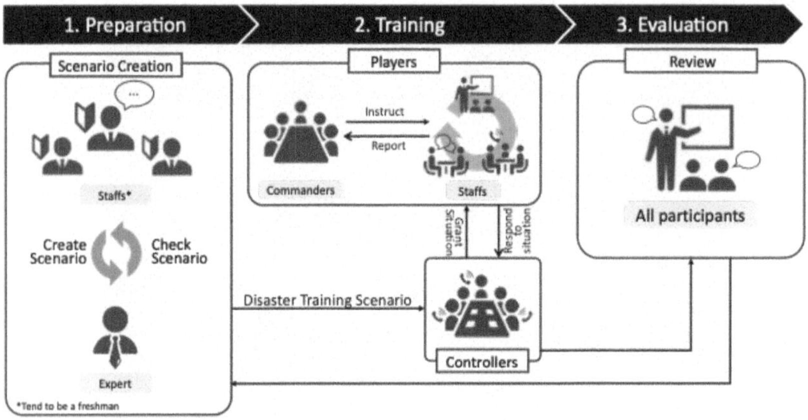

Fig. 2. The overview of scenario based disaster training

The types of disasters that can occur vary greatly depending on geographical factors. In addition, the scenarios used in training tend to be a certain success scenario. However, it is unlikely that there is a fully manageable scenario in the real world.

3. **Time-Consuming Scenario Creation**: The process of developing comprehensive scenarios that consider the various factors mentioned above is time-intensive. This can place a significant burden on municipal offices, potentially disrupting their regular operations. During interviews conducted by the authors with municipal officials, the time required to prepare training scenarios was frequently cited as a major obstacle to conducting effective disaster training.

The ultimate goal of this study is to propose a new disaster training method to develop human resources that can respond to disasters in a real sense. For example, the quality of the training itself can be improved by generating more practical scenarios, such as scenarios that include both realistic and unrealistic responses, and by using a metaverse to separate the trainer from other trainees, making it possible to conduct disaster training without interrupting normal operations. The final objective of this paper is to examine the effectiveness of the current phase.

An overview of the proposed disaster training system is shown in Fig. 3. The fundamental steps remain the same. However, several updates have been introduced.

In the preparation phase, employees interact with the chatbot, which has expertise in disaster management, including local geographical knowledge, to create a disaster scenario. The details are described in the following sections. In the training phase, this scenario forms the basis of a disaster simulation that replaces the controller used in traditional methods. Additionally, agents replace players, allowing for fully automated training within the simulation and

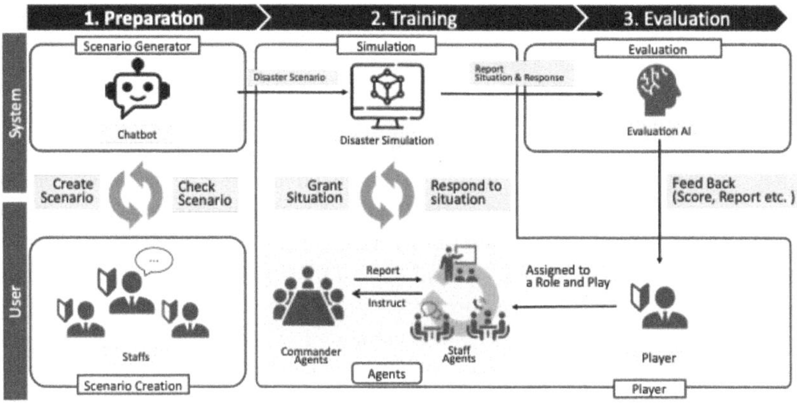

Fig. 3. The overview of the proposed new disaster training system

eliminating the need for full departmental participation. One might ask how human participants are involved in this process. In this system, humans are assigned specific roles, with agents filling their positions within the simulation. As a result, only a few human participants are needed, with the remaining roles filled by NPCs.

Since the training is conducted in a simulated environment, actions taken by both agents and human participants can be recorded, enabling automatic generation of training reports. Feedback is also provided, helping participants identify any unrecognized areas for improvement.

There are three main novelties of the proposed method.

1. **Gain knowledge interacting with AI Expert(Chatbot)**: Even if the local government does not have experts, the knowledge of disaster management can be gained by interacting with the chatbot in the process of creating training scenarios. This solves the challenges of lack of experts and formalization of the scenario.
2. **Full automation of end-to-end disaster simulation**: The disaster simulation from the occurrence to recovery and the evaluation of the training allows the full automation of training. This addresses the challenges of formalization of the scenario and the training time.
3. **Solo training with arbitrary scenarios and roles**: As mentioned earlier, in the proposed system, users are assigned to one of the disaster management roles and all others are NPCs. This allows training to be conducted in one aspect, so that users can stop and restart training at any time. This addresses the challenge of training time.

As for the phase 1, we focused on solving the problems in the conventional scenario-based training method. To address the problems of the conventional method, we propose the interactive training scenario generation system. This system contributes by generating disaster training scenarios using large language models (LLMs) through user interaction, as illustrated in Fig. 3. The use of LLMs for scenario generation offers significant advantages, including enhanced creativity, contextual relevance, efficiency and scalability [4]. Therefore, they are expected to contribute to scenario generation in various fields, such as simulated patient agents in the medical field [5] or test scenarios for autonomous driving [6]. Disaster management is no exception. The use of LLMs is expected to significantly reduce the time and expertise required to create scenarios, ensuring that training remains relevant and effective across different regions and types of disaster. Although the capabilities of LLMs are rapidly improving to the point where the quality of the output generated is indistinguishable, there is a gap to fully automated scenario generation [7,8]. Therefore, by integrating the step of manually checking the generated results using a chatbot-style human-in-the-loop (HITL) method, we can eliminate meaningless outputs and generate highly accurate scenarios in a short time by communicating with users about their needs. We believe this will contribute to the generation of high quality and valuable training scenarios in a short period of time.

In this paper, the feasibility of the proposed method is tested by analysing the generated scenarios and interviewing users.

2 Literature Review

2.1 Disaster Scenario Generation

Disaster training is critical to mitigating the effects of natural and man-made disasters. The generation of realistic disaster scenarios is an essential element of such training. Several methods have been developed, each with its own strengths and weaknesses.

The first method uses expert knowledge. This is the classic method that involves creating scenarios based on the insights of disaster management experts. It reflects the experience and insights of experts, allowing for the creation of fully customized and realistic scenarios that take into account regional characteristics. This method has actually been used in Kumamoto Prefecture or Hirakata City, where scenarios created by local government officials were overseen by experts [9]. However, it requires significant manual effort, and not all municipalities have experts on staff. Many municipalities either have no or only a few dedicated disaster management personnel, making implementation challenging.

The second method is the simulation modeling method. This method uses computer simulations to generate disaster scenarios. It has the advantage of being able to manipulate various parameters to create diverse scenarios [10]. However, it requires advanced computing resources and specialized knowledge, making it time consuming to execute.

The third method is the historical database method. This approach overcomes the challenges of the previous methods by using past disaster data. It generates a scenario by combining the fragments of disaster reports. A key feature of this method is its high reliability due to the use of actual historical data. For example, Sakahira et al. [11] developed the cascading disaster networks using natural language processing (NLP) from the newspaper. These cascading disaster networks can be used as a disaster scenario. However, this type of method relies heavily on past data, which poses a challenge in dealing with new types of future disasters and limits the variety of scenarios that can be generated. In addition, as noted in Sect. 1, a conventional training scenario may not be ideal because the conventional scenarios used are certain to succeed, so a greater variety of scenarios and situations is needed.

In recent years, advances in generative AI, represented by LLMs, have opened up new possibilities for disaster scenario generation. By using generative AI, it is possible to efficiently process large amounts of data and automatically generate highly accurate scenarios. The ability to generate scenarios for unknown disasters is particularly important, providing a means to overcome the limitations of traditional methods. In addition, by using an interactive natural language user interface, even municipal employees without specialized knowledge can easily try it out. Therefore, this paper proposes a method for generating training scenarios using generative AI.

2.2 Large Language Models(LLMs)

LLMs have revolutionized natural language processing(NLP) and artificial intelligence (AI). These models, characterized by their vast number of parameters and extensive training data, have demonstrated remarkable proficiency in a wide range of linguistic tasks.

The development of LLMs can be traced back to the introduction of neural network-based approaches for language modeling. Early models, such as the long short-term memory(LSTM) networks [12], laid the groundwork for subsequent advancements. The advent of the Transformer architecture [13] marked a significant milestone, enabling the creation of models like Bidirectional Encoder Representations from Transformers(BERT) [14] and Generative Pre-trained Transformer(GPT) models [15–17].

LLMs have found applications across various domains, from healthcare to finance. Their ability to understand and generate human-like text has enabled advancements in machine translation, chatbots, and content creation. The generative capabilities of LLMs stem from their ability to learn patterns and structures in the training data, enabling them to produce text that is contextually relevant and semantically meaningful. For example, OpenAI's GPT-3 model has shown exceptional ability to generate human-like text based on given prompts [17]. This ability can be particularly useful in creating disaster scenarios that are both plausible and detailed.

In disaster management, having access to a wide range of potential scenarios is critical for preparedness and response planning. Traditional methods of scenario generation often rely on historical data and expert judgment, which can be time-consuming and may not cover all possible situations. By using LLMs, it is possible to automate the generation of disaster scenarios, thereby expanding the range and diversity of scenarios considered. This can lead to more robust preparedness plans and better training for responders.

Despite their impressive capabilities, vanilla LLMs face several limitations that hinder their broader applicability and effectiveness [7,8]:

1. **Domain Knowledge Deficit:** A language model may lack extensive knowledge of a particular domain to which it has not been exposed.
2. **Outdated Information:** LLMs always have a cutoff date determined by their training dataset. Any events, discoveries, or changes that occur after the last training update will not be within the model's knowledge without access to external sources.
3. **Memorization:** Sometimes a model is exposed to knowledge during its training process, but does not retain it. This is especially true for rare facts that are infrequently encountered in the training data set.

2.3 Retrieval-Augmented Generation

To address the inherent limitations of conventional Large Language Models (LLMs), the Retrieval-Augmented Generation (RAG) framework has emerged as a robust solution [18]. RAG synergistically combines the capabilities of information retrieval with generative modeling to significantly improve the accuracy and applicability of LLMs. By incorporating a retrieval mechanism, RAG models dynamically access and integrate up-to-date information from external sources during the generation process. This dynamic integration enhances the relevance and accuracy of the responses generated by LLMs.

RAG models offer several notable advantages for domain-specific applications. Firstly, they deliver more precise and pertinent responses to the domain specific tasks by retrieving the latest information from external databases [19]. Secondly, these models excel at managing extended contexts and maintaining coherence over prolonged interactions, thereby enhancing the quality of responses in complex and long-duration scenarios. Thirdly, a significant benefit of RAG is its capability to mitigate hallucinations—instances where models generate incorrect or nonsensical information. By grounding the generated content in relevant retrieved documents, RAG models ensure that the information provided is both accurate and verifiable [20]. This aspect is particularly crucial in high-stakes fields such as healthcare and legal services as well as disaster management where accuracy is paramount.

3 Interactive Training Scenario Generator System

3.1 Interview to Users

Before developing the system, interviews were conducted with the users, who are the local government staff. We visited Hirakata City in Osaka Prefecture and Kumamoto Prefecture, and in Kumamoto we also attended the actual training. We shared the concept of the system and got the initial feedback from them. In the initial plan, the whole scenario is generated in time series, but from the interview, the need for the interactive interface is high, so the system design was updated.

3.2 Overview of the System

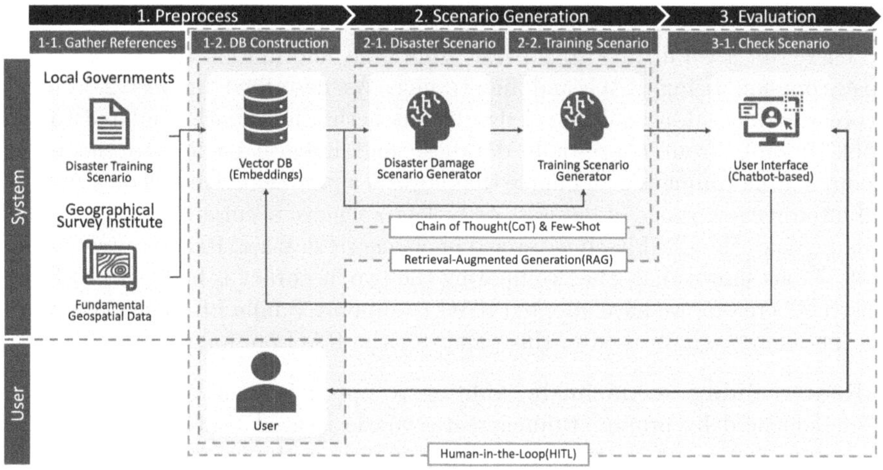

Fig. 4. The system overview

As mentioned in Sect. 1, Creating the training scenario is the key to scenario-based training since it controls the aim and the difficulty of the training, but it is also the bottleneck of these three steps. However, the creation of the training scenario tends to be freshmen who have almost no expert knowledge of both disaster training and disasters themselves. In addition, the creation of the training scenario is time-consuming for the government staff who are already busy with ordinary tasks.

Therefore, we proposed an interactive training scenario generator system that aims to reduce the workload in scenario creation by providing the semi-automated scenario generator with an interactive user interface, as illustrated in Fig. 4. The notable points of this method are; First, the use of LLMs to generate the scenario, which allows for creative scenario generation and also allows users to direct the generation in natural language. The second point is the adoption of several techniques to enhance the reality of the generated scenario, such as RAG, the details of which will be explained in the following sections.

In the first step, documents related to scenario generation are vectorized and stored in a database to facilitate easy retrieval, details of which are discussed in the following sections. Then, vector similarity search is used to extract data relevant to the user's input and integrate it into the input prompt. This enables the generation of scenarios that match the type, scale, and region of the disaster the user is trying to generate. Finally, the scenario is generated by LLM based on the prompt. Note that the interaction between the system and the user is done through the chatbot-style interface, which allows easy access to the generated scenario and give feedback to the system.

3.3 Reference Data for RAG

In principle, vanilla LLMs have the ability to generate the general information learned from the extremely large datasets. However, vanilla LLMs face several limitations (see Sect. 2.3).

There are several ways to provide additional information to the LLM, the most common being RAG and fine-tuning. As described in Sect. 2.3, RAG involves adding additional knowledge by extracting information related to the input prompts from a pre-built database and integrating it into the input prompts. Fine-tuning is a technique that adjusts a pre-trained model on a specific and often narrow range of datasets or tasks to achieve accuracy for a particular domain, since the LLM itself is trained on a generic dataset. Research by Ovadia et al. [7] has shown that when comparing the two, accuracy is higher when RAG is used. Therefore, we have adopted RAG to support vanilla LLMs in this paper.

The reference data used in this paper for the RAG are followings.

1. **Real training scenario**: In addition to specifying the output format is implemented by prompt tuning, real scenario is used as a few-shot to give the knowledge of how the format of the scenario to be used in disaster training and the granularity of the generated scenario are described at the time of scenario generation. The training scenarios used in this research are provided by Hirakata City and Kumamoto Prefecture. The example of a specific training scenario from the Hirakata City is shown in the Fig. 5.
2. **Local Disaster Prevention Plan**: A Local Disaster Preparedness Plan is a document prepared by each community that outlines preparedness and response to natural and man-made disasters. This document is considered helpful in creating disaster scenarios because it contains information on anticipated disasters and their damage for each region.
3. **Geographical data**: Geographic information was collected using the basic geospatial data provided by the Geospatial Information Authority of Japan (GSI). This basic geospatial data includes various types of information such as building outlines, roads, and rivers. For the purpose of this paper, the information used included representative point data for wards, elevation data for each point, and river trajectory information related to disaster scenarios.

3.4 Embedding Model

Embedding is a necessary step in vector search, one of the most important steps in RAG. Vector search is a search method for finding relevant content by converting unstructured data such as text, images, and audio into a distributed representation (vector). Embedding is the process of converting unstructured data into a vector in the above process.

The choice of embedding model greatly affects the accuracy of vector search. Some well-known embedding models are Word2Vec [21] and text-embedding-ada-002 from OpenAI. text-embedding-ada-002 supports not only English but many

Category	Important	Granting time	Responsible for calling	Event Location	Report Content	Detail	Responsible Department	Expected Response
Citizen Report	★	10:30	Citizen	Konan Town	(1) The cliff east of the Tanaka family's muku tree seems to have collapsed, sending earth and sand into the house. (2) The water has also been cut off, although it is not known if this is the cause.		(1)Civil Engineering Department (2)Water Services Department	(1) After inspecting the site, remove earth and sand from the road section. (2) Water truck support
Citizen Report		10:31	Regional Development	10-27, Kusuba-Asahi 1-chome	The road on the Hirakata-Katano Neyagawa line is flooded. I want you to fix the situation.	(In case asked) It is flooded by about 5cm. Cars can still pass through.	Civil Engineering Department	Inspecting the site
Citizen Report	★	10:32	Social Education	1-1-57, Mikuri 1-chome	The roads along the Keihan main line are flooded and there seems to be a problem with the Keihan train service.	(In case asked) It's flooded below the knees.	Secretariat	Answer based on lifeline status.

Fig. 5. The example of training scenario from Hirakata, Osaka (Translated to English)

other languages as well. However, it is not a Japanese-specific model. Therefore, cl-nagoya/sup-simcse-ja-large developed by Tsukagoshi et al. large is used. This embedding model has 2 to 4% higher score than text-embedding-ada-002 in the Japanese Massive Text Embedding Benchmark (JMTEB), a benchmark for Japanese embedding.

3.5 LLM Models

The LLM used to generate the scenarios in this paper is OpenAI's GPT-4 [22] by default, which is the latest gpt-based model. Currently, only GPT-based models are implemented because they have higher performance among other open source LLMs. However, it is possible to implement other choices such as Japanese language specialized model if needed. In the system, chain of thought (CoT) [23], which is one of the innovations to improve the accuracy of generation from LLM such as RAG, is adopted to improve the accuracy of generation. CoT allows models to decompose multi-step problems into intermediate steps, which means that additional computation can be allocated to problems that require more reasoning steps. In the case of the disaster training scenario generation, it is divided into two steps. The first step is instructed to generate the damage scenario based on the referenced geographic data or damage assumptions in regional disaster management plans. Then, the second step generates the training scenario based on the damage scenario generated by the first step and the reference data.

In addition to this, in the prompt for the both models, the example of the disaster damage or the training scenario is given as the few-shot example [17], which is another innovation to improve the accuracy of generation.

3.6 User Interface

In order to implement the interactive user interface, we adopted an open source library in Python called Streamlit. As shown in Fig. 6, the interface is a chatbot that can generate scenarios while interacting with LLMs. Users have to enter the

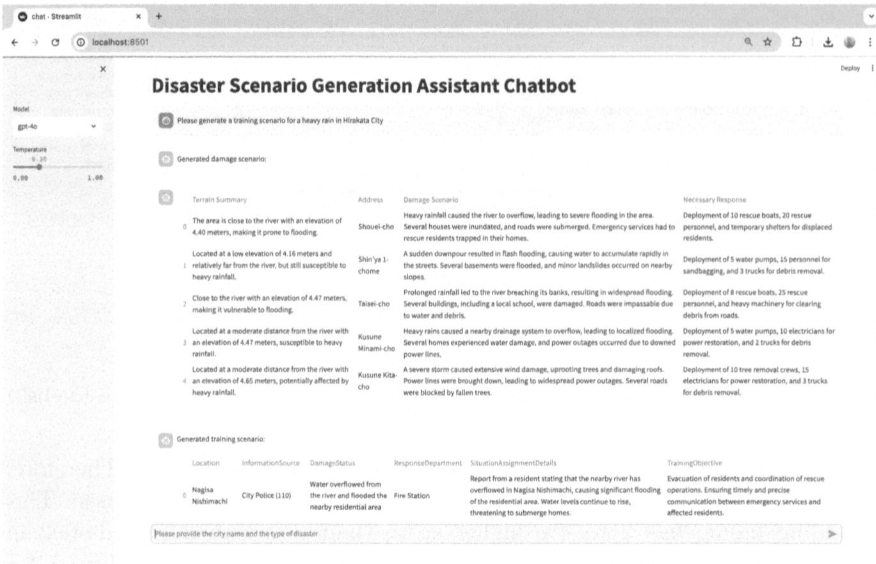

Fig. 6. The user interface of the system

name of the city and the type of disaster as basic information. Based on these information, the system generates several candidate scenarios. The generated scenarios can be downloaded as a CSV file using the Download button.

On the left side of the screen, there is a settings section for the chatbot. Users can select the LLM model, which currently supports GPT-3.5 and GPT-4o, and the temperature of the model, which controls the randomness of the generation, so if you set this parameter to high, then the generated scenario would be more diverse and creative, but the possibility of having meaningless output would be higher. These parameters are expected to be used by advanced users as additional settings to have ideal by tuning.

4 Generation Results

The operation of the system of the proposed method was verified under the generated 25 scenarios of a heavy rain disaster in Hirakata City. The details of the generation results are discussed in the next section.

4.1 Generation of Damage Scenario

Table 1 shows the example of a generated damage scenario based on the references described in Sect. 3.3. In the damage scenario generation step, the summery of geographic information based on the reference, the location where the damage event occurs, the damage scenario, and the expected response to the scenario are generated.

Table 1. The example of generated damage scenario(Translated from Japanese)

Column Name	Content
Geographic Summary	High risk of flooding due to low elevation and proximity to rivers
Location	Kuzuha-Asahi
Damage Scenario	Heavy rains caused flooding in residential areas in the Kusuba-Asahi district. Ten houses were flooded above ground level and 30 houses were flooded below ground level. Roads were also flooded, temporarily paralyzing traffic
Expected Response	Ten workers and three drainage pumps are needed to drain flooded houses. One heavy machine and 5 workers are needed to repair flooded roads.

Kuzuha-Asahi in Hirakata City is located about 22 m away from the nearest river and its elevation is about 14 m, which indicates that the risk of flooding is relatively higher. As shown in the *Geographic Information Summary* column in the table 1, the information retrieval and LLM model successfully understand the geographic information so that it understands that Kuzuha-Asahi in Hirakata City is exposed to the high risk of flooding due to its low elevation and proximity to rivers. Therefore, flood-related damage scenarios are generated, such as residential flooding and traffic paralysis due to flooding.

On the other hand, in the *Expected Response* column, one of the solutions generated by a LLM is *Ten workers and three drainage pumps are needed to drain flooded houses.*, which is probably the unrealistic solution to the problem. Although the water needs to be drained at the end of the disaster, this may not be the best disaster management solution in the middle of the situation. The example shows that information about the state of the situation must be included in a prompt for a LLM to generate a more accurate solution.

4.2 Generation of Training Scenario

Table 2. The example of generated training scenario (Translated from Japanese)

Column Name	Content
Location	Kuzuha-Asahi
Information Source	Reported to police by citizens
Given Situation	Heavy rains caused rivers to overflow, flooding residential areas in the Kuzuha-Asahi. Ten houses were flooded above floor level and 30 houses were flooded below floor level. Roads are also flooded, making it difficult for vehicles to pass through
Corresponding department	Fire station
Expected Response	A local resident reported flooding in the Kuzuha-Asahi area, prompting the response team to evacuate residents and begin emergency operations. Ten workers and three pumps were deployed for drainage, while flooded roads were closed, and traffic was controlled
Aim of training	Prompt evacuation guidance and reduction of flood damage. Strengthen enforcement of traffic control and provision of information to residents. Improve efficiency of drainage operations

Table 2 shows the example of a generated damage scenario based on the damage scenario discussed in the Sect. 4.1. In the training scenario generation step, which is the output of the proposed system, has the following columns; the location where the damage event occurs, information source of the situation, training scenario for the local government staff, the corresponding department to the situation, the expected response to the scenario, and the aim of training with the generated scenario. The generated columns are designed based on the interview with the local government staff in both Hirakata City, Osaka and Kumamoto Prefecture, and the real scenario from Kumamoto Prefecture.

5 Feedback from Users

In order to evaluate the prototype of the system and the quality of the generated scenario, we have visited the Hirakata City, Osaka again. In general, the concept was accepted but if they look closely, there are some flood scenarios that cannot happen because it is located on the relatively higher place in real which non-locals could not judge. This is due to the lack of geospatial information, so additional information is needed. Further needs for the system are identified, such as adjusting the assumption of the scenario or the time frame, etc. (Fig. 7).

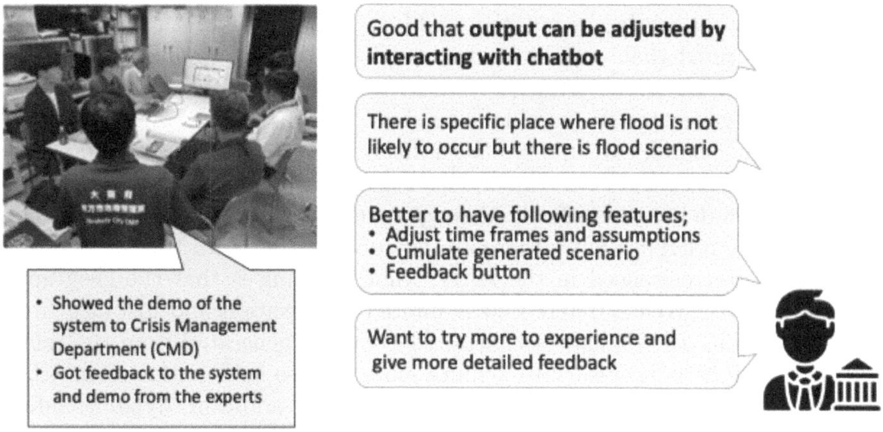

Fig. 7. The interview to local government staffs in Hirakata City.

6 Discussion

Table 3. The summery of generated training scenarios

	Damage Scenario	Training Scenario
Generation Speed	0.1 s to 1 s	0.5 s to 2 s
Number of overlapped location	0/25	
Number of non-existent cities	0/25	
Number of unreal scenarios	5/25	
Number of overlapped scenarios	5/25	0/25

The summery of the generated training scenarios are shown in Table 3. The time required for generating one training scenario is approximately 1 s, which is almost the realtime and much faster than the scenario generated by humans. This indicates that the proposed method has the potential to drastically reduce the scenario creation time which is one of the critical problems in scenario-based training.

In general, the quality of the generated training scenarios is high. The RAG system developed with the proposed structure successfully retrieves the information related to the requests from the user, so that there is no overlap in the selection of the location and geographical information, as confirmed in Sect. 4.1. There is some overlap between the disaster damage categories. Of the 25 scenarios generated, 1/5 of the damage scenarios are the same as others, i.e. flooding of rivers and sewers, landslides, high winds and earthquakes. Since the type of disaster is fixed to heavy rain, the generated damage scenarios cover possible categories, so this overlap is not the problem. In fact the generated training scenarios confirmed that even the category of the disaster damage is limited, location and the details of damage scenario are very vary, so that there is no overlapping in generated 25 training scenarios.

On the other hand, earthquakes are unlikely to occur in a heavy rain event. The reason that scenario of an earthquake is generated is that even the prompt tell the LLM model to diversify the damage category, the actual category is not vary and in the reference data, there are documents related to the earthquakes so that they are referenced in the RAG. Another thing is that the geographical information currently referenced is limited to elevation and distance from rivers. This limits the damage scenarios that can be generated from the reference. Therefore, it is necessary to acquire more diverse information from other databases such as soil databases or hazard maps. In addition, dynamic information such as topographic information and human movements are needed to be added to the input by linking with disaster simulations to generate more practical scenarios.

For the future work, we believe that the accuracy of the scenarios can be improved by adding reference information, and that detailed evaluations of the generated training scenarios require interviews with actual users, such as local government officials and disaster response experts, to evaluate the scenarios.

7 Conclution and Future Work

In this paper, we propose the interactive disaster training scenario generation system using LLMs as generative AI to tackle the problem of generating scenarios for disaster training, and confirm that it is possible to generate scenarios tailored to specific disaster and regional characteristics by referring to actual training scenarios and geographic information, using RAG methods to provide domain knowledge specific to disaster response, which vanilla LLMs do not have.

Future work will include a thorough evaluation by members of the local government to ensure that the scenarios generated by LLM and the chatbot-based UI are practical, effective, and aligned with actual needs. This evaluation will help refine the system and envision the ideal of a new disaster preparedness training. Another future work is to work with simulation. Currently, evacuation scenarios are created statically using hazard maps or other pre-existing data. As an extension of this work, we aim to develop a dynamic system that can collect real-time data on terrain and damage conditions to generate responsive evacuation scenarios. This advancement would allow us to better understand how different response strategies affect citizens. In addition, if non-participating actors can be simulated using agents, it would eliminate the need for coordination with different departments, allowing training sessions to take place without interrupting regular operations.

Acknowledgement. The authors are grateful to the Crisis Management Measures Promotion Division of Hirakata City, Osaka and the Crisis Management and Disaster Prevention Division of Kumamoto Prefecture, especially K. Mikamoto, for their willingness to share the disaster training scenario for this paper.

References

1. Kobayashi, I., et al.: Development of risk management training system for natural disaster (2001). (in Japanese)
2. National Protection Emergency Response Office, Fire Disaster Prevention Division, Ministry of Internal Affairs Disaster Management Agency, and Communications. Study on the guidelines for earthquake disaster prevention training for local public organizations(in japanese). Technical Report 10-52, Fire and Disaster Management Agency, Ministry of Internal Affairs and Communications. Research Report (Fiscal Year 2007) (2008)
3. Kato, T., Asou, H., et al.: Quantitative evaluation of interdepartmental collaboration capabilities in municipalities using map-based simulation training (2020)
4. Wu, J., et al. A survey on llm-generated text detection: necessity, methods, and future directions (2025)
5. Li, Y., et al.: Leveraging large language model as simulated patients for clinical education (2024)
6. Tian, H., et al.: An llm-enhanced multi-objective evolutionary search for autonomous driving test scenario generation (2024)
7. Ovadia, O., Brief, M., Mishaeli, M., Elisha, O.: Fine-tuning or retrieval? comparing knowledge injection in llms (2024)
8. Wang, C., et al.: Survey on factuality in large language models: knowledge, retrieval and domain-specificity (2023)
9. Cabinet Office for Disaster Management. Disaster information: Implementation of disaster training in kumamoto prefecture (2023). (in Japanese). Accessed 20 June 2024
10. Kodama, N., Hada, Y.: Prototype disaster scenario generation system. In: Proceedings of the Conference of the Japanese Society for Disaster Information Research, vol. 11, pp. 295–300 (2009). (in Japanese)
11. Sakahira, F., Hiroi, U.: Designing cascading disaster networks by means of natural language processing. Int. J. Disast. Risk Reduct. **66**, 102623 (2021)
12. Sutskever, I., Vinyals, O., Le, Q.V.: Sequence to sequence learning with neural networks. In: Ghahramani, Z., Welling, M., Cortes, C., Lawrence, N., Weinberger, K.Q. (eds.) Advances in Neural Information Processing Systems, vol. 27. Curran Associates, Inc. (2014)
13. Vaswani, A., et al.: Attention is all you need (2017)
14. Devlin, J., Chang, M.W., Lee, K., Toutanova, K.: Bert: pre-training of deep bidirectional transformers for language understanding. arXiv preprint arXiv:1810.04805 (2018)
15. Radford, A., Narasimhan, K., Salimans, T., Sutskever, I.: Improving language understanding by generative pre-training. OpenAI Blog **1**(8) (2018)
16. Radford, A., Wu, J., Child, R., Luan, D., Amodei, D., Sutskever, I.: Language models are unsupervised multitask learners. OpenAI Blog **1**(8) (2019)
17. Tom, B., et al.: Language models are few-shot learners (2020)

18. Lewis, P., et al.: Retrieval-augmented generation for knowledge-intensive nlp tasks (2020)
19. Sharma, S., et al.: Retrieval augmented generation for domain-specific question answering (2024)
20. Béchard, P., Ayala, O.M.: Reducing hallucination in structured outputs via retrieval-augmented generation (2024)
21. Mikolov, T., et al.: Efficient estimation of word representations in vector space (2013)
22. OpenAI et al. Gpt-4 technical report (2024)
23. Wei, J., et al.: Chain-of-thought prompting elicits reasoning in large language models (2022)

Evacuation

Between Early Warning and Fatigue: Exploring Evacuation and Crisis Management in the 2023/24 Volcanic Eruptions in Iceland

Lucia Castro Herrera[1], Ingimar Ari Jensson[2], and Terje Gjøsæter[1](✉)

[1] University of Agder, Kristiansand, Norway
{lucia.c.herrera,terje.gjosater}@uia.no
[2] Multiconsult, Oslo, Norway
inaj@multiconsult.no

Abstract. This paper investigates the case of the recent volcanic eruptions in Iceland, with the perspective of how the local communities were affected by the early warning and crisis communication, and the long stretches of time with little or no change in the situation, and the perception of danger eventually fading among some of the evacuees. Qualitative methods are used, and in particular, the authors use content analysis on local and international news articles to recreate a story line of an ongoing crisis from the first early warning, the events leading to each of the three eruptions up until mid-February 2024, seeing this from the perspectives of on one hand early warning crisis communication best practices, and on the other hand, cultural issues in crisis communication, normalcy bias, and warning fatigue.

Keywords: Early warning · volcano · crisis communications · evacuation · normalcy · fatigue

1 Introduction

One of the most common practices in disaster management is early warning. Which implies fomenting awareness and taking preventive actions before crisis events to protect and minimize damaging consequences to human life, property (including infrastructure) and the environment [1, 2]. Early warning transcends from authorities only monitoring, coordination and managing a potential situation into a relationship with the potentially affected communities through public information, decision making and required actions. The involvement of the public usually means that a hazard has become a threat. However, *timing is everything* and finding the balance between warnings, calls for action and response is a well-known wicked problem for civil protection authorities [3]. On one hand, *too little time* between warnings and calls for action might have devastating consequences and *too little warning,* and lack of information might fuel confusion and anxiety in potentially affected communities. On the other hand, warnings *issued in advance* and with ample time in anticipation to the potential event, might trigger behaviors of distrust and restlessness, and *too many alerts* can yield information overload and alert fatigue,

Published by Springer Nature Switzerland AG 2026
W. Seböck et al. (Eds.): ITDRR 2024, IFIP AICT 752, pp. 117–128, 2026.
https://doi.org/10.1007/978-3-031-97115-0_8

which can result in the public not following the instructions from the authorities which could lead to harm and severe consequences should a mass scale disaster occur. The element of uncertainty characteristic of crisis events such as volcanic eruptions makes it difficult to predict when events will effectively happen [4]. Which begs the question: how early is too early for early warning and public communication of hazards? Furthermore, are mass alerts sufficient?

This is not an easy question to answer, however, this work in progress study attempts to explore how early is too early in evacuation matters. We do so by contrasting the events of the most recent volcanic eruptions that occurred in the Reykjanes peninsula in Iceland, a country prone to disasters such as earthquakes, severe weather and recurrent volcanic activity. In the course of fourth months from October 2023 to February 2024, this case evidenced the challenge of balance between warnings, actions and hazardous events. Initial evacuation orders were perceived as too early and unnecessary before actual volcanic eruptions started to emerge. In addition, an emergency evacuation took place hours before the most threatening of the eruptions. Furthermore, a third eruption caused damage to critical infrastructure which left households without access to warm water to heat their houses in the midst of winter. The research team followed the development of the ongoing crisis through news reports, press releases from civil protection authorities and social media content related to the incidents. Then, the early warning process was distilled and analyzed in contrast with the academic recommendations on best practices for early warning communication to answer the following research question:

What features can be identified from the actions and reactions of authorities and the potentially affected communities to the process of communicating the threat posed by geological activity and subsequent early warning and evacuation actions during the 2023–2024 volcanic eruption in the Reykjanes Peninsula of Iceland?

The objectives of this work-in-progress are twofold. First, this article seeks to explore early warning through an almost real-time analysis of current events. Second, this work serves as an initial step for future research in early warning that integrates other types of anecdotal and observational data to advance knowledge and best practices that contribute to solve current challenges experienced by civil protection authorities and the communities they serve. Therefore, the remaining sections of the paper are structured as follows: First, a brief literature review is presented as a theoretical framework for the analysis. Then a methodology section explains our research design and approach for analysis. Then, our findings are presented and discussed. Finally, conclusions and future research avenues are presented.

2 Theoretical Background

Early warning systems for natural hazards such as volcano eruptions and seismic activities have been important aspects of emergency management for a long time. For example, the Yokohama Strategy and Plan of Action for a Safer World states that "Early warnings of impending disasters and their effective dissemination using telecommunications, including broadcast services, are key factors to successful disaster prevention and preparedness" [2]. However, communicating these early warnings is not only about mode of dissemination, but also when and how the warning is being communicated and adapted to the local communities in question in order to be effective [5–7].

According to the United Nations Office for Disaster Risk Reduction, early warning systems are "An integrated system of hazard monitoring, forecasting and prediction, disaster risk assessment, communication and preparedness activities, systems and processes that enable individuals, communities, governments, businesses and others to take timely action to reduce disaster risks in advance of hazardous events" [8]. Early warnings are thus the result of these systems and must be communicated and followed up with appropriate actions like evacuation of the areas at risk. However, appropriate timing, decision making and communication are challenging. Because of the uncertainty and fast paced environment in which decisions are made, the rule for determining when the danger is over is not clear. The decision point for lowering the risk and allowing people to return to the affected areas is not always obvious, and the deliberations concerning the decision is not easy to communicate to the affected public. In addition, while there is abundant literature on evacuations [9, 10], there is slightly less focus on the return phase after the end of the crisis in the literature [11, 12]. This aligns well with the observation by Herrera [13] that research in emergency management mostly focuses on the transition from non-crisis to crisis but rarely on the return to non-crisis after the crisis.

A strong factor that can affect the public's willingness to act on an early warning is the *normalcy bias*. This is a cognitive bias that can lead members of the affected public to disbelieve or underplay disaster warnings [14]. Normalcy bias is the minimization of the probability of potential threats and their subsequent implication [15]. *Abnormalcy bias* on the other hand is when authorities or other stakeholders assume that affected communities or survivors of disasters are incapable of rationally coping with shocks and exhibit behaviors of panic, shock, and looting [15]. Abnormalcy bias is not as problematic currently as there is a recognition that survivors are not victims and act as the very first responders in times of crises [16–18].

Another complicating factor is the *alert fatigue* or *warning fatigue* phenomenon. When we experience many warnings and most of them turn out to be near misses or even false alarms, we may become more reluctant to respond to them. This is well-known and made famous by "The boy who cried wolf", one of Aesop's Fables, but was already exploited in 331 B.C. by Alexander the Great, who intentionally used false attacks against Porus in an attempt to reduce their alertness [19].

The effects of alert fatigue have been most extensively researched within the health sciences [20–23]. While the concept of alert fatigue is clearly relevant in the context of the control room and also clearly relate to Endsley's demons of situational awareness [24], the alert fatigue among the public, and in particular alert fatigue caused by early warning systems, is also of particular importance when implementing an early warning communication strategy [25, 26].

Furthermore, disasters can no longer be considered as isolated events. The increasing interdependencies, global networks and uncertainty in determining risk call for a multi-hazards approach to risk management and more specifically, to early warning. A multi-hazard approach goes beyond the sum of potential or eminent hazards, by addressing diverse hazards, risks and impacts occurring in different or similar contextual situations [27]. Diverse hazards in a multi-hazard approach [28, 29] can be:

- *Compound*: two-or more events occurring simultaneously or together amplifying overall impact.

- *Interconnected*: interdependencies between social, environmental, organizational and technological systems evolving in time
- *Cascading*: two or more events occurring as a consequence of the other as ripple effects or domino effects.
- *Cumulatively* over space and time.

While international organizations and country authorities recognize the need for a multi-hazards approach, challenges remain in assessing, managing and formulating processes with multi-hazard methodologies and data to support such approach [28].

3 Methodology

This article follows a qualitative approach that applies content analysis to reconstruct and describe the trajectory of the crisis and unveiling underlining meanings and features to help us help understand the management of uncertainty through early warning and crisis communication [30]. Data sources were news articles published in Icelandic and English from main International and Icelandic media outlets, social media posts from Almannavarnir and Logreglan profiles, risk assessments and press releases from Almannavarnir and the Icelandic Meteorological office, listed on Table 1. We conducted a search using keywords such as volcano, Iceland, evacuation (in English) and Eldgos Reykjanes, Eldgos Grindavík, Eldgos tímalína (in Icelandic). The Icelandic results were more targeted to the Reyklanes region as volcanic activity is common in the rest of the country. For the search in English, only the term Iceland was sufficient to find relevant articles. Initial searches yielded 8–10 news articles per site, however, as events were unfolding at the same time as our data collection, articles were collected and analyzed reiteratively. Social media analysis was done in content posted by the main coordinating authorities, we conducted content analysis and noted sentiment and reactions from social media users interacting with the posts. Risk assessments and official press releases were also included as the main source of communication and advice from authorities. We coded and analyzed our data inductively, thematically, and reiteratively by both constructing a timeline of events and contrasting the content with early warning constructs such as alerts, evacuation, fatigue, and public reactions. To avoid discrepancies in our coding results, the research team worked together in collection and analysis of constructs. Figure 1 represents our ongoing analysis methodology with emphasis on the reiterative nature of our process. Our results are presented in the following section.

Table 1. Sources of information.

Type	Name	Website
Social media	Almannavarnadeild ríkislögreglustjóra	facebook.com/Almannavarnir
	Local Police (Lögreglan á Suðurnesjum)	facebook.com/lss.abending
Authorities' websites and communications	Press releases	almannavarnir.is/frettir/
	Risk assessments	en.vedur.is/about-imo/news/
Icelandic news	RÚV, The Icelandic National Broadcasting Service	ruv.is
	Visir	visir.is
International news	Reuters	reuters.com
	BBC	bbc.com
	CNN	cnn.com

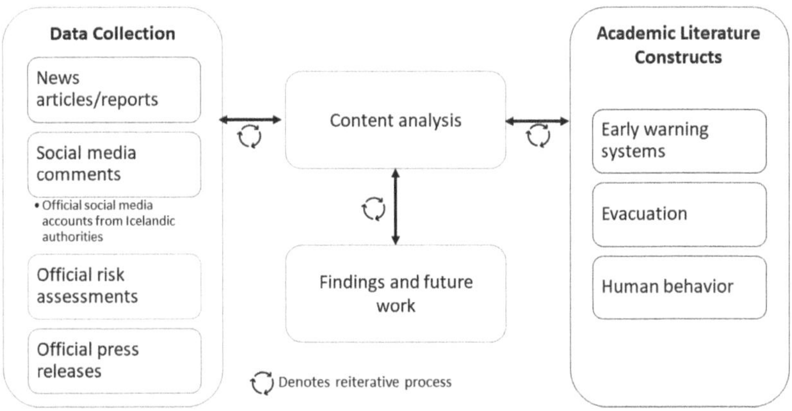

Fig. 1. Ongoing Analysis Methodology.

4 Findings

4.1 Reconstruction of the Events

Iceland is a volcanic active region situated on the Mid-Atlantic where the North American and Eurasian tectonic plates separate. Icelandic geology is characterized by recurrent seismic activity caused by magma (lave underneath the surface of the earth) movement beneath the earth's crust. A volcanic eruption is plausible when magma finds a path to the surface, thus forming a volcanic eruption [31].

In the prelude of the late 2023 and early 2024 volcanic eruptions at the Reykjanes peninsula near the town of Grindavik in Iceland, citizens were restless and eager to return home, they had been evacuated about a month before out of signs of severe increased volcanic activity in the area [32]. The peninsula is not foreign to geological activity that produces earthquakes and minor "tourist" volcanic eruptions, due to the location of a fault line just under the area. In the autumn of 2023, risk assessments revealed the increase of geological activity that prompted the Icelandic authorities to monitoring the area closely [33]. An order of evacuation for residents of Grindavik was issued on November 10th, 2023, together with closures of roads and tourist attractions such as the Blue Lagoon, to prevent potential devastating economic and social losses of an eventual eruption [34]. However, in the absence of volcanic activity from the time of evacuation, the authorities planned and allowed a series of cautionary concessions. The town was allowed to open businesses during the day, including the harbor to boost economic activity but residents were requested to leave the area during nights [35]. Some residents disobeyed the evacuation orders and decided to stay in their homes overnight. At this point residents questioned the validity of the evacuation mandate, criticized the preparedness actions as wasteful and exaggerated, and even threatened to take legal action against the Icelandic Civil Protection (Almannavarnir) as they believed residents should have the right to decide whether to remain in their homes [32].

On December 18th, 2023, the volcano erupted for the first time safely in a remote area away from cities and critical infrastructure. In the aftermath of this eruption, residents of the town were allowed gradually to return to activities 24/7. Authorities recommended the exercise of caution, emphasized the continuous danger of the situation, and monitored the access to the town through checkpoints [36, 37]. However, residents of the town were still eager and restless, they wanted to return to their normal lives [38]. In early January 2024, significant seismic activity was registered, but the Icelandic meteorological office revised down their risk assessments allowing for some return to normalcy. For example, the Blue Lagoon, the popular tourist destination, to open again [39]. On January 10th, a public worker disappeared into one of the craters caused by the eruption [40]. Even though search and rescue operations were activated to find this person, on January 12th the conditions deteriorated with increased seismic and volcanic activity and the efforts to find this person were considered too dangerous to continue. The next day a stricter order of evacuation together with the cessation of all economic activity was re-issued for the town to prevent additional accidents [41]. Given that these new measures were issued on a weekend, the evacuation order was going to be in effect on the following Monday (January 15th). Although residents were encouraged to leave the area at night, those who decided to spend the night at their homes were evacuated early in the morning on Sunday, January 14th, as an imminent eruption was taking place in the proximity of Grindavik [42]. By 8:00 am the lava moved quickly and promptly to the town causing the destruction of some residences and infrastructure [33].

At the time of writing, a new eruption located away from Grindavik has occurred (February 8th - 10th) [33]. However, lava reached a main water pipe which caused parts of the Reykjanes peninsula to miss the warm water supply and electricity which, despite continuous efforts, hasn't been completely restored [43]. Warm water is the main source of heat in the peninsula, which prompted residents to buy alternative sources of heat such as electrical radiators, which were quickly sold out [44]. Authorities recommended residents to ration the use of electricity to avoid power outages and overloading the electricity distribution grid that is not designed to withstand heavy use of energy-intensive electrical appliances [45]. On February 12th, the new pipeline for warm water was completed, however the pipelines are still experiencing damages and service hasn't been completely restored [46]. Almannavarmir announced a zoning plan to allow residents and companies to return to Grindavik during the day to check their properties and possibly save valuables [47], and the authorities continue to closely monitor geological sensors and other seismic activity [33]. It is worth noting that the volcanic activity in the area is ongoing and future eruptions are expected.

4.2 Early Warning Mechanisms and Process

The early warning process during this event follows the progressive cycle of *information → decision → action → information* characteristic of crisis management [48]. From the chronological analysis of our data, we find that in Iceland early warning is exercised by **monitoring sensors** that detect volcanic and seismic activity. The Icelandic Meteorological Office (IMO) oversees the analysis and production of **risk assessments and forecasts of different hazards** which are publicly available on their website vedur.is. The risk assessments include maps and descriptions of relevant updates to the events. When risk levels are deemed significant, authorities activate the Civil Protection Service Levels [31], namely:

- *Uncertainty (Óvissustig)*: in which an event has been identified and has a potential to affect life, communities, or the environment. This level activates collaboration and coordination efforts between relevant stakeholders.
- *Alert (Hættustig):* where the imminent nature of the hazard prompts preventive measures of safety and security and information in form of advice and warning messages is sent to the public.
- *Emergency* (*Neyðarstig*): which is the highest level and immediate actions are in place to "ensure security, save lives and prevent casualties, damage and or loss" [31]

For this volcanic event, the Emergency level was declared on November 10th, 2023. Almannavarnir issues warnings and subsequent mandates for prevention, mitigation, and response to potential or eminent emergencies. The **communication** occurs via press releases, press conferences broadcasted publicly, and social media updates on the official Almannavarnir and Logreglan's Facebook profiles. **Location-based SMS using cell broadcasting** are used to alert the affected communities when **action is required** [31]. Official information is available mostly in Icelandic. Other languages include English and Polish. From our data, it is not possible to infer the frequency of the alerts or community preferences in terms of communications.

4.3 Collaboration

The IMO, the Police (Loreglan), Almannavarnir, the Icelandic Road Administration, and scientists from the University of Iceland continuously monitor the situation and contribute to decision making as events progress. Although the actual relationships and roles are hard to distill from our dataset, Almannavarnir oversees emergency management, the National Crisis and Coordination Centre is in charge of relief and rescue operations at the national level including the communication of alert levels, actions, and recommendations based on preestablished emergency plans [31]. Local Chiefs of Police are in charge of civil protection operations in their region and the organization of crisis management activities is delegated to local Civil Protection Committees [31].

4.4 Evacuation Orders

Evacuation orders are communicated via location-based SMS, social media and traditional media depending on the situation. From our dataset we notice that after an evacuation is ordered, authorities physically monitor the affected area to ensure that no-one is left behind. During the emergency evacuation of January 14th, authorities surveyed the town physically to verify that people left. Residents were instructed to leave a note on the window indicating that the property was empty. At this time, the residents complied with the order to evacuate without problem.

4.5 Public Fatigue vs. Normalcy vs. Compliance

Iceland is exposed to a plethora of hazards that could potentially turn into disasters. Due to the intrinsic geological characteristics of the Icelandic territory, evacuation orders from authorities are followed by the general public in most cases. From the time of the first evacuation order to the first volcanic eruption over a month had passed where significant geological activity was registered but nothing was happening. At this point, the residents of Grindavik started to feel a sense of normalcy which prompted behaviors towards regaining control of stability in day-to-day life, manifested in the desire to return to their homes despite the recommendations from authorities and attempts to sue the authorities in the hopes to regain control and autonomy. Once the second volcanic eruption was eminent, the emergency evacuation was taken seriously, and residents complied with the instructions from the authorities. This behavior continued through the third and most recent eruption. In addition, residents of the Reykjanes peninsula were forced to change their practice of electricity consumption due to the severe damage to the water infrastructure and the potential overload of the power grid. Based on reactions to social media posts from Almannavarnir and the local police, residents are eager to come home and frustrated about the uncertainty perceived through the latest risk assessments and recommendations.

4.6 Multi-hazard Approach

From our dataset, we identified two compound crisis events together with the geological hazards experienced in the Reykjanes peninsula, which called for the mobilization of resources including human capital and new coordination with other relevant stakeholders.

- *Civil unrest*: during the lengthy period of evacuation, signals of potential civil unrest and disobedience were evidenced in the behaviors and actions of potentially affected residents forcing the authorities to take measurements such as house visits to the area in danger. In addition, the communication of extended periods of evacuation and the restrictions to return to the town generated feelings of frustration among affected residents. Which poses a challenge for crisis communication strategies.

- *Critical infrastructure damage*: the damage to the infrastructure pipes for the distribution of warm water caused by the third volcanic eruption triggered an increased use of electricity that threatened to overload the energy distribution grid. Almannavarnir issued recommendations to the public with the aim to limit energy consumption while the infrastructure was being repaired.

Other potential crises that could emerge as the event progresses are of economic and financial nature as the region transitions from response to recovery and the region finds a new normal [49], while not explicitly mentioned in our dataset, we infer that businesses and residents may experience economic losses due to the extended evacuation period. Furthermore, the financial responsibility of the repairs to infrastructure and property could suggest another pressure point that triggers another set of stakeholders and coordination. The lack of evidence in our dataset suggests these events as an avenue for future research.

5 Discussion

Despite the long stretch of time between the first early warnings and the actual eruptions, the Icelandic authorities followed standard crisis management and crisis communication procedures taking into account risk and threat assessments. Alerts, warnings, and evacuation actions with the aim to protect life, property and the environment seemingly prevented disastrous consequences. Residents of Iceland are aware of the potential hazards characteristic of the territory and have high trust in authorities. However, from the analysis, there is a possibility that authorities may have overestimated the residents' willingness to comply with the continued measures over time. The analysis of news articles and social media reactions to content from authorities displays signals of civil unrest and disobedience despite the information provided by authorities and the evidence of the damage caused by the eruptions. Evidence about warning fatigue is not explicitly found in our data set. However, from the first evacuation, we identify the presence of normalcy bias eroding the patience of the evacuated public, and while some social media discussions are applauding the authorities for their work, there are also frustrated voices complaining about the difficulty of the situation as evacuees and the uncertainty of returning home.

Considering the cases of civil disobedience and reluctance to evacuate and stay out of the affected area, digital alerts alone are clearly not sufficient to ensure a complete evacuation. Physical presence and evacuation reminders have been needed to ensure that everyone evacuates, especially in the later periods. This case should also remind us that timing is everything. A too early warning with a premature return to the area at risk can be as bad as a too late warning.

6 Conclusions, Limitations, and Future Research

In this paper, we have investigated, almost in real-time, the case of the recent and ongoing volcanic eruptions in Iceland, using content analysis on local and international news sources, official communication from authorities and social media content to recreate a story line of the crisis from the first early warning until the aftermath of the third eruption in mid-February 2024. We find that the authorities have followed best practices in early warning and crisis management, but the circumstances with long stretches of time between the issuing of the early warning and the following evacuation, and the first eruption – and then again a long stretch of time before the second eruption, seem to have created some fatigue and confusion in the affected public, with tendencies to civil unrest and disobedience leading the authorities to take additional measurements such as physically visit houses to endure that a full evacuation has taken place.

There are limitations to this study, first, the study of media coverage and social media content can be biased as attention is placed to those stories and experiences that represent those who speak louder (in the case of social media) or those who deviate from the norm (the case of media). In addition, the nature of our data limits the depth in which we can analyze and confirm features of early warning. Nevertheless, this initial study serves as a preliminary framing to future research to investigate how warning fatigue, normalcy bias, and potentially big socio-economic losses caused by the actual eruptions as well as the long time in evacuation, conspire to erode the public's willingness to cooperate and comply with authorities' recommendations. Furthermore, as the volcanic situation unfolds continuous analysis (following our continuous analysis methodology explained in Sect. 3) will be performed for new findings and confirmation of the ones presented in this article. Future data sources could include anecdotal interviews from relevant stakeholders who participated in the crisis response, in addition to early warning and crisis management expert discussions to continue advancing the understanding and further improvement of processes around these relevant topics. The current article contributes to the much-needed real-time analysis in crisis management studies as well as the continuous building of theory in early warning and crisis communications.

References

1. Basher, R.: Global early warning systems for natural hazards: systematic and people-centred. Phil. Trans. R. Soc. A: Math. Phys. Eng. Sci. **2006**(364), 2167–2182 (1845)
2. United Nations IDNDR, Yokohama strategy and plan of action for a safer world. United Nations, Yokahoma, Japan (1994)
3. National Research Council. Public response to alerts and warnings on mobile devices: Summary of a workshop on current knowledge and research gaps (2011)
4. Amendola, A.: Management of change, disaster risk, and uncertainty: an overview. J. Nat. Dis. Sci. **26**(2), 55–61 (2004)
5. Twigg, J., The human factor in early warnings: risk perception and appropriate communications. In: Early Warning Systems for Natural Disaster Reduction, pp. 19–26. Springer, Heidelberg (2003)
6. Hamilton, R., Report on early warning capabilities for geological hazards. International Decade for Natural Disaster Reduction (IDNDR) (1997)
7. Horlick-Jones, T., Keynes, M., Jones, D.: Communicating risks to reduce vulnerability. In: Natural Disasters: Protecting Vulnerable Communities: Proceedings of the Conference held in London, 13–15 October 1993. Thomas Telford Publishing (1993)
8. UNDRR. The disaster risk reduction (DRR) glossary. https://www.undrr.org/drr-glossary/terminology

9. Rodríguez, H., et al.: Community processes: Warning and evacuation. In: Handbook of Disaster Research, pp. 183–199 (2007)
10. Buckle, P., Preparedness, warning and evacuation. In: Handbook of Hazards and Disaster Risk Reduction, pp. 493–504 (2012)
11. Siebeneck, L.K., Cova, T.J.: Spatial and temporal variation in evacuee risk perception throughout the evacuation and return-entry process. Risk Anal. Int. J. **32**(9), 1468–1480 (2012)
12. Hidaka, T., et al.: Concerns related to returning home to a "difficult-to-return zone" after a long-term evacuation due to Fukushima Nuclear Power Plant accident: a qualitative study. PLoS ONE **17**(8), e0273684 (2022)
13. Herrera, L.C.: Configuring social media listening practices in crisis management. In: 18th International Conference on Information Systems for Crisis Response and Management (2021)
14. Drabek, T.E.: Human System Responses to Disaster: An Inventory of Sociological Findings. Springer, Heidelberg (2012)
15. Omer, H., Alon, N.: The continuity principle: a unified approach to disaster and trauma. Am. J. Community Psychol. **22**, 273–287 (1994)
16. Wyche, K.F., et al.: Exploring community resilience in workforce communities of first responders serving Katrina survivors. Am. J. Orthopsychiatry **81**(1), 18–30 (2011)
17. Costa, R., et al.: Teachers and school personnel as first responders following disasters: Survivors and supporters. J Trauma Stress Disor Treat **4**(4), 2 (2015)
18. Alexander, D.A., Klein, S.: First responders after disasters: a review of stress reactions, at-risk, vulnerability, and resilience factors. Prehosp. Disaster Med. **24**(2), 87–94 (2009)
19. Breznitz, S.: Cry wolf: the psychology of false alarms. Psychology Press (2013)
20. Ancker, J.S., et al.: Effects of workload, work complexity, and repeated alerts on alert fatigue in a clinical decision support system. BMC Med. Inf. Decis. Mak. **17**, 1–9 (2017)
21. Hassan, W.U., et al. Nodoze: combatting threat alert fatigue with automated provenance triage. In: network and distributed systems security symposium. 2019
22. Cash, J.J.: Alert fatigue. Am. J. Health Syst. Pharm. **66**(23), 2098–2101 (2009)
23. Sutton, J., et al.: Designing effective tsunami messages: examining the role of short messages and fear in warning response. Weather, climate, and society **10**(1), 75–87 (2018)
24. Endsley, M.R., Bolté, B., Jones, D.G.: Designing for Situation Awareness: An Approach to User-Centered Design. CRC press (2003)
25. Mayhorn, C.B., McLaughlin, A.C.: Warning the world of extreme events: a global perspective on risk communication for natural and technological disaster. Saf. Sci. **61**, 43–50 (2014)
26. Yoder-Bontrager, D., Trainor, J.E., Swenson, M.: Giving attention: reflections on severe weather warnings and alerts on mobile devices. Int. J. Mass Emerg. Disasters **35**(3), 169–190 (2017)
27. UNDRR, Words into Action: A Guide to Multi-Hazard Early Warning Systems. Geneva (2023)
28. Šakić Trogrlić, R., et al., Challenges in assessing and managing multi-hazard risks: a European stakeholders perspective. Environ. Sci. Policy **157** (2024)
29. Pescaroli, G., Alexander, D.: Understanding compound, interconnected, interacting, and cascading risks: a holistic framework. Risk Anal. **38**(11), 2245–2257 (2018)
30. Altheide, D.L., Schneider, C.J.: Qualitative Media Analysis. vol. 38. Sage publications (2012)
31. Almannavarnir. Civil Protection Emergency Levels/Phases (2024). Accessed 14 Feb 2024. https://www.almannavarnir.is/english/general-information/emergency-response/
32. Þórhallsson, M.Þ. Íbúa í Grindavík hótað handtöku yfirgæfi hann ekki bæinn. RUV (2023)
33. Icelandic Met Office. Magma accumulation beneath Svartsengi continues (2024). Accessed 15 Feb 2024. https://en.vedur.is/about-imo/news/a-seismic-swarm-started-north-of-grindavik-last-night

34. Almannavarnir, Rýming í Grindavík – Neyðarstig Almannavarna. Reykjavík (2023)
35. Grindavíkurbær, Opnun Grindavíkurhafnar (2023)
36. Lögreglan á Suðurnesjum. Veðurstofa Íslands gaf rétt í þessu út uppfært hættumatskort (2023)
37. Sigurðsson, B. Alls ekkert túristagos. Visir (2023)
38. Pétursson, V.Ö. Undirbúa málshöfðun á hendur ríkinu vegna lokana í Grindavík. Visir (2023)
39. Adam, D.: Blue Lagoon busy on first reopening day. RUV English, 2024
40. Jósefsdóttir, S.D.: Nafn mannsins sem saknað er eftir vinnuslysið. Visir (2024)
41. Almannavarnir, Ríkislögreglustjóri gefur fyrirmæli um tímabundinn brottflutning frá Grindavík / The National Commissioner of Police orders a Temporary Evacuation of Grindavík (2024)
42. Almannavarnir, Eldgos er hafið á Reykjanesinu (2024)
43. Almannavarnir, Hættustig Almannavarna vegna hættu á heitavatnsskorti (2024)
44. Kristjánsson, A.: Hitarar, rafmagnsofnar og gaskútar rjúka út. RUV (2024)
45. Almannavarnir, Allt sem þú þarft að vita vegna núverandi ástands á Suðurnesjum (2024)
46. Almannavarnir, Mikill leki í heitavatnslögninni til Grindavíkur (2024)
47. Almannavarnir, Aukið aðgengi í Grindavík (2024)
48. Benaben, F., Benaben, L.: Science fiction: past and future trends of crisis management. In: 17th International Conference on Information Systems for Crisis Response and Management (2020)
49. Herrera, L.C., et al.: Signals of transition in crisis management: insights from a study of social media use in public service organizations. In: 56th Hawaii International Conference on System Sciences (2023)

Toward the Realization of Resident-Led Tsunami Evacuation Simulation Creation for the Promotion of Community-Based Countermeasures

Kunihiro Nakahara[1(✉)] and Michinori Hatayama[2]

[1] Graduate School of Informatics, Kyoto University, 36-1Sakyo-Ku, Yoshidahommachi 606-8501, Kyoto, Japan
nakahara.kunihiro.33a@st.kyoto-u.ac.jp

[2] Disaster Prevention Research Institute, Kyoto University, Gokasho, Uji-City 611-0011, Kyoto, Japan
hatayama@imdr.dpri.kyoto-u.ac.jp

Abstract. In Japan, there is growing concern about tsunamis associated with potential Nankai Trough earthquakes, which are expected to cause significant damage. As countermeasures implemented solely by administrative bodies are insufficient, it is imperative for individual community residents to consider and implement tsunami countermeasures as their personal responsibility. Previous research has demonstrated that tsunami evacuation simulations can be effective tools in promoting local tsunami evacuation measures. However, due to the complexity of creating these simulations, they have not been widely utilized in communities without ongoing expert involvement. Therefore, this study proposes a resident-led tsunami evacuation simulation approach, aiming to empower local residents to take the initiative in creating tsunami evacuation simulations and to facilitate their consideration and proposal of tsunami evacuation countermeasures within their communities. To achieve resident-led creation of tsunami evacuation simulations, we conducted a validation experiment targeting junior high school students, based on a tsunami evacuation simulation creation method proposed using Scratch. The experiment aimed to determine whether students could configure tsunami animations and create evacuation models, as well as to identify any challenges in the creation process. Results suggest that junior high school students could potentially set up tsunami animations and create evacuation models. Additionally, based on the identified challenges, an auxiliary program to assist in the creation of simulations was implemented for subsequent validation experiments.

Keywords: Tsunami Evacuation Simulation · Visual Programming · Resident initiative

Published by Springer Nature Switzerland AG 2026
W. Seböck et al. (Eds.): ITDRR 2024, IFIP AICT 752, pp. 129–143, 2026.
https://doi.org/10.1007/978-3-031-97115-0_9

1 Introduction

In recent years, there has been mounting concern regarding the potential occurrence of a Nankai Trough earthquake, which, if realized, is projected to inflict extensive damage across vast areas, particularly along Japan's coastal regions, due to both seismic activity and the resultant tsunami. According to the Cabinet Office of Japan [1], in the event of a theoretically maximum-class earthquake, the estimated maximum death toll could reach 323,000 people, with potential maximum economic losses amounting to about 220 trillion yen ($2.2 trillion USD). Given the magnitude of such a disaster, it is impractical for governmental measures alone to adequately address the requisite human and budgetary demands. Consequently, it is imperative for each resident to individually consider and implement specific tsunami evacuation measures. According to the Fire and Disaster Management Agency's report [2], tsunami evacuation measures must be steadily advanced through several key strategies: "thorough enforcement of proactive evacuation actions," "reliable transmission of information promoting evacuation actions," "securing safer evacuation sites," "formulating plans for safe evacuation," and "promoting disaster education that fosters proactive behavior." This underscores the critical importance of community residents actively participating in the consideration of evacuation measures and contributing to the development of local tsunami evacuation plans. In practice, the 2013 amendment to the Japanese Basic Act on Disaster Countermeasures led to the establishment of the "Community Disaster Management Plan System," which aims to actively involve residents in planning and formulating disaster management plans for their districts through a bottom-up approach [3]. This system emphasizes the significance of creating disaster management plans that reflect regional characteristics and leverage local strengths, thereby enhancing the personal relevance of these plans. In this context, "community" refers to "a place where residents live and engage in various activities such as consumption, production, labor, education, health and medical care, recreation, sports, performing arts, festivals, and other forms of social interaction among local residents" [3]. However, despite the recognized importance of residents assuming a leading role in examining district evacuation plans and implementing measures based on them, such initiatives are not sufficiently widespread in tsunami-prone areas. In reality, challenges such as uncertainty about where to begin and a lack of requisite knowledge to carry out activities have been identified as significant obstacles to independently advancing disaster prevention measures [4]. Given this context, there is a pressing demand for tools and strategies that enable residents to conceptualize their own and their community's evacuation plans and translate these plans into concrete measures.

2 Related Study

2.1 Factors Related to Promoting Community Tsunami Evacuation Measures

One of the major challenges in promoting community-led tsunami evacuation measures is the so-called "risk perception paradox," where high risk awareness among residents does not translate into concrete action. According to a study by Wachinger et al., even when people have a high awareness of natural disaster risks, many instances show that this does not lead to actual countermeasures [5]. Additionally, Kakimoto et al. reviewed disaster prevention studies in Japan from the perspective of protection motivation theory and pointed out the existence of the risk perception paradox in Japan's disaster prevention activities [6]. The importance of enhancing self-efficacy and perceived response efficacy as factors to bridge the gap from risk perception to concrete actions or measures has been suggested in theories and models explaining human disaster behavior [7–9]. Protection motivation theory, one of the frequently adopted theories to explain human behavior in the context of disaster prevention, assumes that "protective motivation" is formed through threat appraisal and coping appraisal, and the higher the protective motivation, the more likely protective behavior will be practiced. Threat appraisal is formed from four cognitive factors: perceived severity (recognition of the magnitude of the damage), perceived probability (recognition of the likelihood of damage), perceived external rewards (recognition of social praise for not taking protective action), and perceived internal rewards (recognition of physical pleasure or satisfaction from not taking protective action). Coping appraisal comprises three factors: perceived response efficacy (recognition of how much a specific countermeasure can avoid the damage), perceived response cost (recognition of the financial and psychological cost of taking countermeasures), and self-efficacy (recognition of confidence or outlook on being able to execute the action oneself). Rogers pointed out that enhancing threat appraisal alone, when coping appraisal is low, can hinder the intention to take protective action, emphasizing the importance of increasing self-efficacy and perceived response efficacy [7]. Furthermore, Paton noted that disaster education aimed at raising hazard awareness among residents did not necessarily lead to concrete disaster preparedness actions and proposed the social cognitive preparation model as a model to encourage specific disaster preparedness actions [8]. In this model as well, it is indicated that recognizing self-efficacy and response efficacy are important factors for translating risk perception into concrete disaster preparedness actions. It emphasizes that simply increasing risk perception or crisis awareness only advances to the stage of motivation and that enhancing self-efficacy and perceived response efficacy is necessary to link intention formation to concrete actions. Considering regional needs and challenges is also important for increasing the feasibility of countermeasures. Rowan et al. argued that even technically correct measures that do not consider local opinions and needs result in low satisfaction with the measures and do not lead to concrete actions [10]. For countermeasures that reflect regional needs and challenges, it is necessary to involve residents in the examination and implementation process of the measures. This approach, known as the participatory approach, is recognized for its importance in many disaster management studies [11, 12]. Structuring residents' disaster knowledge is also considered necessary for increasing the feasibility of countermeasures. According to Kobayashi et al., fragmented knowledge and information about a disaster held by the general public may hinder disaster response actions, and structuring disaster knowledge can potentially bridge this gap [13]. In the context of flood disaster knowledge, this structured state means being able to predict subsequent events, such as "heavy rain → runoff → flood → (overflow) → breach → inundation" [14]. Rowan et al. also pointed out that a deep understanding of disaster risks enhances the feasibility of countermeasures and emphasized the importance of visualizing the entire disaster process for residents to recognize it [10]. As indicated in the Community Disaster Management Plan Guidelines, it is crucial to instill a sense of ownership in the community regarding disaster management plans and measures [2]. Sun et al. point out that the underlying cause of the stagnation in local disaster prevention and mitigation activities is the loss of autonomy among the local residents who are ultimately responsible [15]. They suggest that, to promote disaster prevention activities, it is necessary to restore a sense of ownership among the community residents towards disaster prevention activities, as this could be the key to addressing the issue. From the above, to move from the stage of risk perception to the execution of concrete measures, it is essential that each resident can recognize the entire process from the occurrence of an earthquake to the completion of evacuation (recognition of the disaster progression process). They should feel capable of executing the measures themselves (self-efficacy), recognize the effectiveness of the measures when implemented (perceived response efficacy), propose measures based on local needs and challenges (presentation of measures reflecting local circumstances), and feel a sense of ownership over the measures they have devised themselves (ownership of the measures). In the next chapter, based on the framework of the factors related to the implementation of measures mentioned here, we will review the current status and challenges of existing promotion strategies for tsunami evacuation measures.

2.2 Existing Strategies and Tools for Promoting Tsunami Evacuation Measures

A widely implemented strategy for promoting community-based disaster prevention measures is the creation of participatory disaster prevention maps [16–18]. This approach enables people to delineate areas perceived as both prone to hazards and vulnerable. It also allows communities to plot desired and useful risk reduction measures. For example, in Albay Province, Philippines, a model city in the United Nations International Strategy for Disaster Reduction (UNISDR) campaign "Making Cities Resilient: 'My city is getting ready'" (2010–2011), participatory map-making has been actively conducted [19]. This process involves using residents' disaster experiences to create maps, sharing disaster risks, and utilizing the maps as a foundation for community continuity plans. Similarly, participatory map-making has been conducted in Vietnam, Malaysia, and India [20]. The Disaster Imagination Game (DIG), which is a development of disaster prevention mapping, is also widely practiced. DIG involves placing a transparent sheet over a map, imagining potential disasters, and marking predicted damage areas, dangerous spots, evacuation sites, shelters, and useful facilities while considering responses with all participants [21]. This exercise aims to enhance disaster imagination and share local issues among participants. An example of map-making focused on visualizing tsunami evacuation risks is the "Nige-Chizu" (evacuation map), which is a hand-drawn map that illustrates evacuation routes for elderly individuals during disasters, color-coded in three-minute intervals and indicating evacuation directions [22]. This process emphasizes the importance of learning through the creation process, exchanging regional information, visiting sites, considering improvements, and reflecting on disaster prevention plans to contribute to resilient community building. Ushiyama et al. noted that the expected effect of creating local disaster maps is that it allows residents to plot their vague ideas and the opinions of others as concrete positional information on a map, making it easier to devise subsequent measures [23]. Okada and Yamori argued that the map-making process itself promotes risk communication among stakeholders involved in regional disaster prevention [24]. From the above, it is evident that supporting the promotion of measures through map-making has the advantage of facilitating risk communication among participants and visualizing regional dangers and issues on maps. However, it cannot dynamically visualize the entire process from earthquake occurrence to evacuation completion, nor can it sufficiently visualize and verify the effectiveness of countermeasure proposals conceived by residents. Tsunami evacuation simulations can visualize the inundation process and evacuation process of tsunamis and evaluate the effectiveness of proposed measures, making them effective tools for supporting the promotion of tsunami evacuation measures. In reality, local governments in areas vulnerable to tsunamis often publish projected casualty statistics and visual simulations of evacuation behavior on their official websites [25–27]. However, simulations created by municipalities are primarily designed to support disaster prevention measures led by the government and are not suitable for assisting in the examination of disaster prevention measures conducted by residents themselves. As a simulation for residents to consider evacuation measures at the community scale, Kumagai et al. created a tsunami evacuation simulation system in which users can adjust variables like evacuation routes and walking speeds to explore various behavioral scenarios [28]. Similarly, Kawashima et al. developed a simulation system that allows residents to project their own evacuation plans onto the simulation, aiming to promote autonomous evacuation by residents [29]. Furthermore, Hatayama et al. proposed a tsunami evacuation evaluation system that supports community-wide consideration of individual evacuation actions [30]. This study suggests that extracting individual residents' concerns as items to be examined, providing them as animations of evacuation actions, and sharing them among participants can lead to proposals for highly feasible measures. Based on the above, it is evident that utilizing simulation technology to support evacuation measures at the community scale has significant advantages. These include the ability to visualize the evacuation process as an animation, encourage residents to consider evacuation strategies, and facilitate recognition of the effectiveness of proposed countermeasures. On the other hand, simulations created for residents to consider evacuation strategies and measures are conducted by external experts. This process requires significant human and time costs from the collection of local data to the creation of the simulation, posing challenges for deployment in other regions. Kakimoto et al. emphasized that setting up a simulation environment requires considerable effort, and the shortage of skilled personnel limits its application in other communities. [31]. Furthermore, because residents are not involved in the simulation creation process, it is difficult to achieve the risk communication effects seen in resident-led map-making processes. Therefore, to promote community tsunami evacuation measures, a tsunami evacuation simulation that supports residents in leading the data collection, simulation creation, and countermeasure examination, and in proposing feasible measures is necessary. However, such a simulation currently does not exist. Hence, this study proposes a resident-led tsunami evacuation simulation that enables residents to consider and propose tsunami evacuation measures.

3 Resident-Led Tsunami Evacuation Simulation

A conceptual diagram of the resident-led tsunami evacuation simulation is shown in Fig. 1. The creation flow of this simulation begins with the data collection stage, where local residents gather information specific to their area. This includes identifying places that may become impassable during evacuation and individuals requiring assistance during a disaster, through activities such as neighborhood walks and social surveys. In the simulation creation stage, the collected local data is used to construct an evacuation space model and model individual evacuee behaviors in accordance with the local context. The problem identification stage involves sharing the tsunami inundation process and the current evacuation processes considered by the residents as animations to identify issues that need to be addressed. During the measure proposal stage, various local stakeholders discuss the identified issues through simulation creation. They propose measures, reflect them in the simulation, and confirm the results, leading to the proposal of highly feasible measures. Finally, in the measure validation stage, the measures identified in the simulation are verified in the real world through evacuation drills and other means to assess their validity and effectiveness. By repeating these processes under resident leadership, the feasibility of the measures is expected to increase.

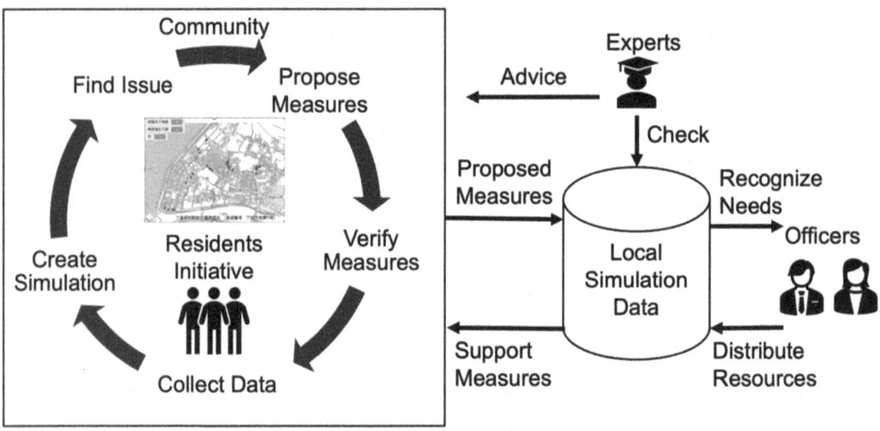

Fig. 1. Resident-led Tsunami Evacuation Simulation Creation Process.

3.1 Regarding the Simulation Creators

To promote a resident-led tsunami evacuation simulation, it is necessary to have personnel with the skills to create such simulations. We consider upper elementary and junior high school students suitable for this role for the following reasons: First, in Japan, programming education has been made compulsory and expanded in elementary and junior high schools since 2020 and 2021, respectively, due to curriculum revisions, alongside the enhancement of disaster prevention and safety education [32, 33]. Therefore, there is a demand for educational tools that incorporate both disaster prevention and programming education. Second, compared to working-age adults, elementary and junior high school students spend more time in their local communities, increasing their potential involvement in community disaster prevention activities. Additionally, if children in the community take the lead, it is easier to gain cooperation across generations [34, 35]. Demonstrating that even young students can create such simulations can increase the likelihood of other generations participating as well.

3.2 Simulation Creation Environment

To enable children and students to create simulations, Scratch3.0 was chosen as the execution environment. Scratch 3.0 was chosen due to its user-friendly interface, which allows beginners to construct programs by connecting blocks in a manner similar to Lego. Additionally, with programming education becoming a compulsory subject in Japanese elementary schools since 2020, the number of Scratch users has been steadily increasing, reaching approximately 1.88 million by August 2023. This suggests that many communities are likely to already have young individuals with strong skills and prior experience using the platform. Nevertheless, it is important to recognize that Scratch has built-in technical constraints—such as a limit of 300 simultaneous sprite instances for representing evacuation agents and overall program size restrictions—which hinder its applicability for large-scale simulations. While Scratch has the aforementioned technical limitations, it was selected as the simulation platform for this study due to its ease of model creation, as our research aims to enable community members to propose specific and concrete tsunami evacuation measures at the community scale.

3.3 Requirements for the Created Tsunami Evacuation Simulation

The requirements for the simulation include visualizing the entire process from tsunami occurrence to evacuation completion as an animation within the scope of a neighborhood association or community association and visualizing the results of the considered evacuation actions. Additionally, as it is intended for use as a tool to examine community tsunami evacuation measures, it must be able to easily reflect individual evacuee actions and dangerous locations within the community in the simulation. The quality of the created simulation need not be highly precise; it should allow rough visualization of the evacuation process and the effects of the measures. This approach aligns with the concept of rough hazard maps proposed by Katada et al., aiming to break the fixation of disaster images and enhance the willingness to search for detailed disaster information subsequently [36].

3.4 Method for Creating Tsunami Evacuation Simulations in Scratch

To visualize the process from tsunami occurrence to evacuation completion, it is necessary to have a road network model for evacuees to move through, an animation representing the tsunami inundation process, and evacuee models moving on the road network model. The operations confirmed to be implementable in Scratch are illustrated in Fig. 2. Generally, a road network model consists of node information (coordinates of intersections and turns) and link information (distances between interconnected nodes). To reflect this information in Scratch, road image data of the area where the simulation is to be created is obtained, resized to fit the Scratch screen size (width: 480px, height: 360px), and uploaded as a background image. The distance ratio per pixel is set from the scale bar on the uploaded image, and the node and link information is stored in lists using a conversion formula to represent it in a one-dimensional list due to Scratch's specifications. For visualizing the tsunami inundation process, many municipalities provide time-series tsunami inundation depth images as open data. These images, matched with the road image's latitude, longitude, and size, are uploaded as backgrounds in Scratch and switched using loop blocks to represent the tsunami animation. The evacuee model can be expressed by setting attributes of an object called a sprite in Scratch and coding the evacuation actions. Evacuee generation can be expressed by combining blocks specifying the appearance location, waiting for seconds, and displaying. The route is represented by entering node numbers from the start node to the target node into a route list. The speed is determined by specifying the travel time between nodes, as the link list already contains the distance values between interconnected nodes. Interaction between evacuees can be expressed by combining conditional blocks with "when touching other objects" blocks to represent speed reduction and other interactions. To visualize the evacuation results, evacuees caught by the tsunami are counted as evacuation failures using conditional blocks combined with "when touching the color" blocks.

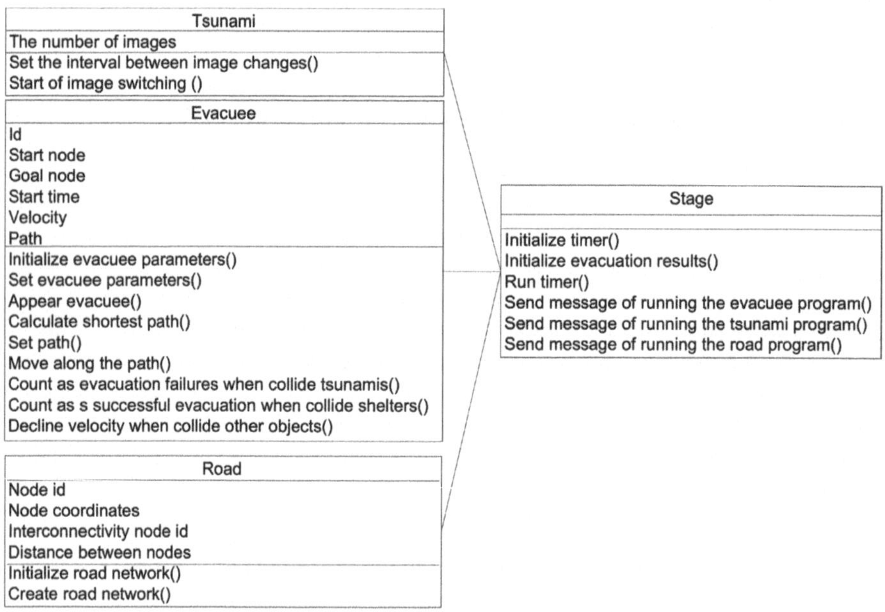

Fig. 2. Scratch Tsunami Evacuation Simulation Class Diagram

4 Verification Experiment for Realizing Resident-Led Tsunami Evacuation Simulation

This study is progressing according to the flow shown in the Fig. 3. So far, in Step 1, a method for creating simulations on Scratch has been proposed to realize a resident-led tsunami evacuation simulation. Step 2 is the part where we verify whether upper elementary to junior high school students can create tsunami evacuation simulations. In this round, we conducted a verification test targeting junior high school students.

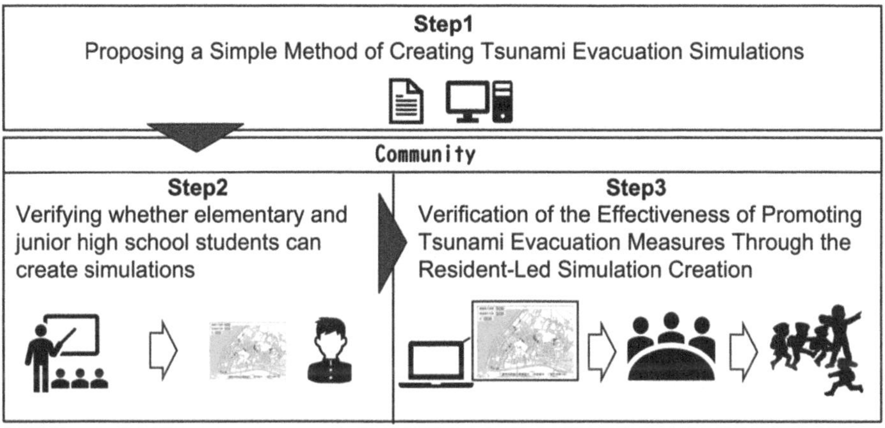

Fig. 3. Research Process Towards the Realization of Resident-led Tsunami Evacuation Simulation Creation

4.1 Purpose and Overview of the Verification Experiment

The verification experiment aims to confirm whether children and students can create tsunami evacuation simulations and to identify any challenging areas in the creation process. Due to a time constraint of 3 h for this verification experiment, the part involving the construction of the road network model was prepared beforehand. The experiment focused on whether junior high school students could create evacuee models and set up tsunami animations. The experiment was conducted over two days, February 19 and 20, 2024, with each session lasting 1.5 h. It was held at a private junior high school in Uji City, Kyoto Prefecture, with six participants on the first day and five on the second day, four of whom attended both days (two attended only the first day, and one only the second day). All participants were second-year junior high school students or younger.

4.2 Flow and Implementation of the Verification Experiment

On the first day, after explaining the dangers of tsunamis and the role of tsunami evacuation simulations, basic operations of Scratch were introduced. Next, coding for the simulation timer and tsunami animation was explained, and the participants implemented it. Following that, the method for coding to make evacuees appear at specified times and locations and setting the routes was explained, and the participants coded their own evacuation actions. Additionally, the method for creating success and failure judgments for evacuation on Scratch was explained, and the participants implemented it. On the second day, the method for duplicating evacuee models, managing multiple evacuation-related parameters in a list, and using a pre-prepared shortest path calculation program was explained. The participants then programmed the actions of multiple evacuee models. Students who completed their tasks quickly were asked to code the evacuee models and tsunami animations for a different area following the previously explained process.

4.3 Evaluation Method

The evaluation method for whether the students could set up tsunami animations and create evacuee models was based on usability testing. According to ISO 9241–11, usability is defined as "the extent to which specified users can achieve specified goals with effectiveness, efficiency, and satisfaction in a specified context of use." Effectiveness refers to the accuracy and completeness with which users achieve specified goals. Efficiency refers to the resources expended in relation to the accuracy and completeness of goals achieved. Satisfaction refers to the comfort and positive attitudes towards using the product. In this experiment, we focused on effectiveness and efficiency. Effectiveness was evaluated by checking the correctness of the submitted code after the lesson, and efficiency was evaluated by the time spent on the tasks. Regarding satisfaction, we did not evaluate it this time due to the small number of experiment participants.

5 Results and Discussion of the Verification Experiment

On the first day, all six participants successfully coded the simulation timer, tsunami animation, and evacuation action programs correctly within 50 min (Fig. 4). Three participants managed to implement the program for counting the number of evacuees who failed due to collision with the tsunami. Regarding the program to represent individual evacuation actions, the students were able to set up start points, times, speeds, and routes for their evacuation objects, suggesting that junior high school students could reflect individual evacuation actions in the evacuation space using Scratch. On the first day, much time was spent entering node numbers in sequence for routes, resulting in three students not reaching the implementation of tsunami collision detection. This indicates the need for a program to assist in creating evacuation models following arbitrary routes within limited time constraints. On the second day, all participating students could duplicate evacuees, manage parameters in lists, and move them within 30 min. Using the pre-prepared shortest path calculation program, they smoothly set routes for each evacuee model. One student successfully set up tsunami animations and created evacuee models for a different area (Fig. 5). This suggests that junior high school students can set evacuation start times, speeds, and move evacuee models to evacuation sites along the shortest path without significant issues.

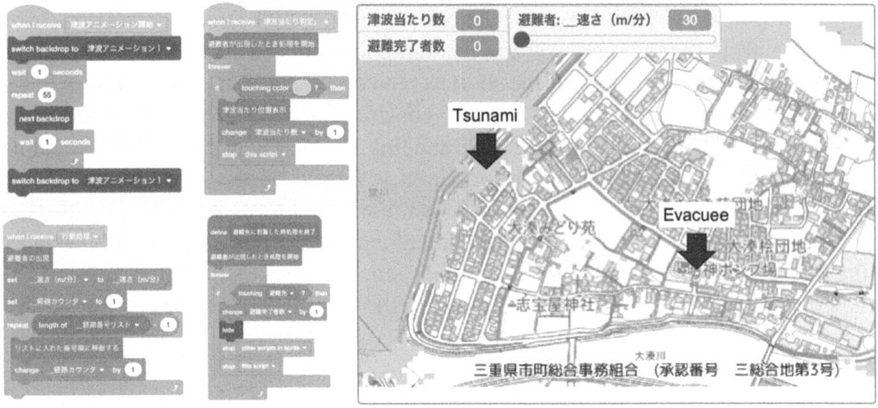

Fig. 4. A Portion of the Code and Tsunami Evacuation Simulation Created by a Student

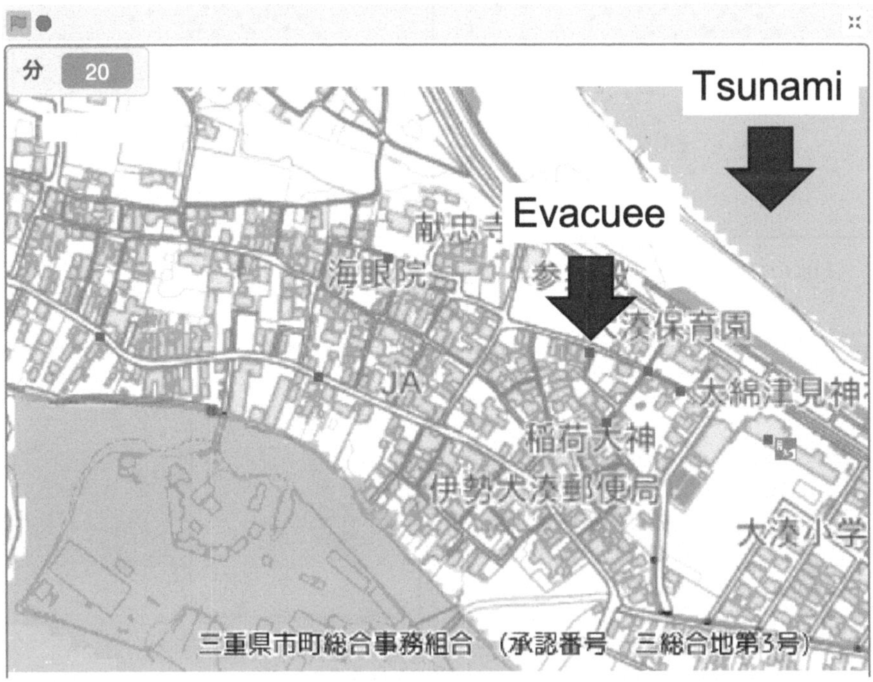

Fig. 5. Tsunami Evacuation Simulation Created by a Student

6 Addition of Auxiliary Programs

Based on the verification experiment results, significant time was spent on setting individual evacuation routes, indicating the need for a program to assist in this process. Since a shortest path calculation program based on Dijkstra's algorithm was already implemented, it was modified to allow calculation of the shortest path by specifying waypoints

(Fig. 6). Specifically, by clicking the Path button on the initial screen, points appear on the screen, and clicking a point to set it as the start point and then another point as the goal or waypoint allows calculation of the shortest path and storage of node numbers in the route list. Additionally, considering students' construction of road network models in the future, a program to assist in creating node and link lists was added (Fig. 7). For adding road nodes, an object to add point information is moved on the screen, and clicking adds the coordinate information to the node list. For link information, clicking the start and end nodes to be connected stores the interconnected node numbers and distances in the link list. For reflecting impassable roads, clicking the Road button on the initial screen displays the road network, and clicking the start and end nodes of impassable roads allows them to be reflected (Fig. 8).

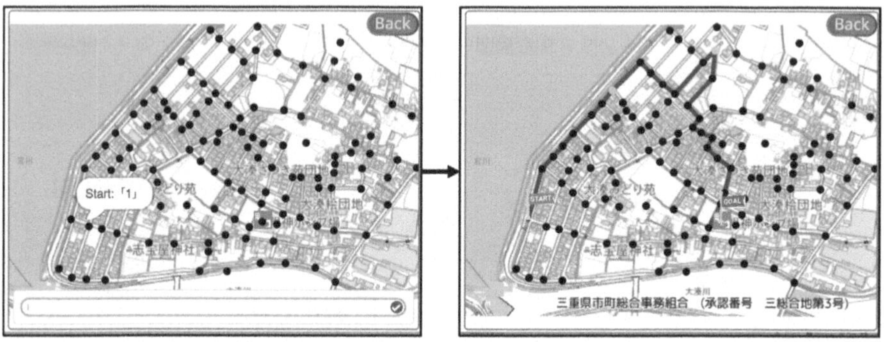

Fig. 6. Shortest Route Search Program that Allows You to Specify a Transit Point

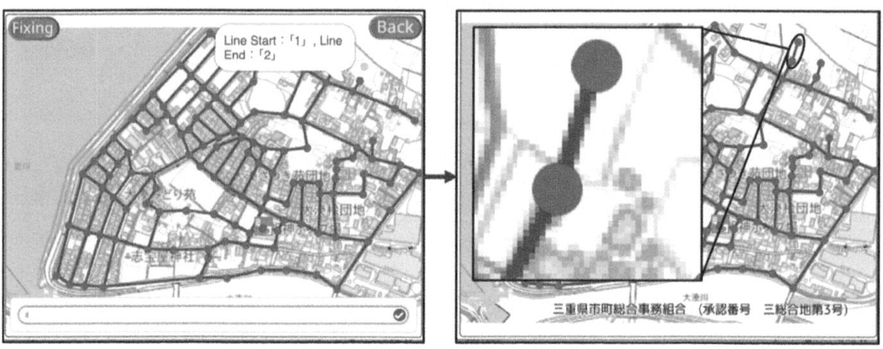

Fig. 7. Programs to Assist in the Creation of Road Network Models

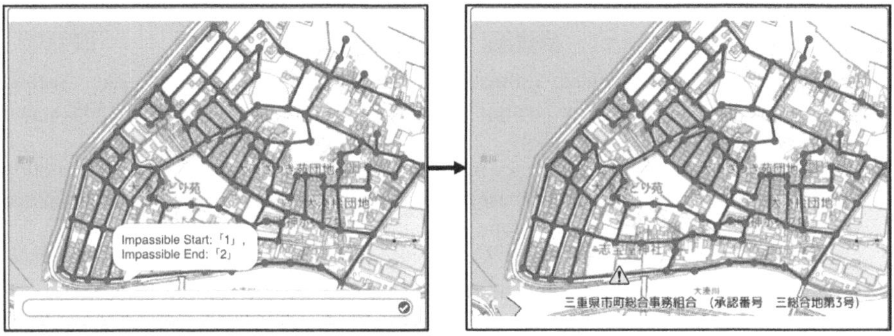

Fig. 8. Programs to Assist in Reflecting Impassible Road

7 Summary

To promote community-driven tsunami evacuation measures, a resident-led tsunami evacuation simulation was proposed. An experiment was conducted to determine if junior high school students, who could potentially be creators, could create tsunami evacuation simulations and to identify any challenging areas in the creation process. The results indicated that junior high school students could program evacuation actions and set up tsunami animations without significant difficulty. Since setting an arbitrary route took a considerable amount of time during the verification experiment, the shortest route program was improved to allow route setting by specifying a transit point. Additionally, to enable elementary and junior high school students to construct and modify evacuation space models, programs to assist in adding roads and reflecting impassable roads on the screen were also implemented. In this verification experiment, the sample size was small, and the ability to create a road network model was not verified. Therefore, it is necessary that further experiments will be conducted at other junior high and elementary schools to verify whether tsunami evacuation simulations can be created, including the creation of road network models. Additionally, after verifying whether elementary and junior high school students can create tsunami evacuation simulations, to evaluate the effectiveness of promoting tsunami evacuation measures through resident-led simulation creation, processes involving data collection, simulation creation, and measure proposals will be carried out in tsunami high-risk areas. These processes will involve children and students as central figures and engage various local stakeholders. The impact of these activities on recognizing the disaster progression process, enhancing self-efficacy, perceiving response efficacy, presenting measures that reflect local conditions, and gaining ownership of the measures will be examined.

Acknowledgements. This work was supported by JST SPRING, Grant Number JPMJSP2110.

References

1. Japan Cabinet Office: Damage estimation of Nankai Megathrust Earthquake: Second report. (in Japanese). https://www.bousai.go.jp/jishin/nankai/taisaku_wg/pdf/20130528_houkoku_s2.pdf.Accessed 27 June 2024
2. Fire and Disaster Management Agency in Japan. Tsunami Evacuation Measures Promotion Manual Study Group Report. (in Japanese). https://www.fdma.go.jp/singi_kento/kento/items/kento106_01_p00.pdf. Accessed 27 June 2024
3. Cabinet Office, Government of Japan. Community Disaster Management Plan Guidelines. (in Japanese). https://www.bousai.go.jp/kyoiku/pdf/guidline.pdf. Accessed 27 June 2024
4. Ministry of Education, Culture, Sports, Science and Technology Homepage, https://www.mext.go.jp/b_menu/shingi/chousa/kaihatu/006/shiryo/attach/1367196.htm. Accessed 26 June 2024
5. Wachinger, G., Renn, O., Begg, C., Kuhlicke, C.: The risk perception paradox—implications for governance and communication of natural hazards. Risk Anal. **33**(6), 1049–1065 (2013). https://doi.org/10.1111/j.1539-6924.2012.01942.x
6. Kakimoto, R., Ueno, Y., Yoshida, M.: Examining the regional characteristics of disaster mitigation behavior to resolve the paradox of natural disaster risk perception. Jpn. Soc. Civil Eng. **73**(5), 57–68 (2017). (in Japanese)
7. Maddux, J.E., Rogers, R.W.: Protection motivation and self-efficacy: a revised theory of fear appeals and attitude change. J. Exp. Soc. Psychol. **19**(5), 469–479 (1983)
8. Paton, D.: Disaster preparedness: a social-cognitive perspective. Disast. Prevent. Manag. Int. J. **12**(3), 210–216 (2003)
9. Rogers, R.W.: A protection motivation theory of fear appeals and attitude change1. J. Psychol. **91**(1), 93–114 (1975)
10. Rowan, K.E., Botan, C.H., Kreps, G.L., Samoilenko, S., Farnsworth, K.: Risk Communication Education for Local Emergency Managers: Using the CAUSE Model for Research, Education, and Outreach. Routledge, New York (2010)
11. Pearce, L.: Disaster management and community planning, and public participation: how to achieve sustainable hazard mitigation. Nat. Hazards **28**, 211–228 (2003)
12. Ranghieri, F., Ishiwatari, M. (Eds.). Learning from megadisasters: lessons from the Great East Japan Earthquake. World Bank Publications, Washington, DC (2014)
13. Kobayashi, H., Tanaka, A.: The influence of disaster knowledge structure on disaster response behavioral intentions: a case study of the torrential rainfall in the Kanto and Tohoku Regions in 2015. Jpn Soc. Disast. Inf. Stud. **15**(2), 137–147 (2017). (in Japanese)
14. Suetsugu, T.: Considering Flood Control from Water Damage: Flood Disaster Mitigation Theory Derived from Lessons Learned. Gihodo Publication, Tokyo (2016). (in Japanese)
15. Sun, Y., Yamori, K., Tanizawa., R.: Action research aimed at restoring the initiative of stakeholders in disaster prevention and mitigation activities. Jpn. J. Exp. Soc. Psychol. **55**(2), 75–87 (2016). (in Japanese)
16. Shaw, R., Takeuchi, Y.: Town Watching Handbook for Disaster Education: Enhancing Experiential Learning. UNISDR, Geneva (2009)
17. Benson, C., Twigg, J., Rossetto, T.: Tools for mainstreaming disaster risk reduction: guidance notes for development organisations ProVention Consortium, Geneva (2007)
18. Cadag, J.R.D., Gaillard, J.C.: Integrating knowledge and actions in disaster risk reduction: the contribution of participatory mapping. Area **44**(1), 100–109 (2012)
19. Toyoda, Y., Kanegae, H.: A study on the effectiveness of community-based disaster prevention maps on community disaster preparedness. Inst. Int. Relat. Area Stud. **35**, 25–43 (2012). (in Japanese)

20. UNDRR Homepage. https://www.undrr.org/publication/making-cities-resilient-my-city-getting-ready-campaign-kit. Accessed 28 June 2024
21. Yana gawa,Y., Takeuchi, I., Jitsuiki, K., Yoshizawa, T.: Disaster Imagination Game at Izunokuni City for preparedness for a huge Nankai Trough earthquake. J. Disast. Mitigation Hist. Cities **17** (2023)
22. Yamamoto, T., Homma, K., Moriwaki, T.: Making of voluntary evacuation maps from various disasters on hazard map. J. Injury Viol. Res. **11**(4), 162 (2019)
23. Ushiyama, S., Abe, Y., Kaneda, M., Imamura, H.: Basic data on workshops for creating community-based disaster prevention maps. Tsunami Eng. **21**, 83–91 (2004). (in Japanese)
24. Okada, N., Yamori, K.: Action research on bosai map cycle–communications and interactions among stakeholders involved in mapmaking activities. J. Disast. Res. **15**(6), 783–793 (2020)
25. Kamakura city homepage. https://www.city.kamakura.kanagawa.jp/sougoubousai/tsunami_simulation/pages/index_meio.html. Accessed 27 June 2024
26. Noshiro city homepage. https://www.city.noshiro.lg.jp/kurashi/bosai-shobo/tsunami-hinankeikaku/12518. Accessed 27 June 2024
27. Matsuzaki town homepage. https://www.town.matsuzaki.shizuoka.jp/docs/2016032400013/. Accessed 27 June 2024
28. Kumagai, K., Oda, K., Hijikata, S., Oka, H.: Development of the Tsunami evacuation simulation system and production trial at the model area (in Japanese). Proc. Infrastruct. Plan. **33**, 270 (2006)
29. Kawashima, K., Tatano, H., Hatayama, M.: A flood risk communication support system to promote safe autonomous evacuation. Proc. Infrastruct. Plan. **23**, 309–318 (2006).https://doi.org/10.2208/journalip.23.309. (in Japanese)
30. Hatayama, M., Nakai, H., Yamori, K.: Tsunami evacuation evaluation system for plan development of community based evacuation. Inf. Process. Soc. Jpn. **55**(5), 1498–1508 (2014). http://id.nii.ac.jp/1001/00101155/. (in Japanese)
31. Kakimoto, R., Yamada, F., Mori, T., Anju, A., Sakajo, H.: Development of learning tools for flood risk communication on support the expansion of areas. Proc. Infrastruct. Planning **41** (2010). (in Japanese)
32. Ministry of Education, Culture, Sports, Science and Technology. Guidelines for Elementary School Programming Education (Third Edition). (in Japanese). https://www.mext.go.jp/content/20200218-mxt_jogai02-100003171_002.pdf. Accessed 28 June 2024
33. Fujii,M.: How Has Disaster Prevention Education Changed in the New Curriculum Guidelines? (in Japanese). https://www-510.aig.co.jp/assets/documents/institute/insight/institute-insight-08-ja.pdf. Accessed 28 June 2024
34. Katada, T., Kanai, M.: Implementation of tsunami disaster education for children and their parents at elementary school. In: Solutions to Coastal Disasters 2008: Tsunamis, pp. 39–48 (2008). https://doi.org/10.1061/40978(313)4
35. Pfefferbaum, B., Pfefferbaum, R.L., Van Horn, R.L.: Involving children in disaster risk reduction: the importance of participation. Eur. J. Psychotraumatol. **9**(sup2), 1425577 (2018)
36. Katada, T., Kimura, H., Kodama, M.: A study on the role of flood hazard maps for disaster risk communication (in Japanese). J. Jpn. Soc. Civil Eng. **63**(4), 498–508 (2007)

Reliability in Decision-Making

Software-Based True Random Number Generator (STRNG) for Reducing Communication Vulnerabilities During Disaster Evacuation and Recovery Within Resilient Urban Development (RUD) Framework

Benny Benyamin Nasution(✉), Rahmat Widia Sembiring, Indra Siregar, and Rina Walmiaty Mardi

Politeknik Negeri Medan, Jalan Almamater No. 1, Kampus USU, Medan 20155, Indonesia
bennynasution@polmed.ac.id

Abstract. Some communication vulnerabilities, such as cryptographic keys generated by a random number generator, have been identified during evacuation and recovery activities of a disaster. Due to some disfunctions of infrastructures and lack of guardiancies, sensitive data and illegal transactions may have occurred uncontrollable. One of the main causes of those communication vulnerabilities is the existence of the Random Number Generator (RNG) within the cryptosystem of network transaction with minimum infrastructures. The communication protection through cryptography cannot access the true RNG as it requires sophisticated and costly devices. To handle the situation, this research has investigated the Software-based True Random Number Generator (STRNG). In contrast to other TRNGs, the STRNG can be deployed using minimum capabilities of a processor, such as a Raspberry Pi. The technology can still generate high-entropy random numbers of unlimited number of digits, and the random number generator bitrate can reach up to 3 kbps. With the STRNG the communication can benefit it for the cryptography that will protect the communication from adversaries. Such secure communication will reduce the capability of potential adversaries that allowed by disaster have a bigger possibility to attack due to the communication vulnerabilities. As part of the bigger research scope, the positive results of the STRNG technology will then increase the quality of the whole framework of the Resilient Urban Development (RUD) project.

Keywords: Software-Based True Random Number Generator (STRNG) · Earthquake Forecasting · Citizen Movement Control System (CMCS) · Single Value Coordinate System (SVCS) · Single Layer Hierarchical Graph Neuron (SLHGN)

Published by Springer Nature Switzerland AG 2026
W. Seböck et al. (Eds.): ITDRR 2024, IFIP AICT 752, pp. 147–162, 2026.
https://doi.org/10.1007/978-3-031-97115-0_10

1 Introduction

A number of disaster incidences taken from UNDRR profiles have shown that infrastructures collapsed, and the evacuation process and first responders' movement took very long time to arrive. The other thing that could not be established properly was the means for communication. Hours after the tsunami of Aceh, people outside Aceh could not figure out how bad the situation was. This example would represent how different the situation compared to the normal situation. For instance, in a normal situation government body would have capabilities to protect and monitor communication, either online or offline [1–5].

Not only during the evacuation processes, when the recovery process started, the infrastructures and communication means were not yet available completely, so the communication and online transactions would not be protected properly [4, 5]. Despite the missing infrastructures, every communication nowadays requires to be protected though a cryptographic technology. This issue has particularly been raised by the Cybersecurity and Infrastructure Security Agency (CISA) in their website (cisa.gov). It is very often discussed that the strength of a cryptography algorithm lies within the symmetric or asymmetric keys generated by the random number generator (RNG) embedded in the cryptosystem. The random number generator is required to generate one or more cryptographical keys. The better the generator is the better quality of keys will be produced.

Not only infrastructures, human resources were amongst resources that cannot be gathered completely to help the evacuation and the recovery processes. Without complete existence of human resources, protecting the communication occurred during those processes was practically impossible. It can be observed from previous disasters that all groups, communities, teams, government bodies did the communication using whatever means they could provide [1–4]. However, it was very difficult to discovers that all the communication and transactions were securely protected. If it is protected, due to limited resources how strong the protection was could not be comprehended.

The other thing that needed to consider during evacuation and recovery was the process time. The evacuation and recovery processes required particular time frames. The technology of Citizen Movement Control System (CMCS) [6] has shown the effect of results caused by different time frames. During a disaster, not only human needs to be evacuated and recovered, animals and important chemical, biological, physical substances must be handled in case it may harm animals or even humans. All those issues must carefully be handled within particular short time limit.

In terms of sending detailed reports through bandwidth consuming data such as pictures or videos, the process time of the communication must be fast. Therefore, the technologies that support the handling through communication should be able to be deployed quickly. This includes particularly the true random number generator (TRNG) used in the cryptosystem that should work in timely manner.

Communication during evacuation and recovery process is the outmost importance. The first and second responders must work and coordinate their work through lots and lots of communication. They have to figure out which part and which one must be handled first and which part or which one must be handled next [5]. In such a work, the target of the communication is just its functionalities. Other issues involved in communication are the protection of data or content in the communication itself. During evacuation and recovery processes, data and information from companies, industries, and government bodies may have been transferred through a communication medium. If the communication is not securely protected, it is very likely that the content may have been stolen, misused, and abused [5].

When the content of communication is not protected properly due to disasters, adversaries may have gained the content and sent it to some kind of storage for the next usage. Some examples of sensitive content or data, that may have illegally been collected during a disaster, are:

- Citizen's private digital properties
- Citizen's personal information
- Company's private digital properties
- Company's business strategies
- Company employee's information
- Company partner's information
- Local government's private digital properties
- Local government's network
- Local government's strategic plans
- Local government's private information

The first and second responder's communication content may also be the attacking target of adversaries. Some efforts to handle the evacuation and recovery processes will no longer be ready to be executed if the communication data or content has been compromised by adversaries. The next section will describe those communication vulnerabilities.

2 Communication Vulnerabilities

It is obvious that the communication system in a hit area can be disturbed or completely paralyzed after a severe disaster. In fact, communication is urgently required in such a situation. People tend to use any means to establish a minimum communication system. As a result, there will be some communication vulnerabilities raising during evacuation and recovery processes. Such vulnerabilities will turn into threats very shortly, depending on how fast people outside the hit area coming in.

The other thing to mention is the existence of people outside the hit area. In case of Aceh's tsunami many people from around the world came in to support and help Aceh's people. In such a situation, it is very problematic to handle the security of the communication. Most people were focusing on evacuating humans, alive or dead. But it is possible that adversaries were also amongst those people at that time. Like in other parts of Indonesia, Aceh's natural resources are tremendous. Since hundreds of years, Indonesia have harvested very expensive bounties across the area. This can still be the main lucrative reason why adversaries might exist during that time.

What make things worst is that after a disaster there is no observation or monitoring that can be established not even by the local or national government, as they are generally focusing on the evacuation of humans and cattle. The citizen might hope that all the people coming in the hit area are good people for helping the citizen and their left belongings. Also, people are aware only of the general assumption that the communication will only be used to coordinate and manage the evacuation and recovery processes [3, 5]. In fact, the existence of people from foreign countries opens up a new opportunity for adversaries to penetrate the country through those people. In short, during a disaster it is difficult to protect sensitive data of the communication using minimum means and minimum systems.

It is one of some difficulties faced when a disaster strikes. The Resilient Urban Development (RUD) research has been run to discover the appropriate model for maintaining the citizen of a city in a good welfare against potential disturbances. In relation to those, the RUD research has worked on the communication issues embedded in a disaster as part of its objectives.

3 Resilient Urban Development (RUD)

The urban development of cities in general, and new cities in particular, does not always run as planned. Uncontrollable and long-lasting urbanization, a systematic and massive terrorist attack, an abrupt pandemic, a frequent landslide, an unpredictable earthquake, etc., are just sources of possible urban development disturbances. The common strategy of handling disturbances in urban development is through response and recovery actions, where ad-hoc solutions are proposed to revise existing the government's plans. These solutions are then implemented as sub-projects that get executed alongside the original plans. Such a strategy takes a long time to define and implement, making it outdated by the time it reaches the execution, due to the fast nature of the disturbances and the slow nature of the treatment processes.

This research is part of the main research of the Resilient Urban Development (RUD), which is an intelligent and adaptive disturbance treatment system that will be able to use data from monitoring systems and dynamically proposes revised government's plans according to the actual situation. The system uses machine learning and pattern recognition algorithms that continuously monitor the time-series data of the key parameters. Once an anomaly from the ongoing urban development is recognized, the system would respond with adapted protocols. The government of the city would need to follow those protocols so, that the resiliency of the urban development can be properly treated and at last the welfare of the citizen in a city hold.

The intelligent system will be trained using a large training dataset acquired from the historical data of other cities, where despite disturbances the urban development has been successfully executed. Since the RUD system uses a data-driven approach to create urban development protocols, it has the huge advantage of requiring less development time and effort, making it more efficient than traditional approaches. Moreover, the RUD system produces protocols containing a list of prioritized steps, leaving some options for the local government to decide which first steps would be the most feasible to implement, depending on other criteria, such as the availability of funding.

To support the recognition capability of the RUD system, the research has previously worked on the machine learning technology of Single Layer Hierarchical Graph Neuron (SLHGN). The technology is capable of successfully recognizing complex patterns. The next technology as part of the RUD research has been inspired due to some difficulties discovered in the current coordinate system when working on the spherical surface of the earth. Those difficulties have been solved through the newly developed Single Value Coordinate System (SVCS) [7, 8], another coordinate system for the earth. The next technology that is involved in the RUD research is the Citizen Movement Control System (CMCS) [6]. This technology will be able to assist the movement of the local citizen to the evacuation area during a disaster, such as an earthquake. The simulation results showed that the CMCS devices could help evacuate up to six hundred people in one square km area within less than 500 s.

To deal with disasters caused by various attacks through transactions on computer networks, the RUD has researched on securing network transactions using the Random Public Algorithm Cryptography (RPAC) technology. The technology differs from the public-key cryptography, in which instead of using public and private keys, the RPAC deploys public and private algorithms. For each session, two new public and private algorithms will be randomly generated. It means that there is no pre-determined way how the new two algorithms would work, making it more secure against commonly known attacks. In case for protecting the owner of data and resources from fraudulence and falsification, the system is protected with Random Steganography Algorithm (RSA) technology. There are two algorithms involved, the first one for generating the steganography and the second one for validating the steganography, and both algorithms are also randomly produced.

An attacker would have lots of difficulties to reveal the RSA algorithms or to modify/fabricate the owner of files, i.e. pictures, audios and videos, without being detected through the RSA technology. The non deterministic nature of the algorithms will increase the strength of the algorithms against common attacks. Lastly, as both technologies of the RPAC and the RSA require a random number generator with high entropy and randomness, the RUD research has worked on the Software-based True Random Number Generator (STRNG) technology.

With such a true random number generator technology, the STRNG will generate high-entropy random numbers despite using minimum means and communication systems. The following section describes the general structure of the STRNG.

4 The Background of STRNG

The main challenge to construct a true random number generator (TRNG) lies in the fact that the generator must have high entropy (randomness) [9–13]. Since a number generated by most of the true random number generators (TRNGs) is a binary number [13], every binary random number must be independent and uniformly distributed [13–15]. Originally, the need for such a random number generator started when the cryptosystem was invented. Since the beginning until now, every cryptography algorithm require one or more keys. At least one of those keys must be generated randomly. So, a random number generator must be there to make a cryptosystem function properly [9].

In principle, it is straightforward to produce a random number. By using a coin, tossing the coin and putting the results (0 for the tail and 1 for the head) for every digit, will generate a binary random number. The same thing applies if instead of a coin, a dice is used. However, the bitrate of the generated numbers will approximately be only 0.2 bps. Which is very low. In terms of using a coin, the entropy can be very high, up to 1.0, and the probability of every digit will be around 0.5. Such a generator will produce every digit independently and the numbers are identically distributed, though.

Yet, modern cryptosystems expect that the key generation can be executed instantly. In a symmetric cryptography, a session key will be generated in every session. If the activity of a session lasts only a second, and every session requires a key of 1000 bits, the key generator must process a bit rate of at least 1 kbps [16].

As a comparison, the number of a pseudo random number generator (PRNG), generated using sequence seeds, can fulfil those requirements. In fact, a PRNG can work very fast. But, once an attacker can gain the seed used to generate random numbers, an attacker may still be able to guess the next-to-be-generated random number without much difficulties [10, 11, 14, 17].

On the other hand, most true random number generators (TRNGs) can also fulfil the requirements. Compared to TRNGs that have difficulties to reach it, a PRNG is guaranteed to have every digit a probability of 0.5. Since all the TRNGs utilize hardware as their entropy sources, an attacker may have an access to the hardware and compromise the entropy and the bias of the generator [17–19].

In order to diminish the drawback identified in PRNGs and to reduce the weakness in hardware-based TRNGs, it is therefore urgently needed to carry out research on a software-based true random number generator. Researchers agree that it is not possible to develop a mathematical formula that will produce a true random number [20]. Therefore, this research has attempted to deploy threads in the new approach for the software-based true random number generator (STRNG).

5 The Software-Based TRNG

The weaknesses and the drawbacks identified within PRNGs and hardware-based TRNGs in principle can be diminished through a software-based TRNG, i.e. the STRNG. So, the STRNG should no longer be prone to an attack and can still have a high bitrate random numbers. The other requirements such as high entropy, 0.5 bias, and NIST statistical tests should be fulfilled. Since it is impossible to develop a mathematical formula that will produce true random numbers, the approach of this research is focusing on the utilization of threads, small software processes.

A random number generated by the STRNG is basically a string of binary values (…0110100…). The length of the string is unlimited. So, in principle any size of random number can be generated. As long as the machine (laptop or mobile phones) is capable of doing it. The generator that produces the string will generate a series of thread pairs. Every pair of threads will be scheduled with the same time point for the execution of a task. In each thread of the thread pair, there is a task of appending a number. One thread will attempt to append a symbol of "1" on particular digit, whereas the other thread will attempt to append a symbol of "0" on the same digit. So, each thread in a pair will compete against each other for gaining an opportunity to append a symbol. The following shows the attempts.

Figure 1 shows two threads competing for appending a 0 or a 1 on a particular digit of a string of binary numbers. The implementation of the competition is equipped

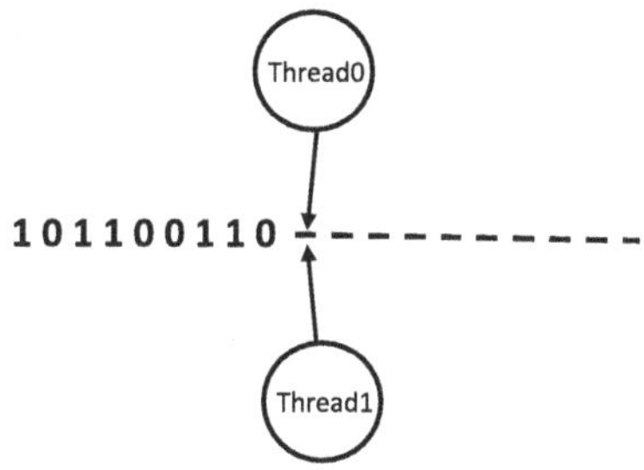

Fig. 1. Two threads are competing to append a 0 or 1

with a mutual exclusion (MUTEX) technique. When Thread0 wins the competition and append a 0, Thread1 would not be able to do anything, it will finish itself. Similarly, when Thread1 wins the competition and append a 1, Thread0 would not be able to do anything, it will finish itself. For the next digit, the generator will generate another pair of threads, and the competition will start again. The following code snippet shows the implementation of the MUTEX.

```
synchronized public void append(String bit)
{
  while (!appendReady)
  {
    try
    {
      wait();
    } catch (Exception e)
    {
    }
  }
  appendReady = false;
  if (!done)
  {
    done = true;
    randString = randString.concat(bit);
  } else
  {
    completed = true;
  }
  if (randString.length() == nrOfBits)
  {
    randReady = true;
    notifyAll();
  }
  appendReady = true;
  notifyAll();
}
```

Within the generator, the thread pair and the scheduling for the threads have been implemented though TimerTask and Timer classes. The Timer object will start a pair of TimerTask objects (Threads) regularly every one millisecond. If the required number of digits for the random number is 1000, the Timer object will schedule itself to start both TimerTask objects regularly 1000 times. The following code snippet shows the implementation of the Timer.

```
synchronized public String rand()
{
  randString = "";
  randReady = false;
  milliSeconds =
    Calendar.getInstance().getTimeInMillis();
  addition = 1;
  timerOne.schedule(new RandomTask("1", this), new
    Date(milliSeconds + addition), 1);
  timerOne.schedule(new RandomTask("0", this), new
    Date(milliSeconds + addition), 1);

  while (!randReady)
  {
    try
    {
      if (completed)
      {
        completed = false;
        appendReady = true;
        done = false;
      }
      wait();
    } catch (Exception e)
    {
    }
  }
  return randString;
}
```

And the following code snippet shows the implementation of the TimerTask class.

```
public class RandomTask extends TimerTask
{
  String value = "";
  TimerRandomGenerator centre = null;

  public RandomTask()
  {
    super();
  }
  public RandomTask(String v, TimerRandomGenerator r)
  {
    super();
    this.value = v;
    this.centre = r;
  }

  @Override
  public void run()
  {
    centre.append(value);
  }
}
```

The string of the random number will be built digit per digit by the pair of threads regularly. Based on the scheduling parameter, with a period of 1 ms, the random number can produce a bit-rate at least 1 kbps. When instead of one digit, two digits are applied in the process of appending a string to the string of the random number, the expected bit-rate would be around 2 kbps. In such a case, the number of threads that will compete is four. Each of all four threads will compete to append a "00", or "01", or "10", or "11" accordingly. Up to three bits can be deployed which means that the bitrate of the STRNG can be up to 3 kbps.

6 The Test Results of STRNG

A number of tests have been carried out for the validation of the STRNG technology. The first test was the percentage of the appearance of each bit in the binary random numbers. To fulfil the uniformness, every bit 0 or bit 1 must have a probability of around 0.5. The following are some results of the tests for the 2-, 3-, 4-, 8-, and 10-bit random numbers (Fig. 2).

According to the results above, it can be validated that the STRNG technology has generated random numbers in which the percentage of the 0 appearance is more or less 0.5 or 50%. This value means that the STRNG technology fulfils the requirement that it is not biased.

The second test was the entropy test. The STRNG has generated tens of thousands random numbers consisting 2, 3, 4, 8, and 10 bits. Their entropy value of every group of those numbers has been measured. The following is the formula for calculating the

The probability of bit 0						
Attempt	Rounds	2-bits	3-bits	4-bits	8-bits	10-bits
1	10000	0.5542	0.5462	0.5247	0.5310	0.4958
2	10000	0.5512	0.5117	0.5067	0.5145	0.5209
3	10000	0.5192	0.5211	0.5365	0.5328	0.5082
4	10000	0.5705	0.5126	0.5361	0.4735	0.5481
5	10000	0.5438	0.5327	0.5353	0.5202	0.5486

Fig. 2. The percentage of the appearance of bit 0

entropy. Note that log 2 is required as the random numbers are binary.

$$H(X) = -\sum\nolimits_{x \in X} p(x) \times \frac{\log p(x)}{\log 2}$$

The following are some results of the tests for the 2-, 3-, 4-, 8-, and 10-bit random numbers (Fig. 3).

The Entropy Values						
Attempt	Rounds	2-bits	3-bits	4-bits	8-bits	10-bits
1	10000	1.9669	2.9678	3.9421	7.6966	9.4528
2	10000	1.9738	2.9571	3.9559	7.7000	9.3165
3	10000	1.9940	2.9797	3.9656	7.7088	9.3123
4	10000	1.9633	2.9858	3.9306	7.7140	9.5537
5	10000	1.9875	2.9443	3.9313	7.7826	9.1334

Fig. 3. The entropy values of random numbers by STRNG

Based on the results above, it can be validated that the entropy of the random numbers generated by the STRNG is constantly higher than 0.9 per bit. The value shows that the STRNG technology can produce very high entropy and fulfil the requirement of a sophisticated random number generator for a symmetric and an asymmetric cryptosystem.

The third test was the distribution of the random values. The expected results should show that in any length of random numbers, the distribution of the generated random number should be uniform and flat.

The following are some test results of the distribution of the generated random values (Figs. 4, 5, 6, 7 and 8).

It can be seen from results above that the distribution of random numbers in various cases is uniformly flat. This validates that the STRNG technology is able to produce uniform distribution of random numbers. In general, there is no bias in random numbers generated by STRNG.

The last test is the complete statistical characteristic tests developed by NIST. The following website provides an online random bit tests based on NIST standards including the result. https://mzsoltmolnar.github.io/random-bitstream-tester/ (Fig. 9).

The data that has been analyzed with the result above was taken from the 80000 20-bit random numbers generated by the STRNG technology. Many tests have been carried out using different data but also of 80000 20-bit random numbers, and the results show the same status. From the result above—green color for all 14 points package—which

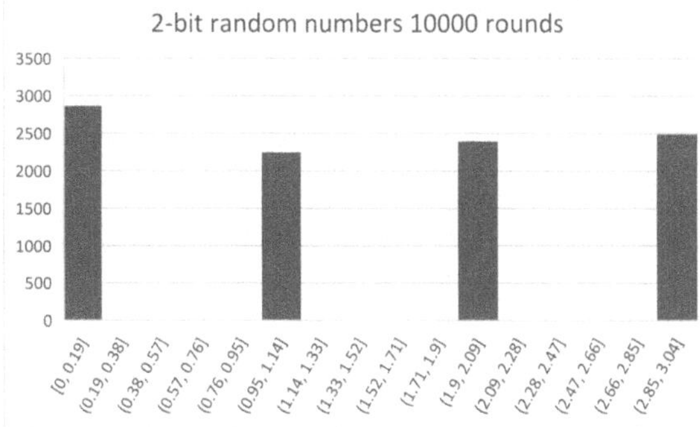

Fig. 4. The distribution of 10000 2-bit random numbers

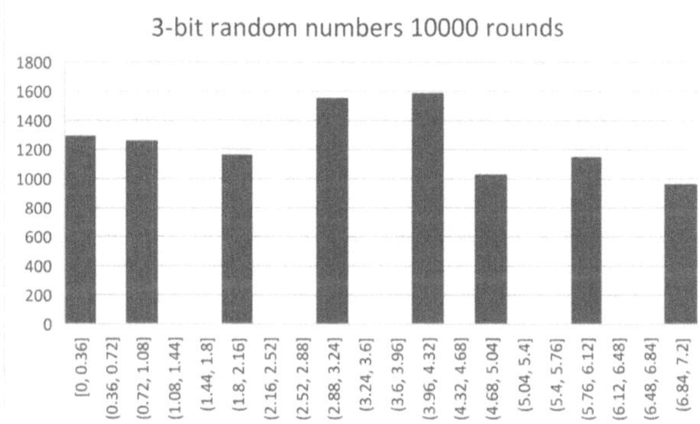

Fig. 5. The distribution of 10000 3-bit random numbers

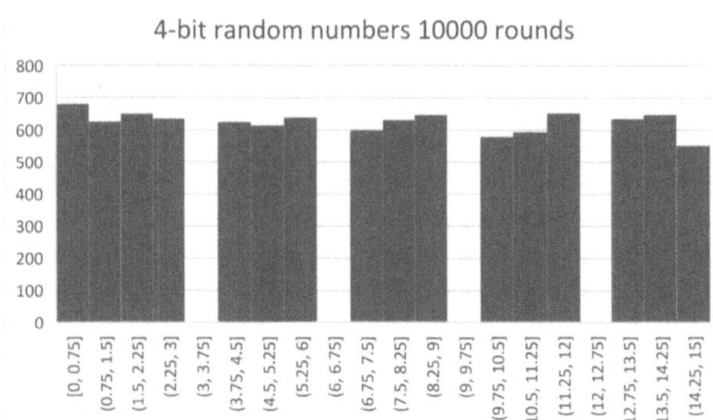

Fig. 6. The distribution of 10000 4-bit random numbers

has been analyzed by the NIST's formulas, it can be validated that the random numbers

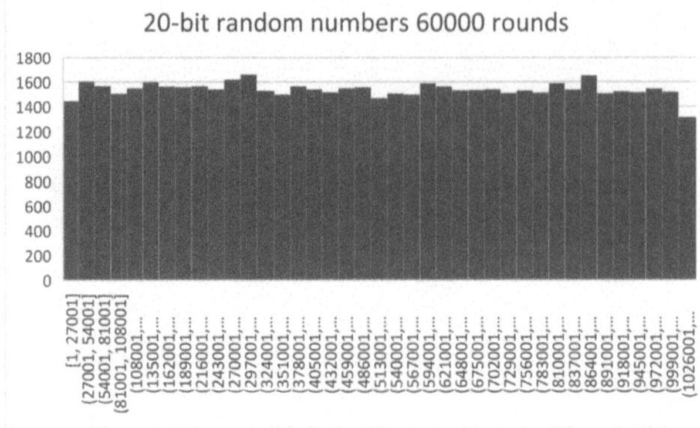

Fig. 7. The distribution of 60000 20-bit random numbers

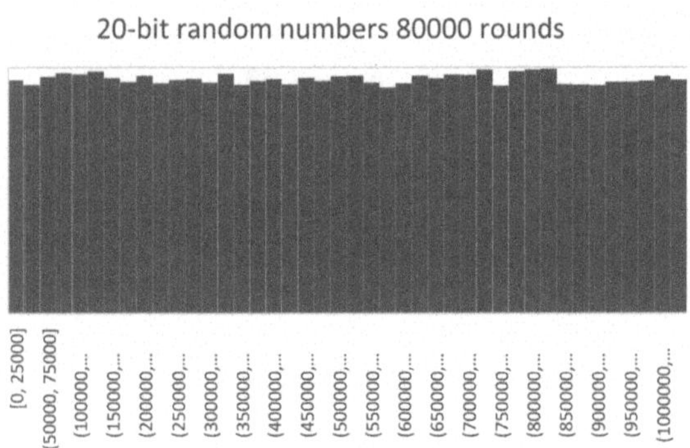

Fig. 8. The distribution of 80000 20-bit random numbers

generated by the STRNG has again fulfilled the requirements of a sophisticated random number generator for a symmetric and an asymmetric cryptosystem.

Interesting to mention is that all publications listed in the references suggest that researchers have not yet attempted to construct some kind of software-based true random number generator. It is therefore unlikely to present the results of the comparison of the STRNG with other types of software-based true random number generators. However, in the website of: https://mzsoltmolnar.github.io/random-bitstream-tester/ there are two parts of true random number samples taken from two different sources of hardware-based true random number generators, from a radioactive decay and from analog to digital converter (ADC) noise. These numbers can also then be tested with the tool.

The following are the results. Note that those random numbers have not passed all the testing parts (indicated by the red color signs) (Fig. 10).

Fig. 9. The STRNG numbers have passed all the 14 points of test

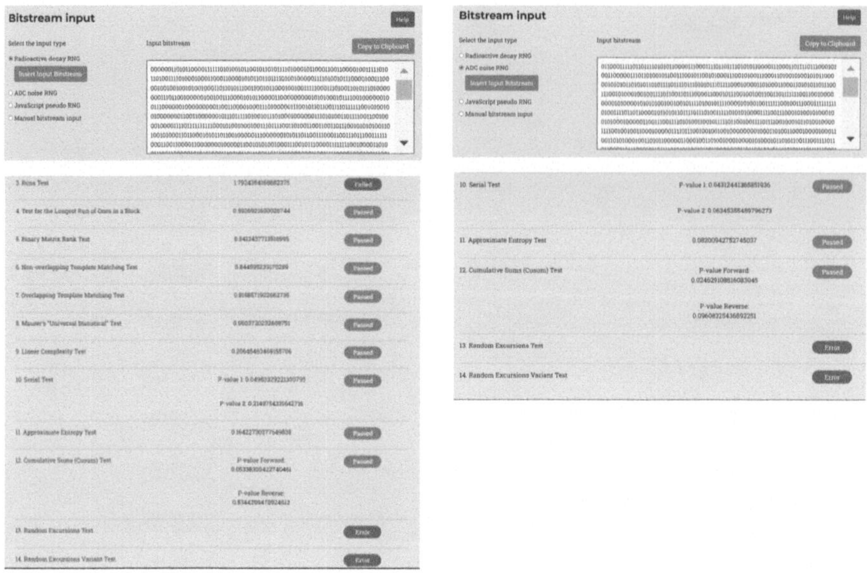

Fig. 10. The result of NIST's test for TRNG using radioactive decay (left) and ADC noise (right)

7 Conclusion

The current problems found within the PRNG and hardware-based TRNG for generating random numbers have been tackled by the STRNG technology. When the problems still exists, a lot of challenges will be faced whenever the implementation aims for critical and sensitive purposes, such as for symmetric and asymmetric cryptosystems in a disastrous situation. The most apparent challenge is about how to prevent attackers from gaining the data or just interfering networked transactions, in which many parties are involved.

The STRNG technology has been so constructed, that the technology is not just cheap and fast enough for minimum means and communication system in a disastrous situation, the statistical characteristics proposed by NIST are fulfilled. As the entropy sources are from threads (non-hardware), attackers would have difficulties to manipulate the activity of the threads. The particular novelty of the research is the existence of threads that, although they are software they can be deployed so that the competition exists. Such competition will naturally generate the entropy that will be benefited by the random number generator part of a cryptosystem.

The good results of STRNG presented through various tests in particular those proposed by NIST have convinced that the contribution of STRNG within the Resilient Urband Development (RUD) research will increase the overall quality of the RUD research.

References

1. Hansson, S., et al.: Communication-related vulnerability to disasters a heuristic framework. Int. J. Disast. Risk Reduct. **51**(1), 1–9 (2020)

2. Raza, M., et al.: Establishing effective communications in disaster affected areas and artificial intelligence based detection using social media platform. Futur. Gener. Comput. Syst. **112**(1), 1–18 (2020)
3. Wisner, B., Blaikie, P., Cannon, T., Davis, I.: At Risk: natural hazards, people's vulnerability and disasters, Unknown: UNDP (2003)
4. Poljanšek, K., Ferrer, M.M., Groeve, T.D., Clark, I.: Science for disaster risk management 2017: knowing better and loosing less. Publications Office of the European Union, Luxembourg (2017)
5. Reardon, G., Galvin, J.: National Emergency Communication Plan. National Homeland Security, USA (2019)
6. Nasution, B. B., et al.: Citizen Movement Control System (CMCS) for handling the evacuation process of an earthquake. In: 2024 IEEE International Conference on Omni-layer Intelligent Systems (COINS), London, United Kingdom (2024)
7. Nasution, B.B., et al.: Transformation of an esvecees (SVCS) value to spherical coordinates as the result of the earthquake forecasting using SLHGN, pp. 261–275. Springer, Kristiansand (2022)
8. Nasution, B.B., Sembiring, R.W., Siregar, I., Seri, E., Mardi, R.W.: Towards single value coordinate system (SVCS) for earthquake forecasting using single layer hierarchical graph neuron (SLHGN). In: Information Technology in Disaster Risk Reduction - 5th IFIP WG 5.15 International Conference, pp. 73–89. Springer, Sofia (2021)
9. Majzoobi, M., Koushanfar, F., Devadas, S.: FPGA-based true random number generation using circuit metastability with adaptive feedback control. In: Cryptographic Hardware and Embedded Systems – CHES 2011, Nara, Japan (2011)
10. Rukhin, A., et al.: A Statistical Test Suite for Random and Pseudorandom Number Generators for Cryptographic Applications, Gaithersburg. National Institute of Standards and Technology, USA (2008)
11. Viega, J.: practical random number generation in software. In: 19th Annual Computer Security Applications Conference, Las Vegas, NV, USA (2003)
12. Ma, Y., Lin, J., Jing, J.: On the entropy of oscillator-based true random number generators. In: Cryptographers' Track at the RSA Conference, San Francisco, California, USA (2017)
13. Johnston, D.: Random Number Generators—Principles and Practices. Walter de Gruyter GmbH, Berlin (2018)
14. Stipcevic, M., Koç, Ç.K.: True random number generators. In: Open Problems in Mathematics and Computational Science, pp. 275–315. Springer, Zurich (2014)
15. Gentle, J.H.: Random Number Generation and Monte Carlo Methods. Springer, USA (2005)
16. Purushotham, B., Manish, K., Prakash, V.B., Dakey, S.: FPGA based 64-BIT true random number generator. Int. J. Creat. Res. Thoughts (IJCRT) **11**(5), 670–673 (2023)
17. Teh, J.S., Teng, W., Samsudin, A., Chen, J.: A post-processing method for true random number generators based on hyperchaos with applications in audio-based generators. Front. Comp. Sci. **14**(6), 1–11 (2020)
18. Jiang, H., et al.: A novel true random number generator based on a stochastic diffusive memristor. Nat. Commun. **8**(3), 1–9 (2017)
19. Cherkaoui, A., Fischer, V., Fesquet, L., Aubert, A.: A very high speed true random number generator with entropy assessment. In: Cryptographic Hardware and Embedded Systems - CHES 2013, Santa Barbara, CA, USA (2013)
20. Lee, K., Lee, S.-Y., Seo, C., Yim, K.: TRNG (true random number generator) method using visible spectrum for secure communication on 5G network. IEEE Access **6**(1), 12838–12847 (2018)
21. Leest, V.V.D., Slui, E.V.D., Tuyls, G.-J.S.P., Handschuh, H.:Efficient implementation of true random number generator based on SRAM PUFs. In: Cryptography and Security: From Theory to Applications, pP. 300–318. Springer, Heidelberg (2012)

22. Marsaglia, G.: Random number generators. J. Mod. Appl. Stat. Methods **2**(1), 2–12 (2003)
23. Narole, N.G., Choudhary, K.B.: Implementation of true random number generator using FPGA based system. Int. J. Trend Res. Dev. **5**(2), 37–40 (2018)
24. Tehranipoor, F., Yan, W., Chandy, J.A.: Robust hardware true random number generators using DRAM remanence effects. In: 2016 IEEE International Symposium on Hardware Oriented Security and Trust (HOST), McLean, VA, USA (2016)
25. Herrero-Collantes, M., Garcia-Escartin, J.C.: Quantum random number generators. Rev. Mod. Phys. **89**(1), 1–55 (2017)
26. Jacak, M.M., Jóźwiak, P., Niemczuk, J., Jacak, J.E.: Quantum Generators of Random Numbers. Scientific Reports, Berlin (2021)
27. Cirauqui, D., et al.: Quantum random number generators: benchmarking and challenges. Quant. Phys. **2206**(1), 1–15 (2022)
28. Moeini, M., et al.: Quantum random number generator based on LED. J. Appl. Phys. **135**(8), 1–10 (2024)
29. Li, Y.-H., et al.: Quantum random number generation with uncharacterized laser and sunlight. npj Quant. Inf. **5**(1), 1–5 (2019)
30. Tamura, K., Shikano, Y.: quantum random number generation with the superconducting quantum computer IBM 20Q Tokyo. In: Workshop on Quantum Computing and Quantum Information, Tokyo, Japan (2020)
31. Mannalatha, V., Mishra, S., Pathak, A.: A comprehensive review of quantum random number generators: concepts, classification and the origin of randomness. Quant. Inf. Process. **22**(1), 1–44 (2023)
32. Xu, F., Qi, B., Ma, X., Xu, H., Zheng, H., Lo, H.-K.: Ultrafast quantum random number generation based on quantum phase fluctuations. Opt. Express **20**(11), 1–12 (2012)

On the Ethical Value of Evidence in Disaster Response

Diogo Sasdelli and Thomas J. Lampoltshammer(✉)

Department for E-Governance and Administration, University for Continuing Education Krems, Krems an der Donau 3500 AT, Austria
{Diogo.Sasdelli,Thomas.Lampoltshammer}@donau-uni.ac.at

Abstract. In the context of disaster response, information is crucial for adequate decision-making. This raises the question of an ethical duty to seek evidence. The paper at hand explores the ethical justification of this duty, addressing the complexities of moral responsibility when morally relevant decisions have to be made and respective actions have to be taken when insufficient information is available. The main ethical problem lies in the potential moral responsibility for actions committed because of ignorance (in the sense of Aristotle), which, intuitively, could be considered as being involuntary. To deal with this issue, the paper at hand proposes an epistemic diachronic ethical duty to seek more evidence in the context of disaster response and justifies it within a consequentialist ethical framework, which, as such, particularly requires minimising the costs and maximising the value of the evidence obtained. While the integration of geo-informatics technologies has the potential to significantly reduce costs and increase the quality of evidence, enhancing decision-making outcomes, it also raises new ethical challenges, including biases, discrimination, and privacy concerns. The paper also briefly addresses possible justification approaches within deontological and aretaic ethics. It is argued that further research on the ethical integration of emerging technologies is needed, which, in particular, involves understanding cultural differences in disaster response and developing comprehensive training programs for disaster professionals to navigate these ethical dilemmas effectively.

Keywords: ethics of disaster response · disaster management · epistemic duties · duty to seek evidence · epistemic condition for moral responsibility · ignorance and moral responsibility · geo-informatics

1 Introduction

The relationship between morality and knowledge is an old question at the intersection between two core areas of philosophy, namely ethics and epistemology. It concerns, *on the one hand*, the epistemic value of ethics, i.e., the question of whether wisdom with respect to moral duties or other ethical concepts such as virtues and vices constitute a form of knowledge – thus being something one can

Published by Springer Nature Switzerland AG 2026
W. Seböck et al. (Eds.): ITDRR 2024, IFIP AICT 752, pp. 163–178, 2026.
https://doi.org/10.1007/978-3-031-97115-0_11

teach or learn – or not, as famously discussed, e.g., in Plato's dialogue "Protagoras" [27]. *On the other hand*, the question concerns the ethical value of knowledge, i.e., broadly speaking, the role of knowledge in identifying moral duties and, in particular, in determining moral responsibility. In this respect, one could investigate, e.g., whether there is a general (epistemic) moral duty to expand and perfect one's knowledge – e.g., in the form of a duty to "inquire" or to "seek evidence" (cf., e.g., [11,20,21]) –, or how ignorance affects one's moral responsibility with respect to their actions, as discussed, e.g., by Aristotle in Book III of the Nicomachean Ethics [3]. These latter questions, i.e., the ones pertaining to the ethical value of knowledge, seem to be entangled in a practical-philosophical paradox (for an overview of the philosophical debate concerning this so-called *epistemic condition* for moral responsibility, cf. [29]): while a more conservative (and in general also intuitively valid) notion of responsibility seems to imply that one may only be held accountable for one's voluntary actions, which would exclude liability for actions that, committed due to lack of knowledge, are to be seen as not being truly voluntary, a more proactive (and intuitively equally valid) notion of responsibility would also include the requirement that a moral agent has enough knowledge (or *is aware*) of certain elements concerning their action, which would imply a duty to seek knowledge or evidence and, *a fortiori*, the moral responsibility for one's lack of knowledge as well as for the actions committed thereby. This seems to be particularly valid with respect to agents that are entrusted with the oversight or duties of care with respect to other agents or objects such as, e.g., parents with respect to their children, as well as, in general, the government, public authorities or other comparable institutions with respect to public safety and security.

These ethical questions concerning the duty to seek evidence and the moral responsibility for actions committed as a consequence of *ignorance* (i.e., a lack of knowledge) implied therein are particularly relevant for the field of disaster response: within disaster response, entrusted actors (usually public institutions and authorities) are confronted with difficult, morally relevant decisions (often in *life-or-death* situations) that have to be made in paucity of time, resources and, especially, of knowledge or information in general. The situation is all the more complex, as the use of technical solutions – in particular artificial intelligence (AI) – to mitigate this paucity might incur violations of other rights and duties, e.g., with respect to privacy or to biased or discriminatory decisions. This complexity poses a substantial challenge to the ethical assessment of decisions and actions taken in the context of disaster response.

The paper at hand aims to analyse the role of the duty to seek evidence within the ethics of disaster management, especially with respect to the use of new technologies – in particular within the field of *geo-informatics* – to gather more information; in particular, the paper at hand proposes a framework to guide the ethical assessment of actions and decisions taken within disaster response scenarios. For this purpose, Sect. 2 first discusses the general ethical justification of the duty to seek more evidence – as well as of the respective moral responsibility for actions committed due to ignorance implied therein – in the context of disaster response. While it will be briefly argued that the duty to seek evidence in the context of disaster response has promising foundations both on aretaic and deontological grounds, the paper at hand shall focus on a consequentialist justification of this duty. This sets the *ethical methodology* adopted within the paper at hand. It shall be shown that, within a consequentialist framework, the justification of the duty to seek more evidence in the context of disaster response requires minimising the costs involved and maximising the quality and the overall value of the evidence obtained. Following this analysis, Sect. 3 shall discuss how technical solutions offered by *geo-informatics* can contribute to these factors, and Sect. 4 shall discuss further ethical challenges raised by the use of geo-informatics technologies. Here, a particular focus shall be set on possible conflicts emerging between the duty to seek evidence and other ethical duties, in particular with respect to protecting the privacy of individuals and avoiding biased or discriminatory decisions. Based on the results of the previous sections, Sect. 5 shall demonstrate how the ethical framework discussed in the paper at hand can be applied to perform ethical assessments related to the management of information for disaster response purposes in three stages: (1) *before*, (2) *during* and (3) *after* a disaster situation. Finally, Sect. 6 summarises the conclusions and refers to future work.

2 Ethical Justification of a Duty to Seek Evidence in the Context of Disaster Response (Ethical Methodology)

It is usually assumed that moral responsibility presupposes some sort of control, e.g., in the form of the agent's free will or agency; in other words, an agent can only be held morally responsible (or liable or accountable) for actions committed under their conscious control, i.e., actions committed willingly and freely [34]. Following Aristotle, one could speak of *voluntary* actions, i.e. actions that have their (causal) origin in an agent, who is also aware of the relevant circumstances concerning the actions (cf. [3,8]). Due to this latter condition, lack of knowledge would, at least *prima facie*, exclude voluntariness and, thus, responsibility.

This might, however, depend on the nature of the ignorance involved. In chap. 3 of the Nicomachean Ethics [3], Aristotle distinguishes between two kinds of actions committed due to ignorance or lack of knowledge or awareness: (1) actions performed *in ignorance* and (2) actions performed *because of ignorance* (for details, c.f., e.g., [8]). In general terms, an agent acts *in ignorance* when they commit a certain action while lacking knowledge or awareness of some relevant set of circumstances, which would otherwise lead them to act in a different way, but there is also a further explanation or reason for why they lack this knowledge or awareness, e.g., they were deceived, drugged or physically exhausted. Intuitively, when explaining why the action was committed, one would not simply mention the agent's ignorance but also the reasons leading to this ignorance: if a person driving a car while heavily drunk ignores a red traffic light and causes an accident, the accident was not caused merely *because* of the person's unawareness of the traffic light, but because of their drunken state. In contrast, an agent acts *because of ignorance* when they likewise lack knowledge or awareness of some relevant set of circumstances, but there is no particular explanation or reason for this lack of knowledge, e.g., when a pilot retracts an aircraft's landing gear unaware of people hiding in the landing gear's bay, which could result in them being crushed to death. Overall, an agent's ignorance can concern various aspects of their actions, e.g., the action itself, its consequences, the people affected, or even the notions of good and evil themselves, which, however, would lead back to the question of the epistemic value of ethics, briefly mentioned above in the introduction.

At first glance, it seems reasonable to argue that only actions committed *because of ignorance* are involuntary. Indeed, as argued in [8], assuming that the lack of knowledge lies beyond the agent's control, such actions seem to be analogous to, or rather even a type of, random – lucky or unlucky – events. With respect to actions committed *in ignorance*, on the other hand, it seems necessary to inquire whether the origin of the ignorance lies within the agent or not. If the lack of knowledge follows from, e.g., a self-induced state of drunkenness, the origin of the ignorance lies within the agent's control; hence, the action is to be seen as voluntary. Indeed, as noticed in [8], Aristotle himself endorses the attribution of moral responsibility (and of punishment) for such actions. This would not be reasonable if, instead, the agent had been deceived or poisoned, thus having no real control over their state of ignorance (for a detailed discussion, cf. [6], in particular Chap. 6).

A particular challenge concerning the ethical justification of the duty to seek more evidence involves the fact that it seems to imply (at least indirectly) moral responsibility even for actions committed *because of ignorance*, i.e., actions that would often be considered involuntary. If an agent acts against the evidence available to them *at a certain time* – either by consciously ignoring it or (assuming doxastic voluntarism [4]) by choosing not to believe it –, it seems reasonable to say that the agent acts *in ignorance*, as the origin of the lack of knowledge lies within the very agent. If, however, the same action is performed in the absence of any evidence against it, then the agent could not have known, *at the time* in which the action was performed, that their action was wrong, i.e., they acted *because of ignorance*. In the first case, one could say that the agent violates a synchronic epistemic duty to *believe well* [20], i.e., to align their beliefs to the evidence available to them at a certain time – and to choose their actions accordingly; in the second case, the agent violated a diachronic epistemic duty to seek for the missing evidence [11]. Following Hall and Johnson [11, p.133], this duty could be stated as follows:

(D) For any proposition that is less than certain on one's present evidence, one has an epistemic duty to seek more evidence about that proposition.

The ethical justification of a duty like (D) – and of epistemic duties overall –is, at least when considered in more general terms, a matter of philosophical controversy (cf. in particular [20] as well as the literature referred to there). This general ethical question cannot be tackled here. Instead, the paper at hand shall investigate the ethical justification of a more restricted version of (D), limited to the context of disaster response:

(D') In the *context of disaster management*, for any proposition that, *despite being relevant for the decision-making within the management of the disaster situation*, is less than certain on one's present evidence, one has an epistemic duty to seek more evidence about that proposition.

Good arguments for justifying (D') can be developed based on all three main established ethical theories, i.e., *deontological*, *aretaic* and *consequentialist* ethics. A brief overview of possible deontological and aretaic approaches to the justification of (D') is provided below in Sect. 2.1; notwithstanding, the paper at hand shall focus on the consequentialist approach, which is discussed in more detail in Sect. 2.2. Furthermore, for the purposes of the paper at hand, it shall be assumed that a proposition is to be considered as *certain* in the sense of (D) or (D') if it surpasses a given certainty threshold, i.e., if there is enough evidence supporting it (cf. also [11]).

2.1 Aretaic and Deontological Approaches

Aretaic or *virtue* ethics are based on the idea that moral activity is characterised by the development and practice of certain qualities of character, i.e., of virtues. One usually also assumes a kind of moral wisdom or prudence (*phronesis*, φρονησις), which is responsible for the coordination of these virtues in the sense of moral activity towards a good or fulfilled life (*eudaimonia*, ευδαιμονια) [13]. Generally speaking – and following the strong Socratic and Platonic influence in the virtue ethics tradition (cf. [10]) –, knowledge plays an important role in aretaic moral theories, and ignorance or lack of knowledge is often considered a main cause for evil. Hence, it seems fairly evident that a virtuous agent in the field of disaster response should be knowledgeable of information relevant to the field and decide their actions accordingly. Justifications for (D') could build on these ideas. Moreover, since modern approaches to improve disaster management rely heavily on the usage of new technologies involving the usage of large amounts of data, considerations pertaining to the modern fields of *computer-*, *information-*, and *data ethics*, which are heavily influenced by classic value and virtue ethics (cf., e.g., [5,32]), are also expected to play a fundamental within the ethics of disaster management in the 21th century.

Deontological ethics, in their turn, conceive ethical duties as being of a relatively more primitive nature, allowing for actions to be deemed as morally wrong even if they lead to positive consequences (for an overview, cf. [1]). Classic examples are Habermas' *discourse ethics* [9], *contractualist theories* (cf., e.g., [28]) and *Kantian ethics* [15]. Solid foundations for (D') can also be found in the deontological tradition. E.g., Kantian ethics includes the so-called *imperfect duty* (towards oneself) to develop and increase one's own natural perfection (*Naturvollkommenheit*), which explicitly includes an intellectual dimension related to reason, understanding, and science (cf. [16, AA VI 444–446]). A particularly promising deontological approach for the justification of (D') draws from contractualism's natural focus on the justification of institutions. For example, it seems reasonable to assume that rational agents put in an *original position* akin to the one proposed by Rawls in [28] would be inclined to accept (D') – or some variant of it – as a guiding principle of institutionalised disaster response.

2.2 Consequentialist Approach

Consequentialist ethics evaluate the moral value of actions based on their consequences [31]. In simple terms, the goal of disaster management is to optimise the positive effects of disaster response, which could be measured on various different proxies such as the mitigation of the damages caused to humans, animals and property as well as the efficient management of rescue teams, distribution of humanitarian aid resources etc. A consequentialist approach to the ethics of disaster management would, therefore, at least from an *objective* perspective, command all those actions that lead to the best possible fulfilment of this optimisation goal – assuming its general positive moral value. For a clearer overview, this can be modelled by the formula:

$$\forall a((a \in \mathfrak{A} \land \mathfrak{A} \xmapsto{\max} \Gamma) \rightarrow \boldsymbol{O}(a)) \tag{1}$$

Where $\mathfrak{A}$ is a set of actions, Γ is a set of conditions (e.g., the proxies mentioned above) representing the fulfilment of the goal of disaster management, and $\boldsymbol{O}(a)$ means the fact that the action a is morally obligatory. In its essence, formula (1) corresponds to the conception of epistemic duties developed in [11]. From a consequentialist perspective, the core element of this formula is the subformula:

$$\mathfrak{A} \xmapsto{\max} \Gamma \tag{2}$$

This subformula states that the actions in $\mathfrak{A}$ optimise the fulfilment of the goals in Γ.

Assuming $\mathfrak{A} \xmapsto{\max} \Gamma$ and the validity of the goals in Γ (the question of their justification will be addressed below in Sect. 3.2), the general *objective duty* imposed upon the disaster management or disaster response structure shall be to perform the actions in $\mathfrak{A}$. From a subjective perspective, however, due to the voluntariness restrictions discussed above in Sect. 2, one can only require from an agent p that they act according to their best beliefs, i.e., that agent p performs the actions in a set $\mathfrak{A}'$ for which they *believe* that $\mathfrak{A}' \xmapsto{\max} \Gamma$ holds (for short, $\boldsymbol{B}_p(\mathfrak{A}' \xmapsto{\max} \Gamma)$), even if this is, in fact, not the case [11]. Let, in this context, two additional key assumptions be added: (K1) that the costs of seeking more evidence are negligible, and (K2) that the fulfilment of (D') will necessarily lead to $\boldsymbol{B}_p(\mathfrak{A} \xmapsto{\max} \Gamma)$. Then, it follows that fulfilling (D') will necessarily lead to the maximisation of Γ. Even in the extreme case in which p's original beliefs already corresponded to the optimal case, Γ will still be maximised nonetheless, at least when one neglects the costs of seeking more evidence. Hence, a rational agent p should necessarily believe that fulfilling (D'), i.e., seeking for more evidence, leads to the maximisation of Γ – even if it is still possible to maximise Γ by other means, e.g., randomly. Hence, (D') is justified based on the duty to maximise Γ.

For example, suppose a situation in which a number x of people are trapped in a collapsing building (e.g., due to a fire or structural damage caused by a flood). Assuming that Γ is maximised when as few lives as possible are lost, that the agent p is a coordinated group of 10 firefighters, and that the actions in $\mathfrak{A}$ with $\mathfrak{A} \xmapsto{\max} \Gamma$ consist of an optimal distribution of the firefighters with respect to the floors and sections of the building in which the people are located, then the required information leading to $\boldsymbol{B}_p(\mathfrak{A} \xmapsto{\max} \Gamma)$ and to the corresponding course of action are the number and the position of the trapped people inside the building. If, for some reason, e.g., due to outdated information or sheer guessing, the firefighters are led to believe that a different course of action $\mathfrak{A}'$ will lead to the most lives saved (i.e., if $\boldsymbol{B}_p(\mathfrak{A}' \xmapsto{\max} \Gamma)$ holds), they could spend too much time searching in empty floors, which could lead to the building collapsing before everybody is brought to safety, probably also jeopardising the lives of the firefighters themselves. A particularly tragic scenario would be the loss of firefighters' lives while searching an otherwise completely empty building. Thus, if adequate information, i.e., information leading to the correct belief that $\boldsymbol{B}_p(\mathfrak{A} \xmapsto{\max} \Gamma)$ can be obtained at a negligible cost of time and resources (as assumed above), the agents involved should strive to obtain this information, i.e., the should fulfil the duty (D') to seek for more evidence.

Evidently, this justification is heavily dependant on the two key assumptions made above, i.e., (K1) the assumption that the costs of searching for more evidence are negligible and, conversely, (K2) the assumption that searching for more evidence (i.e., fulfilling (D')) will necessarily lead to the correct belief and the maximisation of the goal Γ. If assumption (K1) is dropped, one could conceive of scenarios in which the cost of searching for more evidence does not justify the eventual gains later obtained. For example, in the scenario proposed above, if obtaining proper information on the whereabouts of the trapped people takes too long, the building could collapse before the firefighters take any action. Moreover, dropping (K1) seems to strengthen the idea that there is one absolutely optimal set of actions with respect to the goal Γ, which maximises this goal at the smallest possible costs, which incidentally corresponds to the so-called *limit assumption*, which plays an important role in many systems of so-called *deontic logic*, in particular in those based on non-monotonic logic or on the logic of preference (cf., e.g., [7,22]). On the other hand, if one drops (K2), i.e., the assumption that searching for evidence always leads to the best results, one could (especially if (K1) is also dropped) conceive of scenarios in which searching for more evidence actually leads to the best possible course of action being missed, e.g., if the introduction of more evidence leads to confusion or uncertainty concerning actually correct beliefs.

In their essence, assumptions (K1) and (K2) respectively minimise the costs of searching for and maximise the value of evidence. In practical terms, (K1) refers to the ease of obtaining new evidence and (K2) to the quality (and to the positiveness of the effects) of this evidence. The reason why (D') is considerably easier to justify than (D) is the fact that (D') is contained within the context of disaster response. Within this context, it is easier to assume that evidence and knowledge will substantially impact the actions taken. Moreover, since the stakes are so high (human lives and substantial material value), it is also reasonable to assume that the costs involved in searching for evidence shall be relatively low, at least when enough time is available.

Thus, since (D')'s justification depends on the abstract assumptions of (K1) and (K2), its validity with respect to a concrete scenario will depend on how strongly this scenario approaches the ideal circumstances represented by these assumptions. In general terms, the employment of new technological solutions, in particular from the field of *geo-informatics*, promotes the fulfilment of both (K1) and (K2), i.e., lower the costs and increases the quality and overall value of evidence in the context of disaster response. Hence, in the digital Age, (D') is all the more valid.

3 Geo-Informatics' Impact on Costs and Quality of Evidence

The field of geo-informatics, and recently GeoAI, has changed the way we interact with spatio-temporal data. This paradigm shift is true particularly regarding emergency management and disaster response. Related emerging technologies have not only reduced costs concerning seeking evidence but also improved the overall quality of information gathered, a critical aspect of data-driven decision-making [37].

3.1 Reduction of Costs in Evidence Seeking (K1)

Conventional methods of disaster data gathering, such as manual surveys, are labour-intensive and expensive. Geo-informatics technologies provide the means to gather large amounts of data quickly and cost-effectively. These technologies provide critical information without the need for extensive fieldwork, enabling rapid assessment of disaster-affected areas (cf., e.g.,[17]). Concerning the automation of geospatial analysis, GeoAI can dramatically reduce costs. With improved accuracy over manual methods, machine learning algorithms can process large amounts of data. For example, automated loss assessment models can classify the severity of damage to buildings following a quake, eventually speeding up the decision-making process (cf., e.g.,[19]). In addition, GeoAI can also enhance predictive modelling capabilities, which are critical for disaster preparedness and mitigation. Predictive modelling enables better resource allocation and risk management by forecasting the potential impact of natural disasters such as floods and hurricanes. This proactive approach results in a reduction in the overall cost of disaster response and recovery (cf., e.g., [14]).

3.2 Increase in Quality and Overall Value of Evidence (K2)

Critical to accurate disaster assessment, geospatial technologies provide high-resolution, accurate data. For example, authorities can identify the most affected areas and prioritise response efforts using satellite imagery and Geographic Information Systems (GIS). This precision helps to allocate resources more effectively and reduce the time needed for recovery. Geospatial information enables the integration of multiple data sources, including satellite imagery (cf., e.g.,[33]) or social media feeds (cf., e.g.,[12]). This provides a comprehensive view of the disaster scenario. This multi-source approach ensures that decisions are based on the most complete and up-to-date information, improving the overall quality of the response (cf., e.g.,[36]).

4 Ethical Challenges Raised by Geo-Informatics

While geo-informatics has the potential to substantially decrease the costs of obtaining new evidence while increasing its quality and overall value, its usage also leads to new ethical challenges. In particular, these concern (1) the risk of biased or discriminatory decisions and (2) conflicts with other ethical principles, e.g., data protection and privacy. These issues shall be discussed in the following two subsections.

4.1 Avoiding Biased or Discriminatory Decisions

Avoiding biased and discriminatory decisions is one of the main challenges raised by the use of algorithms that rely on large datasets, in particular with respect to machine learning approaches (cf. [32,35]). One of the core issues is the fact that – potentially hidden – biases already contained in the data collected are bound to be perpetuated by a machine trained based on this data.

In the context of disaster response, these challenges might manifest themselves in various ways. E.g., as already discussed above, information concerning the probable whereabouts of humans in need of rescue is crucial for guaranteeing efficient resource allocation and successful rescue operations. Making important decisions on these matters based on substantially biased or even incomplete data might lead to fatal consequences. Defective data is to be expected, especially in places with high social and economic inequality. For example, the lack of correct data on the number of residents in a certain neighbourhood – e.g., a particularly poor neighbourhood or one inhabited mainly by immigrants or refugees – in an affected area might lead to an underestimation of the resources needed for rescue operations, thus discriminating against certain groups. Hence, rather than optimising disaster management as a whole, the mere introduction of new technologies could lead to further exclusions of areas and neighbourhoods already systematically neglected by public authorities, further increasing the social gap between different groups in a society.

These circumstances would strongly jeopardise the fulfilment of the abovementioned assumption (K2), i.e., the assumption concerning the quality and thus the overall value of the evidence gathered, which in turn would question the validity of (D'), i.e., of the duty to seek for more evidence in the context of disaster situations, as discussed above. Conversely, one could argue that (D') compels us not only to seek evidence but to seek good-quality evidence. Guaranteeing good data quality – in particular with respect to possible biases – is, therefore, an essential requisite for the duty to seek more evidence in the context of disaster situations. This might require overcoming social and economic inequalities, especially in the global south. In this regard, approaches from the field of *Smart Cities* might offer valuable solutions (cf. [23–26]).

4.2 Dealing with Ethical Antinomies

Another key issue of modern computer and data ethics concerns data protection and privacy. This issue is particularly relevant for disaster response and management because the data involved is usually personal. In many cases, the information required to guarantee an optimal allocation of resources during a disaster situation would be comparable to a comprehensive surveillance of citizens by public authorities, which is bound to constitute a major violation of their privacy. E.g., data concerning life signals of people trapped under a collapsed building – which could be provided by smart wearables – could be essential for making decisions regarding rescue operations. During a health crisis like the coronavirus pandemic, analysing personal contact information is crucial for accurately tracking the development of infection chains. In general, especially when new geo-informatics technologies enabling the analysis of large datasets are involved, access to nearly every kind of personal data could be useful for optimising disaster response.

Hence, this situation amounts to a conflict or ethical antinomy between two basic ethical principles, i.e., individual privacy and data protection on the one hand and the life and the physical and psychological integrity of the victims on the other. Within a consequentialist framework, this antinomy would correspond to the fact that while both the promotion of individual privacy and saving the victim's lives lead, individually considered, to a maximisation of utility, the satisfaction of one of these goals would usually lead to a violation of the other. In effect, this would amount to a violation of assumption (K2) because the overall value of the gained evidence would be diminished by the violations caused thereby.

In cases where the fulfilment of both principles is (at least practically) impossible, a decision will have to be made – one principle will have to give way to the other. For this purpose, ethics and argumentation theory offer corresponding decision frameworks and procedures. A good example from legal theory for dealing with a similar problem of conflicts between legal principles is discussed by Alexy in [2, p. 81–83]. Following Alexy, one can state the reasoning behind the weighing of principles by the formula:

$$(P_1 \boldsymbol{P} P_2)C \tag{3}$$

where P_1 and P_2 are principles, $\boldsymbol{P}$ is a preference operator, and C is a set of conditions. Intuitively, the formula states that the principle P_1 overrides the principle P_2 under the given conditions C. Being a kind of *prima facie* normative reasoning, two aspects have to be emphasised: firstly, the fact that a principle overrides another under certain conditions does not affect the general validity of the overridden principle. It remains generally valid and applicable. Secondly, as a direct consequence, it is possible that under different conditions, C', the opposite might hold, i.e., principle P_2 might override principle P_1. To determine which principle prevails, one often distinguishes between an abstract weight (i.e., the general importance of a principle *in abstracto*) and a concrete degree of fulfilment or violation of the principles. The main idea is that a heavy violation of a weaker principle might override a light violation of a stronger one. Literature offers various (automated or at least partially automated) implementations of these theories (cf., e.g., [18,30]), which could be employed in order to guarantee an optimal fulfilment of relevant principles, thus further promoting the satisfaction of assumption (K2).

5 An Ethical Framework for Information Gathering in Disaster Response

The practical philosophical discussion of the moral validity of (D') leads to an ethical framework that can be used to enhance and guide decision-making with respect to information gathering in the context of disaster response. The application of this framework is briefly outlined in the following subsections within three stages: (1) *before*, (2) *during*, and (3) *after* a disaster situation.

5.1 Before a Disaster Situation

Assuming its *prima facie* validity, duty (D') commits to *preparatory measures* aiming at optimising the fulfilment of (K1) and (K2) in case a disaster situation occurs. Overall, with respect to (K1), (D') prescribes that all information potentially relevant for disaster response be properly identified as such, and that an information infra-structure be built on the basis of which this data may be efficiently accessed (if already available) or gathered by disaster response actors. With respect to (K2), (D') complies to measures that guarantee both a high quality of the data and its proper usage, e.g., through measures that mitigate possible errors arising from a false interpretation of the data. For concrete examples, the ethical framework surrounding (D') can be used to justify:

- Measures leading to a better integration of public registers, as well as to an easier and overall more efficient access and use of such data by disaster response actors. E.g., information on the inhabitants of an area affected by a flooding might be relevant for coordinating rescue operations. It could, thus, be paramount that this information is made readily available to the respective rescue agents.

- Research and development of new technologies and methods for gathering, processing and sharing potentially relevant data. This could include, e.g., in case of a pandemic like COVID-19, health and contact data; in case of a flooding, models that predict the development of the flooding and likely escape routes and rescue paths. In particular, (D') justifies a relevant ethical value for research on geo-informatics with applications to disaster response.
- The training of disaster response personnel with respect to the usage of data and of new technologies (especially AI) in disaster response scenarios. In particular, this includes the development of ethical decision-making guidelines for situations with limited information, lightening the decision burden of disaster response agents faced with such difficult situations.

In particular, (D') and its surrounding ethical framework can be used within politics to provide arguments for corresponding changes in the disaster response infra-structure and methodologies employed in a country; For example, it could be used to modify legislation (e.g., introducing more flexible legal frameworks for the processing of personal data for disaster management purposes). In any case, challenges such as the ones discussed above in Sect. 4 also have to be taken into account.

5.2 During a Disaster Situation

When applied *during* a disaster situation, (D') concerns basically a decision between two alternatives: (1) to act on the basis of the already available evidence; (2) to gather more evidence before committing to a definitive decision. Circumstances in which both (K1) and (K2) are likely fulfilled to a high degree justify searching for more information before committing to a decision. In contrast, situations in which (K1) and (K2) are not fulfilled to a sufficient degree would more likely profit from immediate action. Hence, within the ethical framework surrounding (D'), the decision to act immediately or to gather further information depends on an assessment of the concrete situation with respect to (K1) and (K2). This is partially the reason why (D') commits to measures that optmise the way information is gathered, processed, evaluated and shared, including, in particular, a better training of disaster response personnel, and the establishment of decision-making guidelines. This makes clear that knowledge about *how* to handle information is as important as the information itself, at least when it comes to decision-making within disaster response.

5.3 After a Disaster Situation

Finally, when applied after a disaster situation, (D') commits to a thorough investigation of the response given to a disaster, focussing both on positive and on negative aspects of the usage of information in decision-making situations. In particular, the investigation should analyse the quality of the data, its availability, the efficiency of the data infra-structure, and the proficiency with which disaster response agents handled information. The main goal of this investigations would be to reveal potential flaws in the management of information for disaster response purposes.

6 Concluding Remarks and Future Work

The paper at hand examined the ethical justification of the duty to seek evidence in the context of disaster response (D'), discussing the view that moral responsibility hinges on an agent's control over their actions, which would only imply a duty to *believe well* and to act accordingly. The ethical complexities of assigning responsibility for actions committed not only *in ignorance*, but also to those committed *because of ignorance* necessitate a nuanced approach, and, hence, the ethical status of a general duty to seek for more evidence is a matter of philosophical debate. For the specific case of a duty to seek evidence in the context of disaster response (D'), an ethical justification seems to be more plausible. The paper at hand considered a consequentialist approach to the justification of this duty while also briefly discussing possible deontological and aretaic perspectives to justify an epistemic diachronic duty to seek evidence in disaster management scenarios. The consequentialist approach, focusing on the optimisation of disaster response outcomes, supports the duty to seek evidence by illustrating how accurate and timely information can maximise positive results, such as saving lives and efficiently allocating resources. This argument relies on the assumptions that the costs of seeking evidence are negligible (K1) and that more evidence invariably leads to better decision-making outcomes (K2). These assumptions are often realistic in disaster scenarios due to the high stakes involved and the advances in geo-informatics technologies. The plausibility of these assumptions can be further increased by the adoption of modern technologies, especially within the field of geo-informatics. However, while geo-informatics significantly reduces the costs and increases the quality of evidence, it also introduces ethical challenges, such as the risk of biased or discriminatory decisions and conflicts with privacy rights. Addressing these challenges requires ensuring high-quality, unbiased data and carefully balancing privacy concerns with the imperative to save lives. The philosophical discussion on the validity of (D') leads to an ethical framework for information gathering within disaster response, which can be applied to support decision making before, during, and after a disaster situation, as briefly discussed in Sect. 5.

The matters discussed in the paper at hand show that further research investigating the role of emerging technologies, such as AI and machine learning, in enhancing disaster response is needed. These technologies have the potential to significantly improve decision-making processes by providing real-time analysis and predictions. However, their integration into disaster management practices also raises ethical questions that need careful examination. Future research should explore how AI and machine learning can be integrated within a disaster-ethics framework, ensuring that their use is transparent, accountable, and beneficial to all affected populations.

Disaster response and the ethical duty to seek evidence can vary significantly across different cultural contexts. Therefore, future research should also examine these cultural differences and develop ethical guidelines that are globally applicable while respecting local norms and values. This involves conducting comparative studies across different regions and cultures to understand how ethical principles are interpreted and applied in various contexts. The findings can help create flexible frameworks that accommodate diverse ethical perspectives, enhancing the effectiveness and acceptance of disaster response efforts worldwide.

Finally, developing comprehensive training programmes for disaster response professionals that emphasise the ethical considerations of evidence-seeking is another crucial area for future research. These programs should include educational materials that highlight the importance of obtaining high-quality evidence while navigating ethical dilemmas. Research should focus on the best practices for training delivery, including the use of simulations, case studies, and interactive modules. Additionally, evaluating the effectiveness of these training programs in real-world scenarios can provide valuable insights for continuous improvement. Finally, the establishment of widely recognised disaster response guidelines for decision-making under limited information could increase the objectivity and the overall quality of decisions made under such circumstances, while also lightning the ethical burden of disaster response actions responsible for making such decisions.

Acknowledgements. The research leading to the paper at hand was carried out within the project "GeoCROW", which has received funding from the FORTE programme under grant no. FO999895161. FORTE is a research, technology, and innovation funding programme of the Republic of Austria, Federal Ministry of Finance. The Austrian Research Promotion Agency (FFG) has been authorised to manage the programme.

References

1. Alexander, L., Moore, M.: Deontological Ethics. In: Zalta, E.N. (ed.) the Stanford Encyclopedia of Philosophy. Metaphysics Research Lab, Stanford University, Winter 2021 edn. (2021)
2. Alexy, R.: Theorie der Grundrechte. Suhrkamp, Frankfurt a.M., Germany, 2 edn. (1994)
3. Aristotle: Nicomachean Ethics. Oxford University Press (2002)
4. Clarke, M.: Doxastic voluntarism and forced belief. Philos. Stud. Int. J. Philos. Anal. Tradit. **50**(1), 39–51 (1986). http://www.jstor.org/stable/4319842
5. Davis, K.: Ethics of Big Data. O'reilly (2012)
6. Echeñique, J.: Aristotle's Ethics and Moral Responsibility. Cambridge University Press (2012)
7. Fehige, C.: The Limit Assumption in Deontic (and Prohairetic) Logic, pp. 42–56. De Gruyter, Berlin, Boston (1994). https://doi.org/10.1515/9783110885675-006
8. Grgić, F.: Ignorance, involuntariness, and regret in aristotle. Int. J. Philos. Stud. **29**(3), 351–369 (2021). https://doi.org/10.1080/09672559.2021.1970790

9. Habermas, J.: Erläuterungen zur Diskursethik. Frankfurt a.M., Germany, Suhrkamp (2020)
10. Hackforth, R.: Moral evil and ignorance in plato's ethics. Class. Q. **40**(3–4), 118–120 (1946)
11. Hall, R.J., Johnson, C.R.: The epistemic duty to seek more evidence. Am. Philos. Q. **35**(2), 129–139 (1998). http://www.jstor.org/stable/20009926
12. Huang, Q., Xiao, Y.: Geographic situational awareness: mining tweets for disaster preparedness, emergency response, impact, and recovery. ISPRS Int. J. Geo Inf. **4**(3), 1549–1568 (2015)
13. Hursthouse, R., Pettigrove, G.: Virtue ethics. In: Zalta, E.N., Nodelman, U. (eds.) The Stanford Encyclopedia of Philosophy. Metaphysics Research Lab, Stanford University, Fall 2023 edn. (2023)
14. Jin, H., Liang, Y., Lu, H., Zhang, S., Gao, Y., Zhao, Y., Zhu, Z.: An intelligent framework for spatiotemporal simulation of flooding considering urban underlying surface characteristics. Int. J. Appl. Earth Obs. Geoinf. **130**, 103908 (2024)
15. Kant, I.: Grundlegung zur Metaphysik der Sitten. Felix Meiner, Hamburg, Germany (2016)
16. Kant, I.: Metaphysische Anfangsgründe der Tugendlehre. Felix Meiner, Hamburg, Germany (2017)
17. Lampoltshammer, T.J., Scholz, J.: Citizen-driven geographic information science. In: Analyzing the Role of Citizen Science in Modern Research, pp. 231–245. IGI Global (2017)
18. Lu, Y., Yu, Z., Lin, Y., Schafer, B., Ireland, A., Urquhart, L.: An argumentation and ontology based legal support system for ai vehicle design. In: Borges, G., Sorge, C., Francesconi, E. (eds.) Legal Knowledge and Information Systems. Proceedings of the 35th JURIX Annual Conference, pp. 213–218 (2022)
19. Matin, S.S., Pradhan, B.: Challenges and limitations of earthquake-induced building damage mapping techniques using remote sensing images-a systematic review. Geocarto Int. **37**(21), 6186–6212 (2022)
20. McWilliams, E.C.: Evidentialism and Epistemic Duties to Inquire. Philos. Q. **73**(4), 965–982 (2023). https://doi.org/10.1093/pq/pqad061
21. Nelson, M.T.: We have no positive epistemic duties. Mind **119**(473), 83–102 (2010). http://www.jstor.org/stable/40865208
22. Parent, X.: Maximality vs. optimality in dyadic deontic logic. J. Philos. Logic **43**(6), 1101–1128 (2014). https://doi.org/10.1007/s10992-013-9308-0
23. Pereira, G.V., Cunha, M.A., Lampoltshammer, T.J., Parycek, P., Testa, M.G.: Increasing collaboration and participation in smart city governance: a cross-case analysis of smart city initiatives. Inf. Technol. Dev. **23**(3), 526–553 (2017). https://doi.org/10.1080/02681102.2017.1353946
24. Pereira, G.V., Eibl, G., Stylianou, C., Martínez, G., Neophytou, H., Parycek, P.: The role of smart technologies to support citizen engagement and decision making: the smartgov case. Int. J. Electron. Gov. Res. (IJEGR) **14**(4), 1–17 (2018). https://doi.org/10.4018/IJEGR.2018100101
25. Pereira, G.V., Klausner, L.D., Temple, L., Delissen, T., Lampoltshammer, T., Priebe, T.: Smart cities and digital twins in lower austria. In: Proceedings of the 24th Annual International Conference on Digital Government Research, pp. 644–645 (2023)
26. Pereira, G.V., Parycek, P., Falco, E., Kleinhans, R.: Smart governance in the context of smart cities: a literature review. Inf. Polity **23**, 143–162 (2018). https://doi.org/10.3233/IP-170067, 2

27. Plato: Protagoras. Oxford University Press (1976)
28. Rawls, J.: A Theory of Justice. Harvard University Press, Cambridge, USA (1999)
29. Rudy-Hiller, F.: The Epistemic Condition for Moral Responsibility. In: Zalta, E.N., Nodelman, U. (eds.) The Stanford Encyclopedia of Philosophy. Metaphysics Research Lab, Stanford University, Winter 2022 edn. (2022). https://plato.stanford.edu/archives/win2022/entries/moral-responsibility-epistemic/
30. Sartor, G.: Normative conflicts in legal reasoning. Artif. Intell. Law **1**(2), 209–235 (1992). https://doi.org/10.1007/BF00114921
31. Sinnott-Armstrong, W.: Consequentialism. In: Zalta, E.N., Nodelman, U. (eds.) The Stanford Encyclopedia of Philosophy. Metaphysics Research Lab, Stanford University, Winter 2023 edn. (2023). https://plato.stanford.edu/archives/win2023/entries/consequentialism/
32. Spiekermann, S.: Ethical IT innovation : a value-based system design approach. Auerbach Book, CRC Press, Boca Raton, Florida, 1st edition edn. (2016). https://doi.org/10.1201/b19060
33. Sui, C., Hong, D.: Multimodal deep learning for geoai. In: Advances in Machine Learning and Image Analysis for GeoAI, pp. 165–199. Elsevier (2024)
34. Talbert, M.: Moral Responsibility. In: Zalta, E.N., Nodelman, U. (eds.) The Stanford Encyclopedia of Philosophy. Metaphysics Research Lab, Stanford University, Fall 2023 edn. (2023). https://plato.stanford.edu/archives/fall2023/entries/moral-responsibility/
35. Varona, D., Suárez, J.L.: Discrimination, bias, fairness, and trustworthy ai. Appl. Sci. **12**(12) (2022). https://www.mdpi.com/2076-3417/12/12/5826
36. Zou, L., Chen, F., Huang, X., Kar, B.: Big earth data for disaster risk reduction (2023)
37. Zou, L., et al.: Geoai for disaster response. In: Handbook of Geospatial Artificial Intelligence, pp. 287–304. CRC Press (2023)

Autonomous Systems: Towards an Assessment of the Reliability

Tullio J. Tanzi and Sophie Coudert(✉)

LTCI, Télécom Paris, Institut Polytechnique de Paris, Paris, France
{TullioTanzi,SophieCoudert}@telecom-paris.fr

Abstract. The use of autonomous systems equipped with the latest technological advances greatly facilitates response operations after a disaster. They can intervene, for example, in places that are inaccessible or dangerous for human rescuers. To be effective, these systems integrate increasingly advanced sensors and therefore become more and more linear. This considerably increases their capabilities but also the cost.

It is therefore necessary to ensure the reliability of the system. The objective of this evaluation is to verify that the system survives and completes the mission or aborts it in time to return to its base. For this we propose the use of formal methods.

The Event-B method allows us to prove properties on a very abstract model of the system, which is then incrementally refined to a detailed specification of a correct implementation by construction. We also illustrate an approach using graphics specifications using Avatar. These two approaches are illustrated in a very simplified description of our Rover.

Keywords: Autonomous System · Simulation · Formal Methods · Models · Cyber-physical Systems · Disaster

1 Introduction

In the chaotic and dangerous context caused by a disaster, the speed of action is directly linked to the survival of victims. It is unanimously recognized that the first 72 h are crucial for rescue. The use of autonomous systems (AS) has advantages even if this use may have limitations (for example, a LIDAR sensor can be disturbed by light sources, a magnetometer can be influenced by metal masses, etc.).

Poor architectural choices in the design or configuration of these systems can make them not only useless, but also potentially dangerous and likely to produce erroneous data that will then be used by rescuers. The objective is therefore to obtain a high level of reliability from the design stage, both hardware and software.

Published by Springer Nature Switzerland AG 2026
W. Seböck et al. (Eds.): ITDRR 2024, IFIP AICT 752, pp. 179–191, 2026.
https://doi.org/10.1007/978-3-031-97115-0_12

1.1 Disaster Management and Autonomous Systems Usage

Disaster management can be improved thanks to recent technological advances. These techniques make it possible to establish plans (rapid mapping), detect and locate victims, and contribute to the restoration of pre-disaster conditions [1]. The affected area may have undergone significant changes (e.g. destruction, soil changes, debris). These environments are chaotic and dangerous, not only for the victims, but also for everyone involved in the rescue process. For example, low visibility can lead to erroneous decisions based on incomplete or unreliable data. Completeness and accuracy of information are necessary for the decision-making process required by emergency responses [2].

The use of autonomous systems (A.S. in the following text), such as rovers or drones, can facilitate information retrieval operations for many tasks. For example, an A.S. can be used, among other things, to make rapid mapping or to scan the affected area for survivors. The need for autonomous measuring systems has existed for a long time, but sufficiently precise measuring techniques did not yet exist. In the past, acquired data was not frequently updated, partly because earlier technologies allowed only a snapshot of the environment and not permanent monitoring. Today, wired and mobile communications networks make it easy to collect distributed measurements as well as acquisition systems dedicated to real-time data collection [3, 4]. However, these systems require the deployment of a fixed infrastructure that needs to be well maintained in order to function. The advent of autonomous vehicles incorporating modern technological sensors (LIDAR, radar, ground-penetrating radar, camera, etc.) [5, 5] offers new opportunities in this area. These devices offer more sophisticated and powerful means, allowing the acquisition of information of heterogeneous types, to explore a chaotic environment. This approach allows operations to overcome the constraints imposed by the existence of fixed infrastructure. In addition, it tolerates communication difficulties [6], for example, in the event of failure or destruction of existing infrastructure following accidents or disasters.

In order to integrate the capabilities of modern sensors, it is necessary to define new approaches. The input of information allows (i) to understand and therefore model the (real-time) environment for mission success, (ii) to reuse the same information to guide the decision-making processes of response teams [7, 8]. The data are produced by a set of heterogeneous sensors deployed for real-time collection: calculation of distance, microwave and LIDAR values, determination of the position or plate using inertial measurement units (IMU), control of data by odometers [9], etc. The use of ground penetrating radar (GPR) enables new detection methods, applicable, for example, to the detection of victims buried after an earthquake [10, 11, 11, 12], thus increasing the likelihood of locating survivors.

1.2 Objectives of the Verification

In our previous work, we validated the mechanical architecture of our ArcTurius rover designed to locate survivors after an earthquake [13].

In this article, we will present different methods to ensure, by design, that embedded software will perform as intended and remain within a safe operating range. A wrong decision on the part of the embedded system can be disastrous and lead to its downfall. Modern autonomous systems are increasingly complex, incorporating increasingly sophisticated sensors, their increasing cost is becoming more and more significant (several tens, or even hundreds of thousands of euros). Their loss therefore has a financial impact but not only that. The loss of such a system sends rescue teams back to their traditional operations with all the risk that this entails for humans. It is therefore important to ensure that the decision-making process is not corrupted and has backup functions.

In our Laboratory, we are currently developing an autonomous rover, Arcturius, and we are experimenting with formal methods to enforce the reliability of some of its aspects [2, 22]. Although occasional (formalization is not the heart of the Arcturius Project), these experiments have proven beneficial in aiding the rover's design.

In this article, we present a simplified example and briefly discuss the perspectives offered by recent developments in formal methods.

- Section 1 succinctly introduces the context and defines its framework. It then presents the expectations of the use of such systems in Disaster Management. The section concludes with the audit objectives.
- Section 2 presents the methods that can be used to verify our systems as well as their theoretical framework.
- Section 3 presents the example used to illustrate the verification. The example chosen consists of validating the ability of a Rover to interrupt its mission and return in the event of a major failure, in this case a sudden loss of part of its electrical energy: physical loss (breakage, accident, etc.).) or electrical (malfunction of the on-board electronics).
- We have used a very simplified model for this article. In our work our models are more complex in order to take into account the reality of our systems. According to the Event B approach used, the abstract model presented is intended to be progressively refined until a detailed specification of a correct implementation by construction is obtained.
- Section 4 conclude the paper.

2 Formal Methods and Cyber-Physical Systems

For all the above reasons, A.S. must be developed while ensuring strong guarantees about their reliability. The approaches that use formal methods are recognized as the ones that offer the strongest guarantees about the developped systems. For example using the B formal method [14] for software development may allow to reach the strongest safety integrity level (SIL4 certification) of the European.

Functional Safety standards. Thus, although the use of such methods for.

cyber-physical systems (what the A.S. generally are) is quite recent, we believe that their contribution is important for our purpose.

Formal methods provide the strength of mathematical proof to system design. They address multiple aspects. They are widely used in electronic design and more partially to ensure software safety, system robustness against attackers (i.e., security), SoC design reliability, System behaviour correction, etc. All these features are relevant for A.S and formal methods may be applied to them. A.S also make new difficult challenges emerge for these methods such as the interfacing with models of the physical (continuous) world, and this is a currently dynamic research topic.

2.1 Formal Reasoning

Formal methods and verification techniques [15] rely on logic, i.e., the idea that the validity of an argument or a proof can be ensured by only checking its form, without needing to "understand" it. Since the end of the 19th century, with the aim of achieving rigor in new mathematics, logic and sound reasoning have been mathematically characterized, leading to formal logic, which allows reasoning by applying rules and techniques whose relevance is determined solely by considering the syntax of the properties to be proved, not their meaning. This opens the door to reliable, computer-monitored proofs, which can be interactive or fully automated in some cases.

The reliability of computer-implementable reasoning rules is established by mathematical proof: they must only allow the proving of properties that are actually true. More explicitely, an implemented proof calculus "$\vdash$" must be sound, i.e., if $M \vdash \Phi$ ($\vdash$ proves that the property Φ holds in the model M) then $M \models \Phi$ (mathematically, Φ actually hold in M). $\Psi \vdash \Phi$ ($\vdash$ proves that the property Φ follows from the property Ψ) must reflect a true mathematical consequence $\Psi \models \Phi$ ($\forall M$, $M \models \Psi =\ > M \models \Phi$). As a toy example, the rule $x = y/2 \vdash y = 2*x$ can be proven (and thus used) for reals but not for integers. Proving tools are sometimes also complete, i.e. "what is true is provable", when considering limited sets of properties.

2.2 Formal Methods

Originally, formal proofs were defined for mathematical logic's (whose models are close to algebras). The idea has since been extended to numerous formal techniques, targeting different kinds of properties (axioms, temporal properties, etc.), different kinds of models (algebras, state machines, etc.), and different application domains (dedicated languages). There are three main approaches.

The axiomatic approach, close to traditional mathematics, allows for deducing properties from other properties ($\Psi \vdash \Phi$), generally with interactive proofs. The model-checking approach allows for verifying that a finite state machine model satisfies a property ($M \vdash \Phi$) by automatically exploring all its relevant states. The equivalence-checking approach uses techniques to establish that two different representations of the same function actually have the same observable behavior. There is no universal "easy to read and write" language provided with efficient tools, and all approaches face complexity problems (multiple tedious proofs, a huge number of states). Moreover, using formal languages requires expertise that is not very widespread in industry, although it is increasing. Thus, specialized approaches have been developed together with associated tools and methodologies that offer not only proof systems but also integrated development environments and interfaces to tackle these obstacles.

Formal modeling widely uses abstraction, aiming to obtain that formal models contain only the information relevant to the properties being proved. This simplifies models and verification. However, as a trade-off, the relevance of the system model concerning the real system becomes harder to verify. Formally mastered refinement can reduce the gap between the model and the real world by adding details in a secure way, but it may be tedious, and in any case, the models must be checked by humans, a process known as validation. Tools are provided for this purpose, such as model animation, simulation, etc. Moreover, other verification approaches benefit from abstract formal models, such as fast simulation or automated test generation, for example. Thus, formal approaches are highly relevant for improving the reliability of developed systems.

In practice, they are widely used in electronic design automation (EDA). They are increasingly used for software development but are often still limited to critical parts, as software complexity remains a challenge. Autonomous vehicles are generally cyber-physical systems, i.e., systems merging digital and physical aspects, which makes modeling more difficult. Among other challenges, defining interfaces between the logical model of the system and the physical model of its environment remains problematic. Moreover, formal methods generally model discrete system, but some approaches exist fo handling continuity in proofs, as for example [16, 19]. [19] proposes a review of these different approaches. A.S. are often not too large (although this is evolving), and they involve sensitive aspects requiring strong reliability. For example, they must not harm people, and since remote intervention on them is not always possible, they must be more robust than typical software. This concern includes, for example, fault detection or the triggering and implementation of recovery procedures. In this context, formal methods for cyber-physical systems are promising.

3 ArcTurius Illustration

While developing the ArcTurius Rover, we experimented with several formal approaches and associated tools. In particular, we used the TTool environment [18], an open-source tool developed by our team for the design of embedded systems (particularly SoCs). The DIPLODOCUS profile of TTool is used to describe the tasks of a system and map them onto the components of a hardware architecture. The resulting abstract model is verified using timed model checking, simulation, and interactive animation. Then, embedded sotware is more precisely designed using the dedicated Avatar Profile of TTool, which also offers model checking and animation. Finally, C code is generated from the Avatar model. In [22], for example, we use this approach to model the obstacle detection mechanism of the rover and ensure that the response time is sufficient to avoid collisions.

More recently, we conducted some experiments using the Event-B approach [19], a system-specific derivative of the B method [16] (dedicated to software development). Using Event-B, systems are described as general state machines using set-theoretic notations, with an interactive prover to demonstrate properties and formally monitor refinement. Using the ProB tool, model checking on Event-B systems is also available when the described state machines are finite. The main interest of the Event-B method is its refinement process, which leads to the progressive development of a detailed implementation that is correct by construction, as all refinement steps are proved. Abstract models describe the system's behavior in a simple way that is generally easy to understand. For example, it states that the rover does not get too close to obstacles without detailing the techniques used for this. The progressively introduced implementation details explain how it does this, i.e., introduce sensors, specify controllers, and distribute the calculations. Another advantage of this approach is that it allows the specification of complete systems comprising both the target machine and its environment, modeling their interactions. For all these reasons, this approach seems interesting with respect to our goals. The main drawback is that Event-B developments are very expensive. Although high-level specifications are simple, introducing all details and proving them (interactively) is a long process that requires strong expertise and significant manpower.

Here, we do not present a full development but we provide an insight into the possibilities offered by these methods for our application domain. In our simplified example, the abstract level is the expected behavior of the rover, which corresponds to the most abstract description level of an Event-B approach. Thus, we describe it using Event-B and the associated Rodin environment. We then use the Avatar profile of the TTool environment, not in the usual way (software design), but to describe a similar model to the Event-B one, to illustrate graphical modeling. Avatar allows for the description of finite state machines and offers, among other features, model checking.

During a mission, our simplified rover repetitively chose between three activities modeled by three actions: it can move (`travel`), it can use its radar (`radar`) and it can use its lidar (`sensor`). Each of these actions consumes energy, abstracted by an interval of possible consumption in our model. Thus, our Event B model comprises, among others, the following axioms:

```
@actions Actions = {travel, radar, sensor}
@energy max_energy = 32
@min_type min_consumption ∈ Actions → ℕ
@max_type max_consumption ∈ Actions → ℕ
@travel_min min_consumption(travel) = 4
@travel_max max_consumption(travel) = 5
@radar_min min_consumption(radar) = 3
@radar_max max_consumption(radar) = 3 ...
```

Our goal is to ensure that the rover can always return, i.e., it keeps sufficient energy. In both Avatar and Event-B models, the behavior of the rover is decomposed into steps: "events" for Event-B and graphical arrows (i.e., state transitions) for Avatar. We maintain two variables, `energy_to_return` and `remaining_energy`, and we ensure that the property `energy_to_return≤ remaining_energy` holds at all time (thus it is an "invariant"). However, we also consider a possible energy incident while traveling, such as the loss of a battery, which may break the invariant. In this case, the rover enters a "`refill`" state where it uses photovoltaic sensors until it is able to return. In the Event-B model, this leads to the following invariants that must be proved during the verification process:

`@refill1 state= refill ⇒ remaining_energy < energy_to_return.`

```
@refill2 remaining_energy < energy_to_return ⇒ state = refill
```

Property `@refill1` states that we only refill when required, and property `@refill2` ensures that we always refill when required. We must prove that no event of our abstract model compromises these invariants. For example, the "critical incident" event above ensure this.

```
event Critical_energy_loss
any loss // the lost energy
where...
@max loss ≤ remaining_energy
@critical remaining_energy − loss < energy_to_return
then
@update remaining_energy := remaining_energy − loss
@state state := refill
end
end
```

With respect to Event B semantics, this event may only occur when the **where** clause is satisfied, and it is easy to check that if the invariants hold before, then they also hold after the event (such simple proofs are automatic).

The Action event below, for an action in `{travel, radar, sensor}`, is only allowed when it does not compromise invariants, in particular by guard `@allow`. The `energy` parameter represents the consumed energy, and `back` is the increase in `energy_to_return`, which exists only for the travel action and in our simplified model, this increase is equal to the consumed energy (c.f., `@back` and `@return`).

```
event Action
any action energy back
where ...
@action_t action ∈ {travel, radar, sensor}
@min energy ≥ min_consumption(action)
@max energy ≤ max_consumption(action)
@back ( action = travel & back = energy or
action ≠ travel & back = 0 )
@allow remaining_energy−energy ≥ energy_to_return + back
then ...
@update last_action := action
@energy remaining_energy := remaining_energy − energy
@return energy_to_return := energy_to_return + back
end
```

The other events, which are not detailed here, are `Return, Abort, Refill` and `Benign_Energy_Lost`. The full specification of this very simplified rover is about 130 lines long, and all proofs were automatic. Notice that although the model is simplified, it provides a relevant illustration of the simplicity of Event B models at a high abstraction level. Following the methodology, the `Action` event can be refined by being split into three events: one event per different action. Further refinements add details specific to each action (fuel level sensors, radar controller, etc.), while preserving the invariant proved on our abstract model. Then the refined system, correct by construction, provides low-level specifications for each rover component.

As our model describes a finite state machine, we can also use the ProB model-checker on it to verify the invariants and some temporal properties. In particular, we verify that the model does not remain blocked in some state (no deadlock). In our model, with max_energy = 32, 2628 different reachable states have been identified within 3 s. We are also able to check more complex temporal properties written in CTL logic, such as, for example, `AG EF ({state= home})` and `AG AF e (Action)`. The first one says that whatever the current state is (`AG`), there exists a way (`EF`) to reach the `home` state. It is established by model checking. The second one says that from any state, we necessarily reach a state in which an action is enabled. Model checking fails because it is possible to enter an infinite loop due to successive incidents.

Experience shows that even simple models may contain mistakes. Some errors are detected while trying to prove properties, but not all. For validation, we can use step by step animation using ProB. It is also possible to add secondary (non critical) invariants to increase the confidence in the model by verifying that its behaviour respects some expected properties. For example, adding the invariant `energy_to_return≤ max_energy` and trying to prove it helped us to find an error in our model. So using such a method allows to strongly improve system reliability but does not prevent from all mistakes. Moreover refining provides an interpretation of high level concepts and properties in a more concrete implementation, which must be relevant. That's where expertise matters and may introduce bias.

A way to make specification more accessible to human is to use graphical representations, as in Avatar, which we used to develop another model of the Rover. As the two formalisms do not have exactly the same features, both models are not equivalent but very similar. The graphical view of the Avatar rover model is in Figs. 1 and 2. The (blue) block view in Fig. 1 defines the used variables and constants, and the (pink) pragma defines temporal properties that are expected to hold. Figure 2 specifies the state machine (just for an overview).

On arrows, conditions for enabling the denoted transition are written in dark green, and blue lines denote actions associated to this transition. The choice of consumption values in the allowed ranges for actions is done with a random operator. Technically, the Avatar model is a bit more complex than the Event B one. However it is not a problem for the efficient model-checking associated to Avatar, which supports billions of states. With max_energy = 32, the model-checking found 21833 reachable states within about 2 s, but only 2121 states after graph minimization (2–3 min).

Figure 3 shows the different verification options, and once the model-checker has run, the results appear in the graphical views. As usual, deadlock freeness can be checked. The two letters "LR" over blue boxes in Fig. 2 show the result of the liveness (L) and reachability (R) checks for each box: green for "success", and red for "failure". Reachability means that it is possible to reach the node. Liveness means that it is certain.

In Fig. 2, as expected, all blue boxes are reachable. The travel box is live, as travel is the single authorized action when starting a mission.

The `radar` and `sensor` boxes are not live (red L), as they can be never chosed. More complex properties can be verified, described by way of CTL formulas.

Here it is the case of the safety pragmas (pink box in Fig. 1), whose verification can be invoked (in Fig. 3). The two first ones are similar to the `@refill1` and `@refill2` invariants of the Event B model. The first one is `@refill2`: we always refill when required, and it is true, as shown by the geen "check" on its left (see .

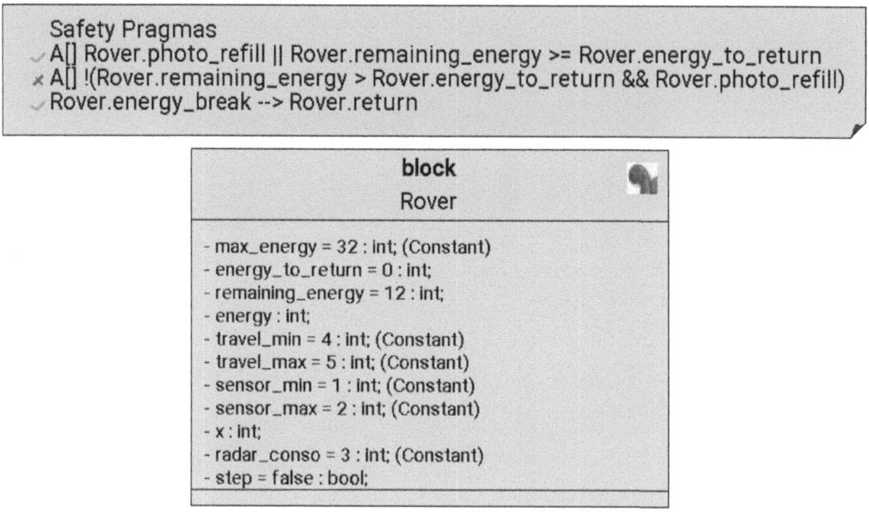

Fig. 1. Avatar Block and Pragma Declarations (color figure online)

Figure 1).

The second one (`@refill1`: we only refill when required) is false (red cross on left). Indeed, in the Avatar model, any energy incident leads to the refill state, even if the remaining energy is sufficient to return. Thus, this verification reveals a clumsiness in our modeling. The last pragma use the temporal operator "`p -- > q`", which means that whenever `p` is verified in a state, we are certain that `q` will be verified in some future state. Here we ensure that after any energy incident (`energy_break` box), we always finally reach the `return` box.

Notice that in case of failure, the model-checker provides a trace representing a path (a succession of states) that breaks the property, so that the human can analyze it to understand the problem. Moreover, Avatar also provides tools to support model validation such as random simulation and step-by-step human driven animation.

Figure 4 shows an example of trace obtained with this interactive animation.

In the framework of the Arcturius Project, we developed several small models, essentially with TTool, to address specific issues (security of communications, system-on-chip architecture, some expected high-level behavior) [13, 15]. They were a bit more complex than the one presented here, but not too much. As formalization was not a central topic, these models were developed a posteriori or alongside the project (which is not methodologically optimal). Of course, an ambitious approach would require more manpower and greater maturity in formal approaches for cyber-physical systems. However, as also noted in other contexts, even occasional use of formal methods provides significant benefits in terms of reliability. Writing high-level (thus simple) models brought out many questions, as mathematization does not allow blur or ambiguity. These questions were often relevant, helped address forgotten cases, and lead to discussions that clarify numerous expectations at a high level in the design process, which is highly useful for a development process targeting strong safety.

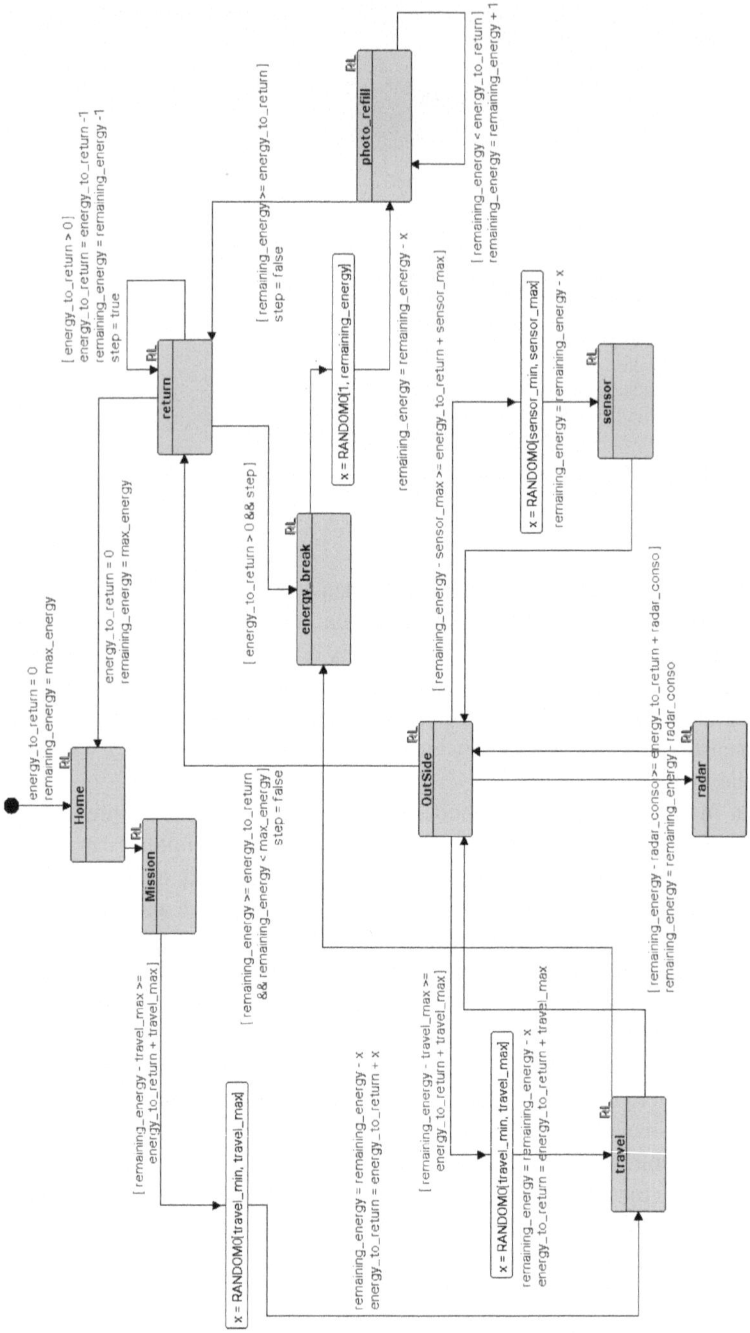

Fig. 2. Avatar State Machine description

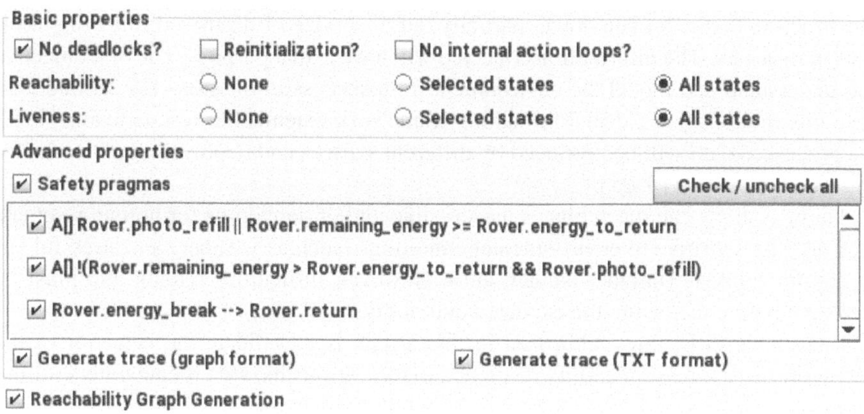

Fig. 3. Avatar Model Checking Options

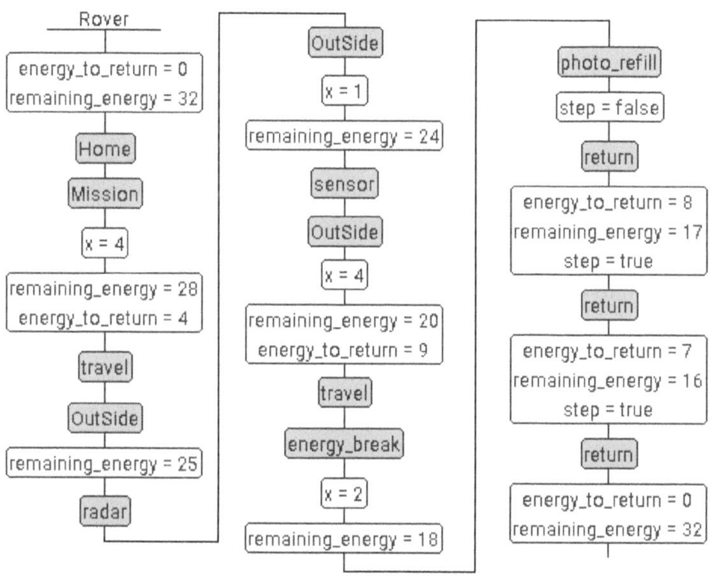

Fig. 4. Avatar Interactive Animation

4 Conclusions and Perspectives

The use of autonomous systems integrating modern technological sensors (LIDAR, radar, video, etc.) opens new perspectives for disaster management [5, 21]. This equipment constitutes an increasingly sophisticated means of acquiring all kinds of information in order to explore a given environment. In this regard, the use of sensors coupled with an autonomous system makes it possible to carry out a mission without external intervention. This approach makes it possible to overcome the constraints of existing infrastructure or communication difficulties [6], such as degraded environments with infrastructure that is broken down, partially out of service or destroyed following accidents or disasters. The information collected will have a dual purpose. The first objective is to understand and model the environment for a successful mission. The second is to reuse this modeling in a decision-making framework extended to rescue teams [7, 8]. The processed data will be produced by different sensors and deployed in networks for real-time collection [19–21].

These systems can reach places inaccessible and/or dangerous for human rescuers. They are less sensitive to environmental conditions (such as weather) and stressful situations for humans (fatigue, danger, etc.). However, difficulties remain and must be overcome before achieving the expected autonomy.

One of the difficulties addressed in this article is to validate the behavior of the system during its mission and its resilience to the various hazards it encounters during its mission.

We explore the use of formal methods for this purpose and confront their usual limitations: i) complexity of modeling and verification; ii) human bias, with modeling generally being carried out by experts; iii) and finally, a significant implementation time. This is what justifies the extreme simplification of the example used to illustrate the text (Sect. 3).

This is also why we use them partially on targeted aspects, such as with the Ttool tool intended for SoC design. We also explore more general methods, such as Event-B, which requires much more labor (interactive proof), but in return offers very strong guarantees of reliability of the developed and proven system, provided that the abstract model is formally refined to a level of detail close to the final implementation.

Note that, to process the continuous, it would be necessary to use the latest developments and extensions around Event-B. These advances are recent and are not completely stable or fully documented. However, they offer great potential for the future.

References

1. Mukhopadhay, B., Bhattacherjee, B.: Use of information technology in emergency and disaster management. Am. J. Environ. Prot. **4**, 101–104 (2015)
2. Tanzi, T., Isnard, J.: Autonomous system for data collection: location and mapping issues in post-disaster environment. C. R. Phys. **20**, 204–217 (2019)
3. Stormont, D., Allan, V.: Managing risk in disaster scenarios with autonomous robots. J. Systemics Cybern. Inform. **7**, 66–71 (2009)
4. Tanzi, T.J., Isnard, J.: Public Safety Network: an Overview, chap. 1, in: Wireless Public Safety Networks 1, edited by: Câmara, D., Nikaein, N. (2015). ISBN 9781785480225
5. Tanzi, T., Chandra, M.: Propagation modelling towards the design of drone borne GPR for humanitarian applications. In: XXXII General Assembly of the International Union of Radio Science, pp. 19–26, Montreal (2017)
6. Chandra, M., Tanzi, T.: Propagation Issues Relevant to the De- sign of a Drone Borne GPR (Ground Penetrating Radars), Klein- heubacher Tagung 2016 (KHB 2016), 26–28 September 2016. Miltenberg, Germany (2016)
7. Tanzi, T., Roudier, Y., Apvrille, L.: Towards a new architecture for autonomous data collection, ISPRS Geospatial Week 2015: Workshop on civil Unmanned Aerial Vehicles for geospatial data acquisition, 1–2 October 2015, La Grande Motte (Montpellier) (2015)

8. Apvrille, L., Tanzi, T., Roudier, Y., Dugelay, J.L.: Drone humanitaire: état de l'art et réflexions, Revue Française de Photogrammétrie et de Télédétection 213–214, 63–71 (2017). ISSN 1768-9791
9. Tanzi, T., Chandra, M., Isnard, J., Camara, D., Sebastien, O., Harivelo, F.: Towards "drone-borne" disaster management: future application scenarios. In: ISPRS Ann Photogramm. Remote Sens. Spatial Inf. Sci., vol. III-8, pp. 181–189 (2016). https://doi.org/10.5194/isprs-annals-III-8-181-2016
10. Thrun, S., Burgard, W., Fox, D.: Probabilistic Robotics, The MIT Press, Cambridge (2005). ISBN 9780262201629
11. Chandra, M., Tanzi, T.: Feasibility Assessment of a Drone borne Ground Penetrating Radar Sensor for Humanitarian Applications in the context of Disaster Management, 1st URSI Atlantic Radio Science Conference (URSI AT RASC), 16–24 May 2015. Gran Canaria, Spain (2015)
12. Li, Z., Zhu, Q., Gold, C.: Digital terrain modeling: principles and methodology. CRC Press, Boca Raton, USA (2005)
13. Chandra, M., Tanzi, T.: Drone-borne GPR design: propagation issues. C. R. Phys. **19**, 72–84 (2018). https://doi.org/10.1016/j.crhy.2018.01.002
14. Chandra, M., Tanzi, T.: Drone-Borne GPR Design: Propagation Issues, in: Journées scientifiques de l'URSI-France (JS'17), 1– 3 February 2007, Sophia Antipolis (2017)
15. Bertolino, M., Tanzi, T.: Advanced Robot 3D Simulation Inter- face for Disaster Management, Kleinheubach Conference, 23– 25 September 2019, Miltenberg, Germany, pp. 1–4 (2019)
16. Abrial, J.R.: The B-book: Assigning Programs to Meanings. New York, NY, USA: Cambridge University Press (1996)
17. Coudert, S., Legros, D.: Formal methods and abstraction for a safe and feasible Design, Journées Scientifiques U.R.S.I., Sophia Antipolis, France (2017)
18. Platzer, A.: A complete axiomatization of quantified differential dynamic logic for distributed hybrid systems. Logical Methods Comput. Sci. 8(4), 1–44 (2012)
19. Dupont, G., Aït-Ameur, Y., Pantel, M., Singh, N.K.: An event-B based generic framework for hybrid systems formal modelling. In: Integrated Formal Methods, pp. 82–102. Springer (2020)
20. Abrial, J.-R.: Modeling in Event-B: System and Software Engineering. New York, Cambridge University Press, 1st ed., (2010)
21. Pedroza, G., Apvrille, L., Knorreck, D.: AVATAR: A SysML Environment for the formal verification of safety and security properties. In: 2011 11th Annual International Conference on New Technologies of Distributed Systems, pp. 1–10 (2011). https://doi.org/10.1109/NOTERE.2011.5957992
22. Genius, D., Li, L., Apvrille, L., Tanzi, T.: Multi-level latency evaluation with an MDE approach. In: Proceedings of the 6th International Conference on Model-Driven Engineering and Software Development (MODELSWARD 2018), pp. 295–302 (2018). ISBN: 978–989–758–283–7
23. Liu, J.W.S.: Real-time Systems, 1st edn., Prentice Hall, Upper Saddle River, NJ, USA https://dl.acm.org/doi/book/10. Accessed 9 Dec 2020
24. Berger, A.S.: Embedded Systems Design: An Introduction to Processes, Tools, and Techniques, CMP Books, Berkeley, CA (2002). ISBN 1578200733
25. Shukla, S.K.: Introduction to Embedded Systems, TEQIP Course at IITK, IIT Kanpur, 29 August 2016. Kanpur, India (2016)

War and Safety Issues

Military Perspectives on CBRN Drone Autonomy: Balancing Trust and Control

Bettina Biron[1(✉)], Stephan Schraml[2], Gerald Bauer[3], and Walter Seböck[1]

[1] University for Continuing Education Krems, 3500 Krems, Austria
bettina.biron@donau-uni.ac.at
[2] AIT Austrian Institute of Technology GmbH, 1210 Vienna, Austria
[3] Austrian Federal Ministry of Defence, 1090 Vienna, Austria

Abstract. The threat of CBRN (chemical, biological, radiological and nuclear) incidents has become a growing concern for military and emergency response organizations, requiring innovative strategies to improve preparedness and mitigate risks. One promising approach is the use of reconnaissance drones - agile unmanned aerial vehicles (UAVs) - to support CBRN incident response. Reconnaissance drones can quickly provide an overview of CBRN incidents and gather information without risking people. However, the increasing autonomy of drones requires high levels of trust in the technologies used by emergency services. This paper examines attitudes toward autonomous reconnaissance drones among Austrian military personnel, with a specific focus on how different levels of autonomy affect trust and acceptance. As part of the Semi-autonomous chemical aerial reconnaissance system (C-SALS) research project, soldiers and conscripts of the Austrian Armed Forces specializing in CBRN-Defence were surveyed. The results reveal a generally positive perception of drone technology, with speed of results, clear presentation of information, and accuracy rated as the most important characteristics. The study reveals nuanced preferences regarding autonomy levels, with variations between different personnel groups. The findings challenge some common assumptions about technology acceptance and provide important insights for the responsible integration of autonomous reconnaissance drones into CBRN defence preparedness and emergency response planning.

Keywords: CBRN · UAV · drones

1 Introduction

Chemical, biological, radiological, and nuclear (CBRN) threats are among the most severe security challenges today. Whether arising from accidents or deliberate attacks, such incidents pose significant challenges to military forces. The consequences extend beyond immediate health and infrastructural damage, often leading to long-term social, economic, and environmental repercussions [1–3]. This study examines how professional soldiers and conscripts of the Austrian Armed Forces perceive autonomous reconnaissance drones for CBRN detection. The central focus is on how different levels

Published by Springer Nature Switzerland AG 2026
W. Seböck et al. (Eds.): ITDRR 2024, IFIP AICT 752, pp. 195–209, 2026.
https://doi.org/10.1007/978-3-031-97115-0_13

of autonomy—ranging from manual operation to semi-autonomous ("human-on-the-loop") and fully autonomous ("out-of-the-loop") systems—influence trust in and acceptance of such technologies. In the context of the increasing significance of automated systems in defence technology [4, 5], this research provides essential insights for the future integration of drone technology into CBRN defence approaches.

This research was funded by the Austrian defence research program FORTE (Federal Ministry of Finance) in cooperation with the Austrian Federal Ministry of Defence. The authors thank the Austrian Armed Forces for their support in conducting the survey.

2 Lessons from CBRN Incidents

Historical CBRN disasters show that inadequate reconnaissance capabilities have repeatedly intensified the consequences of such events. The Chernobyl disaster (1986) demonstrated how underestimating radioactive contamination delayed evacuations and exposed first responders and civilians to hazardous radiation [6, 7]. Timely use of modern reconnaissance drones could have enabled faster data acquisition and improved protective measures. Similarly, during the Fukushima disaster (2011), assessing nuclear contamination in real time posed major challenges [2, 9]. After earthquake-triggered meltdowns, uncertainty about radiation dispersion delayed critical decisions. Although drones were later used to map radiation, earlier deployment could have facilitated quicker evacuations and containment efforts [3, 23].

Chemical and biological threats had similarly grave consequences. The Bhopal gas leak (1984) caused thousands of deaths and severe long-term effects [7, 12]. The lack of immediate information on the toxic substance hindered medical response efforts. Unmanned systems capable of rapid hazard identification could have enabled faster and more effective countermeasures. These cases highlight the need for real-time, accurate situational awareness in mitigating CBRN incidents [13]. Autonomous reconnaissance drones offer a promising technological means to enhance emergency response and operational safety [10].

3 CBRN Drones: Benefits and Barriers

Autonomous reconnaissance systems are gaining strategic importance in modern security and defence operations [8, 10]. Particularly in the context of CBRN threats, which represent a tangible and complex danger [1, 9], drones offer the potential to enhance situational awareness, accelerate risk assessments, and reduce personnel exposure in hazardous environments. For the Austrian Armed Forces, which play a key role in civilian protection during CBRN events, drone technology enables faster, safer decision-making. Equipped with specialized sensors, drones can detect chemical agents, monitor radiological spread, and map contaminated areas in real time [7]. These capabilities support the timely coordination of protective measures and evacuation planning [1].

However, successful deployment depends not only on technological capacity but also on the trust and acceptance of those who use these systems [14, 17]. As levels of autonomy increase—from manual operation to AI-driven analysis—so do concerns regarding reliability, transparency, and human oversight. In high-stakes scenarios such as evacuations, responders must be able to rely on drone-generated data without hesitation [11, 13]. Thus, the integration of such technologies requires attention to both system performance and human factors, particularly trust and perceived legitimacy.

4 Research Question and Methodological Approach

Understanding user perceptions is essential for responsible integration of new technologies into security and defence settings [6]. Within the C-SALS research project, this study addresses the following research question:

"How do professional soldiers and conscripts of the Austrian Armed Forces perceive autonomous reconnaissance drones for CBRN detection?"

The central hypothesis explores whether varying degrees of autonomy influence trust levels among military personnel, and whether perceptions differ between professional soldiers and conscripts. The study examines how perceived controllability and reliability shape attitudes toward different autonomy levels. The methodology employs a structured online survey developed with subject matter experts from the Austrian Ministry of Defence. The questionnaire design was informed by literature on trust in autonomous systems and refined through expert discussions to ensure applicability to military contexts. The selection of professional soldiers and conscripts enables comparison between experienced personnel and those representing younger, potentially more technology-savvy generations who may operate such systems in the future. The Austrian Armed Forces play a central role in national CBRN emergency response as one organization equipped with specialized capabilities. This investigation contributes to the CBRN SaaS initiative within the PESCO framework [22], which promotes advanced semi-autonomous reconnaissance solutions for cross-border disaster preparedness and defence.

5 Signal Processing in the Context of Drone Autonomy

In recent years, significant progress has been made in the field of drone autonomy, particularly in autonomous navigation and control [4, 5]. For better classification, autonomy can be divided into several areas: signal processing, navigation, collision avoidance, decision making, communication, self-diagnosis and maintenance. This section focuses on efficient sensor data analysis, which is an essential element in achieving a higher degree of autonomy by providing the basis for informed decisions. Although decision-making remains the responsibility of humans, it could increasingly be used by technical systems to carry out missions autonomously in the future [20].

The subject of this study is the development and application of methods for the automatic analysis of measurement data to improve the decision-making basis of emergency services in critical situations.

5.1 Approach to Understanding Autonomy Perceptions

This research focuses on understanding user perceptions and trust in autonomous systems within the CBRN defence context. While the technical aspects of data processing and sensor capabilities form an important foundation, the primary concern is how these technological advances are perceived and accepted by potential operators. The challenges explored include how different levels of autonomy affect trust, acceptance, and perceived usefulness of drone systems among military personnel. The study examines how factors such as reliability, control preferences, speed of information delivery, and clarity of presented data influence the willingness of CBRN specialists to rely on increasingly autonomous drone systems in mission-critical scenarios.

5.2 System

The system developed in this project is based on the drone Schiebel CAMCOPTER® S-100 equipped with additional sensors, which already has the ability to fly automatically (via waypoints). The additional sensors include a high-precision laser scanner for scanning the terrain, a stand-off detector capable of detecting and identifying hazardous chemical substances from a great distance, and a sampling system on a platform carried 30 m below the UAV, capable of taking gas samples from hard-to-reach locations. As a flexibly deployable UAV-based reconnaissance system, the drone is intended to assist emergency services in tactical mission planning and monitoring in two ways:

i) By detecting and identifying a gas cloud with a stand-off detector and determining potentially exposed areas, reconnaissance and mitigation can be accelerated.
ii) By determining safe sink channels and autonomously taking samples, detailed chemical analyses can be carried out without endangering personnel.

The core elements of this system include:

Real-time 3D modelling of terrain profiles to identify subsurface depressions. Such depressions are of particular interest for gas measurement as they are more prone to heavy gas accumulation and therefore potentially higher gas concentrations. A depression is defined as a continuous area of terrain that has a positive gradient (rising terrain) in any direction from the lowest local point. The method starts by identifying these lowest points and uses a 'flood filling' algorithm that iteratively increases the target height until a negative gradient is reached.

Analysis of the 3D terrain to identify suitable sampling areas and facilitate automated sampling. The objective is to identify areas of the terrain where the UAV can safely descend to a low altitude in order to take samples, while maintaining a minimum distance from obstacles to avoid collisions. Additionally, navigation support during ground manoeuvres while sampling helps minimise the risk of accidents, further enhancing the UAV's safety.

6 Autonomous Drones, Scepticism and Trust

Although autonomous drone technologies offer significant advantages in terms of efficiency and operational flexibility, their acceptance and successful implementation still depend heavily on individual and institutional attitudes. Concerns about such systems are shaped by a range of issues, including technical reliability, safety, ethical implications, and broader operational consequences.

Trust in technological systems is a complex, multidimensional construct. Hoffman et al. [14] argue that trust goes beyond conventional safety metrics and includes factors such as predictability, performance stability, and the presence of control mechanisms. Lee and See [17] define trust as "the attitude that an agent will help achieve an individual's goals in a situation characterized by uncertainty and vulnerability," emphasizing the interplay of cognitive and emotional dimensions. Camp [6] stresses that trust must be an integral design element of technical systems—especially in high-stakes domains such as the military—rather than a secondary consideration. In line with this, Endsley [13] links trust to shared situational awareness, highlighting the importance of aligned understanding in human-machine interaction, particularly during complex emergency responses. Building on this foundation, Mayer et al. [19] identify three dimensions of trust: ability (technical competence), benevolence (intent to support the user), and integrity (adherence to acceptable principles). When applied to autonomous systems, ability primarily reflects perceived technical reliability. In the current study, participants rated **accuracy of results** as one of the most important attributes of reconnaissance drones in CBRN scenarios ($M = 4.68$ on a 6-point Likert scale), underlining the central role of perceived ability in fostering trust. In military environments, trust acquires specific characteristics due to the critical nature of operations. Holzinger et al. [15] describe a concept of "calibrated trust," developed through training and operational experience, which allows personnel to assess system performance without falling into overtrust or blind scepticism. This perspective is echoed in the survey results: while respondents overall express positive views on drone use, they remain cautious about fully autonomous systems and prefer solutions that retain some level of human oversight.

6.1 Autonomy Levels and Their Impact on Trust Formation

The autonomy of reconnaissance drones spans a spectrum, each level bearing distinct implications for trust and acceptance. Parasuraman et al. [20] distinguish four stages of automation: information acquisition, information analysis, decision selection and action implementation. Each can be realized with varying degrees of human or machine involvement. Building on this model, Endsley [13] introduced a taxonomy of automation levels, ranging from manual control—where all tasks are performed by humans—to full automation, where systems operate entirely independently. Between these poles lie several configurations of human-machine interaction, reflected in the categories used in the survey:

- Human-in-control: All decisions and operations are made by humans, with minimal system support
- Human-in-the-loop: The system executes tasks autonomously but requires human input for key decisions
- Human-on-the-loop: The system acts autonomously, while humans monitor and intervene if needed
- Human-outside-the-loop: The system functions entirely independently, with little or no human involvement

Survey results reveal a pronounced preference for human control: 38.75% of respondents favour a "human-in-control" model, indicating a basic scepticism toward full automation. The "human-in-the-loop" model is preferred by 31.25%, while 25% support the "human-outside-the-loop" configuration. Only 5% favour the "human-on-the-loop" model, making it the least popular option. Previous research by de Visser et al. [22] suggests an inverse relationship between autonomy and trust—higher autonomy often leads to reduced trust, especially among inexperienced users. The findings partly challenge this assumption. While there is a clear preference for human oversight, a significant share (25%) is open to highly autonomous systems. Moreover, the differences between professional soldiers and conscripts suggest that the connection between experience and trust in autonomy may be more nuanced than expected.

6.2 Challenges to Trust in Autonomous Military Reconnaissance Drones

Trust in autonomous reconnaissance drones—especially in complex CBRN scenarios—is shaped by several interrelated challenges: Technical reliability remains a key concern. AI-driven systems may struggle with interpreting unpredictable or atypical situations, particularly under the variable conditions typical of CBRN environments (e.g., shifting atmospheric conditions, unknown chemical compositions, and physical obstacles). Survey respondents reflected this scepticism: accuracy of results ($M = 4.68$) and clarity of information presentation ($M = 4.70$) were identified as essential system characteristics (Fig. 2). Algorithmic opacity poses another challenge. The often non-transparent decision-making processes of AI models—the so-called "black box" phenomenon—undermine operator confidence [16]. In military operations, where situational awareness and accountability are critical, unexplained decisions reduce the system's perceived reliability. Tensions around control allocation further complicate the issue. Decision-makers must determine how to balance automation with human oversight in a way that maintains operational efficiency and trust, without disrupting established command structures. This tension is particularly pronounced in CBRN reconnaissance, where both speed and precision are vital, and errors may have severe consequences. Ethical and regulatory issues also influence trust perceptions. Although not the focus of this study, the potential misuse of autonomous drones—for unauthorized surveillance or deployment beyond their intended purpose—adds to broader societal and professional scepticism. Finally, experience and expertise asymmetries play a role. Rieger et al. [21] argue, trust formation varies between experts and novices: experts focus on performance metrics and system transparency, while novices are more influenced by interface usability and general ease of operation.

6.3 Strategies for Enhancing Trust in Autonomous Reconnaissance Drones

To establish and maintain trust in autonomous reconnaissance drones, the challenges outlined above must be addressed through carefully tailored technical and organizational strategies. A core principle is the implementation of human-centred design. The human-in-the-loop (HITL) concept ensures that humans remain actively involved in decision-making processes. Research by Chen and Barnes [7] shows that HITL systems enhance trust by allowing AI-driven decisions to be reviewed and corrected when necessary. This aligns with the survey results, where 31.25% of respondents favoured human-in-the-loop models—indicating a preference for retaining human control at critical decision points. Transparency is another key factor in building trust. Explainable AI methods can help make algorithmic decisions more understandable. Doshi-Velez and Kim [11] argue that explanations should be tailored to users' expertise and operational context. For CBRN drones, this could include visual representations of sensor data, confidence ratings for hazard detection, and clear indicators distinguishing between automated and human-confirmed assessments. The high importance attributed to clear information presentation (M = 4.70) in the survey supports the relevance of transparency mechanisms (see Fig. 2). Operational speed also emerged as a critical criterion. With a mean score of 4.81, speed of results was rated the most important factor among all drone characteristics. In CBRN emergencies, timely data is essential for effective decision-making and life-saving interventions. Thus, drone systems must balance speed and efficiency with adequate human oversight. Systems that accelerate data collection and analysis while allowing human validation at key points may best address these dual requirements. Training and user familiarization are equally vital. Prior research by. [10, 15] demonstrates that trust in autonomous systems improves significantly through training that strengthens users' mental models. Although the difference in preference between professional soldiers and conscripts was not statistically significant, it suggests that experience and exposure may influence attitudes toward autonomy. Comprehensive training programs could help foster calibrated trust across diverse personnel profiles.

Finally, gradual introduction of autonomy can support incremental trust development. Parasuraman et al. [20] recommend adaptive automation—adjusting autonomy levels dynamically based on task complexity, user workload, or context. Given the diverse autonomy preferences in the data, flexible drone systems capable of switching between modes may prove most effective for real-world CBRN operations.

6.4 Trust in Autonomous Systems and High-Risk Environments

This study tested the hypothesis that higher autonomy in CBRN reconnaissance drones results in lower trust among military personnel. Survey results partially support this hypothesis, with 38.75% of respondents favouring "human-in-control" systems. However, the relationship is not strictly linear, as 25% of respondents are open to "human-outside-the-loop" systems with minimal human intervention. Contrary to expectations, professional soldiers did not exhibit significantly more scepticism than conscripts ($p = 0.283$), challenging assumptions about generational differences in technology acceptance. Reliability and controllability were emphasized by respondents, with high importance placed on accuracy (M = 4.68) and clear information presentation (M = 4.70). Trust dynamics are particularly complex in CBRN environments due to heightened risks. Respondents rated drones highly for ensuring safety of operational forces (M = 4.89), with speed of results (M = 4.81) being rated as the most important factor. These findings suggest that systems balancing speed, accuracy, and clear information presentation, while maintaining appropriate human oversight, achieve optimal trust levels in high-risk contexts.

7 Research Methodology

To empirically investigate the acceptance of reconnaissance drones, a structured quantitative questionnaire was developed as part of the collaboration between the University for Continuing Education Krems (UWK), the AIT Austrian Institute of Technology, and the Austrian Armed Forces. The questionnaire design was informed by a thorough review of existing literature on trust in autonomous systems, human-machine interaction, and CBRN-specific risk perception. Experts from the Austrian Armed Forces provided input to adapt the survey to military operational contexts. The finalized questionnaire underwent rigorous validation. Content validity was ensured through expert reviews by CBRN specialists and survey methodology experts. Refinements were made based on feedback from the pilot phase, improving question phrasing, response options, and survey flow. After approval, the questionnaire was distributed to military barracks with the support of the Austrian Armed Forces. The survey targeted both professional soldiers and conscripts, especially those specializing in CBRN operations. Data collection occurred online between November 2023 and February 2024, resulting in 86 valid responses. Demographically, 90% of respondents were male, 4% female, and 6% did not specify their gender. 91.7% were born in Austria, with the remaining respondents from the EU (7.1%) and outside the EU (1.2%). 74% of respondents were under 30 years old. The majority (45.3%) had completed an apprenticeship, with most working in basic military service (53%), professional soldier roles (44%), and 3% in unspecified positions. 96.5% focused on CBRN defence, with 23.3% expressing interest in becoming drone pilots. While the study provides valuable insights, the sample size of 86 may limit generalizability to broader military contexts. Additionally, the cross-sectional nature of the study captures attitudes at a specific point in time, without tracking potential changes in perceptions with increased exposure to autonomous systems.

8 Results

8.1 General Attitudes Toward Drones

Figure 1: The overall attitude towards drones among the surveyed participants is highly positive. Reconnaissance drones are particularly valued for their ability to ensure the safety of operational forces, especially among CBRN defence specialists, with a mean rating of 4.89 on a 6-point Likert scale. The civilian population also recognizes the safety benefits of reconnaissance drones, particularly in safeguarding human lives, with a mean score of 4.42. In Austria, the primary focus for drone applications is on addressing chemical hazards, followed by nuclear threats, despite the absence of nuclear power plants in the country. Drones are generally perceived as technologically advanced and appealing. Negative perceptions, such as ethical concerns or doubts about reliability, are minimal. Only a small proportion of respondents expressed discomfort with drones, with a mean score of 2.48. Scepticism about reliability is similarly low, with only 2.44 agreeing that drones "cannot be trusted because they are too faulty." These results suggest that concerns about drone technology play a relatively minor role in the overall evaluation.

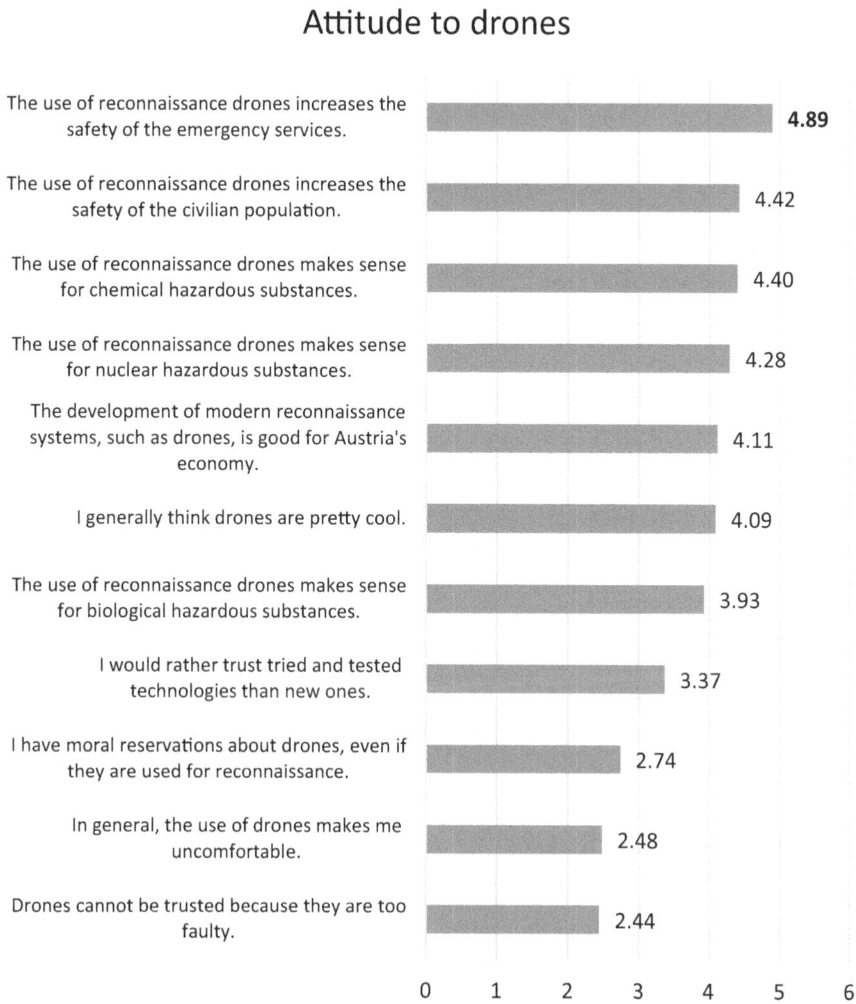

Fig. 1. Attitudes of drones; n = 0,86, 6-point-Likert-Scale, n = 86, mean

8.2 Important Characteristics of Reconnaissance Drones

Figure 2: Among the evaluated factors, the speed of results is considered the most important, with a mean score of 4.81 on a 6-point Likert scale. It is followed closely by the clear presentation of information (M = 4.70) and the accuracy of results (M = 4.68), indicating that users prioritize both efficiency and data reliability in reconnaissance drones. The relatively small differences between these scores suggest that respondents seek a comprehensive solution rather than focusing on a single feature. Automation ranks lowest, with a mean score of 3.99, reflecting a preference for retaining control over drone operations. This finding suggests a degree of scepticism about full automation but not

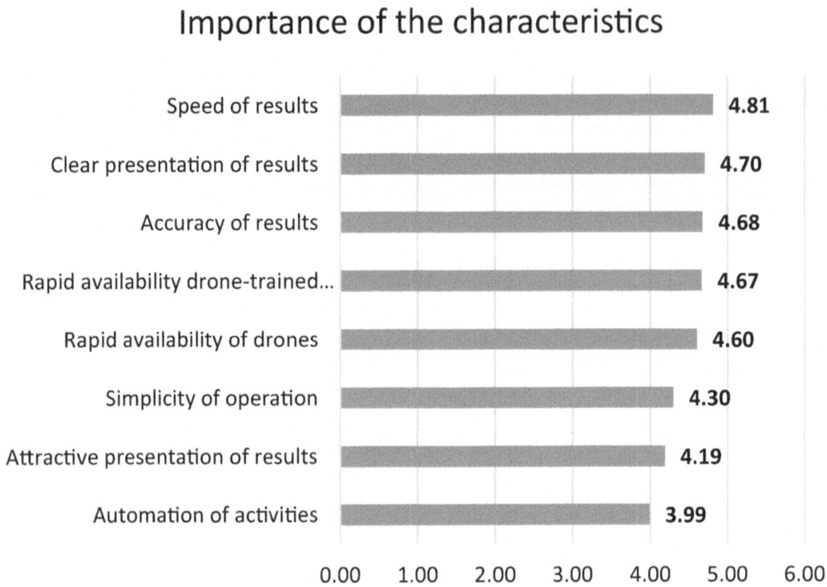

Fig. 2. Importance of the characteristics of reconnaissance drones for CBRN-cases; 6-point-Likert-Scale, $n = 86$, mean

outright rejection. Automation is seen as useful, though not as a primary requirement for effective deployment.

8.3 Trust in Autonomous Systems

Figure 3: There is no absolute trust in autonomous systems among the surveyed participants. While reconnaissance drones are generally well-received, respondents tend to favour retaining decision-making authority rather than fully delegating operational control to autonomous systems. A comparison between conscripts and professional soldiers shows that conscripts display slightly less scepticism toward autonomous decision-making. However, statistical analysis using the Whitney U test ($p = 0.295$) reveals no significant difference, suggesting that younger soldiers are not notably more inclined to trust autonomous systems than their more experienced counterparts.

8.4 Preferred Levels of Autonomy

Figure 4: The data show that 38.75% of respondents prefer to maintain the highest level of control over drones, reflecting a fundamental but nuanced scepticism toward fully automated processes. Among the different levels of autonomy, 31.25% favour a "human-in-the-loop" approach, requiring human input for critical decisions. A slightly smaller proportion, 25%, prefer a "human-outside-the-loop" system, where drones operate with minimal human intervention. Only 5% of respondents favour a "human-on-the-loop" model, where operators supervise and intervene only when necessary.

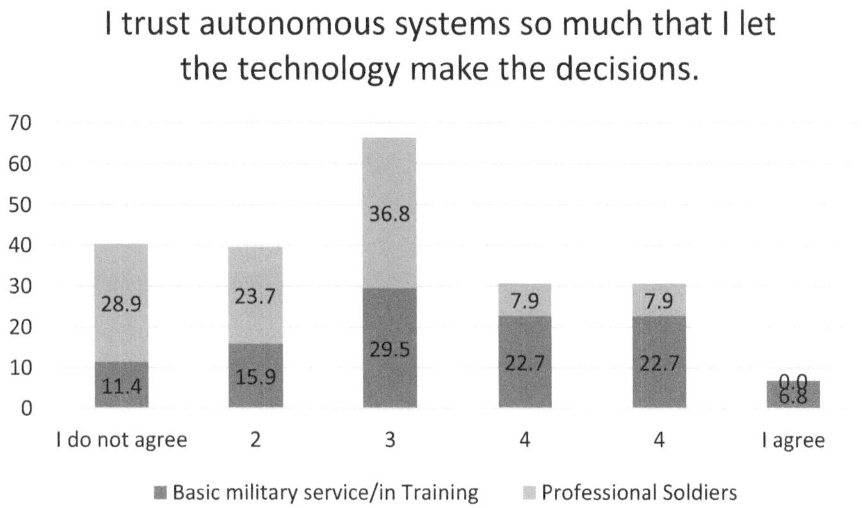

Fig. 3. Trust in autonomous systems, n = 86, in %, p = 0,295 (non-significant)

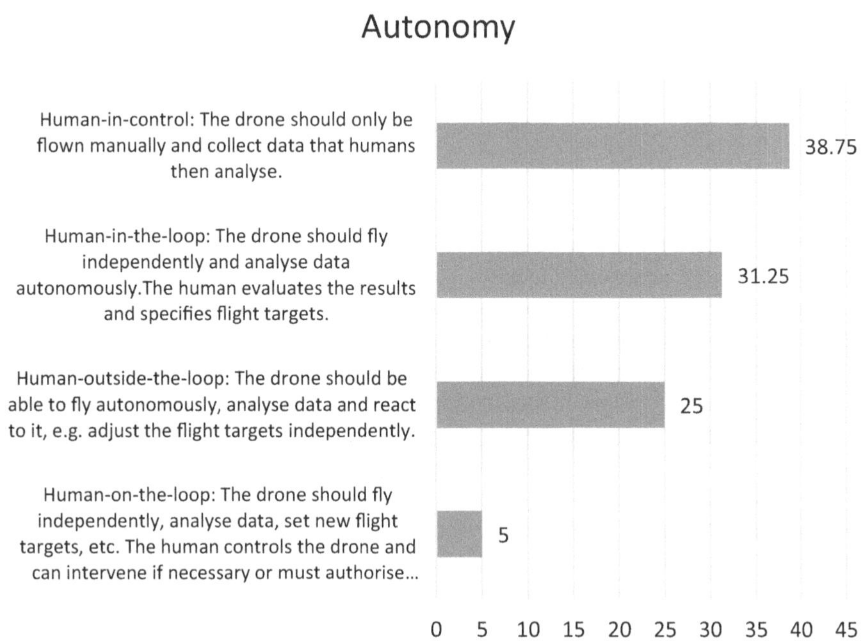

Fig. 4. n = 86, 6-point Likert-Scale, in %,

8.5 Differences Between Professional Soldiers and Conscripts

Figure 5: A noticeable difference emerges in the preferences for drone automation levels when comparing professional soldiers, conscripts, and trainees. Active service members

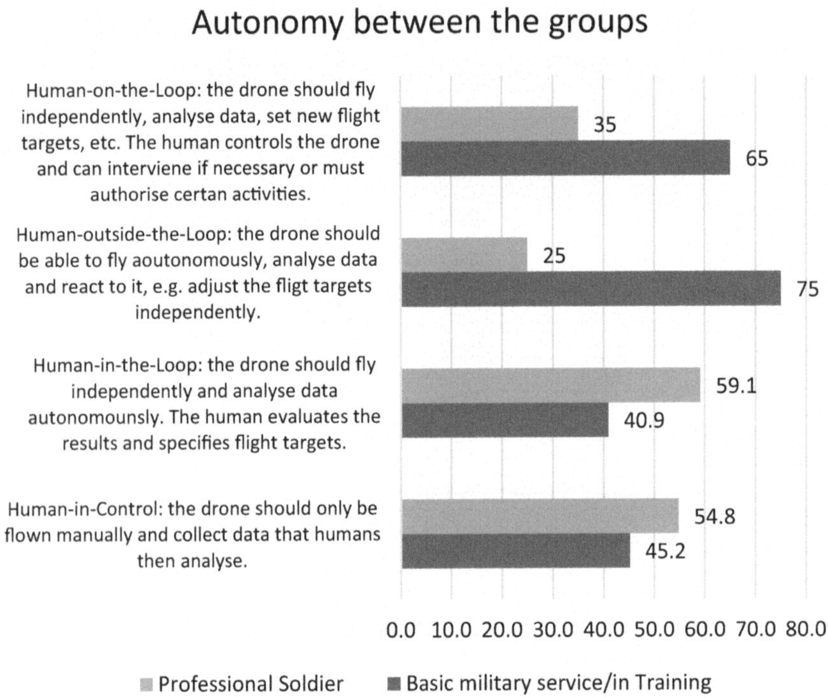

Fig. 5. Autonomy between the groups, n = 86, 6-point Likert-Scale, in %,

show a stronger preference for the "human-on-the-loop" approach, while older individuals tend to prefer direct control. This could reflect a generational effect, as younger individuals are more accustomed to automated processes. However, the difference is not statistically significant ($p = 0.283$), suggesting that age and experience may influence trust in autonomous systems, but do not lead to fundamentally different attitudes toward drone autonomy. The "human-in-the-loop" approach, requiring human input at key decision points, sees a more balanced distribution: 59.1% of professional soldiers and 40.9% of conscripts/trainees favour this level of oversight. Similarly, for full human control ("human-in-control"), 54.8% of professional soldiers and 45.2% of conscripts/trainees prefer retaining the highest level of authority. These findings indicate a general preference for human oversight in military settings but no definitive generational divide in attitudes toward autonomy. Professional experience and familiarity with automated systems appear to play a more significant role in shaping perspectives on the balance between autonomy and control in reconnaissance drone operations.

8.6 Testing the Central Hypothesis

The central hypothesis suggested that higher autonomy levels would correlate with decreased trust, with a more pronounced effect among professional soldiers than conscripts. The data partially supports this hypothesis. A clear preference for higher human control was observed (38.75% favouring "human-in-control"), aligning with the first part of the hypothesis. However, the anticipated difference between professional soldiers and conscripts was not statistically significant ($p = 0.283$), challenging assumptions about experience-based trust formation. Regarding the mediating factors of perceived reliability and controllability, the data confirms their influence on trust, as predicted. The high importance ratings for accuracy ($M = 4.68$) and clear information presentation ($M = 4.70$) highlight the continued significance of performance-based trust factors in the CBRN context. The low agreement with statements suggesting that drones are unreliable ($M = 2.44$) further supports that perceived reliability is not a major barrier to trust in this population.

9 Discussion and Conclusion

The study results indicate that the overall attitude toward reconnaissance drones is highly positive. Military personnel specializing in CBRN defence rate them as particularly beneficial for the safety of operational forces, with a mean score of 5.08 on a 6-point Likert scale. The civilian population also acknowledges the protective benefits of reconnaissance drones, particularly in enhancing public safety ($M = 4.42$). A more detailed analysis of key drone features reveals that speed and rapid availability are considered the most important factors ($M = 4.81$), followed by the clear presentation of information ($M = 4.70$) and accuracy of results ($M = 4.68$). The automation of activities, however, ranks lowest ($M = 3.99$), reflecting a preference for maintaining control over drone operations rather than fully relying on automation. Despite the generally positive perception of drones, there is no absolute trust in autonomous systems. Respondents tend to hesitate when it comes to fully delegating decision-making authority to autonomous drones, favouring some degree of human oversight. The finding that most respondents prefer human-in-control (38.75%) or human-in-the-loop (31.25%) approaches warrants a nuanced interpretation beyond simple technophobia or conservatism. Rather than indicating distrust in the technology itself, these preferences likely reflect "appropriate trust calibration"—the alignment of trust with system capabilities and limitations. Military personnel operate in contexts where accountability for decisions is paramount, and their preference for maintaining human control may represent a sophisticated understanding of current technological limitations rather than resistance to innovation. An approach that could address these concerns might involve automation for standard tasks, such as autonomously transporting drones from the starting point to the deployment area, while retaining human oversight for more critical tasks, such as conducting detection operations upon arrival.

The distribution of preferences across different autonomy levels reflects the theoretical tension between control and efficiency. The strong preference for human-in-control and human-in-the-loop approaches demonstrates what Lyons and Stokes [18] termed the "trust gap"—the mismatch between users' mental models and the actual capabilities of autonomous systems. Notably, the relatively low preference for the human-on-the-loop model (5% overall) challenges assumptions about graduated autonomy adoption and suggests that military personnel may prefer either clearly defined boundaries of human control or a more complete delegation of certain tasks to autonomous systems.

The absence of statistically significant differences between professional soldiers and conscripts challenges common assumptions about generational digital divides in technology acceptance. While digital natives are often presumed to be more accepting of automation, the findings suggest that in specialized military contexts, operational considerations may override generational tendencies. This aligns with Holzinger et al.'s [15] concept of "calibrated trust," which emphasizes that trust in high-stakes environments develops through professional socialization and risk assessment rather than generational factors alone. The strong emphasis on speed of results ($M = 4.81$) coupled with preferences for human oversight suggests that CBRN reconnaissance drone development should prioritize systems that accelerate data acquisition and preliminary analysis while maintaining clear mechanisms for human review and decision authority. These findings indicate that autonomous capabilities should be implemented in ways that enhance human decision-making rather than replace it, particularly for high-consequence decisions. The relatively low interest in human-on-the-loop systems (5% overall) further suggests that semi-autonomous approaches where humans passively monitor system actions may be the least effective implementation strategy.

10 Outlook

The central hypothesis posited that higher autonomy levels would correlate with decreased trust, particularly among professional soldiers. The data partially supports this hypothesis. While a clear preference for human control was observed (38.75% favouring "human-in-control"), the expected difference between professional soldiers and conscripts was not statistically significant ($p = 0.283$), challenging assumptions about experience-based trust formation. Future research should expand to include other first responder groups, such as firefighters, EMS, and civil protection agencies, to understand how professional backgrounds influence drone acceptance. The current focus on military personnel provides valuable insights as they are the primary operators of CBRN reconnaissance drones and directly engage with the technology's autonomy features, unlike other responders who may primarily use the information gathered rather than operating the systems themselves. Additionally, future studies could explore how attitudes evolve as autonomous drone technology becomes more prevalent in real-world applications.

References

1. Alawad, W., Halima, N.B., Aziz, L.: An Unmanned Aerial Vehicle (UAV) system for disaster and crisis management in smart cities. Electronics **12**(4), 1051 (2023)
2. Aoki, M., Rothwell, G.: A comparative institutional analysis of the Fukushima nuclear disaster: Lessons and policy implications. Energy Policy **53**, 240–247 (2013)
3. Bonetti, P., Cho, C.H., Michelon, G.: Environmental disclosure and the cost of capital: evidence from the Fukushima nuclear disaster. Eur. Account. Rev. **33**(5), 1693–1721 (2024)
4. Brundage, M., et al.: The Malicious Use of Artificial Intelligence: Forecasting, Prevention, and Mitigation (2024)
5. Brynjolfsson, E., McAfee, A.: The second machine age: work, progress, and prosperity in a time of brilliant technologies. WW Norton & company (2014)

6. Camp, L.J.: Design for Trust. In: Trust, Reputation and Security: Theories and Practice, Springer-Verlag (2003)
7. Chang, A.H., Chen, A.P., Hsu, E.B.: Chemical Disasters. Public Health Emergencies Case Studies Competencies Essential Services Public Health 82 (2021)
8. Chen, J.Y.C., Barnes, M.J.: Human-agent teaming for multirobot control: a review of human factors issues. IEEE Trans. Hum. Mach. Syst. **44**(1), 13–29 (2014)
9. Coleman, C.N.: Fukushima and the future of radiation research. Radiat. Res. **179**(1), 1–8 (2013)
10. Cortright, D., Fairhurst, R., Wall, K.: Drones and the future of armed conflict: ethical, legal, and strategic implications. University of Chicago Press (2017)
11. Doshi-Velez, F., Kim, B.: Towards a Rigorous Science of Interpretable Machine Learning (2017)
12. Eckerman, I., Børsen, T.: Corporate and governmental responsibilities for preventing chemical disasters: lessons from Bhopal. In: Ethics of Chemistry: From Poison Gas to Climate Engineering, pp. 113–140. World Scientific (2021)
13. Endsley, M.R.: Toward a theory of situation awareness in dynamic systems. Hum. Factors J. **37**(1), 32–64 (1995)
14. Hoffman, L.J., Lawson-Jenkins, K., Blum, J.: Trust beyond security: an expanded trust model. Commun. ACM **49**(7), 94–101 (2006)
15. Holzinger, A., et al.: Calibrated trust in military AI systems. IEEE Intell. Syst. **38**(5), 78–85 (2023)
16. Kissinger, H., Schmidt, E., Huttenlocher, D.P.: The age of AI: and our human future. Little, Brown and Company (2021)
17. Lee, J.D., See, K.A.: Trust in automation: designing for appropriate reliance. Hum. Factors **46**(1), 50–80 (2004)
18. Lyons, J.B., Stokes, C.K.: Human-human reliance in the context of automation. Hum. Factors **54**(1), 112–121 (2012)
19. Mayer, R.C., Davis, J.H., Schoorman, F.D.: An integrative model of organizational trust. Acad. Manag. Rev. **20**(3), 709–734 (1995)
20. Parasuraman, R., Sheridan, T.B., Wickens, C.D.: A model for types and levels of human interaction with automation. IEEE Trans. Syst. Man Cybern. Part A Syst. Hum. **30**(3), 286–297 (2000)
21. Rieger, T., Kugler, L., Manzey, D., Roesler, E.: The (Im)perfect automation schema: who is trusted more, automated or human decision support? Hum. Factors **66**, 1995–2007 (2023). https://doi.org/10.1177/00187208231197347
22. De Visser, E., Pak, R., Shaw, T.: From 'automation' to 'autonomy': the importance of trust repair in human–machine interaction. Ergonomics **61**, 1409–1427 (2018). https://doi.org/10.1080/00140139.2018.1457725
23. Yoshimura, H., et al.: Categorization of disaster-related deaths in Minamisoma city after the Fukushima nuclear disaster using clustering analysis. Sci. Rep. **14**(1), 2946 (2024)

The Virtualization of Terrorism and its Consequences for Counterterrorism

Nicolas Stockhammer(✉)

Danube University Krems, 3500 Krems, Austria
nicolas.stockhammer@donau-uni.ac.at

Abstract. This conference paper investigates the "virtualization of terrorism," highlighting how digital technologies facilitate extremist activities along the entire value chain of ideologically motivated violence- from radicalization to attack execution. It emphasizes that terrorists now extensively utilize online platforms for secure communication, recruitment, and operational planning, significantly altering the landscape of modern terrorism. Referring to case studies of notable attacks, such as the 2017 Manchester Arena bombing and the 2019 Halle synagogue shooting, the study aims at illustrating how perpetrators leveraged online resources for radicalization and attack preparation. The research paper also discusses the rise of Generation Z as a new wave of perpetrators, influenced by platforms like TikTok, which has become a tool for recruiting and radicalizing youth. Encrypted messaging apps further complicate counterterrorism efforts by enabling secure communication among extremists. Conclusively, the study underscores the urgent need for adaptive counterterrorism strategies to address the challenges posed by the virtualization of terrorism, which allows for greater anonymity and operational flexibility for terrorists. The findings call for a reevaluation of current approaches to effectively combat the evolving threat landscape shaped by digital technologies.

Keywords: counterterrorism · virtualization · technology · disaster

1 Introduction

Terrorism is inarguably a man-made disaster [1]. As such it is distinguished not only by its human origin but also by its intentional infliction of harm for political, ideological, or religious targets. Unlike natural disasters, which are rooted in environmental or biological processes, terrorism arises from deliberate human agency and calculated choices. It is characterized by the use of violence or the threat thereof to instill fear, disrupt societal order, and coerce states or populations into compliance or change. The man-made nature of terrorism places it within the realm of preventable and controllable phenomena, contingent on addressing the underlying sociopolitical grievances, ideological motivations, and mechanisms of radicalization that drive individuals or groups to commit such acts. This is where counter-terrorism to a greater extent becomes a preventive task.

Published by Springer Nature Switzerland AG 2026
W. Seböck et al. (Eds.): ITDRR 2024, IFIP AICT 752, pp. 210–227, 2026.
https://doi.org/10.1007/978-3-031-97115-0_14

From a theoretical standpoint, terrorism challenges the boundaries of conventional disaster frameworks, requiring an intersectional approach that integrates political science, psychology, and sociology. The conceptualization of terrorism as a man-made disaster necessitates a shift from viewing it solely as a security threat to understanding it as a complex social process shaped by individual decision-making, group dynamics, and structural conditions. This perspective not only broadens the analytical scope but also informs more effective prevention strategies rooted in social resilience, inclusive governance, and targeted counter-radicalization efforts.

Against this backdrop, in terrorism research there are basically four argumentative strains for the claim of terrorism as man-made disaster:

1. The intentional nature of terrorism: Terrorist attacks are deliberately planned and executed by individuals or groups [2], unlike natural disasters.
2. Human agency: Both, cause and implementation of terrorist acts are entirely dependent on human decisions and actions [3].
3. Societal impact: Terrorism can have severe and long-lasting effects on communities, infrastructure, and social structures [4].
4. Prevention and mitigation: Counterterrorism efforts primarily focus on human factors, such as addressing radicalization, improving security measures, and intelligence gathering [5].

Considering that terrorist-induced events require similar mitigation strategies as disaster management suggests- all related to preparedness, detection, response, and recovery [6]. The British Counterterrorism Strategy "CONTEST" for example, puts this approach into four Ps: "**P**reventing" (from becoming terrorists or supporting terrorism); "**P**ursuing" (terrorists to disrupt their plots is designed to reduce the threat);"**P**rotecting" (against a terrorist attack reduce [...] vulnerability) and "**P**reparing" (to mitigate the impact of any attack are designed to reduce the impact) [...] [7].

Terrorism qualifies as a man-made disaster due to its intentional design to inflict harm, disrupt societies, and instill fear. Unlike natural disasters, which arise from environmental phenomena, terrorism is a deliberate act orchestrated by individuals or groups to achieve political, ideological, or religious goals. This intentionality is crucial to understanding its classification as a man-made disaster, as it reflects a calculated effort to exploit vulnerabilities in human systems—be it through attacks on critical infrastructure, mass gatherings, or economic targets.

Terrorism's societal impact parallels that of natural disasters in terms of disruption and devastation, but with an added layer of psychological manipulation. While natural disasters create fear due to their unpredictability, terrorism's fear stems from its targeted and purposeful nature, aiming to destabilize communities and undermine confidence in governance and security systems. The human toll in terms of lives lost, injuries, and psychological trauma is compounded by the cascading effects on social cohesion, economic stability, and public trust—effects that are directly engineered by the perpetrators.

The classification of terrorism as a man-made disaster is further supported by its potential impact on critical infrastructure. Terrorist attacks often target essential systems such as power grids, water supplies, transportation networks, and communication systems [8]. Such kind of attacks are meticulously planned to exploit vulnerabilities in these vital structures, demonstrating the human element in both the conception and execution of such acts. The deliberate targeting of critical infrastructure underscores the intentional nature of terrorism and its aim to cause maximum disruption to society. The long-term effects on community cohesion, social trust, and individual mental health further emphasize the man-made nature of this disaster.

The aim of this research paper is to analyze the impact of rapidly evolving digital technology on the terrorist landscape and evaluate its far-reaching ramifications for counterterrorism efforts [9]. Contemporary manifestations of terrorism indicate that the phenomenon of extremist violence has gradually become virtualized [10]. What does that mean? Terrorists operating clandestinely regularly use various digital technologies to set up secure peer to peer-communication networks where they exchange on subversive issues like terrorist plotting, targeting or tactics [11]. They host and share illegal extremist content on social media channels, consume online tutorials, look for support to learn the terrorist skills and disperse terrorism related information within closed channels [12]. What's more, radicalized individuals are frequently using online resources to create weapons and to gather information how to execute attacks. Both, terrorist organizations as well as inspired or affiliated lone actors increasingly exploit the entire digital value chain of terrorism [13]. Starting from a first virtual contact with extreme positions, narratives, and ideologies, from recruitment, propaganda and radicalization to the direct planning and organization of attacks- nearly everything is mandated online. This phenomenon may be referred to as the "virtualization of terrorism". It implies the immersion of terrorists into the sphere of cyberspace across the entire pathway (from the initial contact with extremist ideology to the planning and execution of attacks). The World Wide Web has in the past decade become the prime space – a digital ecosystem – for fostering all kinds of terrorist activities [13]. Not only on a motivational level but also in terms of capabilities, it describes the virtual ability to conduct online operations ranging from providing propaganda platforms to preparing attacks: An essential criterion on all spectrums is "*the role of the internet and the associated virtualization of terror - from initial contact with extremist propaganda, to radicalization and recruitment, to planning and logistical support, including the exchange of information on the effective execution of an act of terror - almost everything takes place online*" [14]. Recent terrorist attacks illustrate such a more and more fashionable online procurement of terrorism. In most cases the first contact responsible for a further radicalization process takes place online [15]. Online radicalization refers to a process by which individuals are influenced or encouraged to adopt extremist ideologies through the internet [16].

However as a distinguished group of radicalization scholars has pointed out, "*online extremism at the level of the user work with the assumption that radicalization, while it can be impacted by things that happen online, does not come purely as a result of online behaviors*" [16].Therefore we should preferably speak of "dual radicalization", both on- and offline, whereas the online part is steadily playing a more important role for the complex and evolving process of turning towards extremism [18]. Particularly jihadist and far-right extremist movements, exploit virtual platforms to spread propaganda, recruit new members, and incite violence. Online forums are misused as incubator for extremist ideologies, while algorithms often amplify radical content, potentially speeding up the process of radicalization [17]. Radicalization occurs across multiple online platforms, including social media networks, encrypted messaging apps, and forums on the dark web [18].

These spaces enable extremist groups to disseminate ideologies without geographical limitations, and they can more easily target vulnerable individuals who may feel isolated or disenfranchised [19]. All these three aspects- vulnerability, isolation, and disenfranchisement- on a psychological level applied to some extent for Salman Abedi, the Manchester suicide bomber.

The Ariane Grande Concert Attack

The Ariana Grande concert attack in Manchester on May 22, 2017, serves as a grim example of how terrorist attackers are able to exploit online resources for the consequent procurement and preparation of violent acts [20]. Not very surprisingly, the perpetrator's radicalization was reportedly influenced by online extremist content, including jihadist propaganda from IS [21]. The suicide bombing, which killed 22 people and injured over 800, was carried out by the attacker, Salman Abedi, a British-born individual of Libyan descent, who constructed an improvised explosive device (IED) using materials he sourced both locally and online. Abedi's bomb was constructed using readily available components, many of which were purchased online. Abedi used online platforms to research bomb-making techniques, and he acquired various components necessary for constructing the explosive device [22]. These materials included chemicals, electronic components, and other items that, while innocuous on their own, were combined to create a deadly weapon. Investigations confirmed that the easy online access to these materials played a critical role in enabling the attack. Undoubtedly, the Manchester case underscores the growing trend of terrorists relying on online platforms to facilitate the planning and execution of their operations, from ideological indoctrination to the procurement of weapons and bomb-making materials. The use of encrypted communications and online tutorials allows for the decentralization of terror plots, enabling individuals or small cells to carry out attacks with minimal direct contact with organized terror groups, making prevention and detection more challenging for authorities.

The Halle Synagogue Attack

The Halle Synagogue Attack on October 9, 2019, also demonstrates how terrorism is facilitated by online radicalization and what impact the use of digital platforms nowadays has for planning, procurement, and promotion of attacks [23]. While staging the terrorist assault, the perpetrator Stephan Balliet, a German right-wing extremist, attempted to enter the synagogue, but failed to breach the fortified door. Frustrated, he turned his attention to surrounding people on the street and at a nearby kebab shop, where he opened fire on bystanders. His rampage was partially thwarted by the security measures at the synagogue, but the attack still resulted in causalities. Balliet was radicalized through online far-right communities, where antisemitic, racist, and homophobic content is rampant. His radicalization was not the result of in-person recruitment or group dynamics but rather a solitary process fueled by digital propaganda. The attack demonstrated the growing problem of online "lone wolf" radicalization [24]. From the perspective of counterterrorism there were two interesting gradually "innovative" specifics of the terrorist assault: permanent live streaming on Twitch and the use of 3D-printed weapons. Balliet livestreamed his attack on the gaming platform Twitch, emulating the Christchurch shooter Brenton Tarrant who livestreamed his own attack on Facebook. Though fewer people watched Balliet's livestream in real-time (around five people), the video was quickly spread on extremist forums and social media, garnering tens of thousands of views [25]. The use of livestreaming to broadcast acts of terrorism is a tactic aimed at amplifying the psychological impact of the attack and recruiting like-minded individuals. A second significant element of the Halle attack was Balliet's use of homemade, 3D-printed firearms [26]. Although he had some traditional weapons, he experimented with producing guns using 3D printers, following blueprints available on the internet. The use of such technology allowed the perpetrator to circumvent stricter gun laws in Germany. While many of his improvised weapons malfunctioned during the attack, the incident underscored the increasing danger posed by emerging technologies in the hands of terrorists. The Halle attack is firm evidence of the growing threat posed by emerging technologies such as 3D printing in terrorism [27]. While access to digital blueprints for weapons increases, it poses new challenges for law enforcement agencies trying to prevent attacks. The use of homemade weapons makes it more difficult for authorities to track and prevent the acquisition of lethal devices [28]. As these two exemplary case analyses suggest, capability and deeply rooted motivation go hand in hand, as extremists use the diverse opportunities offered by cyberspace for their activities in every conceivable way. Anonymity and clandestine operations favor organizations and lone actors who take advantage of sub-conventional, asymmetric tactics, and vice versa. Based upon the assumption that these extremists manage to escape or bypass the countermeasures of counterterrorism investigators, they can create a virtual hub that allows them to quickly adapt and use it as a weapon. Fundamentally, the toxic combination of strong motivation and existing capabilities poses a constant threat to security. Unfortunately, the likelihood of establishing such attack scenarios is relatively high. With the help of virtualization, terrorists are increasingly able to remain anonymous and untraceable, making it significantly more difficult for law enforcement agencies to uncover and prevent their activities.

Focusing on Europe, most of the key developments, dynamics and trends shaping the terrorist threat landscape are largely determined by four parameters: *shifting ideologies, technological advancements, tactical modifications/adaptions,* and *geopolitical influence.* Based on statistics extrapolated from Europol's most recent *TE-SAT 2023* report [29] and other relevant data sources ("*Global Terrorism Database*", "*Global Terrorism Index*", "*RAND Database of Worldwide Terrorism Incidents*", C-REX "*RTV*", FFI "*JPED database*" etc.) [30] operationalizing the future projection methodologies of "Strategic Foresight Cockpit", the author has in a joint effort collaboratively identified and analyzed pivotal phenomena respectively key trends that are very likely going to manifest for the next 3–5 years [31]. The following trend phenomena—initially identified as 105 and later refined to 35—have been systematically analyzed (see Fig. 1) in recent months using software-driven trend research. This approach aimed to forecast dynamics that are either emerging or currently unfolding across Europe.

Based on six relevant trends to describe constellations of digital technologies misused to foster terrorism, rated with a high permeance validity and stability, but also high probability and significant impact ("*Increased Use of Encrypted Platforms*", "*Virtual Plotting*", "*Virtual Targeting*", "*Generation Z as Perpetrators*", "*TikTok-Radicalization,*

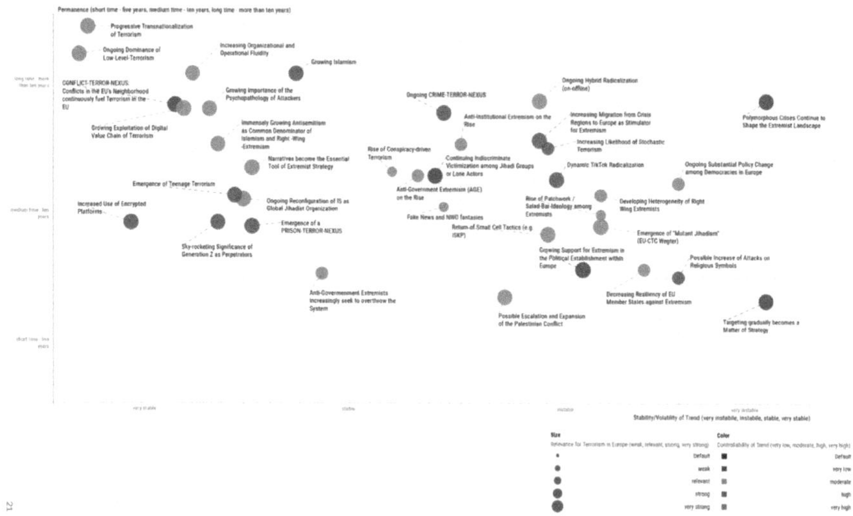

Fig. 1. EICTP Strategic Foresight Cockpit Trend Matrix (Screenshot, Work in Progress)

and "Catastrophic Terrorism"), the significance of virtualization for terrorism will be described and further examined.

2 Increased Use of Encrypted Platforms

Extremists and terrorists like Abedi or Balliet use peer-to-peer encrypted messaging platforms for several reasons, all of which revolve around enhancing their ability to communicate securely and evade detection by law enforcement and intelligence agencies [32]. Encrypted platforms are constantly available, easily accessible, and not hard to maintain [33]. Moreover, the vast availability of different platforms, apps and tools adds to this development. They can be used as hideaway for terrorists and safe space for communication, as they are hard to detect and penetrate. End-to-end encryption ensures that messages are scrambled during transmission and can only be decrypted by the intended recipient. This level of encryption makes it very difficult for third parties, including service providers or law enforcement, to read the messages, even if they are intercepted. Many encrypted platforms like Telegram allow for secure group communications, enabling extremists to coordinate within larger cells or networks without fear of their conversations being monitored. According to recent important research by Reuben Dass, "*in at least 44 percent of the 57 virtually directed Islamic State plots between 2014 and 2020, Telegram was used as a method of communication*" [11].

Encrypted platforms and apps are used to recruit new members by providing a safe space for potential recruits to engage with extremist content and communicate with recruiters without fear of being monitored. Extremists frequently use encrypted messaging to distribute propaganda materials such as videos, audio messages, or written manifestos, bypassing traditional social media platforms that might censor or remove such content. Regarding the rise of the so-called "Islamic State" (IS, also Daesh) as the Norwegian scholar Thomas Hegghammer asserts that: "*[IS, note NS] propaganda spread so quickly that the state security authorities were unable to keep track of all new sympathizers. This led to one of the worst waves of terrorist violence in modern European history. In three years, from 2015 to 2017, jihadists killed almost 350 people in Europe, more than had been killed in jihadist attacks in the previous 20 years [...]*" [34]. This was just a first tipping point regarding the exploitation of virtualization, also in terms of encryption: "*Finally, the new online ecosystem offered rich opportunities for clandestine communication. Encrypted messaging apps proliferated, and jihadi communication ran across a variety of platforms. It was a nightmare for the intelligence services*" [34]. And it still is, one might add.

Operations are securely coordinated on these platforms. Planners and perpetrators can discuss sensitive plotting details, such as target selection, logistics, and timing, without worrying that their plans will be intercepted by authorities. Peer-to-peer encrypted platforms are particularly useful for small, decentralized cells or lone actors who need to communicate with handlers or other operatives while maintaining operational security. By means of encrypted communication, terrorist plotting has undoubtedly gone virtual.

3 Virtual Plotting

Virtual plotting (terrorist planning) involves the process where one or more coordinators provide remote guidance to operatives in other countries to execute attacks [35]. Such guidance can vary in scope, including assistance with selecting targets, choosing attack methods, and offering ideological or logistical support through digital communication channels. Diffusion and decentralization are the guiding principles for the IS' virtual plotting (in particular that of its powerful branch ISKP, short for IS-Khorasan Province) [11]. ISKP appears to be one of the relevant terrorist groups utilizing virtual planning to coordinate its attacks. They have continued to use virtual plotting techniques, where operatives are directed remotely, often through encrypted communication platforms like Telegram. Virtual planning involves any kind of support to attackers without ever meeting in person, a trend that has recently been identified as "cyber- coaching" [36]. The rationale behind this approach is simple: terrorist groups are keen to avoid traditional organizational structures hence reducing the ability of law enforcement to track their activities. In the case of the March 2024 Moscow Crocus City Hall assault ISKP terrorists killed 145 people and wounded another 551 at the venue, making it one of the most devastating terror attacks on Russian soil, reminiscent of attacks by Chechen militants at the Moscow Theatre (2002) and Beslan School (2004) [37]. One of the ISKP perpetrators was reportedly in contact with individuals using the pseudonyms "Abdullo" and "Muhammad," though their true identities yet remain unclear [11]. Other reports indicate that the attackers were recruited through a Telegram group linked to ISKP, with a figure known as "Sayfullo" allegedly serving as the primary tele-commanding "entrepreneur" orchestrating the attack [11].

Targeting is by definition a critical component of terrorist plotting because it determines the impact and success of an attack in achieving the group's objectives. Selecting the right target allows terrorists to maximize psychological impact, create widespread fear, and attract media attention. High-profile locations, such as government buildings, transportation hubs, or landmarks, often serve as prime targets because they symbolize authority, societal stability, or cultural significance.

4 Virtual Targeting

Remote virtual plotting substantiates the parallelly rising trend of virtual targeting, where attackers exchange on potential targets for different values (material, real i.e., casualties or symbolic) and feasibility of the attacks. Targeting or "material" (economic value), "real" (object-related i.e., for their practical asset value) "symbolic" targets has always been a question of terrorist strategy [38]. Such preference is subject to strategic thinking and organizational decision-making. Terrorist targeting becomes a matter of strategy in several key respects (political messaging, psychological impact, provocation, etc.), involving the careful selection of targets to achieve broader political, psychological, and ideological goals [39].

When selecting targets, a distinction must be drawn between "hard targets" and "soft targets". "Hard targets" are targets, organizations, facilities, people, buildings that are relatively well to very well protected. Whereas the classification as "soft target" refers to locations or individuals that are vulnerable to attacks due to minimal security measures and high concentrations of people. This includes civilian areas like public gatherings, schools, hospitals, shopping centers, and playgrounds, where defenses are weak or nonexistent. These sites are particularly appealing to terrorists seeking to cause widespread fear and chaos, as they provide opportunities for high casualty rates with relatively low risk of resistance. The lack of robust security at such places makes them easier targets for mass-casualty attacks [40].

Designated perpetrators are sometimes informed by entrepreneurs, as relates to the preferred category when it comes to target selection. High profile attacks like 9/11 or the Bataclan plot usually cover various targeting aspects and are therefore more effective. Being a significant part of virtual plotting – targeting has also been transcended to the sphere of (mostly) encrypted online communication. The ISKP has in the past two years brought this virtual terrorist targeting approach to "perfection". Many of the recent attack scenarios, either executed or thwarted suggest a prior virtual exchange on target selection and related to it on *modi operandi.* [37].

5 Generation Z as Perpetrators

Generation Z (those born roughly between 1997 and 2012) presents a unique profile as potential terrorist attackers, shaped by their digital-native upbringing, access to advanced technology, and exposure to global online platforms. Unlike previous generations, Gen Z has grown up with unprecedented access to social media, which has become a breeding ground for radicalization. Terrorist organizations exploit these platforms to disseminate propaganda, recruit members, and provide training materials. Moreover, Gen Z attackers are leveraging emerging technologies in ways that reflect their digital fluency. The use of encrypted messaging apps, cryptocurrencies, and online marketplaces on the dark web has made it easier for young radicals to acquire resources, plan operations, and evade detection.

Recent terrorist plots- both executed and foiled indicate a rising significance of perpetrators belonging to Generation Z for attack planning and executing. Teenagers across the ideological spectrum have engaged as online innovators and influencers, and violent offline activists. Independently of adults, adolescents have succeeded in producing terrorist propaganda, influencing towards violence, and preparing to engage in terrorist violence both domestically and abroad. Current data suggest that terrorists in Europe may eventually become younger. According to latest data by Peter R. Neumann, among the app. Sixty jihadist suspects arrested in Western Europe in the last ten months, two thirds were teenagers - some of them very young teenagers [41].

In terms of radicalization, we increasingly observe 13–17-year-old teens that develop firm intentions to commit terrorist attacks. The emergence is deeply linked with the rise of virtual platforms which can be regarded a disruption. In the field of jihadism, the so called "*TikTok–Jihad*" has become a prototypical manifestation of this trend to virtualization of extremist violence [42]. TikTok has become the fastest growing application in the world, largely thanks to its popularity among kids and teenagers. Regarding extremist exploitation, the tools are now more commonly used in both dimensions: to recruit and radicalize. In this case, the "*gamification*" of terrorism thesis has maintained some legitimacy due to the impact of memes and symbols [43]. Also in the ideological sphere of right-wing extremism, teenagers increasingly play a role as perpetrators, either in relevant terrorist groups such as Atomwaffen- and Feuerkriegsdivision or as lone actors. Adolescents are not merely passive consumers of content created and shared by adult counterparts but firmly ideologically driven in the light of radicalization processes and networks *sui generis*. When addressing the issue of youth vulnerabilities to radicalization, online social media such as TikTok and YouTube- among others- are in the epicenter of the problem. Research does indicate that young extremists are more likely to engage with social media and other virtual platforms compared with adults who are charged for terrorism [44]. Moreover, notorious extremist epigones such as the Norwegian terrorist Anders Behring Breivik are in the specific extremist scene celebrated as heroes and role-models.

6 Virtual TikTok–Radicalization

In the last years radicalization has mostly gone online [45]. TikTok has become a major platform, where radicalization of young individuals now takes place. Its customized content targeting youth suggests that extremists may be taking over and exploit this platform for their purposes. It already happens. Islamist preachers and influencers are using the Middle East conflict and the raging war in Gaza in particular as an opportunity to convince young people of their extremist ideology. Moreover, the video streaming app TikTok is increasingly deployed by political stakeholders, also populist and sometimes extremist, to reach younger voters. TikTok grants social media users the opportunity to create and share short videos of between 3 and 60 s with added music and audio-visual effects. In the past years, extremists of all ideological backgrounds have continued to exploit this platform as a space for propaganda to foster radicalization among adolescents. In early August 2024, the arrest of two teenagers, aged 18 and 19, in Austria, who had pledged allegiance to the Islamic State (IS) and likely plotted a terrorist attack at a

Taylor Swift concert in Vienna [46], has underscored a growing concern: the recruitment of young individuals into Islamist and far-right terrorist groups through social media, especially TikTok [47]. The trend of "TikTok-Jihad" becoming a low-threshold catalyst of religiously motivated extremist violence has sparked a resurgence of jihadist activities across Europe. In the past year, the continent has experienced meanwhile more than ten terrorist attacks, including the most recent attacks in Munich and Villach—mostly small in scale but some fatal—with security and intelligence services thwarting over 20 planned attacks [41].

Intelligence experts highlight TikTok's role as a major recruiting platform for young lone perpetrators and virtual terror cells, thanks to its extensive reach and algorithmic influence [48]. In many cases radicalized teenagers switch platforms and resort to Telegram for further extremist activities.

Telegram is often used for planning and coordinating attacks. This shift in recruitment strategies poses significant challenges for law enforcement. Europol has set up a collaboration to remove extremist content from the platform [49]. Yet, monitoring online interactions and identifying virtual meeting places is far more complex than tracking face-to-face meetings between recruiters and recruits. Besides that, radical online preachers are intentionally dispersing content that is deliberately prepared to remain below a threshold, where extremism is easily detected by algorithms. Moreover, many of their messages are conveyed in such a manner that adolescent recipients may easily interpret them as a call for action and engagement with extremist ideologies [52]. As the Swedish scholar Simon Sorgenfrei put it: "*The Salafi missionaries of interest here are not primarily selling tangible products (even though that is also the case) but rather a set of values, i.e., the idea of an authentic Islam*" [50].

7 Catastrophic Terrorism

The sixth trend stands apart from the preceding ones and does only superficially not appear to share a direct connection with them. Upon closer examination, however, it becomes evident that each of the preceding trends may potentially exhibit a direct connection.

Catastrophic terrorism refers to terrorist attacks designed to cause widespread destruction, often using weapons of mass destruction (WMDs) such as nuclear, chemical, or biological weapons, though simpler methods like "dirty bombs" can also be used. These attacks aim for mass civilian casualties and the disruption of societal order by targeting particularly critical infrastructure or economic facilities. The primary goal is to exert political pressure through the devastation caused. Catastrophic terrorism differs from conventional terrorism by the magnitude of the damage intended, often involving multiple coordinated teams and complex logistics to maximize impact. The United Nations have expressed concern over the threat of "catastrophic terrorism," particularly involving nuclear, chemical, and biological weapons. The UN Security Council, through resolutions like 1540 and 2325, has addressed the need for global efforts to prevent non-state actors, including terrorists, from acquiring or using WMDs. The UN's High Representative for Disarmament Affairs, Izumi Nakamitsu, warned that technological advancements such as 3D-printing, drones, and the Dark Web have made it easier for terrorist groups to gain access to these dangerous materials [54]. This reinforces the obvious nexus between high casualty terrorist attacks and technological innovation.

Since the coalition warfare against the IS in Syria and Iraq, drones have become a preferred weapon of terrorists [51]. The increasing use of drones by terrorist organizations highlights a shift toward adopting more advanced technologies for catastrophic attacks [52]. Initially designed for military purposes, drones have become easily accessible and affordable, with various models available for purchase: "*The rapid popularization of drones for average consumers and businesses has created a market that will continue to drive the technological improvement of drones for the foreseeable future. Improvements will extend to sizes, form factors, energy storage, techniques for propulsion, sensors, and the ability to utilize and integrate advanced computer capabilities*" [52]. Terrorist groups continuously exploit the simple accessibility to deploy drones equipped with explosives or biological and chemical weapons to target both soft and hard targets, such as civilian populations and critical infrastructure. Against this backdrop, terrorist attacks on critical infrastructure pose a significant disastrous threat. Critical infrastructure encompasses essential systems and assets such as power grids, water supplies, transportation networks, and communication systems. These vital components form the backbone of modern societies, making them attractive targets for terrorists seeking to cause widespread disruption and instill fear in the population. The potential consequences of successful attacks on critical infrastructure are far-reaching and multifaceted. Disruptions to power grids can lead to widespread blackouts, affecting hospitals, emergency services, and daily life. Attacks on water supplies may compromise public health and sanitation. Targeting transportation networks can paralyze cities and disrupt supply chains, while compromising communication systems can hinder emergency response efforts and create chaos [53]. The interconnected nature of these systems means that an attack on one sector can have cascading effects across others, amplifying the impact and complicating recovery efforts [54]. Given the high stakes involved, protecting critical infrastructure from terrorist attacks requires a comprehensive and multidisciplinary approach. This includes implementing robust physical security measures such as pollards in order to preempt vehicular rampage attacks, enhancing cybersecurity protocols, developing resilience and redundancy in critical systems, and fostering cooperation between public and private sectors. Continuous risk assessment, intelligence gathering, and the development of rapid response capabilities are also crucial elements in safeguarding these vital assets against evolving terrorist threats.

The potential of autonomous drones for "catastrophic terrorism" is particularly concerning due to their versatility [59]. They can carry out complex, multi-phase attacks (e.g., using drone swarms), acting as a second or third wave of assault, causing further casualties and confusion after an initial strike. Drones also allow terrorists to strike from a distance, reducing their personal risk and eliminating direct contact with victims. This makes them ideal for targeting difficult or isolated locations, such as tankers, where chemical or oil spills could cause widespread environmental and economic damage.

Although acquiring drones capable of such catastrophic uses requires advanced technical skills, the continued development of unmanned aerial technology – especially in its autonomous variant – renders their future use in large-scale terrorist attacks highly plausible. Drones may be used not just for destruction but also for terrorist propaganda.

Terrorists could film their attacks using drones, creating footage that amplifies their extremist message of fear and chaos when disseminated online, fulfilling their goal of widespread psychological shock effects, creating fear and destabilization.

The virtually induced aspect of catastrophic terrorism extends beyond physical destruction. Drones and other technologies may further be used for psychological warfare and increasingly– as mentioned– also for propaganda purposes. Combined with the growing sophistication of cyber capabilities, such virtually induced components redefine the landscape of catastrophic terrorism, posing profound challenges to global security frameworks.

8 Conclusion: Counterterrorism Options and AI

Counterterrorism closely resembles disaster management in its emphasis on preparedness, mitigation, and response to high-stakes scenarios that threaten lives, infrastructure, and societal stability [55]. Both fields intrinsically involve anticipating potential threats, developing strategies to minimize risks, and coordinating swift responses to minimize harm when incidents occur. For example, counterterrorism planning includes intelligence gathering, risk assessments, and scenario planning [56] —parallel to how disaster management anticipates and prepares for natural calamities like hurricanes or earthquakes. In both cases, the focus lies on reducing vulnerabilities and building resilience to withstand crises effectively [57].

Another similarity lies in the importance of multi-agency coordination. Just as disaster management requires collaboration between emergency services [58], governments, and humanitarian organizations, counterterrorism relies on seamless coordination among law enforcement, intelligence agencies, military units, and international partners. Both fields operate under the understanding that no single entity can address the complexity of these crises alone. Effective communication and a clear division of roles are vital for successful interventions, whether responding to a terrorist attack or managing a natural disaster's aftermath.

Both counterterrorism and disaster management also prioritize rapid and effective responses to minimize damage and save lives. In the event of a terrorist attack, as in a natural disaster, time is of the essence. Emergency services must act quickly to secure affected areas, provide medical aid, and restore order. This similarity underscores the shared reliance on well-trained personnel, robust communication systems, and pre-established contingency plans to respond to dynamic and unpredictable events.

Finally, counterterrorism and disaster management both emphasize recovery and resilience-building as critical post-crisis priorities [64]. Beyond immediate response efforts, both fields focus on rebuilding affected communities, restoring confidence in institutions, and preventing future incidents. In counterterrorism, this includes deradicalization programs, enhanced security measures, and policy adjustments, while in disaster management, it involves rebuilding infrastructure and improving preparedness for future events. In essence, both disciplines share a cyclical process of preparation, response, recovery, and adaptation, underlining their structural and functional parallels.

As demonstrated during this examination, counterterrorism strategies must increasingly consider the vast array of options and new tactics emerging from the virtualization of terrorism. An ongoing digital transformation of extremist activity, fueled by disruptive advancements in technology, requires organizational adaptiveness by counterterrorism institutions in response. While terrorists are increasingly exploiting online platforms, encrypted communication, and virtual networks to radicalize, recruit, and coordinate attacks, law enforcement and intelligence bodies must acquire skills to counter these online-driven tactics. It is no secret that such strategies are particularly influential among younger generations, such as Generation Z and Alpha, who are more deeply integrated into digital ecosystems. Extremists from these adolescent cohorts employ a completely different technological toolkit—ranging from social media manipulation to encrypted messaging apps—to spread their ideology and plan operations. Using old-fashioned counterapproaches does not lead to anywhere. Law enforcement and intelligence agencies must therefore evolve in tandem with these tectonic shifts to become more resilient and effective. Traditional methods of monitoring extremist activity are becoming obsolete in the face of decentralized (Sageman: "*leaderless jihad*") [59], virtually networked terrorist cells. Investigative bodies need to develop or expand existing specialized techniques to counter these threats, including enhanced cyber-surveillance, artificial intelligence for detecting radicalization patterns, and international cooperation in monitoring dark web activity. Furthermore, the increased accessibility of sophisticated technologies, such as 3D-printed weapons and drones, compounds the complexity of the threat, requiring new forms of intervention and prevention.

The rapid evolution of extremist violence, particularly in its digital forms, calls for a reevaluation of existing counterterrorism frameworks to address not only physical threats but also the virtual spaces where terrorism incubates and thrives.

In the light of terrorist manifestations and capabilities, Artificial intelligence (AI) is widely regarded as a game changer. AI is in many aspects a double-edged sword [60]. On the one hand, AI is likely to enhance security measures by automating threat detection through advanced data analysis, pattern recognition, and the monitoring of online spaces for radical content. AI tools are able to process vast amounts of data to identify potential threats in real-time, making it easier for law enforcement to detect radicalization early or trace suspicious communications on encrypted platforms. For example, AI algorithms can help to flag extremist content on social media, analyze behavioral patterns indicative of radicalization, and even simulate attack scenarios to improve response strategies.

On the other hand, terrorists themselves are beginning to exploit AI for their own purposes, such as creating deepfakes to disseminate propaganda, bypassing traditional surveillance with advanced encryption algorithms, and potentially even using autonomous systems like drones in attacks [61]. While traditional forms of extremist propaganda rely on trained personnel to plan, create, and disseminate content, the rise of AI generative models could enable a broader range of extremist non-state actors to produce significantly more sophisticated propaganda with far less effort. Emerging generative AI technologies have the potential to revolutionize both mainstream and extremist media production, spanning areas such as video games, digital content, music, and other audio formats [62]. This evolution may open avenues to reach new audiences and facilitate radicalization through innovative propaganda techniques. The accessibility of AI-driven technologies like chatbots and language models such as "ChatGPT", "MS

Copilot", "Apple Intelligence", "Perplexity", "Claude" and many others could enable extremist groups to automate recruitment, spread misinformation, or even direct terrorist attacks through virtual means, further complicating the threat landscape.

Thus, while AI offers significant promise in enhancing counterterrorism efforts, it also poses new security challenges. But it raises also ethical questions. Governments and intelligence agencies need to stay ahead of how extremists might leverage AI and adopt preemptive regulations and countermeasures to mitigate these risks while harnessing the technology for defensive purposes. Balancing the benefits and risks of AI will be crucial in shaping the future of counterterrorism strategies. Without doubt, the future of extremism and terrorism is virtual.

References

1. Waugh, W.L.: Terrorism as Disaster. In: Handbook of Disaster Research. Handbooks of Sociology and Social Research. Springer, New York (2007). doi: 10.1007/978-0-387-32353-4_22, last accessed 2025/04/7. See also: Samuel, K.L.H., Banks, W.C., Richemond-Barak, D.: "Improving Disaster Risk Mitigation: Towards a 'Multi-Hazard' Approach to Terrorism." In: Samuel, K.L.H., Aronsson-Storrier, M., Bookmiller, K.N. (eds.) The Cambridge Handbook of Disaster Risk Reduction and International Law, pp. 464–498. Cambridge University Press, Cambridge (2019)
2. Gartenstein-Ross, D., Joscelyn, T.: Enemies Near and Far: How Jihadist Groups Strategize, Plot, and Learn (Columbia Studies in Terrorism and Irregular Warfare), pp. 107–164. Columbia University Press, New York (2022)
3. Horgan, J.: Terrorist Minds: The Psychology of Violent Extremism from Al-Qaeda to the Far Right (Columbia Studies in Terrorism and Irregular Warfare). Columbia University Press, New York, pp. 163–180 (2023)
4. Byman, D.: Terrorism and the Threat to Democracy, Brookings Policy Brief (2019) https://www.brookings.edu/articles/terrorism-and-the-threat-to-democracy. Accessed 4 Jul 2025
5. Warnes, R.: Human Factors in Effective Counter-Terrorism: A Comparative Study, 1st ed., Routledge, London (2024). More general on prevention: Schmid, A.P.: Handbook of Terrorism Prevention and Preparedness. ICCT Press, The Hague (2021)
6. National Academies of Sciences, Engineering, and Medicine: Countering Terrorism: Lessons Learned from Natural and Technological Disasters. Washington, DC The National Academies Press (2002). https://doi.org/10.17226/10414. Accessed 4 Jul 2025
7. CONTEST. The United Kingdom's Strategy for Countering Terrorism, UK Government Publishing (2023). https://assets.publishing.service.gov.uk/media/650b1b8d52e73c000d54dc82/CONTEST_2023_English_updated.pdf. Accessed 4 Jul 2025
8. Gabriel, A., et al.: Process modelling of physical and cyber terrorist attacks on networks of public transportation infrastructure. In: Aurélie Montarnal, A., et al.(eds.), Proceedings of the 14th International Conference on Information Systems for Crisis Response and Management, pp. 390–399. Albi, France: Iscram (2017)
9. Katz, R.: Saints and Soldiers: Inside Internet-Age Terrorism, From Syria to the Capitol Siege. Columbia Studies in Terrorism and Irregular Warfare) Columbia University Press, New York (2022)
10. Awan, A.N.: The Virtual Jihad: an Increasingly Legitimate Form of Warfare. CTC Sentinel 3(5) (2010). https://ctc.westpoint.edu/wp-content/uploads/2010/08/CTCSentinel-Vol3Iss5-art3.pdf. Accessed 4 Jul 2025

11. Dass, R.: Islamic State-Khorasan Province's Virtual Planning. Lawfare (2024). https://www.lawfaremedia.org/article/islamic-state-khorasan-province-s-virtual-planning. Accessed 4 Jul 2025
12. Ingram, H.J.: Learning from ISIS's Virtual Propaganda War for Western Muslims: A Comparison of Inspire and Dabiq (2017). https://www.icct.nl/publication/learning-isiss-virtual-propaganda-war-western-muslims-comparison-inspire-and-dabiq. Accessed 4 Jul 2025
13. Stockhammer, N.: Introduction. In: Nicolas Stockhammer (ed.): Routledge Handbook of Transnational Terrorism, Routledge, Abingdon, Oxon; New York (2023)
14. Nesser, P.: Introducing the Jihadi Plots in Europe Dataset (JPED). J. Peace Res. **61**(2), 317–329 (2024)
15. Stockhammer, N.: Trügerische Ruhe. Der Anschlag von Wien und die terroristische Bedrohung in Europa. Amalthea, Vienna (2023), p. 30. Also refer to Dass, R.: Islamic State-Khorasan Province's Virtual Planning. Lawfare (2024). https://www.lawfaremedia.org/article/islamic-state-khorasan-province-s-virtual-planning. Accessed 4 Jul 2025
16. Weimann, G., Dimant, R.: The Metaverse and Terrorism: Threats and Challenges. In: Perspectives on Terrorism, 17(2), (2023). https://pt.icct.nl/sites/default/files/2023-06/PT%20-%20Vol%20XVII%2C%20Issue%20II%20-%20June%202023%20A5.pdf. Accessed 4 Jul 2025
17. Winter, C., et al.: Online extremism: research trends in internet activism, radicalization, and counter-strategies. Int. J. Conflict Violence **14**(2), 2 (2020)
18. See mutatis mutandis, ual Radicalization: The Making of Jihad in Chechnya. In: Hughes, J.: "From Nationalism to Jihad", Philadelphia, pp. 94–127 (2007). https://doi.org/10.9783/9780812202311.94. Accessed 4 Jul 2025
19. The Soufan Center IntelBrief: he Evolution of the Online Violent Extremist Landscap (2022). https://thesoufancenter.org/intelbrief-2022-october-20. Accessed 4 Jul 2025
20. Chen, H.: Exploring extremism and terrorism on the web: the dark web project. In: Yang, C.C., et al.: Intelligence and Security Informatics. PAISI 2007. Lecture Notes. In: Computer Science, 4430. Berlin (2007). https://doi.org/10.1007/978-3-540-71549-8_1. Accessed 4 Jul 2025
21. Malik, N.: Terror in the Dark: How Terrorists use Encryption, the Darknet, and Cryptocurrencies. In: The Henry Jackson Society Henry Jackson Society (2018). https://henryjacksonsociety.org/wp-content/uploads/2018/04/Terror-in-the-Dark.pdf. Accessed 4 Jul 2025
22. Anderson, D.: Attacks in London and Manchester March-June 2017 SSRN (2017). https://ssrn.com/abstract=4833522. Accessed 4 Jul 2025
23. Manchester Arena Inquiry Volume 3: Radicalisation and Preventability. Report of the Public Inquiry into the Attack on Manchester Arena on 22nd May 2017, UK Government Publishing (2023). https://assets.publishing.service.gov.uk/media/63ff865ae90e0740dc92d1d8/MAI_Final_PDF_Volume_3.pdf. Accessed 4 Jul 2025
24. Benedek, E., Simon, N.: The 2017 Manchester Bombing and the British-Libyan Jihadi Nexus". CTC Sentinel, 13(5), 28–39 (2020). https://ctc.westpoint.edu/wp-content/uploads/2020/05/CTC-SENTINEL-052020.pdf. Accessed 4 Jul 2025
25. Koehler, D.: The Halle, Germany, Synagogue Attack and the Evolution of the Far-Right Terror Threat. CTC Sentinel, 12(11), 14–21 CTC (2019). https://ctc.westpoint.edu/wp-content/uploads/2020/02/CTC-SENTINEL-112019.pdf. Accessed 4 Jul 2025
26. Hartleb, F.: Das Phänomen des virtualisierten rechten Terrors. SIAK-Journal – Zeitschrift für Polizeiwissenschaft und polizeiliche Praxis (4), 17–27 (2022). https://doi.org/10.7396/2022_4_B. Accessed 4 Jul 2025
27. Pozzoli, N.: POV: Wearable Cameras and the Gamification of Lone-Actor Terrorist Violence. GNET Insights (2024). https://gnet-research.org/2024/02/28/pov-wearable-cameras-and-the-gamification-of-lone-actor-terrorist-violence. Accessed 4 Jul 2025

28. Basra, R.: The Future is Now: The Use of 3D-Printed Guns by Extremists and Terrorists. GNET Insights (2022). https://gnet-research.org/2022/06/23/the-future-is-now-the-use-of-3d-printed-guns-by-extremists-and-terrorists. Accessed 4 Jul 2025
29. Basra, R.: Behind the Mask: Uncovering the Extremist Messages of a 3D-Printed Gun Designer. ICSR London (2023). https://icsr.info/wp-content/uploads/2023/10/ICSR-Report-Behind-the-Mask-Uncovering-the-Extremist-Messages-of-a-3D%E2%80%91Printed-Gun-Designer.pdf. Accessed 4 Jul 2025
30. Chase, R. J., LaPorte, G. (2018): The Next Generation of Crime Tools and Challenges: 3D Printing. NIJ Journal 279 (2018). https://nij.gov/journals/279/Pages/next-generation-of-crime-tools-and-challenges-3d-printing.aspx. Accessed 4 Jul 2025
31. Europol.: European Union Terrorism Situation and Trend Report (2023). https://www.europol.europa.eu/cms/sites/default/files/documents/European%20Union%20Terrorism%20Situation%20and%20Trend%20report%202023.pdf. Accessed 4 Jul 2025
32. Among other sources refer to Global Terrorism Database (https://www.start.umd.edu/gtd); "Global Terrorism Index" (https://www.economicsandpeace.org/wp-content/uploads/2024/02/GTI-2024-web-290224.pdf); "RAND Database of Worldwide Terrorism Incidents" (https://www.rand.org/nsrd/projects/terrorism-incidents.html); C-REX "RTV Report" (https://www.sv.uio.no/c-rex/english/groups/rtv-dataset/2023-rtv-trend-report.pdf); FFI Jihadi Plots in Europe Dataset (https://www.prio.org/journals/jpr/replicationdata); Hacker, Erik (2023*):* Jihadi Attacks in Europe. Trends and Features 2014 – 2022, Scenor (2023). https://www.scenor.at/_files/ugd/ff9c7a_7e48f92a024e46f582ee0556c80fe0ce.pdf. Accessed 4 Jul 2025
33. The European Trend Report on Terrorism 2025 report is expected to be published in the first quarter of (2025)
34. Graham, R.: How Terrorists Use Encryption. CTC Sentinel, 9(6), (2016). https://ctc.westpoint.edu/wp-content/uploads/2016/06/CTC-SENTINEL_Vol9Iss614.pdf. Accessed 4 Jul 2025
35. Clifford, B., Powell, H.: Encrypted Extremism. Inside The English-Speaking Islamic State Ecosystem on Telegram. Program on Extremism (GWU) (2019), GWU Program on Extremism. https://extremism.gwu.edu/sites/g/files/zaxdzs5746/files/EncryptedExtremism.pdf. Accessed 4 Jul 2025
36. Hegghammer, T.: Resistance is futile: the war on terror supercharged state power. Foreign Aff. **100**(5), 50 (2021)
37. Gartenstein-Ross, D., Blackman. M.: ISIL's Virtual Planners: A Critical Terrorist Innovation. War on the Rocks (2017). https://warontherocks.com/2017/01/isils-virtual-planners-a-critical-terrorist-innovation. Accessed 4 Jul 2025
38. Mueller, J.: The Cybercoaching of Terrorists: Cause for Alarm? CTC Sentinel, 10 (9), 29–35 (2017). https://ctc.westpoint.edu/wp-content/uploads/2017/10/CTC-Sentinel_Vol10Iss9-21.pdf. Accessed 4 Jul 2025
39. Stockhammer, N., Clarke, C.P.: Learning from Islamic State-Khorasan Province's Recent Plots. Lawfare (2024). https://www.lawfaremedia.org/article/learning-from-islamic-state-khorasan-province-s-recent-plots. Accessed 4 Jul 2025
40. Hoffman, B.: Terrorist targeting: Tactics, trends, and potentialities. Terrorism and Political Violence 5(2), 12–29 (2024). https://doi.org/10.1080/09546559308427205 Brooks, R.: How Community Ties Influence Terrorist Targeting of Civilians. National Consortium for the Study of Terrorism and Responses to Terrorism (2013)
41. Marchment, Z., Gill, P.: Spatial Decision Making of Terrorist Target Selection: Introducing the TRACK Framework. Studies in Conflict & Terrorism, 45(10), 862–880 (2020). https://doi.org/10.1080/1057610X.2020.1711588. Accessed 4 Jul 2025
42. Goertz, S., Stockhammer, N.: Terrorismusbekämpfung und Extremismusprävention. Springer, Wiesbaden, p.235 (2023)

43. Neumann, P.R.: Substack Channel Die Terrorlage"- „5 Punkte zur Terrorismusbekämpfung. https://prneumann.substack.com/p/5-punkte-zur-terrorismusbekampfung. Accessed 4 Jul 2025
44. The Soufan Center IntelBrief: TikTok Jihad: Terrorists Leverage Modern Tools to Recruit and Radicalize (2024). https://thesoufancenter.org/intelbrief-2024-august-9. Accessed 4 Jul 2025
45. Schlegel, L.: As You Like It: User Types in Digital Gamified Radicalisation Processes. GNET Insights (2021). https://gnet-research.org/2021/09/01/as-you-like-it-user-types-in-digital-gamified-radicalisation-processes. Accessed 4 Jul 2025
46. Gunton, K.: The Impact of the Internet and Social Media Platforms on Radicalisation to Terrorism and Violent Extremism. In: Montasari, R., Carroll, F., Mitchell, I., Hara, S., Bolton-King, R. (eds.): Privacy, Security and Forensics in the Internet of Things (IoT). Cham. (2022). https://doi.org/10.1007/978-3-030-91218-5_8. Accessed 4 Jul 2025
47. Binder, J., Kenyon, J.: Terrorism and the internet: How dangerous is online radicalization? Front Psychol. **13**, 997390 (2022). https://doi.org/10.3389/fpsyg.2022.997390. Accessed 4 Jul 2025
48. Stockhammer, N., Clarke, C.P.: The August 2024 Taylor Swift Vienna Concert Plot. CTC Sentinel **18**(1), 8–18 (2025). https://ctc.westpoint.edu/wp-content/uploads/2025/01/CTC-SENTINEL-012025.pdf. Accessed 4 Jul 2025
49. CNN: These TikTok videos are concerning counterterrorism experts. Here's why, (2024). https://edition.cnn.com/2024/08/15/world/video/abul-baraa-tiktok-islamist-radicalization-digvid. Accessed 4 Jul 2025
50. Ayad, M.: The original sounds of terrorist leaders: A TikTok feature enables terrorist content to flourish. Institute for Strategic Dialogue (ISD) (2024). https://www.isdglobal.org/digital_dispatches/the-original-sounds-of-terrorist-leaders-a-tiktok-feature-enables-terrorist-content-to-flourish. Accessed 4 Jul 2025
51. EUROPOL: Europol and TikTok collaborate to bolster efforts against terrorist content. https://www.europol.europa.eu/media-press/newsroom/news/europol-and-tiktok-collaborate-to-bolster-efforts-against-terrorist-content. Accessed 4 Jul 2025
52. Guhl, J., Comerford, M.: Understanding the Salafi Online Ecosystem: A Digital Snapshot, Institute for Strategic Dialogue (ISD) (2021). https://www.isdglobal.org/wp-content/uploads/2021/11/Snapshot-study.pdf. Accessed 4 Jul 2025
53. Sorgenfrei, S.: Branding Salafism: Salafi Missionaries as Social Media Influencers. Method & Theory in the Study of Religion **34**(3), 211–237 (2021). https://doi.org/10.1163/15700682-12341515. Accessed 4 Jul 2025
54. United Nations Office for Disarmament Affairs: Open Consultations on the Comprehensive Review of the Status of Implementation of Resolution 1540, (2004). https://www.un.org/en/sc/1540/documents/ODA%20HR%201540%20OC%20Remarks%202022.pdf. Accessed 4 Jul 2025
55. Larter, D.B.: SOCOM commander: Armed ISIS drones were 2016's most daunting problem. Defense News (2016). https://www.defensenews.com/digital-show-dailies/sofic/2017/05/16/socom-commander-armed-isis-drones-were-2016s-most-daunting-problem. Accessed 4 Jul 2025
56. Pledger, T.G.: The Role of Drones in Future Terrorist Attacks. Land Warfare Paper (137), (2021). https://www.ausa.org/sites/default/files/publications/LWP-137-The-Role-of-Drones-in-Future-Terrorist-Attacks_0.pdf. Accessed 4 Jul 2025
57. Gabriel, A., et al.: Process modelling of physical and cyber terrorist attacks on networks of public transportation infrastructure. In: Montarnal, A., et al (eds.): Proceedings of the 14th International Conference on Information Systems for Crisis Response and Management, pp. 390–399. Albi, France (2017). https://idl.iscram.org/files/alexandergabriel/2017/2028_AlexanderGabriel_etal2017.pdf. Accessed 4 Jul 2025

58. Jenkins, B., Butterworth, B: Train Wrecks and Track Attacks: An Analysis of Attempts by Terrorists and Other Extremists to Derail Trains or Disrupt Rail Transportation. Maleta Transportation Institute (2018). https://transweb.sjsu.edu/sites/default/files/1794_Jenkins_Train-Wrecks-Train-Attacks.pdf. Accessed 4 Jul 2025———: How Sophisticated Are Terrorist Attacks on Passenger Rail Transportation. https://transweb.sjsu.edu/sites/default/files/SP0520-Jenkins-Terrorist-Attacks-Passenger-Rail-Transportation.pdf. Accessed 4 Jul 2025
59. Blanchard, A., Hall, J.K.C: Terrorism and Autonomous Weapon Systems: Future Threat or Science Fiction?, Centre for Emerging Technology and Security (CETaS) Expert Analysis (2023). https://cetas.turing.ac.uk/sites/default/files/2023-06/cetas_expert_analysis_-_terrorism_and_autonomous_weapon_systems_-_future_threat_or_science_fiction.pdf. Accessed 4 Jul 2025
60. Schmid, A.P.: Handbook of Terrorism Prevention and Preparedness. The Hague, ICCT Press, 2020/21. https://icct.nl/handbook-of-terrorism-prevention-and-preparedness. Accessed 4 Jul 2025
61. Crelinsten, R.: Counterterrorism, pp. 90–94. CUP, Cambridge (2009)
62. Coaffee, J.: From Counterterrorism to Resilience. The European Legacy, 11(4) 389–403 (2006). https://doi.org/10.1080/10848770600766094. Accessed 4 Jul 2025
63. Court, M., et al.: Counter-terrorism medicine: creating a medical initiative mandated by escalating asymmetric attacks". Prehosp. Disaster Med. **35**(6), 595–598 (2020)
64. Hardy, K.: Resilience in UK Counter-Terrorism. Theoretical Criminology 19(1), 77–94 (2015). https://doi.org/10.1177/1362480614542119. Accessed 4 Jul 2025
65. Sageman, M.: Leaderless Jihad: Terror Networks in the Twenty-First Century. University of Pennsylvania Press, Philadelphia (2008)
66. See Harari, Y.N.: Nexus: A Brief History of Information Networks from the Stone Age to AI. Random House, London (2024)
67. Schori-Liang, C.: Terrorist Digitalis: Preventing Terrorists from Using Emerging Technologies. Global Terrorism Index 2023 Report, 72–75 (2023). https://www.visionofhumanity.org/preventing-terrorists-from-using-emerging-technologies; further: https://www.visionofhumanity.org/wp-content/uploads/2023/03/GTI-2023-web-170423.pdf. Accessed 4 Jul 2025
68. Siegel, D., Doty, M.B.: Weapons of Mass Disruption: Artificial Intelligence and the Production of Extremist Propaganda. Global Network on Extremism and Technology (GNET) Insights (2023). https://gnet-research.org/2023/02/17/weapons-of-mass-disruption-artificial-intelligence-and-the-production-of-extremist-propaganda. Accessed 4 Jul 2025

Air-Raid Shelters – Painful Memory (from the Cold War) with New Actuality

Jaziar Radianti[1](✉), Stella Polikarpus[2], Priit Laaniste[2,3], and Terje Gjøsæter[1]

[1] University of Agder, Kristiansand, Norway
jaziar.radianti@uia.no
[2] Estonian Academy of Security Sciences, Tallinn, Estonia
[3] Estonian Ministry of the Interior, Tallinn, Estonia

Abstract. The article discusses the renewed importance of air-raid shelters or sheltering sites in contemporary times, acknowledging insights from the conflict in Ukraine and the historical neglect of shelter maintenance since the Cold War. In later years, a knowledge gap on understanding the role of air-raid shelters has developed among younger generations, and a full war in Europe requiring air-raid shelters was almost unthinkable for many, especially in Western Europe. Background history and today's practices concerning air-raid shelters in Estonia and Norway is explored, and experiments are performed to develop training for handling potential air-raid situations. To examine perceptions on need to seek shelter during air raid attacks and the perceived preparations needed for staying in such shelters, two workshops were conducted in Estonia and in Germany, each with 12 participants. The participants were introduced to the topic of air-raid shelters through fact-based presentations about air-raid shelters in Norway and Estonia, and assigned two tasks, to use the internet to find information about public air-raid shelters in their country and assess the quality of the information, and to identify and go to the closest safe place to seek shelter from the workshop site, while discussing essential items to bring. Furthermore, the distinction between shelter, bunker and sheltering site and their requirements is discussed. Finally, it is noted that the participants seemed to rely to a large degree on IT infrastructure and mobile communications, which may be unavailable in basements and shelters, or disrupted.

Keywords: Sheltering · Bomb Shelter · Bunker · Sheltering Place · Air-Raid Attack · Technology-enhanced Learning

1 Introduction

Despite the armed conflict in Ukraine having erupted in 2014 after the annexation of Crimea by Russia [1], only the recent attack in 2022 has raised the "alarm" that the war is real and "near" in Europe, after the painful memory of the second world war and the cold war are almost forgotten. One of the left-behind "civil defense artefacts" [2] from the second world war and the cold war was the abandoned bomb shelters in some

Published by Springer Nature Switzerland AG 2026
W. Seböck et al. (Eds.): ITDRR 2024, IFIP AICT 752, pp. 228–243, 2026.
https://doi.org/10.1007/978-3-031-97115-0_15

countries in Europe. These "forgotten" shelters were a result of citizens having enjoyed living side-by-side mostly peacefully with their neighboring countries. Of course to claim that no armed-conflict has occurred in Europe after the cold war is not necessarily true, as several minor and major armed conflicts, intermediate armed conflict to war, had occurred in 1990's and before, especially in the former Yugoslavian countries, Romania, Chechnya, Basque (Spain) and Northern Ireland [3].

Current concern of the war situation triggers the needs for understanding of the function of air raid shelters that can be relevant as a part of disaster scenarios, risk and preparedness. Increased attention of such issues has also been raised in the scholarly literature, but many of these literatures discuss more on the repurposing such shelters into different functions as a part of the urban or regional design and even tourism [4–6] and leave behind such scenario in the emergency management plan. In brief, there is a knowledge gaps among generations on understanding the civil defense artefact in terms of air-raid shelters, as such scenarios are unthinkable. Assuming that air raid scenario has not yet been calculated risk in the emergency management plan, nor the part of the individual preparedness plan and civil defense, in this article, we try to address this issue. Note that we exclude Chemical, Biological, Radiological, Nuclear and Explosive (CBRNE) that may always be a part of military threat scenarios and armed conflicts or wars. Moreover, despite using war as scenario, we focus more on the civil protection domain, particularly on individual knowledge on preparedness against air raid attack scenario than about the war itself.

The relevance of this chosen research angle is strengthened by the fact that the experience of Ukrainian war showed that most civilian casualties occurred due to flying shrapnel during drone or bomb attacks, as people were outside and not sheltered [7, 8]. Indeed, the likelihood of casualties is significantly lower if people take shelter indoors in such air raid attack. In this case, individuals are protected from flying shrapnel, and a direct hit on or near the building is much less likely. However, understanding of such scenario may not be considered by many people nowadays and especially younger generation that has no experience with war. Moreover, previous experiences with building massive shelters makes the perception of such shelters as "facilities to prevent air raids that never happen" [2, 9]. Assuming that threat scenario for escalated war outbreak is high, when looking back to existing "civilian defense artefact", people are realizing that such infrastructure can be important part of defense and to protect the populations. However, civilian people are not trained [10] anymore against such armed-conflict and air-raid scenarios well-documented in the history[11, 12], not even exposed to the existence of such infrastructure as the function has been converted, for example into parking place, storage, or even tourist attraction. Moreover, the development of information and communication technology in air-raid scenarios should be considered when looking into this theme.

In this article, we explore the background history and today practices of the air-raid shelters in two countries neighboring to Russia, i.e., Estonia and Norway, and conduct a couple of simple experiments to develop training for the potential air-raid situation. Thus, the main research questions are:

- RQ1 How is the need to seek shelter during air-raid attacks perceived nowadays?
- RQ2 What are the perceived needs to prepare to seek shelter during the air-raid attack?

The organization of this paper is as follows: Sect. 2 looks for the literature on the role of shelters in the history and current public debates on their existence and usage. Section 3 reveals the method used in this study. Section 4 reports the results from the experiments in two countries and then the implications of the results are discussed in Sect. 5. Section 6 concludes the overall findings and limitations of this article and the future works.

2 Literature

2.1 Shelter Use

The initial thought on the bomb shelters was triggered by the need to sheltering the population from atomic bombs, especially after observing the destructive power of atomic bomb in Hiroshima and Nagasaki [13], damages in the Europe after the bomb raid in the second World War, and arm race in the cold war [14]. Bomb shelter or bunker was considered as a field in the defense sector that involved the design of high-performance damage-limiting systems [15]. The shelters should protect the citizens against the effects of blast and radiation and relied on existing buildings in the safest areas. The shelters should be accessible, located in the buildings that can withstand blast at plausible distance, including shielding from radiation and falling debris, be free from the potential hazard such as glass, heavy ceiling features and nearby explosive, and unobstructed exits [13]. Moreover, an early study in the US military on evaluating potential shelters pointed out the recommended use of high quality of mine space, also potential use of tunnels and caves as an alternative shelters [15]. In some cities in Europe, the shelters were above the ground or private shelters that are basically basements such as in Hamburg [16] or bunker infrastructure in Switzerland [9].

Switzerland has constructed significant number of bomb shelter within private homes since 1960s. Additionally, a significant number of shelters have been built in Finland and Sweden since World War II, where the corresponding requirement has been a part of mandatory building regulations. In the Netherlands Noodertunnel in Utrecht has a part could function as an air-raid shelter that can accommodate up to 2000 people who can stay in this tunnel for 48 h. In 2009 the technical room of the shelter was made visible to public by installing a glass wall, but it has no longer visible now to public, and only presented as graphical references in the tunnel to the shelter function [17]. There were actually underground shelters in the Netherlands built in the strictest secrecy during the beginning of 1960s. The construction was combined with other construction work to obscure the shelter building. It was a building with concrete walls and thick doors under squares, parking garage and public buildings [18].

2.2 Public Debates on Shelters

Indeed, there are pro and contra on the efficacy of the bomb shelters. Dyson [14] argues that shelters are inadequate to save the citizens from the effects of a nuclear attacks, fallout, blast, firestorms, even though the shelters are properly designed. Dyson [14] warns that effective bomb shelter might escalate the arms race and increase the likelihood of nuclear conflict. The author urges against the large-scale construction of bomb shelter, argues that an effective shelter system could lead to a self-reinforcing cycle of escalation.

Other arguments that deemed bomb shelters as useless because it cannot prevent the firestorms [19]. On the contrary, Lucas et al. [16] are against this opinion and argues that properly constructed shelters could save the lives, even in the event of a nuclear attacks. By studying Hamburg and other cities in the World War II, Lucas et al. [16] points out that the properly constructed shelters can prevent most deaths due to fire, even in the areas of intense firestorms. The Switzerland's experience gives different story. Despite the state's efforts to engineer a "bomb-proof" society through these shelters, the endeavor was largely unsuccessful. Swiss citizens began to undermine the shelters' intended purpose as early as the 1970s, underwent processes of deterritorialization, and losing their function as secure passage [9].

Despites these disagreements on the efficacy and efficiency of the bomb shelters, several recent studies have made the bomb shelter thought is becoming relevant, and event contextualized with the current modern time such as energy-efficient technologies for temporary and longer-term stay in the shelters [20], and urban planning context. Pomortseva and Kobzan [21] have proposed the use of the Geographical Information Systems (GIS) to design and locate bomb shelters. Apparently, the notion of "bomb shelters" is becoming actual nowadays.

There is a study that considers the experiences of ordinary individuals whose everyday lives are examine at—or below—the grassroots within bomb shelters in the heavily attacked cities of Chernihiv, Kyiv, and Kharkiv [22]. The paper reveals how Ukrainian nationalism has manifested and (re)produced amidst the conflict. Manifestation is illustrated with children's drawings on a bomb shelter walls and different examples of social media use to promote activities related to public sheltering and war in Ukraine. There are courses for teachers to maintain their mental health and well-being to support children and their education during the war in Ukraine [23].

Another study about historical event Bethnal Green Shelter indicates that already in history there are examples that public bomb-shelters have been attacked [24]. During the Russia-Ukraine war many public places have been attacked by the drones and missiles, for example hotel [25] energy infrastructure [26], children hospital [27] and a school shelter [28]. Therefore, it could not be expected that public shelters that are marked with civil protection signs are excluded from direct attacks.

During the Cold War, many shelters were built in West Germany because it was understood that a military conflict between the Soviet Union and Western countries would primarily occur on German territory. Until recently, Western European countries do not perceive that a military conflict is likely to break out primarily on their territory. However, societies in Northern and Eastern European countries are more concerned about the possibility of a military conflict on their territory. Therefore, the primary conclusion is that although the war in Ukraine is happening in Europe, the perception of war, including the understanding of the need for shelters, varies across different European countries.

Therefore, the urgency of looking at this civil defense' infrastructure is not homogeneous in different European countries, but countries that are located near the warzone seems to have raising discussions on the relevance of such shelters. The relevance of air raid shelters has been a part of public debates over the years in some countries.

Bennersved [2] for instance, have examined historically the public debate on air raid shelters in Sweden, where such artifacts are perceived of having symbolic and political meaning to citizens such as a symbol of preparedness and a way to ensure the safety of individuals and communities in the event of attack [29]. Shelters perceived as a part of Sweden's welfare system and the emphasis on equal distribution of shelters across the country. The deficiency in the shelter system was seen as evidence of built-in inequality in welfare services. Shelters were also considered as a symbol of welfare nostalgia, highlighted the historical past of shelters, particularly during the Cold War, and how they were seen as a symbol of higher ambitions for the welfare of the people and the willingness to protect. The debate also shifted towards individual responsibility and the idea of prepping. Shelters were seen as places for individuals to seek protection and prepare for crisis situations. Bennersved [2] also points out the role of media in shaping the debates on shelters. Media used local settings and the proximity to shelters to anchor and make it newsworthy and influenced the spread of shelter-related news. Shelters became a surface for projecting moral, political, and cultural issues, and discussions focused on responsibilities and power relations rather than the risks that shelters are built to protect from.

In Norway, the construction of new shelters followed the cold war, and when the requirement that public buildings needed to have a shelter was removed in 1998, the construction of new public shelters came to an abrupt halt. In the public debate before the breakout of the Ukraine war, the focus was on lack of maintenance [30] lack of plausible alternative use during peace time and a general agreement that the concept was outdated [31]. It was also pointed out that the capacity was too small in any case [32], and only covered the densely populated parts of Norway [33]. In 2020, the Norwegian Government White Paper nr. 5 (2020–2021) on Societal Security in an Uncertain World [34] states that the government planned to substitute the shelter scheme with a new scheme for safe spaces, but without going into details on what this new concept would entail. Recently, the discourse moved towards a new reality of the shelters, and the reintroduction of the requirement to build public shelters has been discussed [35], particularly in vulnerable areas [36].

Estonia became independent after the collapse of the USSR and in 1993, the Estonian government decided to abandon the maintenance of previously established civil defense shelters and ceased the construction of new ones [37]. However, the need for public places to seek shelters in Estonia as a neighboring country to Russia became particularly evident in 2022 following the outbreak of full-scale war in Ukraine. Same year the Estonian government decided to map and mark suitable locations for sheltering based on existing infrastructure in public spaces. These are not traditional bomb shelters or bunkers, but a *sheltering place* (Estonian: "varjumiskoht"). A sheltering place is a structure or part of a structure adapted for sheltering that protects against dust, blast and flying objects [38]. All these shelter places are marked with civil protection sign and the word "Varjumiskoht" in existing structures that provide minimal protective cover. However, as the war in Ukraine carried on, already two years later in 2024, the government gave its preliminary approval to establish a mandatory requirement for building shelters in new larger or public buildings [38]. Currently, preparations are underway for the new law and technical regulations.

3 Methodology and Workshop Design

To answer our RQs in this study, we employed an interpretive stream of the qualitative method [39, 40] as understood in the information systems field. Qualitative research enables us to study social phenomena, and socio-cultural and organizational context in relation to the air-raid shelters. The study is an interpretive in nature as it tries to focus on complexity of human sense making and actions as situation emerges [40]. In this interpretive position, we assume that the knowledge is gained through the social constructions such as language, consciousness, shared meanings, documents, tools and other artifacts.

We assumed that:

1. Participants have not thought about need to seek shelter during air-raid attack before the workshop.
2. Social connection will play a role during shelter seeking.

3.1 Workshop Procedure and Design

Two different workshops were implemented, the pilot workshop in Estonia and the main workshop in Germany with similar scenario. The Estonian workshop procedure was that students were dived into two groups, and they were given a group task to find a safe place to hide from air-raid attack in the building they were. Once they had agreed the place is safe, they were asked to discuss several questions. The Germany workshop procedure was as follows. First, the participants were introduced to the topic of air-raid shelters, based on the facts on air-raid shelters in Norway and Estonia through a presentation. Two tasks have been pre-prepared for the group works:

In the first task, we posed several questions such as the participants' country of origins, if they have lived there before Ukrainian war (and not recently moved to the country), if there are active infrastructure for public shelters. They were asked to check the website of each country concerning the information about public air-raid shelters, if the information is available for foreign language, if there are specific information on maintenance and upgrading of the public shelter to the public. We also asked participants to assess the quality of the information.

In the second task, we told the participants the following information:

There is an air-raid warning happening right now! You need to identify in your group as soon as possible the safest place to seek shelter!

In Estonia, pilot 90 min workshop vocational education students were given the task during their regular English class, after the teacher had divided students into two groups. Both groups were followed by a researcher, when they moved out of the second-floor classroom to find a safe place. Participants of the pilot workshop had attended classes together, so they knew each other. Workshop was held in multistory schoolhouse that is listed at Estonian Rescue Board website as sheltering place to seek shelter during air-raid attacks [41].

At the workshop held in Germany, the participants were gathered in an old 91-m-long three-wing complex with multiple storeys. A practical exercise was conducted in which participants had to find a suitable room for shelter within or near the seminar building within five minutes. They chose the basement of the building as the suitable sheltering room. And afterwards we observed together the areas assumed to be safe for sheltering.

Discussion themes in this practical exercise centered around the following themes: If the participants knew someone local in the group that know the building where the workshop was held, and the safe place to hide in the next 4 h. The participants were also asked to pick the priority to bring with them into a public shelter in such scenario, and to assess the tolerable duration to stay in the public shelter in case they need to stay longer than 4 h, and interaction needed in such situation. We also asked if such a shelter (the building they were in) was suitable for people in wheelchairs, or any other disability. Moreover, we asked how they would communicate that they had arrived at a safe place and potentially survived the air-raid attack.

3.2 Data Collection and Participants

The data was collected in the Estonian workshop from 12 participants and the scheduled English class lasted all together 90 min. All students were IT students and had some experience before on how to use CoTrack. We used web-based "CoTrack" tool [42] as a part of data collection activities to document the dialogues, with the participants' consents. CoTrack is an experimental tool made by University of Tallinn for digital collaboration. The tool requires users to sign-in, while the administrators (the researchers) could assign participants into groups digitally. The tool generated unique codes for each group such as "90E3DB". Those who belongs to the same group should then enter this code. The advantage of using this tool is that researchers could keep track the conversation occurring in each group simultaneously. When participants logged in to the tool, they were asked permission to use their own device to record the text they type in and audio. Note that CoTrack was not the only means to collect data as we also rely on the group discussion. Thus, in the event of the CoTrack recording stopped in one of the exercises, we still could elicit information through the group discussion.

Main data collection was implemented through a 120-min international workshop and focus group discussion. In the German workshop, there were 12 participants in total representing various countries in Europe, especially Norway, the Netherlands, Estonia and Germany. The participants were combined academic and emergency management practitioners divided into four groups. Each participant needs to login in a predefined group division and enter the specific code to join one of the groups. We also used recording devices for extra backup, in case the co-track did not function well. Note that the exact workshop locations are anonymized to a country level.

On the data analysis, we follow the principles of interpretive research as proposed by Klein and Myers [39], i.e. by trying to achieve a mutual understanding between parts and the whole and contextualizing the findings by considering country of origins of the participants and historical contexts (such as whether or not the participants have exposed to shelter ideas). Moreover, Klein and Myers [39] suggest that analyzing the data should consider how the interaction between the researchers and the subjects contributed to constructing the data. In our case, such interaction indeed was a key for obtaining the necessary data. We tried to identify possible contradictions between findings and existing practices, or contradictory among participants' perception on a specific issue. The possibility of existence of multiple interpretations for certain findings were taken into account. There is also the suspicion principle [39] required to understand the potential biases and distortion for the collected data. In the analysis process, the data was treated in different ways for analysis like breaking data into meaningful parts, aggregate date that have similar content and coded them into themes.

4 Findings

This section will present the findings from the workshops and experiments in Germany and Estonia.

4.1 Pilot Experiment in Estonia

High level themes appeared from the Estonian experiment, such as *discrepancies on evacuation decision making*, the existence of an *"expert" member in a group, priority choices to bring in sheltering action,* and *the differences in understanding of information needs and the role of technology* in such air raid scenarios.

In the Estonia experiment, one group decided to go to the gym. The reason was that the gym has no windows, located below the first floor. The group members agreed that the gym is a safe area. In this group, one of the students were a refugee from Ukraine and had experience of seeking shelter because of the war experience, thus was considered as an expert. The group checked an online list of public shelters, and decided that the closest place to the group location was the same bulding they were, i.e., the vocational college. However they did not notice the signed location in the building existed. The group deemed the most important things to bring are water, food, medicine and communication devices such as mobilephone.

The other group decided to go to the underground floor, after they also had checked the list of sheltering places in the hallway, as the classroom had windows. In cellar there were no windows, and no school wireless connection, and mobilephone signals were vanished. In the cellar, there was tap-water, toilet and laundery room, however the group members stood or sat on the corridor. Later, when returing to the classroom where the teacher waited for them, it turned out that the chosen place was the part of the building that had a sign shelter place on of the doors leading to it. No-one from these six people had noticed the sign before, even if the students had participated in classes in that building already for several months.

When participants were asked who they would like to contact, they named family, friends and classmates. The question was proposed in a way that they should let them know that they have found a safe place to hide until air-raid warning is finished. They thought they wanted to inform their close ones with mobile phones, and in the cellar the mobile reception was available during the simulation. One group also thought they could write a letters or write a message through gmail and if the internet happens to come back, there may be a chance to send it. The participants thought that the chosen sheltering place was quiet, people could start talking to each other about the situation and get to know their opinion about the situation everyone are forced into. They imagined that there would be a possibility to talk about personal life and stories.

4.2 Experiment in Germany

High level themes appeared from the Germany workshop and experiment. The four main themes especially: *the urgency of raising "shelter" into public debate, assessment on adequacy of sheltering infrastructure, priority to bring in sheltering, and communication vulnerability.* There was a disagreement on the need for entering public debate concerning the shelter topic. According to participants, this is a topic that, although part of the public debate, "no one wants to touch." The general public doesn't want to deal or feel challenged intellectually with questions of threats, and potential threats. An opposite opinion advocated the curiosity and willingness to understand better the actual picture on air-raid scenario, as expressed by one of the participants:

> *"... if the general public wants or doesn't want to deal with it, it's an open question. Because... these days, ... I think a half of the world at least here [In Europe], is aware that there is a severe rupture of the eternal peace, [and perceived as], the end of the Cold War, etc... or at least has to be challenged to some degree. The more we know the better informed we are, the more protected safe I feel..."*

The basement rooms were quickly located and easily accessible, allowing for rapid movement to that location. Participants assessed that the basement rooms were suitable for sheltering because they had thick stone walls and massive support pillars. Additionally, the basement had restrooms, available drinking water, and functioning mobile communication.

Although a detailed engineering assessment of the rooms' suitability was not conducted, the seminar organizing team also spoke about the building's history. The specific university building had been bombed to the ground during World War II, (pointing to the anonymized location of the workshop). The university building was rebuilt by students using readily available materials, which varied in quality. As a result, participants were unsure whether the shelter room provided sufficient protection against flying shrapnel, overpressure, vibration, and whether the building was collapse-resistant. Furthermore, the shelter location was not marked within the building, as Germany has not started marking suitable sheltering rooms (and the fact, there is no corresponding political decision or legal requirement).

The participants were asked what are important to have with them in such severe air-raid scenarios. One on the top of the list was to bring any form of identification materials that allow them to be recognized, if something happened to them. The idea of carrying identification is efficiency and time-saving action, e.g., it could expedite the registration process. They specified a method that to some extent reflect the younger generation's mind living in a digital world, for example, the use of electronic devices for identification purposes. Indeed, more traditional personal documents were listed as important such as ID card or bank card. An opinion even mentioned the need of having dental records as the dental features can identify individuals. While the majority agreed on the idea of the importance of the identification, but the debate emerged: *First*, the issue of the practicality and necessitate to carry identification at all times. It was deemed plausible logic that dental record could identify individuals, but in panic situation, very few people would consider bringing dental records, or even having them at home. As said by one participant:

> "...*If you are aware that you are running for your life, if you think that grabbing for your ID card would make sense, do it. But you are running for your life, if you have to waste time searching for it, don't. Then, people would be making informed decisions...*"

Second, the existence of multiple methods for identification during the chaotic sheltering process. A participant argued that in such situation, one might lose the means for identity checking, or even had no internet for conducting identification electronically, thus the ID is not always the most important thing to bring:

> "*.... ID is not so important because if something happen and we are missing in that situation, is still there is a way to do the cross check with the family for example:...—oh my son is not yet coming today so something might happen—and it means that ID is not so crucial. There's another thing that I didn't think about it the first time I had to evacuate the building ...There was fire alarm... late at night. I was already gone to bed. I just put on my trousers and a shirt and went outside. ... It took approximately 10 seconds before I was thinking, okay, that was a mistake not bringing my jacket, it was winter. And ... in a basement, it could also be quite a lot colder than you expect. So actually, a jacket, I thought about it this time, as a priority to bring, but I might have forgotten if I was not trained to think that way...*"

One of the bigger themes derived from this prioritizing-under-pressure exercise was awareness for being individually resilient, which many had understood this as the ability to adapt and prepare in emergency situations, but it needed to be extended into "having essentials readily available. There is also an observation on the gender differences in habits and behaviors, such as how males are more likely to carry essentials or keep them in their pockets, while female often put them in the purse. This could affect someone's speed and awareness of receiving updated information, i.e., putting essentials in the pocket allowed one to react faster, which is crucial in emergencies.

Lastly, one participant addresses the concern on the communication infrastructure vulnerability, by recalling the history of training as rescue officer where all the trainees should visit an underground bomb shelter from the former Soviet Union. And they were told that there were a special ventilation system and a separate communication system, a landline phones. But how many landline phones are available nowadays? In fact, the majority of people in highly digitalized country are using internet-based or mobile-based communication. Moreover, TV is often used as a channel for public communication, however, a participant mentioned that in his country, many people do not have TV anymore and it will be a challenge to communicate to the right channel for emergency communication to the public in situations like this air-raid scenario.

To sum up, the findings show some important themes derived from our experiments in two countries and provide majority answers to our research questions but left with some open questions we discussed in the next section and eventually the future research.

5 Discussion

The urgency and perceived threat of air raids varied significantly among the workshop participants, particularly those in the second workshop, which included participants from multiple countries. Focus group discussions conducted after the workshop revealed that the perception of the threat posed by Russian aggression —emphasizing the necessity of shelters—, is stronger in Northern and Eastern European countries, such as Estonia and Norway. In contrast, Western European countries such as Germany and the Netherlands have not taken steps to restore existing shelters or made political decisions to construct new ones.

Moreover, we also would like to take the discussion one step further. These experiments show that the terms "shelter" and "sheltering" have distinct meanings and requirements. During the workshops, however, the term was not introduced to the participants, as the theme itself is relatively new, particularly for the younger generation. The discussion about the usage of various terms was instead conducted in a more guided manner through leading questions, such as, 'Do you think this building is adequate as a shelter, or is it merely sufficient to protect people from injury during a raid?' At this point the facilitator could introduce the differences, but they were not fully aware of the differences.

Estonian crisis management seems to be more precise in distinguishing between these two concepts and which is considered essential to clarify the differences between "shelter," "sheltering," and their specific meanings. For example, in English, Norwegian, and Estonian, "shelter" is a broad term, which can lead to varying interpretations of what it means to take shelter during air-raid attacks. Our discussion with a shelter expert suggests that the terms "shelter," "bunker," and "sheltering place" should be more clearly defined and expanded to encompass multiple meanings.

A bunker or shelter is defined as a reinforced underground facility, typically constructed to protect the public during wartime, including from nuclear attacks. Such structures often feature independent ventilation systems and other essential infrastructure to ensure the survival of those seeking refuge. The primary function of a bunker or shelter is to safeguard human life during conflict. In the case of Ukraine, the shelter systems fell into disrepair after the collapse of the Soviet Union.

A sheltering place, on the other hand, is a structure or part of a structure adapted to protect against dust, blasts, and flying objects. Such places can include subways, tunnels, and garages, which can be adapted to provide temporary cover during conflicts. In Ukraine, during the war, the use of these shelters has been widespread. Additionally, specific requirements must be met for shelters and sheltering sites.

Moreover, the dialogue with the expert participant highlights again, what are the requirements for shelter and sheltering place, which can be seen in Table 1. This comparison is based on a draft legal act from the Estonian Emergency Act[1]. It is limited to

[1] https://eelnoud.valitsus.ee/main/mount/docList/81ef7ad8-14e2-4d3d-9c4e-83a841c1b8b4.

a very high-level requirements, without going deep into the engineering requirements. We notice the differences between *shelter* and *sheltering place*, where shelter has tighter requirements than sheltering site. Understanding about shelter and sheltering sites should be clearly communicated to the public that the primary use of sheltering places is not to take cover from atomic attack. However, the primary use of bunkers often is to work and live in a safe place during war times.

Moreover, in a more typical disasters beyond the war, there are also situations where sheltering places are practically an "ad-hoc" sheltering, i.e., people carefully locate a safe place to protect themselves against dangers such as in earthquake, floods, and school shooting. It is not always a formal infrastructure, but rather any places where people can seek refuge.

Table 1. Comparison of requirements for shelters and sheltering places.

Requirement	Shelter	Sheltering place (minimum requirements)
Construction, Wall thickness and materials)	✔ minimum thickness of reinforced concrete walls, ceilings etc.	✔ preferably stone walls
Overpressure resistance	✔ shelter must be airtight and maintain overpressure	✔ emergency exit via another door or window
Emergency exit		✔ sufficient air exchange
Ventilation	✔ Second exit required	-
Airtightness	Specific filtered ventilation which operates also in case of power loss	-
Collapse resistance	✔	-
Electricity supply	Airtight construction and door	-
Hygiene conditions	✔	-
Contaminated outdoor air filtration	Structure of building and shelter is collapse-proof	Short-term (hours)
Duration of stay	✔	✔ preferably stone walls

It is also worth to mention that our experiments show the importance of paying attention to communication infrastructure. Todays' generation are heavily depending upon the availability of internet and mobile phone. However, our experiment showed that such things may not work in the basement, thus communication is becoming very crucial as one should be able to comminate their whereabout in the scenario of air raid attack.

Lastly, we are aware of the potential biases introduced in this research, among others: 1) *response biases due to gap between generations*: as the workshop participants are combined young generations with no experience with the cold-war, and those were who still have memory from the fear during the cold war. Thus, for younger generation, the existence of the of air-raid shelters are unknown. 2) *Self-selection (volunteer) bias*: it may lead into greater discrepancy in the results due to variation in the participant knowledge. This is related to response bias. However, the nature of this study is explorative, and we discuss about the participants' perceptions, which to some extent, open to variations of the participants' backgrounds. Moreover, the participants came from different countries, and having different perception on what threats are more pressing, and thus has been trained and thought differently on immediate dangers that they can protect themselves. Thus, there are potential that the cultural background and country of origin, different part of the countries (near Russian border or not) may affect the discussion results; 3) *Recall bias:* this topic falls into infrequent event, but due to a little experience dealing with sheltering, or little knowledge about it, it may lead into inaccurate answers. To anticipate these biases, we asked participants in the beginning of the workshop to check online sources concerning this topic from their own countries to enable more balanced discussions. The authors also check more credible sources where the participants were unsure and rely on memory on specific information. In some cases, discrepancies of the cultural background have enriched the discussions and results.

6 Conclusions and Future Work

This article is answering the research questions on today's perception regarding the need to seek shelter and to prepare during air-raid scenario. Apparently, we found nuance regarding the realism of the threats, or it has been perceived as a part of the public debate that most people are reluctant to be involved in, and especially because they thought that the threat might not happen. But even with this different opinion, when doing simulations for seeking shelter to avoid air raid attacks, interesting discussions occurred, and learning process happen on the importance of understanding information needs and priority of items to bring when sheltering should occur. As this knowledge and understanding is actually applicable not only under the air raid attack scenario, but also other scenarios that require ones to move quickly and decide what to prioritize.

Likewise on the information needs and communication infrastructure in crises, we also found that the opinions vary from one to another. The information technology (IT) solutions are the most compelling channel to manage information and communication flows among different people who were affected by the disasters. IT solutions (apps, websites, map applications, notification solutions via mobile phones, etc.) have been deemed as effective tools for finding shelters and informing the public. However, IT solutions have been associated with risks. First, IT solutions may not function during a crisis, meaning that public notifications and finding the nearest shelter cannot solely rely on IT solutions. Otherwise, the population dependent on these IT solutions may become helpless during power outages, communication disruptions, or other crises that cause IT solutions to fail. Another significant risk associated with IT solutions is the concentration of information about all existing shelters in one place. While residents may be hidden from air raid when sheltering, they may remain visible to the enemy from an IT perspective. Concentrating the population in a location known to a military adversary or terrorist organization creates additional risks, and at some point, the shelter itself could become a target.

Concerning the limitation of this study, there are several points can be listed. *First*, methodologically, the findings and discussion were derived from participants representing European countries, and represented many corners of European countries (e.g., southern, eastern and central Europe). We also cannot directly compare the results from the first and the second workshop directly given we did not have the same requirements of participants. In the Estonian workshop, the participants were more homogeneous in terms of nationality, age and study background. In the second workshop, the participants were highly diverse: nationality, age range, background (practitioners and academia) and experience with emergency management works. While the comparison was not the main goal of this study but comparing the threat perceptions on air-raid scenarios in different countries in Europe and beyond with similar criteria would be one way to improve this limitation. Second, this work is practical oriented paper. For the improvement, applying a theoretical perspective can bring the data into a certain direction that will provide higher level, and generalizable results and a solid theory-based results.

On the future work, we consider simulation as a good technique to raise awareness and communicating risks to citizen on such unimaginable air raid attacks, especially for younger generations. This also can be a compelling approach, as we discussed earlier, TV is no longer fully a source for entertainment and education, also crisis communication channel. The use of augmented reality, for example, allows us to do visualization and showing the air-raid attack training that can improve our understanding on such situation, and trained to take informed decision for sheltering. Moreover, theoretical concept originating from situation awareness literature [43, 44] and environmental psychology, especially spatial and ecological aspects of social behavior and crowding [45, 46] will be used actively to guide and deepen this research theme.

Acknowledgements. Big thank you to the workshop participants who provided valuable and thought-provoking insights.

References

1. CFR War in Ukraine. Global Conflict Tracker (2024)
2. Bennesved, P.: Shelter news: affordance, place and proximity in news media representations of civil defence artefacts. Crit. Mil. Stud. **10**(1), 1–18 (2024)
3. Wallensteen, P., Sollenberg, M.: After the cold war: emerging patterns of armed conflict 1989–94. J. Peace Res. **32**(3), 345–360 (1995)
4. Matacz, P., Świątek, L.: The unwanted heritage of prefabricated wartime air raid shelters—underground space regeneration feasibility for urban agriculture to enhance neighbourhood community engagement. Sustainability **13**(21), 12238 (2021)
5. Rosser, P., Soler, S.: From oblivion to life: the recovery of intangible cultural heritage through the anti-aircraft shelters of the spanish civil war. Heritage **7**(2), 817–828 (2024)
6. Bryant, D.: Main London blitz local response: the suburbs. In: Agency and Locality in the London Blitz, pp. 165–224. Springer (2024)
7. HRMMU, Report on the Human Rights Situation in Ukraine 1 March 2024–31 May 2024. 2024, United Nations Human Rights Office of the High Commissioner
8. The State of the World's Human Rights. Amnesty International: London, UK (2024)

9. Berger Ziauddin, S.: (De) territorializing the home. The nuclear bomb shelter as a malleable site of passage. Environ. Plan. D Soc. Space **35**(4), 674–693 (2017)
10. Donahue, A., Tuohy, R.: Lessons we don't learn: a study of the lessons of disasters, why we repeat them, and how we can learn them. Homel. Secur. Aff. **2**(2) (2006)
11. Hayward, J.: Air power, ethics, and civilian immunity during the first world war and its aftermath. Glob. War Stud. **7**(2), 102–130 (2010)
12. Clapson, M.: The emerging terror, in Blitz Companion: Aerial Warfare, Civilians and the City Since 1911: Aerial Warfare, Civilians and the City Since 1911. University of Westminster Press London, pp. 13–36 (2019)
13. Hayes, T.J.: Evaluating atomic bomb shelters. Mil. Eng. **43**(295), 344–346 (1951)
14. Dyson, F.J.: Thoughts on bomb shelters. Bull. Atomic Sci. **18**(3), 14–15 (1962)
15. Krupka, R.A.: An evaluation of the shelter potential in mines, caves and tunnels, vol. 1. Hudson Institute (1965)
16. Lucas, K.A., et al.: Efficacy of bomb shelters: with lessons from the Hamburg firestorm. South. Med. J. **83**, 812–820 (1990)
17. UtrechtAltijd 'Voordat de bom valt': de Koude Oorlog in Utrecht (2019)
18. Rijkswaterstaat Koude Oorlog: de geheime schuilkelders van Rijkswaterstaat (2023)
19. Leaf, A.: New perspectives on the medical consequences of nuclear war. N. Engl. J. Med. **315**(14), 905–912 (1986)
20. Zhidkova, T, Selikhova, Y., Kazachenko, V.: Urban-aspects aspects of organization of energy-efficient underground space for protection. Theory Pract. Des. **25**, 140–148 (2022)
21. Pomortseva, O., Kobzan, S.: Geospatial modeling of the location of bomb shelters in residential areas of the city. In: IOP Conference Series: Earth and Environmental Science. IOP Publishing (2023)
22. Howlett, M.: Nation-building from (below) the grassroots: everyday nationalism in Ukraine's bomb shelters. Nations Nationalism **29**(1), 63–69 (2023)
23. Gromova, Z., et al.: Supporting educators' mental health from a Ukrainian bomb shelter. Child. Educ. **99**(6), 48–53 (2023)
24. Moore, S.: The Bethnal green shelter disaster. War Soc. **43**(2), 187–199 (2024)
25. Kennedy, N., et al.: British safety adviser for Reuters killed in Russian strike on Ukraine hotel (2024)
26. Gillet, F., Vernon, W.: Seven killed in 'most massive' Russian air attack, Ukraine says (2024)
27. Aljazeera Photos: At least 31 killed as Russia bombs Ukraine; children's hospital hit (2024)
28. HRW "Tanks on the Playground": Attacks on Schools and Military Use of Schools in Ukraine (2023)
29. Bennesved, P., Norén, F.: Urban catastrophe and sheltered salvation. Media Hist. **26**(2), 167–184 (2020)
30. Oslo, K.i., Rapport 19 Tilfluktsrom, in Kommunerevisjonens rapporter. Oslo Municipality: Oslo (2023)
31. TU Utspilt sin rolle. Teknisk Ukeblad Media (2001)
32. Hanssen, R.I.: Beredskap uten tilfluktsrom. ND, Nordnorskdebatt (2022)
33. Finnset, K.A., Hoseth, B., Sveen, E.H.: Har ikke bygd nye offentlige tilfluktsrom i Norge på over 20 år (2022)
34. Meld.St.5, Samfunnssikkerhet i en usikker verden, J.-o. beredskapsdepartementet, Editor. Norway (2020)
35. Husebye, O.C.: Hvor drar vi om krigen kommer? Forsvarets Forum (2024)
36. Olsen, Ø.F.: Regjeringen vil prioritere tilfluktsrom i utsatte områder. In Forsvarets Forum (2022)
37. Tross, J.: Elanikkonnakaitse areng Eestis iseseisvuse taastamise järgsel perioodil (2023)
38. ERR Interior ministry's draft shelter regulation raises construction costs of buildings (2024)

39. Klein, H.K., Myers, M.D.: A set of principles for conducting and evaluating interpretive field studies in information systems. MIS Q. 67–93 (1999)
40. Myers, M.D., Avison, D.: Qualitative research in information systems: a reader. Sage (2002)
41. Päästeamet Avalikud varjumiskohad Tartus - Avalikud varjumiskohad (2023)
42. CoTrack Track collaboration across digital and physical spaces (2024)
43. Endsley, M.R.: Measurement of situation awareness in dynamic systems. Hum. Factors **37**(1), 65–84 (1995)
44. Endsley, M.R.: Situation awareness misconceptions and misunderstandings. J. Cogn. Eng. Decis. Making **9**(1), 4–32 (2015)
45. Aiello, J.R., Thompson, D.E.: Personal space, crowding, and spatial behavior in a cultural context. In: Environment and Culture, pp. 107–178. Springer (1980)
46. Altman, I., Taylor, D.A., Wheeler, L.: Ecological aspects of group behavior in social isolation 1. J. Appl. Soc. Psychol. **1**(1), 76–100 (1971)

Information and Community Disaster Management

Proposal for a Tourism and Disaster Prevention Information Portal Site for Foreign Tourists Visiting Japan

Jun Sasaki(✉)

Faculty of Informatics, Yamato University, 2-5-1 Katayama-Cho, Suita, Osaka 564-0082, Japan
sasaki.jun@yamato-u.ac.jp

Abstract. In recent years, the number of foreign tourists visiting Japan has increased. However, Japan is prone to natural disasters, such as earthquakes and tsunamis, as well as river flooding caused by typhoons and heavy rains. When such natural disasters occur, foreign tourists visiting Japan may suffer serious harm because of a lack of language proficiency and information on how to respond. This paper proposes a tourism and disaster prevention information portal site to enable foreign tourists visiting Japan to have a safe and enjoyable sightseeing trip. This portal site allows users to search for sightseeing trip plans in Japan, learn disaster prevention knowledge to deal with natural disasters in Japan, and obtain multilingual smartphone apps with guidance for actions to take for disaster prevention during sightseeing trips. In this study, the author and students at Yamato University and Iwate Prefectural University built a prototype tourism and disaster prevention information portal site for foreign tourists visiting the 2025 Osaka World Expo. In the future, we will conduct evaluation experiments on this portal site and use them to improve it and build a more ideal system.

Keywords: Natural Disasters · Disaster Prevention Education · Tourism Travel Planning · Portal Site

1 Introduction

In Japan, natural disasters such as earthquakes and tsunamis, as well as river flooding caused by typhoons and heavy rains, occur frequently. In addition, the number of foreign tourists is increasing [1], and there is always the possibility that tourists will be involved in a natural disaster. Because of differences in language and customs, foreign tourists may not be able to respond appropriately to such disasters and may suffer serious harm.

The Japanese government provides many disaster prevention information websites and smartphone apps that would be useful for disaster prevention for foreign tourists. However, few foreign visitors know about these disaster prevention information resources. This is because few tourists are interested in disaster prevention information alone. This study aims to develop an effective way to provide tourists with disaster prevention information by linking it to tourism information. Therefore, this study first built

Published by Springer Nature Switzerland AG 2026
W. Seböck et al. (Eds.): ITDRR 2024, IFIP AICT 752, pp. 247–256, 2026.
https://doi.org/10.1007/978-3-031-97115-0_16

a site for searching tourist travel plans in Japan. Then, a disaster prevention information portal site was added, with disaster prevention information and links to access useful apps with guidance for actions to take for disaster prevention.

In Sect. 2, previous research examples on tourism and disaster prevention information are described, in Sect. 3, the concept of the proposed tourism and disaster prevention information portal site are introduced, and in Sect. 4, an overview of the constructed prototype system is given. Finally, Sect. 5 discusses conclusions and future works.

2 Previous Research on Tourism Support Systems and Disaster Prevention Information Systems

In Japan, the tourism industry was sluggish from 2020 to 2021 as a result of the response to the spread of COVID-19. However, since infection prevention measures such as vaccines became available and behavioral restrictions were relaxed in 2023, global tourism recovered, leading to larger numbers of tourists visiting Japan and, concurrently, increased tourism spending [1]. However, Japan is prone to natural disasters such as earthquakes, tsunamis, typhoons, floods, and volcanic eruptions. For tourists to safely enjoy traveling, it is important that they are aware of the risks of such disasters and take sufficient precautions when traveling.

To date, research on the above issues has largely been divided into research in the tourism field, and research in the disaster prevention field.

Recent research in the tourism field includes tourism recommendations using internet blogs and social media sites and apps (hereafter, social network services; SNS) [2]. In the field of tourism, the author has conducted research on many topics, including an analysis of traveler intent using photos and check-in data posted on the internet, a tourist destination recommendation system using SNS data [3–6], a day trip planning support system for urban and rural areas [7], a day trip planning system with high satisfaction considering travel fatigue [8], and a method for individually recommending attractive tourist destinations suitable for tourists using traveler profile data [9]. In addition, in the field of disaster information, the author has conducted research on a real-time mapping system of evacuation shelter status for safe evacuation [10], a regional information-sharing system for disaster prevention and evacuation [11], and a proposal for an evacuation support system for regional disasters and its evaluation by multi-agent simulation [12].

In their paper on tourism and disaster risks, Ritchie et al. summarize tourism risks [13]. They surveyed and classified 142 papers on tourism risk, crisis, emergency, and disaster management published between 1960 and 2018. Most previous research papers reported responses from the perspective of the tourism industry or individual cases, and there were no examples of research on learning and preparing for disasters from the travelers' perspective. Other examples of research include the behavior of foreign tourists visiting Japan when driving in Japan, and an analysis of the nationalities and causes of traffic accidents [14, 15]. There have also been reports on the construction of a disaster digital archive for use in disaster prevention education in Japan [16].

However, these studies do not link tourism and disaster prevention information, and the number of foreign tourists who tour Japan by car is still fairly small, so the reality is that these studies do not contribute to the safety and security of foreign tourists in general.

3 Tourism and Disaster Prevention Information Portal Site Concept

The Ministry of Land, Infrastructure, Transport, and Tourism provides a wide range of information and basic knowledge on tourism and disaster prevention in Japan, as well as apps that help foreign tourists take disaster prevention measures when traveling [17]. Many disaster prevention apps are available that are useful while traveling [18]. Many local governments also provide tourism and disaster prevention information for foreign tourists in each region [19–22]. In addition, the Ministry of Foreign Affairs of Japan has posted information on natural disasters for Japanese traveling abroad on its website, such as volcanoes and forest fires in Italy [23] and avalanches in Austria [24].

However, because tourists are generally focused on information about tourist spots, gourmet options, transportation, and other things that are important for enjoyment, they tend to be unaware of the existence of disaster prevention information. This is thought to be because creating tourist travel plans is already burdensome, meaning that disaster prevention information is not highly prioritized. Therefore, the author and participating students created a website that lists tourist travel plans and combines information on topics such as tourist spots, hotels, and transportation, with a searchable database. Using this website will reduce the burden of creating tourist travel plans. Furthermore, a system was created whereby disaster prevention information for travel destinations and useful disaster prevention apps with guidance for actions to take for disaster prevention can be obtained. This system is easily accessed by clicking on a link on the tourist information page.

To our knowledge, the proposed concept of the tourism and disaster prevention information portal site will be the first to provide disaster prevention information while focusing on tourism plans.

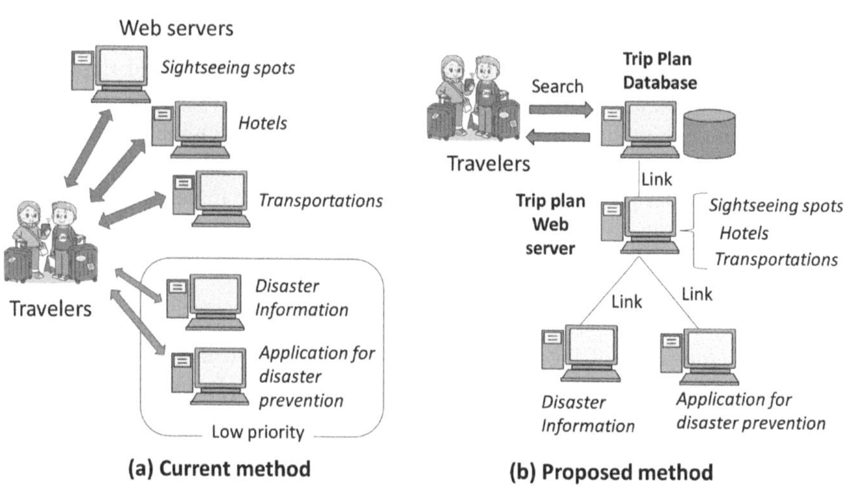

Fig. 1. Comparison of travel planning and disaster prevention information acquisition methods.

Figure 1 compares the conventional and proposed methods for creating tourist travel plans and obtaining disaster prevention information. In the conventional method (see Fig. 1(a)), travelers create travel plans by assembling information from various sources about tourist spots, hotels, and transportation facilities on a piecemeal basis, which places a heavy burden on them. Disaster prevention information and apps related to the specific travel destination must be found by searching different websites, which is a time-consuming task; if the traveler is not interested, it inevitably becomes a low priority. In the proposed method (see Fig. 1(b)), the tourism and disaster prevention information portal site can be used by travelers to create tourist travel plans simply by searching and selecting from a database. At the same time, the necessary disaster prevention information and disaster prevention apps can be easily obtained by simply clicking on links related to disaster prevention information for the travel destination. With the aim of verifying the validity of this proposal, the author decided to first build a prototype system and conduct a usage experiment.

4 Overview of the Prototype System

4.1 Concept of Prototype System Construction

The tourism and disaster prevention information portal site proposed in this study is intended to be ongoing, and not a temporary resource. Instead, it is desirable for the site to be improved continuously through ongoing use. Therefore, we decided to run the Plan, Do, Check, and Action (PDCA) cycle according to the following schedule.

(1) Plan: Concept proposal and research plan creation (2024)
(2) Do: Build a prototype (2024)
(3) Check: Usage evaluation experiment (2025)
(4) Action: Improve the prototype (2026)

By repeating this PDCA cycle, the prototype will become closer to an ideal system. The prototype was constructed considering the fact that the 2025 World Expo will be held in Osaka, Japan, and many foreign tourists are expected to visit the city. For this reason, we will create tourist travel plans for tourists based in Osaka and traveling to various parts of Japan and build a website and database for them. The site will also provide useful disaster prevention information relevant to each region of Japan the user plans to visit.

4.2 Configuration of the Developed Prototype

The structure (site map) of the developed prototype is shown in Fig. 2. When users select the season in which they intend to travel on the travel planning website, a map of Japan appears, with recommended travel destinations (areas) displayed on the map. When they select an area, they can view a slide video of the travel plan, including tourist spots, transportation, schedules, and budgets. There are currently over 74 travel plans; because it would be difficult to view them all, a travel plan database was created that allows users to search for travel plans that match travel conditions by entering the travel conditions such as season, number of nights, number of travelers, and budgets.

The top page of the travel planning website has a button that links to the Japan Disaster Information Portal Site. This portal site allows users to view disaster information for Japan, as well as information on evacuation methods and destinations. The site provides information on evacuation methods and evacuation destinations that users can learn as preliminary knowledge before traveling, such as "SOS cards", pictograms, and hotlines (stock information), and information on apps (e.g., "Safety tips" and real-time information) and emergency contacts that will be useful in the event of a disaster while they are in the area (flow information). "SOS cards" are cards that foreign visitors can carry to show to Japanese people in the event of a disaster to receive help. The "Safety tips" function provides push notifications for emergency earthquake alerts, tsunami warnings, and special weather warnings in Japan. It also provides a collection of links to information needed in the event of a disaster, such as response flow charts and communication cards, and is supervised by the Japan Tourism Agency. The app is available in 15 languages.

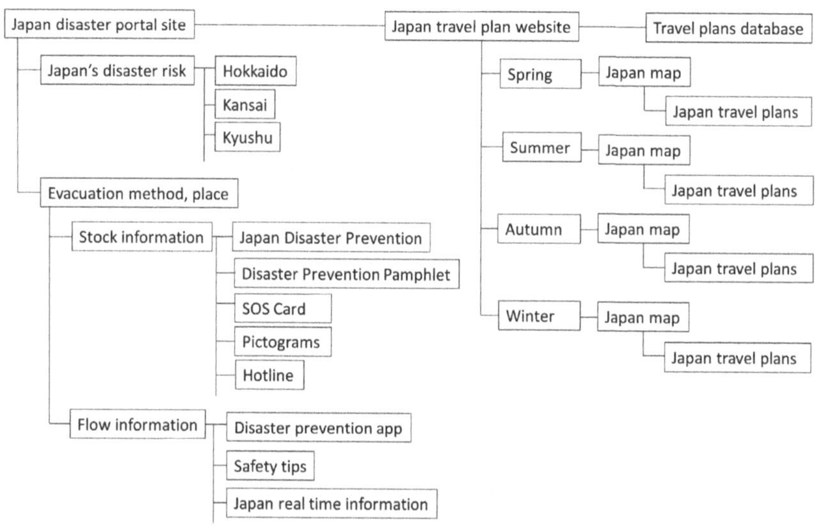

Fig. 2. Structure of the tourism and disaster prevention information portal site prototype (site map).

In the field of social capital, the effects that are immediately useful are called "Flow effects" [25]. Effects that are useful in the long term are called "Stock effects". Therefore, the author defined information that is immediately useful as "Flow information" and information that is useful in the long term as "Stock information".

4.3 Example of Prototype Screen

Figure 3 shows an example of the screen displayed when "Spring" is selected on the top page of the travel planning website. In Japan, March to May is considered "Spring", June to August is "Summer", September to November is "Autumn", and December to February is "Winter". When the user presses the "Yamanashi Prefecture" button on the map of Japan, they can see an overview of travel plans for Yamanashi Prefecture (e.g., start point, destination, number of people, number of nights, and budget) and images of highlights of the trip in slides (videos).

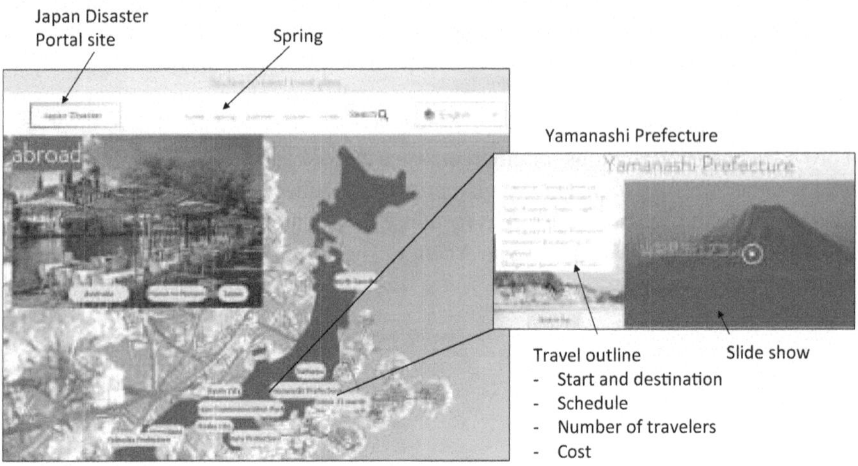

Fig. 3. Example screen of the travel plan website (Spring, Yamanashi Prefecture).

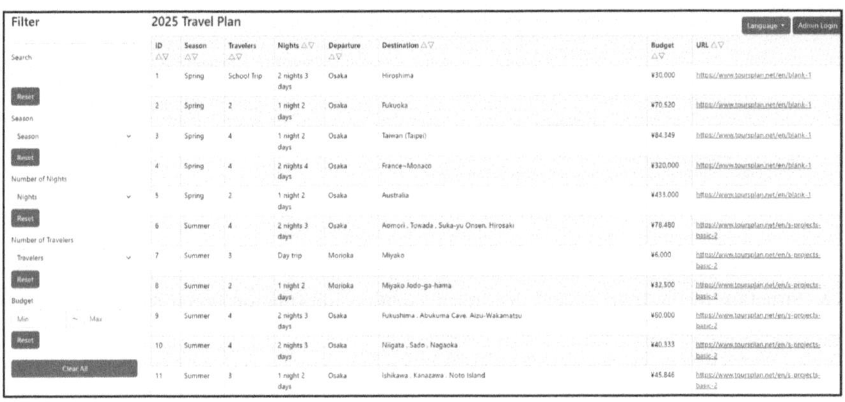

2025 Travel Plan

ID △▽	Season △▽	Travelers △▽	Nights △▽	Departure △▽	Destination △▽	Budget △▽	URL △▽
1	Spring	School Trip	2 nights 3 days	Osaka	Hiroshima	¥30,000	https://www.toursplan.net/en/blank-1
2	Spring	2	1 night 2 days	Osaka	Fukuoka	¥70,520	https://www.toursplan.net/en/blank-1
3	Spring	4	1 night 2 days	Osaka	Taiwan (Taipei)	¥84,349	https://www.toursplan.net/en/blank-1
4	Spring	4	2 nights 4 days	Osaka	France~Monaco	¥320,000	https://www.toursplan.net/en/blank-1
5	Spring	2	1 night 2 days	Osaka	Australia	¥433,000	https://www.toursplan.net/en/blank-1
6	Summer	4	2 nights 3 days	Osaka	Aomori . Towada . Suka-yu Onsen. Hirosaki	¥78,480	https://www.toursplan.net/en/s-projects-basic-2
7	Summer	3	Day trip	Morioka	Miyako	¥6,000	https://www.toursplan.net/en/s-projects-basic-2
8	Summer	2	1 night 2 days	Morioka	Miyako Jodo-ga-hama	¥32,500	https://www.toursplan.net/en/s-projects-basic-2
9	Summer	4	2 nights 3 days	Osaka	Fukushima . Abukuma Cave. Aizu-Wakamatsu	¥60,000	https://www.toursplan.net/en/s-projects-basic-2
10	Summer	4	2 nights 3 days	Osaka	Niigata . Sado . Nagaoka	¥40,333	https://www.toursplan.net/en/s-projects-basic-2
11	Summer	3	1 night 2 days	Osaka	Ishikawa . Kanazawa . Noto Island	¥45,846	https://www.toursplan.net/en/s-projects-basic-2

Fig. 4. Example of screen of the travel plan database.

Figure 4 shows an example of a screen from a travel plan database. This database was developed using MySQL and Php (Web database). Travel plans are uploaded to the app by an administrator, but anyone can search the uploaded travel plans. Users can narrow their search by travel season, number of people, number of nights, and upper budget limit. Each travel plan has a link that takes users to a website that contains the corresponding travel plan.

Figure 5 is an example screenshot of the Japan Disaster Information Portal Site that is displayed when the "Japan's disaster risk" button at the top of the travel planning website is pressed. This page includes the buttons "Japan's disaster risks" and "Evacuation methods, place".

Pressing the "Japan's disaster risks" button allows users to view disaster information for each region of Japan. The prototype contains links to pages for Hokkaido, Kansai, and Kyushu that are available in multiple languages. A current issue with many pages for regional disaster-prevention information is that they are still only in Japanese, and are unavailable in multiple languages. In the future, the author will add links from regions that have created multilingual disaster information pages, such as Kyoto [26] and Tochigi [27].

Figure 6 shows a page with information on how to evacuate and where to evacuate when a disaster occurs. It links Stock information that should be studied in advance and Flow information that would be useful at the time of a disaster. The Stock information allows users to obtain disaster prevention information prepared by the Japanese government, pamphlets on evacuation methods, and contact information (SOS Card and Hotline). The Flow information links to a page where a user can download disaster prevention apps (with information such as "Safety tips") prepared by the Japanese government and view the Japan Meteorological Agency's real-time disaster information page. Although some parts of the information are not yet available in multiple languages, comprehensive links are provided nonetheless given the importance of this information and its usefulness in the event of a disaster.

Fig. 5. Example of screen shot of the Japan Disaster Information Portal Site.

(a) Stock information **(b) Flow information**

Fig. 6. Pages for evacuation methods and evacuation destination information.

5 Conclusion and Future Works

In this paper, the author proposes a tourism and disaster prevention information portal site that foreign tourists visiting Japan can search for tourist plans and obtain disaster prevention information for their destinations and necessary disaster prevention apps simultaneously. By using this portal site, the user can enjoy a safe and secure tourist trip to Japan. The portal site is currently in the prototype stage and will be continuously improved. In the future, further investigation will be needed to verify the usefulness of the site to foreign tourists who have actually encountered a disaster.

This paper describes the developed website from the perspective of foreign tourists visiting Japan. In the future, the author will add a function to introduce the attractiveness of specific areas in Japan for travelers from the perspective of regions that receive tourists. For example, the Tohoku region of Japan is recovering from severe damage caused by the Great East Japan Earthquake on March 11, 2011. However, the population continues to decrease, and reconstruction is still not complete. In addition, the Noto Peninsula in Ishikawa Prefecture in the Hokuriku region also suffered extensive damage from a major earthquake on January 1, 2024. The recovery there is still far from complete, and the region remains severely economically depressed as a result. Therefore, in the future, the site should incorporate tourism information on the Tohoku, Noto Peninsula, and Hokuriku regions for foreign tourists visiting Japan, with a focus on attracting tourists to these areas.

Another consideration is that inconsiderate behavior and crowding as a result of the high volumes of foreign tourists who visit popular tourist spots such as Kyoto, Asakusa, Kamakura, and Mount Fuji can cause distress for local residents. This problem is called overtourism [28]. In the future, the proposed portal site will include features that will allow users to learn etiquette and manners relevant to the Japanese cultural context for famous tourist spots. Furthermore, the site would advise users about points of caution for traveling in rural areas of Japan by rental car, as well as the risks of accidents and other entanglements that may befall foreign tourists in urban areas such as Tokyo and Osaka.

Acknowledgements. The author expresses deep appreciation to students at Yamato University and Iwate Prefectural University for their assistance in creating the prototype site, its many tour plans, and its database. This research is supported by JSPS KAKENHI Grant Number JP24K15554. We thank Edanz (https://jp.edanz.com/ac) for editing a draft of this manuscript.

References

1. Japan Tourism Agency (Tourism White Paper), pp. 15–16. https://www.mlit.go.jp/statistics/content/001512919.pdf
2. Xiang, Z., Magnini, V.P., Fesenmaier, D.R.: Information technology and consumer behavior in travel and tourism: insights from trip planning using the internet. J. Retail. Consum. Serv. **22**, 244–249 (2015)
3. Sasaki, J., Li, S.: A method for classifying photos on tourism websites by color analysis. In: Advances and Trends in Artificial Intelligence from Theory to Practice. LNAI, vol. 11606, pp. 265–278 Springer (2019)
4. Sasaki, J., Takahashi, S., Shuang, L., Komatsu, I., Yamada, K., Takagi, M.: Discovering target users interested in local areas using online advertising and social network services. In: Communications in Computer and Information Science (SOMET 2015), vol. 532, pp. 203–215. Springer (2015)
5. Sasaki, J., Takahashi, S., Yamada, K., Takagi, M.: Analysis of traveler intentions using SNS photos and check-in data. In: SOMET 2016, pp. 50–58. IOS Press (2016)
6. Takahashi, S., Li, S., Yamada, K., Takagi, M., Sasaki, J.: A case study of a tourist course recommendation system using data from social network services. In: SOMET 2017, pp. 339–347. IOS Press (2017)
7. Li, S., Sasaki, J.: Personal trip planning system (PTPS) for use in urban and rural areas. In: SOMET 2018, pp. 259–269. IOS Press (2018)
8. Li, S., Sasaki, J.: A sensibility model for day trips considering satisfaction and fatigue with transportation." In: SOMET 2020, pp. 355–366. IOS Press (2020)
9. Li, M.-H., Sasaki, J.: A method for recommending individually appropriate and attractive travel destinations for tourists using profile data. In: IEEE PIC 2021, pp. 248–252 (2021)
10. Kitsuya, M., Sasaki, J.: Real-time mapping system of evacuation shelter conditions for safe evacuation. In: Springer Nature Singapore, Emerging Technology Practice Cases and Theories for Disaster Resilience, Disaster Risk Reduction Methods, Approaches and Practices, pp. 229–239 (2021)
11. Kitsuya, M., Sasaki, J.: Development of regional information sharing system (RISS) for disaster prevention and evacuation. Inf. Syst. Front. (2020). ISSN 1387-3326
12. Kitsuya, M., Sasaki, J.: Proposal of an evacuation support system for regional disasters and its evaluation using multi-agent simulation. In: Information Technology in Disaster Risk Reduction (ITDRR), IFIP AICT, vol. 575, pp. 45–54. Springer (2020). ISSN 1868-4238
13. Ritchie, B.W., Zhang, Y.: Reviewing research on tourism risk, crisis, and disaster management: launching a curated collection of annals of tourism research on tourism risk, crisis, and disaster management. Ann. Tourism Res. **79**, 102812 (2019)
14. Yoh, K., Okamoto, T., Inoi, H., Doi, K.: Comparative study on foreign drivers' characteristics using traffic violation and accident statistics in Japan. IATSS Res. **41**, 94–105 (2017)

15. Yoh, K., Doi, K., Inoi, H.: A study on foreign drivers' deceleration behavior and traffic accident risk in Japanese popular sightseeing region. In: Proceedings of Eastern Asia Society for Transportation Studies, vol.12 (2019)
16. Sato, K., Okamoto, K., Miyao, M.: Japan, moving towards becoming a multi-cultural society, and the way of disseminating multilingual disaster information to non-Japanese speakers. In: IWIC 2009, pp. 51–60 (2009)
17. Gester, J., Boret, S.P., Morimoto, R., Gordon, A., Shibayama, A.: The potential of disaster digital archives in disaster education: the case of Japan disasters digital archive (JDA) and its geo-location functions. Int. J. Disaster Risk Reduction **77**, 103085 (2022)
18. Japan Disaster Information Page by the Cabinet Office: Disaster Management - Cabinet Office. bousai.go.jp
19. Example of a disaster preparedness app for travel (Safety Tips). https://www.rcsc.co.jp/safety-tips-en
20. Disaster information page of the Union of Kansai Governments: Union of Kansai Governments Wide-area Disaster Prevention Portal Site/Union of Kansai Governments. kouiki-kansai.jp
21. Hokkaido Disaster Prevention Information Portal Site: Hokkaido Disaster Prevention Portal. bousai-hokkaido.jp
22. Kumamoto Prefecture's multilingual disaster prevention information portal site: Disaster prevention brochure (easy Japanese, English, Chinese, Korean, Vietnamese) - Kumamoto homepage for foreign inhabitants. transer.com
23. Ministry of Foreign Affairs of Japan. https://www.anzen.mofa.go.jp/od/ryojiMailDetail.html?keyCd=150731
24. Ministry of Foreign Affairs of Japan. https://www.anzen.mofa.go.jp/od/ryojiMailDetail.html?keyCd=139998
25. Ministry of Land, Infrastructure, Transport and Tourism; Stock effects and flow effects (in Japanese). https://www.mlit.go.jp/sogoseisaku/infra/content/001706051.pdf
26. Kyoto Online Tourist Information Center. https://kyonavi.kyoto.travel/en/
27. Visit Tochigi. https://www.visit-tochigi.com/discover-tochigi/
28. von Goodwin, H.: Overtourism: Cases, Symptoms and Treatment, Tourisms Wissen – quarterly, pp. 110–114 (2019)

The Iberian Orca Interaction Crisis: Disentangling Wild Marine and Human Lives—A Call for Managed Co-existence

Hans J. Scholl(✉)

University of Washington, Seattle, USA
jscholl@uw.edu

Abstract. First observed in 2020, a phenomenon of increasingly damaging proportions has surfaced in need of both emergency managers and seafarers' attention: Some members of the Iberian Residential Orca population have been interacting with and damaging human-operated seagoing vessels mainly in the Western entrance to the Strait of Gibraltar and the Gulf of Cádiz as well as along vast stretches of the Atlantic Iberian coastline. So far, no human losses have been recorded despite the sinking of several sailboats by these orcas. However, it appears only as matter of When rather than of If that such fatalities will be recorded, which will then transfer this particular wild-animal-human interaction onto a new level of urgency and directly into the realm of emergency management. As an effective self-help mechanism, recreational sailors have created social-media groups, which report the location of orca sightings and interactions in almost real time. Local authorities in Portugal, Morocco, and Spain are also on the alert providing advice to the fishing and recreational sailing communities. In this article, a multidisciplinary approach is undertaken that aims at improving the situational awareness of both emergency responders and sailing/fishing communities. It further attempts to identify a pathway towards developing appropriate measures of preparedness, mitigation, response, and recovery.

Keywords: Emergency management · safety at sea · wildlife protection · Orcinus orca · killer whales · Iberian cetaceans · blue-fin tuna · orca attack patterns · situational awareness and preparedness · attack prevention · attack mitigation · attack response · recovery from attack · legal and illegal countermeasures · common operating picture · Madrid workshop · resilience

1 Introduction

1.1 The Orca/Human Interaction Crisis

Orca-human interactions in the waters around the Western Iberian Peninsula must nowadays be seen as a severe emergency and safety crisis in the making. This particularly human-centric view reflects current and future effects on human life and safety at sea; however, on part of the wild animals this crisis might be equally, or even more, severe, which adds to the complexity of adequately managing the situation at hand.

Published by Springer Nature Switzerland AG 2026
W. Seböck et al. (Eds.): ITDRR 2024, IFIP AICT 752, pp. 257–275, 2026.
https://doi.org/10.1007/978-3-031-97115-0_17

The Iberian Residential Orca population has recently been classified as a "critically endangered species" [1], and it is highly protected by both Spanish [2] and Portuguese [3, 4] laws and regulations. Local and international teams have researched whale populations of the Mediterranean Sea and the Eastern Atlantic for decades.

Historically, orcas and humans coexisted relatively peacefully in Iberian and Mediterranean waters. Ancient accounts, such as those by Strabo [5] and Philostratus [6], depict orcas as large and powerful creatures, but their interactions with humans were infrequent and largely benign. Only one exception is found in historical records: In the Bosporus and adjacent waters near Constantinople during the reign of emperor Justinian (527–565 CE), a single large whale known under the name of Porphyrios scared fishermen and seafarers by indiscriminately attacking and sinking numerous fishing and merchant vessels in the span of half a century. Justinian found himself pushed to mobilize Eastern Roman naval forces to find and kill the animal in order to reestablish safety at sea, however, to no avail. The wild animal finally stranded in pursuit of a dolphin unable to retreat from the mud to the safety of open waters, when it was hauled ashore by humans and killed. So far it has not been confidently established that Porphyrios was a supersized orca, although its mammal-hunting behavior serves as an indicator [7]. With this one exception, these early observations suggest that orcas posed little threat to maritime activities, and their presence was more perceived as a curiosity rather than a danger.

However, the contemporary situation paints a starkly different picture. While some Iberian orcas have interacted with fishing vessels for the better part of three decades, sailboats and other non-fishing-related smaller boats, both professional and pleasure, only became targets as late as May of 2020 [8, 9]. Interactions between orcas and human-operated vessels have since escalated dramatically, leading to significant damage and even the sinking of several sailboats [9]. While no human fatalities have been reported so far, the increasing frequency and intensity of these interactions suggest that such an outcome is only a matter of time. The situation has reached a critical juncture, necessitating immediate attention from emergency management professionals and the maritime community.

1.2 Measures to Increase Situational Awareness

Sailors have reacted by forming self-help groups via Social Media channels (groups on Telegram, Facebook, as well as dedicated websites), which report sightings and interactions in real-time inside the community. Also, research groups and governmental and non-governmental organizations have been providing online information to seafarers.

In October of 2022, the website orcas.pt began logging and showing incidents/interactions of sailing vessels with orcas in the Atlantic waters of the Western Iberian Peninsula including the Strait of Gibraltar (SoG). In May of 2023, when incidents and interactions had become more frequent, a Telegram chat channel ("Orcas Locations") was established, whose membership quickly grew up close to 2,000 subscribing members. Subscribers were summoned to strictly report on orca sightings and interactions, if any, as well as provide the exact location along with photo evidence, if possible. Later, another Telegram chat channel was established ("Orca Discussions") with some 1,600 subscribing members, which allowed members to exchange experiences, provide advice, make recommendations, and discuss matters of preparedness and response.

Also, a Facebook channel was established with some 500 subscribers. The orcas.pt website and the related social media channels were recognized and awarded in November of 2023 for their contributions by the Germany-based non-government organization (NGO) Trans-Ocean e.V., which honored the organizer, Rui Alves, and the supporting marine biologist Renaud de Stephanis of CIRCE, Algeciras, Spain, for their voluntary services. Other organizations, such as the UK-based Cruising Association (https://www.theca.org.uk/orcas) are also tracking and reporting interactions (https://www.theca.org.uk/sites/all/misc/orcas/Orca-historical-interaction-location-data.pdf). In Portugal, the Instituto Hidrográfico provides overview maps and advice, which incorporates and consolidates data from the national navigational warning system (ANAV) as well as from orcas.pt and gtiberica.com. In Spain, the inter-organizational working group GT Orca Atlántica provides updates on location and makes recommendations to seafarers (https://www.orcaiberica.org/en). However, these groups and initiatives are still only loosely interconnected, and parts of the seafaring population in the danger zones are still unaware of both aforementioned recommendations as well as the orcas' real-time locations, seasonal migration paths, and avoidance tactics. In other words, situational awareness is dangerously incomplete, and matters of preparedness, mitigation tactics, response behavior in case of an attack, as well as recovery and survival procedures are not comprehensively established and trained.

Under the auspices of the Spanish Government, a workshop on the orca/human interactions was conducted in early February of 2024 that assembled 29 national and international researchers (including representatives from Morocco, Portugal, Argentina, Canada, France, Iceland, Taiwan, UK, United States, and Venezuela) as well as administrators and government officials (including members of the Spanish Coast Guard and the Portuguese Navy) who provided updated recommendations for mariners [10]. Yet, representatives from important stakeholder groups (recreational sailors, whale watch operators, and local fishermen associations) were not included in that workshop.

1.3 Context and Paper Organization

This paper aims to address this looming crisis by adopting a disaster information management perspective. While acknowledging the plight of the critically endangered Iberian orca population and the anthropogenic factors contributing to their constrained situation, the primary focus is on enhancing the safety and preparedness of fishermen and sailors (note: the terms sailors, sailboat operators, and mariners are used interchangeably throughout the article). By improving situational awareness, providing guidance on preventive measures, and outlining response and recovery strategies, this paper seeks to empower the maritime community to navigate this challenging environment more safely and effectively.

The paper is organized as follows: The next section presents the extant related literature succeeded by the methodology section and the research questions. Thereafter, the findings are presented for each research question, which then are discussed. Finally, future research avenues and concluding remarks are presented, which also detail the particular contributions of this research.

2 Literature Review

The Iberian orca population, once considered a rare visitor to the Mediterranean [11, 12], has undergone significant changes in recent decades. While early accounts portray them as infrequent and largely harmless [5, 6], contemporary research paints a more complex picture of a critically endangered population facing numerous threats [13].

The Strait of Gibraltar, a vital migratory corridor for Atlantic blue-fin tuna (ABFT), has become a focal point for orca activity. These apex predators have developed a specialized hunting technique, the "endurance-exhaustion" method, to capture these fast-swimming fish [14]. However, the decline of ABFT stocks due to overfishing has put significant pressure on the orca population, potentially leading to nutritional stress and reduced reproductive rates [15].

Human activities have further exacerbated the challenges faced by Iberian orcas. Vessel traffic, noise pollution, and chemical contamination have all been identified as contributing factors to their declining population and altered behavior [13, 16–18]. Moreover, interactions with fishing vessels, particularly the drop-line fishery targeting ABFT, have created a complex dynamic between orcas and humans [19]. While some orca pods have learned to exploit this fishery technique for easy access to larger tuna, this orca behavior has also led to conflicts with fishermen and potential risks to the smart predators themselves [20].

The complex interplay between ecological factors, anthropogenic pressures, and orca behavior has resulted in a highly differentiated social structure within the Iberian population [21]. Different pods exhibit distinct foraging strategies and social interactions, highlighting the adaptability and cultural transmission within these intelligent creatures [22]. Understanding these nuances is crucial for developing effective conservation and management strategies that address both the immediate safety concerns and the long-term viability of this critically endangered population.

As mentioned above, in February of 2024, a workshop [10] sponsored by the governments of Spain and Portugal convened in Madrid to address the escalating interactions between Iberian orcas and vessels, primarily sailboats, resulting in rudder damage and even vessel sinking. The workshop aimed to understand this phenomenon and develop management recommendations. The primary recommendation for mariners was to avoid hotspots and, in case of encounters, move away quickly towards the coast or a rescue area, while immediately alerting authorities. The use of harmful deterrents was discouraged, emphasizing their ineffectiveness and potential to reinforce the behavior. Importantly, the workshop speculated that these interactions were not aggressive but rather a fad or social behavior, likely influenced by increased prey availability and reduced lethal and hurtful interactions with fisheries.

Other recommendations included: (1) Increased cooperation and consistent advice/reporting systems across the region, along with an international advisory group to provide scientific and technical guidance; (2) improved cetacean stranding responses with rapid necropsies by specialized experts to understand causes of death; (3) Consolidation of existing datasets and research proposals to understand orca movements, vessel overlap, and behavioral variations; (4) development of a Conservation Management Plan for the critically endangered Iberian orca population, considering national plans and involving range states and relevant bodies; and (5) a comprehensive communications strategy targeting all stakeholders, emphasizing the non-aggressive nature of interactions and providing clear guidance on avoidance and mitigation measures [10].

While the workshop emphasized the urgency of addressing this issue through a multifaceted approach, combining research, mitigation, and education to protect both mariners and the endangered Iberian orca population, it remained unclear what actions were supposed to be taken by whom, and how the funding of whatever actions and measures would be secured. Moreover, notably absent from the workshop were key stakeholders: sailboat operators/mariners, whale watch operators, and fishermen (through their respective local organizations), as well as the Portuguese and Moroccan Coast Guards, potentially limiting the perspectives considered.

The absence of both mariners' self-help groups and whale watch operators and their datasets from this workshop is particularly concerning since the vast majority of sighting/interaction data along with photographic documentation has been collected in real time by these stakeholder groups. As Díaz López and colleague observed [23], Citizen Science is essential for marine conservation by providing a large amount of data that help understand marine life and their environments. Mobile technology, especially smartphones and apps, has made it easier for volunteers to collect and share observations. Such collaborative approach generates massive datasets and allows for data collection on a much larger scale than would be possible otherwise [23]. Other Iberian orca-related research has equally heavily relied on datasets mostly provided by Citizen Scientists [17, 18].

3 Methodology and Research Questions

3.1 Research Questions

Based on the review of the literature on wild animal behavior, official recommendations, and the still pending integration of crisis management efforts, the location data collected by sailboat operators' self-help groups and their discussions of preparedness and mitigation measures, as well as response and recovery approaches are important sources of data. In this study a combined dataset of anonymized chat protocols of the "Orca Locations" and "Orca Discussions" Telegram groups is used:

Research Question #1 (RQ #1): *How has the Telegram/orcas.pt group contributed to sailors' situational awareness regarding actual locations of orcas?*
Research Question #2 (RQ #2): *According to the "Discussions," how has the Telegram/orcas.pt sailor self-help group adjusted their behavior and understanding relative to the group's evolved situational awareness?*

3.2 Conceptual Instruments

This study has been conducted by employing the so-called "information perspective," which is a human actor and human action-centric approach to investigating challenges of coordination procedures, processes, and structures as facilitators of human information needs, information behaviors, and information flows, which then lead to decision and actions. In crisis management, when looking at challenges in terms of coordination and collaboration, the information perspective allows a detailed investigation of actions and interactions of responders and communities as they are mediated via the existing and emerging information infrastructures and their various aforementioned elements [24, 25]. In the context of this study, the concept of Information Infrastructures is particularly relevant as it helps understand the effectiveness of communication and information-sharing practices among sailors responding to orca interactions. The principles of redundancy, resourcefulness, robustness, and rapidity as advanced in [25] have been used to analyze how the two Telegram Orcas Locations and Discussions groups have developed strategies to manage and mitigate orca-related risks, contributing to the overall resilience of the sailing community in the face of escalating incidents.

3.3 Data Selection and Analysis

Data Selection, Extraction, and Preparation. In this study the anonymized chat protocols of the "Orca Locations" and "Orca Discussions" Telegram groups have been used as complete datasets. The data range of extracted chat data ranged from the start date in May of 2023 to the end of July of 2024. The data were anonymized.

Data Analysis. The researcher who is member of the two Telegram groups conducted a chronological and thematic context analysis identifying major observations, topical threads, concerns, and their occurrence and reoccurrence over the 14 months of chat history. Along the lines of [25] the researcher also identified aspects of information infrastructure redundancy, resourcefulness, robustness, and rapidity (that is, for example, how fast did the community react to a given interaction). The researcher performed a careful manual read-through the entire dataset to get a feel for the overall conversation and to identify potential themes. Thereafter, a subset of the data was manually coded, labeling individual messages with relevant keywords and categories. This manual coding helped develop a preliminary understanding of the major themes and patterns in the discussions. Based on this manual coding automated techniques (Python) were then used to analyze the entire dataset. The Natural Language Toolkit (NLTK) was utilized for text preprocessing tasks such as tokenization, stemming, and lemmatization. Gensim then was used for topic modeling, specifically the Latent Dirichlet Allocation (LDA) algorithm, to identify clusters of words that frequently appeared together in the messages. This helped identify the major topics of discussion and to group messages into relevant categories. TextBlob was used for sentiment analysis, specifically the PatternAnalyzer algorithm to assess the overall tone and sentiment of the discussions. This way emotional responses of the sailors to the orca interactions were captured, and patterns in sailors' reactions were identified. This content analysis was an iterative process, with manual and automated techniques informing each other. The manual coding helped refine the automated analysis, and the automated analysis helped identify patterns that might have been missed in the manual coding. To validate the findings of the content analysis, a combination of qualitative and quantitative techniques was used, in which the coherence and relevance of the identified themes and patterns was qualitatively assessed, and the frequency and distribution of these themes and patterns was quantitatively determined across the dataset. This validation process helped ensure that the findings of the content analysis were accurate and reliable.

4 Findings

Below the findings are presented in the order of the research questions.

4.1 Ad RQ #1 (*How has the Telegram/orcas.pt group contributed to sailors' situational awareness regarding actual locations of orcas?*)

Overview. Both orcas.pt, the Telegram Orcas Locations chat group along with various smartphone apps, and the British Cruising Association (CA) provide updates on orca locations on a regular basis, the former ones almost in real time. Between the location-focused chats and apps, the updates vary in frequency and precision. The Telegram Orcas Location and Telegram Orcas Discussions groups are closely linked to the orcas.pt website. For all practical purposes, the host/owner decided early on to separate discussions from basic location information, which took members some time to absorb and respect. With growing membership numbers, both the Location and Discussions groups have seen a steady increase in daily posts, which have reached forty to sixty posts a day in peak orca season. Members therefore have to expend some time and care to stay abreast understanding the overall situation and then calibrating the information to their area of operation.

While the website orcas.pt provides a frequently updated overview of orca location information, here and for presentation purposes only, the Cruising Association's overview (see Fig. 1) is used, which offers compact insights into the trends of frequency and distribution of sailor-reported orca interactions with sailboats across different regions around the Iberian Peninsula from 2020 to July 2024.

	January					February					March					April					May					June				
	2020	2021	2022	2023	2024	2020	2021	2022	2023	2024	2020	2021	2022	2023	2024	2020	2021	2022	2023	2024	2020	2021	2022	2023	2024	2020	2021	2022	2023	2024
Marbella - Gibraltar	#	0	0	0	0	#	0	0	0	0	#	0	0	0	0	#	0	0	0	0	#	0	0	0	0	#	0	0	0	0
Gibraltar - Cadiz / Tangier	#	0	3	3	0	#	2	1	3	2	#	1	0	3	1	#	7	8	10	5	#	2	8	20	21	#	13	13	21	11
Cadiz - Cabo S Vicente (Sagres)	#	0	0	1	0	#	1	0	0	0	#	0	1	1	1	#	0	0	2	1	#	0	0	1	2	#	6	5	13	4
Cabo S Vicente - Cascais	#	0	0	0	1	#	0	0	3	1	#	0	0	1	2	#	0	0	0	0	#	0	0	0	1	#	2	1	0	6
Cascais - Viana do Castelo	#	0	0	0	0	#	0	0	0	0	#	0	0	1	1	#	0	0	1	0	#	0	0	0	0	#	0	0	0	0
Viana do Castelo - Galicia coasts	#	0	0	0	0	#	1	0	0	0	#	0	0	0	0	#	0	0	0	4	#	0	0	0	0	#	0	0	0	2
Bay of Biscay	#	0	0	0	0	#	0	0	0	0	#	0	0	0	0	#	0	0	0	0	#	0	0	0	0	#	0	0	0	0
Tangier towards Atlantic Islands	#	1	0	0	0	#	0	0	0	0	#	0	0	0	0	#	0	0	0	0	#	0	0	0	0	#	0	0	0	0
Total per month per year	0	1	3	4	1	0	4	1	6	3	0	1	1	6	5	0	7	8	13	10	0	2	8	21	24	0	21	19	34	23
Total per month overall	9					14					13					38					55					97				

	July					August					September					October					November					December				
	2020	2021	2022	2023	2024	2020	2021	2022	2023	2024	2020	2021	2022	2023	2024	2020	2021	2022	2023	2024	2020	2021	2022	2023	2024	2020	2021	2022	2023	2024
Marbella - Gibraltar	0	0	0	11	0	0	2	0	1	-	0	0	0	0	-	0	0	0	1	-	0	0	0	0	-	0	0	0	0	-
Gibraltar - Cadiz / Tangier	6	36	1	20	15	0	24	1	4	-	0	0	0	0	-	0	0	1	2	-	0	0	0	4	-	0	0	0	0	-
Cadiz - Cabo S Vicente (Sagres)	0	0	0	2	0	2	0	0	3	-	0	8	0	1	-	0	0	3	0	-	0	0	0	1	-	0	0	0	0	-
Cabo S Vicente - Cascais	0	0	3	1	0	5	0	3	6	-	0	9	2	5	-	4	4	6	0	-	2	0	6	2	-	0	0	2	1	-
Cascais - Viana do Castelo	0	0	3	0	0	0	0	0	0	-	0	9	2	2	-	2	0	1	1	-	0	2	0	1	-	0	0	0	2	-
Viana do Castelo - Galicia coasts	0	4	6	5	0	2	0	28	10	-	20	2	12	4	-	2	7	0	3	-	0	0	4	0	-	0	0	0	0	-
Bay of Biscay	0	1	3	1	2	0	0	7	4	-	0	1	1	3	-	0	0	2	0	-	0	0	0	0	-	0	0	0	0	-
Tangier towards Atlantic Islands	0	0	0	0	0	0	0	0	0	-	0	0	0	0	-	0	0	0	0	-	0	0	1	1	-	0	0	0	0	-
Total per month per year	6	41	16	40	17	9	26	39	28	0	20	29	17	15	0	8	11	13	7	0	2	2	11	9	0	0	0	2	3	0
Total per month overall	120					102					81					39					24					5				

Fig. 1. Cruising Association, July 2024 - Orca - historical interaction location data around the Iberian Peninsula—www.theca.org.uk/orcas

The majority of interactions, including both sightings and attacks, are concentrated in the Gibraltar-Cadiz/Tangier region. This area has consistently experienced a high number of interactions throughout the years, indicating its significance as a hotspot for orca activity. The Cadiz-Cabo S Vicente (Sagres) region also shows a notable increase in interactions, particularly in 2023 and 2024. This may suggest a potential shift or an expansion in orca activity towards this area. The Cabo S Vicente-Cascais region has also seen a steady increase in interactions, particularly in 2023 and 2024. In contrast, regions such as Marbella-Gibraltar, Cascais-Viana do Castelo, Viana do Castelo-Galicia coasts, Bay of Biscay, and Tangier towards Atlantic Islands have experienced relatively fewer interactions. The Bay of Biscay stands out with a very low number of interactions, indicating a limited presence of orcas in this area.

The data also reveal a concerning trend of increasing interactions over time. The total number of interactions per month has risen significantly from 2020 to 2024, with a particularly sharp increase observed in 2023 and the first half of 2024. The months of May through October appear to be the most active period for orca interactions, suggesting a seasonal pattern in their behavior.

Table 1. Orca-sunk Sailboats as of July 31, 2024

Sailboat Name/Flag	Date of Incident	Time of Incident	Location	Damage	# Humans (Perished/Rescued)	Type of Keel/length (m)
Name not known/P	31-Jul-22	1200 h	Cabo S Vicente /Cascais	Sunk (Sines, P)	(0/5)	Mono/10.2 m
Smousse/F	1-Nov-22	1200 h	Galicia	Sunk (Viana do Castelo, ES)	(0/4)	Fin w/bulb & spade rudder/12 m
Champagne/CH	4-May-23	0550 h	SoG	Sunk (Barbate, ES)	(0/5)	Mono/15 m
Grazie Mamma II/PL	31-Oct-23	2300 h	SoG	Sunk (Tangier-Med, Morocco)	(0/6)	Mono/13.4 m
Alboran Cognac/ES	12-May-24	0943 h	SoG	Sunk (near Tangier, Morocco)	(0/2)	Mono/15.75 m
Bonhomie William, GB	26-Jul-24	2200 h	SoG	Sunk (near Barbate, ES)	(0/3)	Mono/12 m

Overall, while the Cruising Association's overview provides valuable information about the spatial and temporal distribution of orca interactions around the Iberian Peninsula over time, the Telegram Orcas Location chat channel provides almost real-time updates, which are daily consolidated in orcas.pt maps with monthly breakdowns of interaction locations. The data highlight a certain seasonality pattern with areas of highest orca activity during certain months when sailors have to exercise increased caution. It is noteworthy that despite the increasing situational awareness on part of at least the self-help group members, interactions with serious outcomes (including sinking of sailboats) are on the rise. The increasing trend in interactions underscores the need for continued research and the development of effective mitigation strategies to ensure the safety of both sailors and orcas. As Table 1 shows, each year since 2022, at least two sailboats were sunk as a result of orca interaction, most of which occurred in the Strait of Gibraltar (SoG).

Summary of Findings (ad RQ#1). The Telegram Orcas Locations chat log provides near-real-time information on orca sightings, interactions, and also absence of such occurrences, which in turn is compiled into historical interaction location data presented at orcas.pt or the CA' overview (Chart 1). A strict separation of orca location-related information only and certain, but limited, follow-up exchanges appears to have become the Locations group's norm. However, while the location focus has cleaned up the chat channel from noise, it also demonstrates the need for further informational and contextual exchanges, which add to deeper understanding of the seafaring challenge at hand. The chat log also highlights the importance of community-driven information sharing and collaboration in mitigating the risks associated with these encounters.

4.2 Ad RQ #2 *(According to the "Discussions," how has the Telegram/orcas.pt sailor self-help group adjusted their behavior and understanding relative to the group's evolved situational awareness?)*

The discussions in the Telegram Orcas Discussions chat channel reveal an evolving dialogue among sailors and marine enthusiasts regarding the increasing frequency and severity of orca interactions with vessels, particularly in the Strait of Gibraltar and surrounding areas.

Orca Attack Frequency and Locations. The group members actively shared information about orca attacks and sightings, including the date, time, and location of each incident. The frequency of attacks varied throughout the 14 months, with periods of increased activity followed by periods of relative calm (see Chart 1) probably due to both seasonal migratory passing of orcas and lower frequencies of sailboat passing by known hotspots. As seen, while the attacks were concentrated in certain of these hotspots, primarily around the Strait of Gibraltar and the coast of Portugal and Spain, the Telegram Orcas Discussion group also discussed the possibility of orcas expanding their range and attacking boats in other areas.

Attack Countermeasures and Self-defense. Animated discussions flared up occasionally about the right to (violent?) self-defense. Said one member in response,

> "There is no law that denies me the right to defend myself if I consider my life to be in imminent danger. No Spanish law, no Portuguese law, no American law, no European law. None. It matters not what is putting my life in imminent danger." <quote #01>

And another member responded,

> "The legal case for self-defense is strong, but only if lives are at stake, not if property is at stake. I may be wrong, but I think 0 sailors have died so far due to "interactions" from orcas?" <quote #02>

Various strategies for deterring orca attacks were discussed, including using noise-making devices such as pingers, oikomi pipes, and underwater firecrackers, deploying sand or other substances in the water, and modifying the boat's rudder, or other underwater appendages. The effectiveness of these countermeasures was debated, with some members reporting success and others expressing skepticism:

> "We [have been] using the pinger since Biscay. Currently we are in Lisbon on the way to Almerimar. We put 6 kg diving weights on the pinger with 5m rope to keep it in about 1m depth [at] 5 knots speed. We have had no Orca interaction, and we have [heard] from only one case where a boat with pinger was attacked." <quote #03>
>
> "The general opinion is that pingers don't work. There are boats attacked with pingers, and there are some studies that proves that they don't work." <quote #04>

The legality of some of these measures, particularly the use of underwater firecrackers, was also a topic of discussion.

Sightings and Interaction Behavior. Members shared their observations of orca behavior, including the wild animals' movements, feeding patterns, and interactions with boats. They also discussed the possibility of orcas communicating with each other and learning new behaviors, such as attacking rudders. A range of emotions towards the orcas was expressed, from fear and frustration to admiration and respect:

> "I wan[t] to sail and cruise the coast of Portugal for fun this summer. I am starting to have 2nd thoughts. Doesn't sound like fun to live in fear of being attacked." <quote #05>
>
> "We are all smart human beings and we live the seas and all that is in it. I figure therefore we can find a solution that does not hurt these stunningly beautiful animals." <quote #06>

Speculations About Orca Attack Motivation. The group members discussed various theories about why orcas were attacking boats, including the possibility that they were just playing, or practicing hunting techniques, or protecting their territory.

> "They play also with the propeller and use it as a spa. We have several underwater videos with such a behavior." <quote #07>

The group also discussed the potential impact of human activities, such as fishing and shipping, on orca behavior. The lack of a definitive answer to this question was a source of frustration for many members.

Recommendations and Good Practices. Advice was shared on how to minimize the risk of orca attacks, including staying in shallow water inside the 20m bathymetric line, avoiding fishing areas, and being prepared to take evasive action if necessary. The group also discussed the importance of reporting orca sightings and attacks to the authorities and to the orcas.pt platform. Also emphasized was the importance of responsible sailing practices and respecting the orcas' natural habitat. This following exchange between two members illustrates this particular notion,

> "...Humans think they are above them. Apparently, humans made them starting attack boats. The ocean is their habitat and feeding zone. So, if we can use it both by simply avoiding them, what's the problem?" <quote #08>
>
> "I want to sail as well. But I do think avoiding the orcas is a better solution instead of being stubborn and have a god complex [and] go- straight through the area where they are fishing, and then think I have the right to harm them." <quote #09>

Technology in Orca Monitoring and Mitigation. The use of technology was discussed, such as tagging animals and using GPS trackers as well as acoustic deterrents, to monitor and deter orca interactions. Members also discussed the potential benefits and challenges of using such technologies. The development of new technologies, including the Orcinus app, was seen as a positive step towards improving the safety of both sailors and orcas. However, one member also reported concerns,

> "Interesting to see that the platforms displaying the maps differ from each other. Also, interesting that in Orcinus you can see info about the interaction but in GT orcas you can only see the date. I like the map display of Orcinus but I'm missing more updates." <quote #10>

Government Authorities in Addressing the Orca/Human Interaction Issue. The group members discussed the role of government agencies and also research organizations in addressing the orca/human interaction issue. Some members expressed frustration with the lack of action by the authorities, while others emphasized the importance of collaboration between sailors, scientists, and policymakers to find effective solutions. Said one member,

> "[Governments] do not seem to do their job by completely ignoring an obvious problem and danger to humans." <quote #11>
>
> And another stated,
>
> "It seems necessary that some important politician or government minister would be interested in supporting our class of sailors and obtaining state funds and resources to find a solution to these "interactions/attacks". Without government support we will forever be trying to find ways to protect ourselves but without an effective solution." <quote #12>

The work of organizations such as CIRCE and the GTOA was recognized as being crucial in understanding orca behavior and developing mitigation strategies.

These were *major and recurring* discussion topics that arose in the Orcas Discussion group over the 14 months. The conversations were often lively and passionate, reflecting the complex and challenging nature of the orca/human interaction issue. Most group members demonstrated a strong commitment to finding solutions that would benefit both sailors and orcas, and their discussions provided valuable insights into the challenges and opportunities associated with orca/human interactions.

Apart from the major discussion topics above, several other interesting and relevant subtopics emerged during the 14-month period:

Media and Public Perception. Frequently discussed was how the media portrays orca interactions and the impact of this portrayal on public perception of both orcas and sailors. There was concern that sensationalized reporting could lead to negative consequences for both groups. Members also discussed the importance of educating the public about orcas and promoting responsible sailing practices.

Orca Interactions Impact. The economic impact of orca interactions on the sailing and tourism industries in the Iberian Peninsula was discussed in lively exchanges. Concerns were raised that the fear of orca attacks could deter sailors from visiting the area and negatively impact local businesses. As seen reported before, likewise in this particular context the need was discussed for government support to address the orca/human interaction issue and mitigate its economic impact.

Ethics. Discussants also engaged in lively debates about the ethics and legality of using various deterrents and mitigation measures, such as firecrackers and other more assertive measures, which could potentially create discomfort in the wild animals. Some members argued that these measures were necessary to protect boats and crews, while others expressed grave concern about the potential harm to orcas and the environment. Again, the legality of these measures was also a topic of discussion, with some members arguing that they were justified under the principle of self-defense.

Collaboration and Information Sharing. Sailors, scientists, and policymakers it was discussed had to collaborate and share information to address the orca/human interaction issue. The orcas.pt platform was seen as a valuable tool for facilitating this collaboration and providing sailors with up-to-date information about orca activity. The group members showed much interest for more research to better understand orca behavior and develop effective mitigation strategies.

Need for Coexistence. Some members shared stories of positive encounters with orcas, while others expressed concern about the high potential for conflict between humans and orcas. The need for coexistence between humans and orcas and the importance of finding solutions that benefit both groups appeared to prevail in the discussions.

Adjustment of Group Member Behavior. While members appeared to be split over the nature of preferred self-defense measures (aggressive/non-aggressive), they seemed to converge on the "stay-inside-the-20m-bathymetric-line" recommendation whenever safely possible. However, group members also adjusted their behavior in terms of postings to the two Telegram chat channels. In members' chat behavioral adjustment, Rui Alves, the moderator has played a decisive role in admonishing and cajoling members into, for example, staying away from offensive speech and politics and focusing rather sharply on location information for sightings and interactions, and for orca/human interaction-related discussions, which made the two chat channels readable and maintainable despite its constantly growing membership numbers.

Information Dissemination. The moderator consistently and proactively shared updates on orca sightings, attacks, and research findings, often drawing from various sources, including direct communication with sailors, researchers, and authorities. He also created and maintained the orcas.pt website, which served as a central repository for information about orcas, including maps, safety protocols, and educational resources.

Research Collaboration and Advocacy. The moderator actively collaborated with researchers, such as Renaud de Stephanis from CIRCE, also a member of both Telegram groups, to gather and disseminate accurate information about orca behavior and develop effective mitigation strategies. Also, both the moderator and de Stephanis advocated for increased government support and action to address the orca/human interaction issue and ensure the safety of both sailors and orcas.

Community Building and Support. The moderator further fostered a strong sense of community among the group members, encouraging them to share their experiences, offer support to each other, and work together to find solutions. He also organized events and initiatives, such as the "one flag one member" project, to strengthen the bonds within the community and promote awareness of the orca/human interaction issue.

In summary, the moderator played a multifaceted and indispensable role in the Telegram chat groups. Clear dedication, moderating leadership, and unwavering commitment to the safety of both sailors and orcas were instrumental in creating a widely appreciated platform for information sharing, collaboration, and community building. While no scientific proof can be provided it is highly likely that the moderator's efforts have contributed to reducing the number of orca incidents and to promoting a more harmonious coexistence between humans and orcas in the marine environment.

Summary of Findings (ad RQ#2). Over time the Telegram/orcas.pt sailor self-help group has adjusted its behavior and understanding of orca/human interactions in several ways. Members actively share information about attacks and sightings, discuss countermeasures and orca behavior, and speculate about motivations behind the interactions. The group also shares recommendations for minimizing risks (<20 m rule) and emphasizes the importance of reporting incidents and responsible sailing. Technology for monitoring and mitigation has been embraced. The moderator has been found crucial in shaping group behavior, information dissemination, research collaboration, advocacy, and community building.

5 Discussion, Recommendations, and Concluding Remarks

Lack of a Common Operating Picture. While platforms like orcas.pt, the two Telegram groups, GTOA, Orcinus, the Cruising Association, and various Portuguese and Spanish government agencies all provide updates of various kinds and at various frequencies on the orca/human interaction issue around the Iberian Peninsula, these efforts have not yet amounted to what has been defined as a Common Operating Picture (COP) as defined below.

> "A common operation picture (COP) is a continuously updated overview of an incident compiled throughout an incident's life cycle from data shared between integrated communication, information management, and intelligence and information sharing systems. The goal of a COP is real-time situational awareness across all levels of incident management and across jurisdictions" (https://www.dhs.gov/publication/common-operating-picture-emergency-responders - accessed Aug 1, 2024).

Sometimes it appears as if these information services rather compete for attention than collaborate on the issue by cross-verifying and vetting the information available to them. What may help overcome this situation is an inter-governmentally sponsored and staffed clearing house/pilot center (for example, jointly funded by the European Union, Morocco, Portugal, and Spain), which systematically collects, verifies, and disseminates relevant information to all stakeholders (including sailors, fishermen, whale watch operators, conservationists, marine biologists among others) in real time. Sailboat operators that enter national waters of Iberian and Moroccan waters may need to be required to install and constantly operate Automatic Identification System (AIS) equipment. In this way, it would not only be the mariners' duty to manage their own passage according to available information, but the pilot center could also send targeted warnings to individual vessels in case of orca sightings and interactions including no-passage warnings. Moreover, such clearing house/pilot center could be connected to a to-be-installed network of passive acoustic monitoring devices as has been used in the Pacific Northwest (see https://www.fisheries.noaa.gov/alaska/marine-mammal-protection/passive-acoustic-monitoring-marine-mammals-alaska—accessed Aug 1, 2024). This might not only greatly help reduce the number of satellite tags necessary for marking (while potentially compromising the health [17] of) Iberian orcas, but rather also benefit both marine scientists and seafarers in their respective endeavors alike. Orca pod locations and seasonal geographic distribution would be much better known.

The Behavioral Conundrum. This study has been undertaken from an information scientist's academic perspective (as well as that of a sailboat owner in the Bay of Cádiz). Therefore, through the lens of an academic non-expert in the disciplines of Marine Biology, Marine Wildlife Conservation, Wild-Animal Behavioral Psychology, Fishery Economics and Regulations, the following discussion is performed with much restraint, and it is rather meant to pose questions rather than provide answers.

From the extant literature (see also above literature review section) it appears that major ecological shifts have been observed in the Strait of Gibraltar (known as the zenith orca hotspot) in the past four decades. Measurably, noise [15, 26] and pollution [16] levels have increased (in dramatic and multifold fashion) over these decades. The fierce competition for resources (that is, for example, first and foremost aggressive fishing of ABFT) has also created growing contention between the orca population and humans. While some ABFT fishing quota regulations appear to have provided potentially some short-term ease of food shortages for the orca population [10, p. 4], the extended scarcity of prey appears to have affected orca reproduction rates [13] along with the aforementioned detrimental environmental factors, which ultimately led to the declaration of a "critically endangered" species [27]. It remains unchallenged that humans and orcas are direct and fierce competitors for ABFT.

The role of various human activities imposing significant stressors on orcas and other maritime wild life, in particular, in the Strait of Gibraltar, which is utilized by humans at unprecedented frequencies, must be taken into account when it comes to considering the observed behavioral changes in orca behavior. Reportedly, as early as 2000 [28], close-by whale watching had already significantly increased, which ever since has done so even more contributing to further shrinking the wild animals' habitat despite careful and unobtrusive operations on part of the whale watch operators. However, perhaps way more impactful in the last four decades, commercial and military ship movements through the Strait have been estimated to have doubled from under 60,000 to over 110,000 annual movements (see ShipsGo Blog: https://blog.shipsgo.com/strait-of-gibraltar-ship-traffic-live-map/ accessed Aug 1, 2024). Noise levels (and with them) orcas' sensory orientation capacities can therefore be assumed to be negatively affected [26]. Besides the contamination of food sources leading to exceeding concentrations in Iberian orcas, "at which severe toxic effects are known to occur" [16, p. 5], in its constrained environment the population is suffering from human equipment-inflicted injuries (propellers, fishing lines, gun-shot wounds, among others) as well as observable diseases (emaciation, skin diseases, etc.) [17, 18]. However, despite all protective laws and conservationist regulations, the most-deadly interaction for orcas still remains the interaction with fishing vessels. From the known Iberian orca pods (A1, A2, B, C, D, E, F) it was the A pods who reportedly were the first to opportunistically prey on ABFT caught by fishermen on long lines since the mid 1990s. Orcas were "stealing" some 17 percent of the catch [12]. Both Spanish and Moroccan fishermen reacted with indignation culling eight orcas in 2004/2005 [12]. It is unclear to the non-expert whether or not this enormous extraction can be attributed to the splitting of the A pod into the A1 and A2 pods. Officially, through various laws, orca culling had become illegal in 2007. Esteban's Iberian Orca catalogue lists the aforementioned pods' ancestral lineages up to 2023 [29]. Per animal, the catalogue reports on interaction behavior (fishing boat only, fishing boat and sailboats, sailboats only, and no interaction). It is interesting to notice that although sighted and identified near vessels three pods have had no interaction with humans whatsoever (the C, D, and E pods).

Between 2010 (when the catalogue's tracking started) and 2023, the non-interacting pods had a mortality rate of 18 percent, that is, 2 of 11 individuals deceased. However, the F pod consisting of 5 individuals has no known mortality since its detection. Sixty percent (3 F pod animals) are known to interact with sailboats but not with fishing boats. The mortality numbers change dramatically when looking at the A1, A2, and B pods, which reportedly interact with fishing vessels and actively prey on caught ABFT from fishing lines. According to the Esteban catalogue, in the A1 pod, of 12 individuals 5 disappeared or were found dead (that is, a 42 percent death rate). Among the deceased orcas 1 juvenile individual had not had any interaction with fishing boats, while the four others had. None of these deceased animals had any interaction with sailboats. In the A2 pod of 17 individuals, 6 orcas disappeared or were found dead (that is, a 35 percent death rate). Of the 6 deceased individuals, 5 had interactions with fishing vessels only, and not with sailboats, and the 1 deceased individual with no interaction was a juvenile. The B pod originally had 6 individuals, of which 3 have meanwhile deceased (that is, a 50 percent death rate). All 3 deceased B pod individuals interacted with fishing boats only, and not with sailboats. A total of 9 alive members of the A1 and A2 pods and 1 alive member of the B pod interact with both fishing vessels and sailboats. The high mortality in the A1, A2, and B pods is striking when compared to that in the C, D, and E pods that do not interact with fishing vessels. Likewise, the F pod that only interacts with sailboats has even a mortality rate of zero. It is therefore hard to make the case that contact with fishing vessels (that is, orcas' preying on, or "stealing," fishermen's catches) should be considered totally unrelated to the respective A1, A2, and B pods' extremely high mortality rates since 2010.

The Theories on Orcas' Changed Behavior. Various theories have been offered (playing, fad, juvenile hunter training, malice, and revenge among others). This study is not in a position to support or refute any of these theories However, anthropomorphic explanations of wild animal behavior have repeatedly been called into question by wild animal behavioral scientists, for example, Galef ("it is probably best for scientists to be conservative, to adopt the simplest descriptions and explanations of behavioral phenomena consistent with available evidence") [30, p. 158]. Given the documented pressures and stressors in a shrinking habitat, an increasingly aggressive reaction on part of a group of endangered wild animals does not appear as overly far-fetched when observed through the lens of a non-expert colleague from elsewhere in academia.

Stakeholder Tensions. Stakeholders in this orca/human interaction issue have fairly different levels of salience [31] and resulting stances [32]. As outlined before, so far not all stakeholders have been engaged and integrated in pursuit of a balanced solution, which would have the prospects to successfully disentangle the increasingly dangerous situation. While the February 2024 Madrid workshop convened 29 academic and administrative experts from around the world, it missed out on including important stakeholders (sailboat operators, whale watch operators, and local fishermen associations). Stakeholders are those who can affect and/or can be affected by policy, action, regulation, or other significant outcomes of some kind [31]. So far, marine biologists, marine wildlife conservationists, behavioral ecologists, governmental officials, and other administrators had a major say in shaping recommendations and regulations. As an example, the Madrid workshop convened 11 government officials and administrators, 7 conservation biologists, 6 ecologist and environmental scientists, and 5 marine mammal biologists. It does not even need the burden of proof to detect the inescapable implicit bias in such a composition of an expert panel and its resulting recommendations. Since the aforementioned three groups were omitted from providing their perspectives, it would have been more than surprising had their views, wants, and needs been accurately represented. But they were not. Furthermore, since some conservation biologists have publicly expressed little, if any, sympathy for the causes of the three groups (see the discussion of stakeholder stances in [32]), a balance of interests and practice-ready disentanglement as a solution for de-conflicting the unfolding orca/human interaction crisis is not in sight. From the perspective of any successful and sustainable crisis management, however, such stakeholder-negligent and top-down approaches have rather been known for their systemic failure.

Measures of preparedness, mitigation, response and recovery have been discussed in the Madrid workshop recommendation. However, crisis management experts and mariner practitioners need to develop appropriate plans, measures, and drills, which can be accepted and adopted by the seafaring communities.

Sailboat Operators' Information Infrastructures. As shown above the scientific community has already benefited from sailboat operators/mariners' self-help groups as well as from whale watch operators and their massive data collections. The mariners' current information infrastructure, despite its dispersion and lack of integration, is already providing life-saving and damage-preventing information. In the case of the Telegram groups ("Orca Locations" and "Orca Discussions") and its affiliated orcas.pt website the community has demonstrated quite some resilience, which has been defined by the four ***R's*** in [33]. In terms of ***redundancy***, through multiple communication channels and information sources, the group provides a good degree of redundancy, ensuring that critical information about orca sightings and interactions is disseminated even if one channel experiences disruptions. The group also relies on various external sources, such as the Orcinus app, marine traffic websites, and direct communication with researchers and authorities, further enhancing its redundancy. Members frequently cross-verify reports and share multiple sightings and experiences to create a comprehensive understanding of orca behavior. This redundancy in communication ensures that critical information is available even if one source is unreliable or delayed. When it comes to ***resourcefulness***, the group exhibits this particular capacity by actively seeking and developing strategies to manage orca/human interactions. This includes brainstorming sessions, sharing personal experiences, and discussing potential solutions like the use of deterrents or modifications to boat design. The group's willingness to explore new ideas and adapt its strategies in response to evolving orca behavior also demonstrates its resourcefulness. For example, recommendations to stay within the less than 20-m bathymetric line emerged as a key strategy to reduce the risk of orca encounters. This advice was reinforced by members sharing their experiences and outcomes, allowing the group to refine and disseminate effective tactics quickly. With respect to ***robustness*** the group demonstrated its ability to maintain functionality and cohesion despite challenges and disagreements. The presence of clear rules and moderation helped ensure that discussions remained focused and productive, even when faced with differing opinions or contentious topics. Despite the escalation in the severity of orca attacks, including the sinking of two more sailboats in summer of 2024, the group continued to develop and share robust non-aggressive strategies to minimize risk. Finally, in terms of ***rapidity***, the disseminate information about orca sightings and attacks had been crucial for its effectiveness in mitigating risks. The use of real-time communication platforms like Telegram has allowed for the quick sharing of critical information, enabling sailors to make informed decisions and take evasive action when necessary. Members promptly reported orca sightings, attacks, and near-misses, allowing others to make real-time decisions about their own routes and actions. This rapid dissemination of information contributes to the group's overall resilience, enabling them to respond swiftly to new threats and adjust their strategies as needed.

In summary, while still too loosely integrated and coordinated, the mariners' self-help groups and websites provide a remarkable resilience in their information infrastructure.

Conclusion and Outlook. It has been the object of this study to identify obstacles to coordination and collaboration of efforts in the response to the unfolding orca/human interaction crisis and to identify pathways for recommendations, which help mitigate the negative outcomes of those interactions for both, the wild animals and humans. In so doing, the study contributes to both the academic understanding of the complexities of managing a crisis response and to the practical understanding of measures and choices available to response planners. Marine biologists, conservationists, ecological scientists, government officials, administrators, fishermen associations, whale watch operators, sailboat operators, and their various associations will benefit massively when collaborating and more closely communicating in an integrated fashion, which will finally help produce a 24/7 authoritative common operating picture, from which all interested parties and stakeholders can draw, and which allows anticipative mitigation measures. Disentanglement may be manageable ahead of time, when datasets are better integrated and AI tools support the proactive management of sailboat passages and whale watch parties. Future investigations will follow up with assessing and evaluating the practical measures taken and the choices made by responders.

Acknowledgement. The research was possible through admittance to membership to the lead author who also benefited from numerous exchanges with the moderator of the two Telegram groups and orcas.pt.

References

1. Esteban, R., Foote, A.: Orcinus orca (Strait of Gibraltar subpopulation), Killer Whale (2024). https://www.iucnredlist.org/species/pdf/132949669
2. Real Decreto 1727/2007, de 21 de diciembre, por el que se establecen medidas de protección de los cetáceos B. O. d. Estado Standard 1727/2007 (2007)
3. Decreto-Lei nO. 263/81 de 3 de Setembro M. d. Q. d. Vida (1981)
4. Decreto-Lei nO. 9/2006 de 6 de Janeiro D. O. D. T. e. D. D. R. Ministerio do Ambiente Standard 9 (2006)
5. Strabo, "Book XV, chapter 2, section 13," The Geography of Strabo, H. C. Hamilton and W. Falconer, eds., p. 1, London: George Bell & Sons, 17
6. Philostratus, F.: The life of Apollonius of Tyana (English translation], pp. 1–4: livius.org, 238
7. Szabo, V.E.: Chapter Two. Whales and Whaling From Classical Antiquity to the Middle Ages," Monstrous Fishes and the Mead-Dark Sea, pp. 31–65: Brill (2008)
8. Esteban, R., et al.: Update on the interactions between killer whales and vessel along the Iberian Peninsula, International Whaling Commission: Subcommittee/working Group (2022)
9. Esteban, R., et al.: Killer whales of the Strait of Gibraltar, an endangered subpopulation showing a disruptive behavior. Mar. Mammal Sci. **38**(4), 1699–1709 (2022)
10. Anonymous, Workshop-Interactions Between Iberian Killer Whales and Vessels: Management Recommendations, Gobierno de España, Madrid (2024)
11. Notarbartolo-di-Sciara, G.: Killer whale, Orcinus orca, in the Mediterranean Sea. Mar. Mamm. Sci. **3**(4), 356–360 (1987)
12. Reeves, R.R., Notarbartolo di Sciara, G.: The status and distribution of cetaceans in the Black Sea and Mediterranean Sea, Malaga, Spain (2006)
13. Esteban, R., et al.: Conservation status of killer whales, Orcinus orca, in the Strait of Gibraltar. Adv. Mar. Biol. **75**, 141–172 (2016)

14. Guinet, C., Domenici, P., de Stephanis, R., Barrett-Lennard, L., Ford, J.K., Verborgh, P.: Killer whale predation on bluefin tuna: exploring the hypothesis of the endurance-exhaustion technique. Mar. Ecol. Prog. Ser. **347**, 111–119 (2007)
15. Esteban, R., Verborgh, P., Gauffier, P., Giménez, J., Guinet, C., de Stephanis, R.: Dynamics of killer whale, bluefin tuna and human fisheries in the Strait of Gibraltar. Biol. Cons. **194**, 31–38 (2016)
16. Jepson, P.D., et al.: PCB pollution continues to impact populations of orcas and other dolphins in European waters. Sci. Rep. **6**(1), 1–17 (2016)
17. Herr, H., Burkhardt-Holm, P., Heyer, K., Siebert, U., Selling, J.: Injuries, malformations, and epidermal conditions in cetaceans of the strait of gibraltar. Aquat. Mamm. **46**(2), 215–235 (2020)
18. Hanninger, E.-M., Selling, J., Heyer, K., Burkhardt-Holm, P.: Injuries in cetaceans in the strait of gibraltar: an update for the period 2016–2020. IWC **24**, 143–160 (2023)
19. de Stephanis, R., Cornulier, T., Verborgh, P., Sierra, J.S., Gimeno, N.P., Guinet, C.: Summer spatial distribution of cetaceans in the Strait of Gibraltar in relation to the oceanographic context. Mar. Ecol. Prog. Ser. **353**, 275–288 (2008)
20. Esteban, R., Verborgh, P., Gauffier, P., Giménez, J., Foote, A.D., de Stephanis, R.: Maternal kinship and fisheries interaction influence killer whale social structure. Behav. Ecol. Sociobiol. **70**(1), 111–122 (2016)
21. de Stephanis, R., Giménez, J., Esteban, R., Gauffier, P., García-Tiscar, S., Sinding, M.S., Verborgh, P.: Mobbing-like behavior by pilot whales towards killer whales: a response to resource competition or perceived predation risk? Acta Ethologica **18**, 69–78 (2015)
22. Ford, J.K.: Killer whales: behavior, social organization, and ecology of the oceans' apex predators. In: Würsig, B. (ed.) Ethology and Behavioral Ecology of Odontocetes, pp. 239–259. Springer, Cham (2019)
23. Díaz López, B., Methion, S.: Killer whales habitat suitability in the Iberian Peninsula and the Gulf of Biscay: Implications for conservation. Ocean Coast. Manag. **255**, 107245 (2024)
24. Scholl, H.J., Chatfield, A.T.: The role of resilient information infrastructures: the case of radio Fukushima during and after the 2011 eastern Japan catastrophe. Int. J. Public Adm. Digit. Age **1**(2), 1–24 (2014)
25. Scholl, H.J., Patin, B.J.: Resilient information infrastructures: criticality and role in responding to catastrophic incidents. Transform. Gov. People Process Policy **8**(1), 28–48 (2014)
26. Williams, R., Lusseau, D., Hammond, P.S.: Estimating relative energetic costs of human disturbance to killer whales (Orcinus orca). Biol. Cons. **133**(3), 301–311 (2006)
27. Esteban, R., et al.: Using a multi-disciplinary approach to identify a critically endangered killer whale management unit. Ecol. Ind. **66**, 291–300 (2016)
28. Urquiola, E., De Stephanis, R.: Growth of whale watching in Spain. The success of the platforms in south mainland, new rules. Eur. Res. Cetaceans **14**, 198–204 (2000)
29. Esteban, R.: Iberian Orca (Orcinus Orca) Photo-Identifcation Catalogue. Friendship-orca Project, Fundación Santander-CEMMA-GTOA pp. 1–81 (2023)
30. Galef, B.G.: The question of animal culture. Hum. Nat. **3**, 157–178 (1992)
31. Mitchell, R.K., Agle, B.R., Wood, D.J.: Toward a theory of stakeholder identification and salience. Defining the principle of who and what really counts. Acad. Manag. Rev. **22**(4), 853–866 (1997)
32. Blair, D.L., Whitehead, C.J.: Too many on the seesaw. Stakeholder diagnosis and management for hospitals. Hosp. Health Adm. **33**(2), 153–166 (1988)
33. Bruneau, M., et al.: A framework to quantitatively assess and enhance the seismic resilience of communities. Earthq. Spectraq. Spectra **19**(4), 733–752 (2003)

Integrating Relationality into Community Resilience: Enhancing Disaster Management Strategies

Barbara Gruber(✉)

Department for Security Studies, University for Continuing Education Krems, Dr. Karl-Dorrek-Strasse 30, 3500 Krems, Austria
Barbara.gruber@donau-uni.ac.at

Abstract. Community resilience has become a widely discussed concept in disaster management literature, as it promises to draw on the self-organization capacities of people and shifted the focus from individual and household preparedness to social networks. Relationality is important for community resilience, as community resilience depends on the relationship between institutions and local governance, as well as on the quality of the social bonds of the community members. Rather than focusing on the properties or functions of systems—as is typical in resilience research—relationality examines the relationships that constitute and drive these systems, which is important for disaster communication. This approach helps to understand how relationality can be improved to increase community resilience.

Keywords: community resilience · disaster management · relationality · information technology

1 Introduction

Community resilience has become a widely discussed concept in disaster management literature, as it promises to draw on the self-organization capacities of people and shifted the focus from individual and household preparedness to social networks [1]. It is often associated with improved information processing before, during and after disasters, as disaster communication builds on perceptions of belonging, trust and sharing [2]. This article explores through a literature review the most important factors for community resilience, focusing on relationality.

Recently, scholars [3–5] noted the relevance of relationality for disaster risk reduction, particularly with regards to community resilience. This growing interest stems, in part, from a failed assumption – namely, that strengthening resilience at the local level would automatically translate in a more resilient national community [6]. However, this assumption did not manifest itself as policy makers apparently hoped. Therefore, there was an increased interest on how relationality functions both within communities and between communities and broader organization or state structures.

Published by Springer Nature Switzerland AG 2026
W. Seböck et al. (Eds.): ITDRR 2024, IFIP AICT 752, pp. 276–289, 2026.
https://doi.org/10.1007/978-3-031-97115-0_18

Relationality is a central theme across strands of resilience research. In ecological resilience, the persistence of relationships is considered essential for system adaptability and survival [7]. In psychological resilience research, social bonds are emphasized as a critical factor in overcoming adversity [8]. Community resilience research integrates both perspectives, recognizing the interplay of ecological and social factors. This article builds on these traditions and investigates how relationality is conceptualized in community resilience literature, particularly in the context of disasters.

In this article relationality is defined as "the condition by which individuals (or groups) think and act in coherence with the web of relationships of which they are part.[9]" Rather than focusing on the properties or functions of systems—as is typical in resilience and sustainability research—relationality examines the relationships that constitute and drive these systems [10]. This perspective provides a valuable lens for understanding the dynamics of community resilience, particularly in disaster contexts.

The research question guiding this article is: How is relationality conceptualized in community resilience literature in the context of disasters? Additionally, the article explores how these conceptualizations relate to information technology. The following sections outline the conceptual foundations of relationality and community resilience, critically examining their intersections and implications for disaster risk reduction.

This literature review follows the Preferred Reporting Items for Systematic reviews and Meta-Analysis (PRISMA) methodology widely used for systematic reviews of literature. The review is based on 51 articles. In accordance with PRISMA guidelines, I conducted a systematic search for literature using the Scopus and Web of Science databases. The key search terms were "community resilience," "disaster," and "relationality." The Web of Science search yielded 33 results, while the Scopus search produced four additional results, all of which were already covered by the Web of Science findings. Since the number of hits was insufficient, I expanded the search by systematically reviewing relevant journals, focusing specifically on Resilience and Sustainable Development, which led to the identification of 17 additional relevant articles.

Next, I screened all articles, prioritizing those that conceptualized relationality and/or community resilience in alignment with the research question, with particular attention to studies incorporating both concepts. This process identified 20 articles centered on the concept of community resilience, along with three literature reviews on the topic. These articles formed the core of the literature review, as the goal was to understand how relationality is conceptualized in relation to community resilience.

During the screening process, I excluded one article because it focused on a niche theoretical perspective on poetics by Glissant, making it irrelevant to the topic [11]. I then assessed the remaining 27 articles for their relevance to information technology and/or communication, ultimately including eight. One additional article was included based on a reviewer's recommendation, bringing the total to nine.

I further screened the remaining 21 articles and excluded four due to their limited relevance to disaster resilience. One article was a short advocacy piece promoting intergenerational solidarity for rights-based disaster resilience [12]; while the topic was relevant, the format did not meet the criteria for an academic article. Another article focused on relational health and broader relationships without directly addressing community resilience [13]. Similarly, one article examined relationality in the context of land and Indigenous peoples but lacked a direct connection to disaster resilience [14]. Lastly, [15] was excluded due to its minimal focus on disasters.

The remaining 17 articles were categorized as either system-level resilience or bottom-up resilience, with two articles fitting both categories [16, 17]. In total, the review includes 22 conceptual and literature review articles, along with 17 case studies.

The article proceeds as follows: first I engage with a discussion of definitions covering the question of which resilience is meant in community resilience, defining community and discussing the normative impact of the concept community resilience (in the following CR). Subsequently, I discuss relationality on two levels: a systemic level discussing relational engagement between communities and institutions, and a bottom-up level discussing social relationships between community members. Finally, I engage with how these findings might enhance disaster communication.

2 Community and Resilience: Conceptual Clarifications

Before diving into the findings of relationality, it is important to engage with the definition of community resilience, as this already helps us to discern why relationality matters.

Like other research on resilience, also community resilience literature tends to start with the question: which resilience? Resilience rose to prominence during the past 20 years. Sociologist Ulrich Bröckling [18] even went as far as calling it the most important concept of the 21st century. The term resilience can be traced back to the Latin word "resilire", meaning to recoil. The first conceptualization of resilience can be traced to the material sciences of the 18th century [19]. In material sciences, resilience measures the quality and speed with which a material returns to its prior state, after having been exposed to a severe shock like heat. Approximately in the 1970s, when complexity thinking began to take hold and formed a new paradigm, ecology as well as psychology started to conceptualize resilience as well [20]. Worth mentioning is Buzz Holling who coined the differentiation between engineering resilience, referring to the aforementioned conceptualization of the material sciences, and ecological resilience. Ecological resilience refers to the ability of a system to respond, withstand, absorb and adapt to shocks, without changing its basic functions. The difference between engineering and ecological resilience is, that in the latter resilience is a transformation and an improvement, rather than a return to a former state [21]. As mentioned above, the persistence of relationships within a system is a key factor. However, the definition of ecological resilience is best suited to analyze systemic relationships, rather than personal ones. In psychology it was development psychology which started to engage with resilience, resulting from a study showing that some children developed remarkably normal despite severe environmental stressors [8, 22]. Subsequent studies engaged with the question which characteristics, relational and environmental factors supported the resilience of these remarkable children. Research about psychological resilience is best suited to analyze the relevance of personal relationships for resilience. To conclude, in psychology, as well as ecology, resilience is a process rather than an outcome and it is a transformation rather than a return to a status quo.

Community resilience literature merges these distinct conceptualizations, drawing on ecological as well as psychological features [23]. Community resilience definitions combine those conceptualizations to a "socio-ecological" understanding of resilience [24, 25]. This is due to the issue that ecological resilience is better equipped to understand systemic processes, to see how individuals, groups and organizations or institutions interact and how to enhance resilience on a systemic level. Psychological resilience is better equipped to understand individual and group level characteristics of resilience, like social bonds and supportive relationships. Community resilience needs to bridge both levels, as it needs to understand what connects the community, and how the community engages with other organizational levels and its environment [24]. Therefore, relationality in community resilience literature can refer to analyzing the social bonds between community members, what they consist of and how they influence resilience, but it can also refer to how the community relates to government agencies and/or the environment before, during and after a disaster [23]. As a result, community resilience is often associated with networking capacities, focusing on the interactions between members and collective action.

Before moving on to explore these different forms of relationality and what they consist of, it is also important to shortly discuss the term "community". Similar to resilience, community is a term with an incredibly positive connotation, partially stemming from American political discourse in the 1990s, arguing that there was an erosion of values and local organization which had to be restored [1]. As such the discourse of community is appealing because it indicates "a lost form of sociability, rooted in authenticity, solidarity, trust and shared values" [ibid.]. These connotations of the term are discernable in the CR literature, as community is defined as "a group of individuals having a certain characteristic in common, including being bound to a degree by a specific locality, culture, behaviour, norms, institutions and a 'shared vision" [26]Thus, community is still a feel-good concept and centrally designates to have something in common.

Chaskin [27] provides four conceptualizations of community, which all stress relationality. The first concept is in accordance with the above-mentioned affective understanding of community as an "unit of belonging and identity". The second concept is more functional in that he stresses production and exchange, which nonetheless point toward interconnectedness and dependency for mutual support. The third one focuses on networks, portraying communities as providers of access to information, resources and opportunities, also stressing relationality on a system-level. The fourth concept states that communities are not only social units, but also political ones which can lead to collective action. These conceptualizations shows that relationality is relevant for the concept of community, but relationality can take on different meanings depending on the contextual understanding of community.

A different concern regarding community is, if community is a place-bound concept. Usually, communities are associated with a particular locality that a group of people shares and thus feel "belonging" and an emotional attachment to it [5, 23, 28]. This is particularly prevalent in relation to disaster as this shared experience in the same place is important for CR. However, some authors argue that community might also apply to virtual or imagined communities who do not have to share a place to have something in common [6]. Furthermore, authors emphasize a difference between rural and urban communities, as rural communities in contrast to urban ones often feature closed community ties and a stronger social connection [29]. To sum up, while there is critique regarding the positive connotation of the term community, most literature stresses the relevance of community as a place bound concept transmitting a feeling of security and belonging.

One of the central outcomes of this literature review is that community resilience is a normative concept because authors actively connect it to well-being in different forms [5, 16, 17, 23, 26, 28]. CR literature acknowledges that CR is not per se a normatively good outcome, because communities can divide and exclude people as well [6]. Therefore, CR research strands tie the concept to normatively positive visions of life, albeit in different forms, like "population wellness" or decolonial alternative normative visions like "buen vivir"[1]. Norris et al. [28] tie CR to population wellness, measured through levels of mental and behavioral health, role functioning and quality of life. These measurements depend on the functioning of disaster management, as working disaster management would reduce a negative impact on these factors. Korosteleva and Petrova [26] tie CR to identity and the meaning of a" good life", a vision for a better future which mobilizes communities in times of disaster. They also emphasize the Rwandan concept of "agarico" meaning dignity and self-worth, stressing independence from international aid and self-reliance as well as solidarity [26]. Also, the South American alternative vision of a good life, buen vivir, stresses relational aspects of community and the environment as a whole, as it is based on connectedness and interdependence. Finally, Central Eurasian concepts like "mahalla" stress the importance of formal and informal infrastructures of mutual support in times of need, independent of state structures and thus prime examples for self-organization [26]. Case studies on relationality and CR often had a decolonial perspective and/or used participatory methods giving participants a voice in the research process [30–34].

While CR literature acknowledges that neither community nor resilience refers automatically to a normative vision, authors tie the concept to different understandings of what a good life means. Recently, local concepts of shared visions for a good life and community understandings of relationality became the focus of research, acknowledging that there is not one idea of community resilience or relationality, but these can differ depending on the community.

To sum up, CR stems from socio-ecological definitions of resilience, including systemic factors as well as social factors, aiming at a transformation, rather than a return to a prior state. Additionally, this transformation is tied to a normative vision tying this transformation to an improvement or a better life for the community members. Relationality matters, because CR depends on the relations between different systems (e.g. state-community interaction) and it depends on the relations between community members. In the following, I will engage with the most important factors for relationality, starting with relational factors of top-down and bottom-up organization, demonstrating relationality on two levels.

[1] Buen Vivir is a South American concept designating what a good life for everyone consists of, explicitly naming to live in balance with nature, to reduce social inequality, an economy based on principles of solidarity and civil society participation.

3 System-Oriented Community Resilience

In recent years, interest grew in the question of relationality in CR literature, to better understand how to improve CR. There are two strands in this literature dealing with these questions, corresponding to the above-mentioned dimensions of how people bond with each other to form a community, or how the community interacts with other organizations, as expressed in the following quote: "Communities of place interweave in complex ways with regions, nations, and the globe" [23].

Literature engaging with how CR works as bonds among people usually take a bottom-up perspective, focusing on the self-organization capacities of people enabled through their agency and self-determination [26]. This perspective is in some cases in opposition to international organization or state-led interventions, stemming from civil defence disaster planning as top-down endeavors [35, 36]. In CR literature, such initiatives are at odds with the goals of CR, because they intervene on the local level without knowledge about the particularities of the place or the people within [3, 5]. Quinn et al. [5] for example argue that a government has a"significant role in shaping or mobilizing community resilience" but "responses of communities are often at odds with the aims and wishes of governance institutions, as well as being hindered rather than driven by institutional responses and requirements." Thus, literature points to the issue of top-down governance and how this impedes a mutual relationality. Relational engagement is problematized when it is one-directional. Rather it must be a relational engagement, where both sides are heard and considered.

In this regard, literature points to instances of neglected mutual relationality and its difficult consequences during disaster management. Kan and Lejano [9] show that the ability to self-organize can decline, if governments do not take community voices into consideration. In another case, top-down disaster management disempowered local community agency recovery efforts [3]. However, findings also show that in the absence of institutional support and mutual relationality, communities start to strengthen its own resilience through increased self-organization, although state support would be appreciated [26, 37]. In this case, the relationality of bottom-up resilience was strengthened, while system-level relationality was neglected. Barrios [4] shows that political leaders might abuse their power to distribute resources by punishing or rewarding grass-root leaders for their political behavior. This example illustrates that power relations must be taken seriously when studying relationality. Overall, mutual relationality in which a system is receptive to different levels appears to be important for CR. But there are also studies demonstrating a different outcome. One of them shows that neglect from the government might lead to more bottom-up community resilience and a strengthening of the relations between community members. Therefore, system-level relationality is context bound, meaning the specific context needs to be taken serious to determine how relationality improves CR.

A further discussion in CR centers around the issue of how governments can support the strengthening of supportive relationships of community members. Rather than engaging in a top-down manner, governments act as facilitators of local structures. This discussion arose from the issue that self-organization during and after disasters work best in already established organizational forms, rather than newly emerging ones. This form of strengthening relationality is evident in the discussion about "social capital" and how states can support the strengthening of local social capital [28, 38]. Kan and Lejano [9] differentiate between three types of social capital namely "bonding, bridging, and linking capital". They differentiate these different levels with reference to the family and relative level (bonding), broader community networks like friends and neighbors (bridging) and community-institution relations (linking). The latter is important to obtain resources and formal support, important for recovery. Further research engages with how state-community relationships can be strengthened through inclusion, competency and advocacy, thereby focusing on how to strengthen the agency of the community [16].

The final discussion of system-level CR focuses on community-environment relations mostly from a decolonial or postcolonial perspective. Authors highlight a holistic and circuit understanding of human-nature relations, which should be considered [34, 39]. Datta [34]emphasizes the relevance of relationality by pointing out that "Relational frameworks emphasis the intricate web of relationships that shape Indigenous perspectives on climate change, acknowledging that these perspectives are not isolated but embedded within broader interconnected systems". In this context, the focus on relationality helps to capture the complex web of communities, not only with each other or the state or global governance, but also with nature and which acknowledges worldviews based on reciprocity and interconnectedness. Relationality is not just analyzed, by understanding the relational components of indigenous people's perspective on land and climate change, but also exercised through research methods based on equality. This research is quite sensitive towards power relations regarding Global North and South power imbalances, community-state, community-nature and community-researcher relations.

To address the research question, "How is relationality conceptualized in CR literature?", the literature reveals that relationality is primarily conceptualized at a system level. System-oriented CR literature often focuses on state-community relations, exploring how states can enhance CR. This necessitates serious consideration of power dynamics, as the state is typically the more powerful entity, while the community, as a subset of the state, is less powerful and dependent on it [3]. In this context, the state is portrayed as an external entity that engages with communities either through direct, top-down intervention or through a more mutual, albeit asymmetrical, relationship. As Lejano [10] pointed out, the focus on relationality helps to focus on the relationships that drive the system, rather than only focusing on the properties or functions of the system.

In the former case, the relationship is marked by pronounced power asymmetry and one-dimensionality. In the latter, while power asymmetry remains, it is acknowledged, with the state considering the community's voice and needs, resulting in a more reciprocal dynamic. Another perspective within the literature suggests that relationality is not always direct; instead, the state may influence existing community relationships, such as by strengthening social capital. Equally, particularly decolonial or postcolonial perspectives study relationality through methods and theoretical lenses sensitive to power dynamics.

Overall, system-level relationality contrasts with bottom-up relationality in that it is less characterized by affective traits, such as those found in personal relationships, and more by functional attributes. These include providing services, addressing needs, and facilitating the exchange of knowledge and resources. Nevertheless, the literature on social capital tries to enhance personal relationships between community members. [16] even points out that public administration should develop more empathetic relationships to facilitate CR with regards to disasters.

A shortcoming of this strand of literature is that it is unclear on its definition of community. Differentiating between different conceptualizations, like those articulated by Chaskin [27], would help to understand the context of community: is it seen as a functional entity to provide access to resources and information, or a source for identity and belonging, or a political entity. This would also help to understand how relationality is perceived, and how it can be strengthened.

4 Bottom-Up Resilience – Agency, Solidarity and Support

The richer strand of literature engages with bottom-up community resilience. This strand of literature is concerned with relationality as social bonds between community members and how this facilitates self-organization before, during and after disasters. A few studies point out the limitations of CR and a romantization of the concept, particularly with regards to poverty and the Global Sout [3, 40] h. However, most authors highlight that social relationships are crucial for CR as social connection facilitates preparedness and evacuation and is important to deal with loss [5, 17, 28]. Most authors engaging with bottom-up process of resilience emphasize social relationality, particularly three concepts stood out: agency, solidarity and support.

The first key characteristic of relationality in bottom-up CR is agency, as it enhances adaptive responses and leverages opportunities for transformation or recovery [23, 41, 42]. Within the concept of agency, I capture forms of agency such as self-determination, self-help, self-organization and participation. The common element of these forms of agency is that they refer to community members acting on their own volition together in the interest of the community. Brown and Westaway [43] similarly refer to community agency as the capacity of community actors to act independently, proactively and collectively for their own interest. This is important because agency is essential in countering feelings of powerlessness and victimhood in the face of disaster. It is also crucial to determine local needs and control capacity building processes, mitigating disasters more effectively [44]. By fostering community agency, collective empowerment and hope are strengthened.

To illustrate the crucial role of agency, effective disaster management is often dependent on already existing self-organization in civil organizations which can be mobilized in a coordinated fashion for disaster managemen [28] t. Such pre-organization in turn can help in situations when collective action and decision-making are necessary as people already have prior experience in such processes. Furthermore, the existence of voluntary organizations helps to foster social connections of communities in the first place, as they create a sense of belonging, identity, reciprocity and inclusiveness [17].

The second key characteristic of relationality in bottom-up CR is solidarity, as shared experiences of trauma and loss can strengthen connectedness, fostering a collective willingness to support one another and actively engage in CR efforts. Solidarity is a concept that needs to be distinguished through social, civil and political spheres, in which social refers to a shared interest and membership, civic as an obligation in a civil society to protect the community, and finally political solidarity as activism against injustice or oppression [44]. Social and civic solidarity can be observed during disasters as interest between different groups and social classes align in the shared need during disasters and the effort of recovery [5]. Solidarity is also an important factor for social identity [45]. Political solidarity is quite dependent on the particular circumstances, and most likely also depend on the government in place.

To illustrate political solidarity, Meriläinen et al. [46] show in their case study about India where individual requests for rehabilitative assistance were unsuccessful, that, regional communities started to organize themselves and collectively advocate for rehabilitation to ease displacement. In this case political solidarity led to better settlements and recovery. In contrast, Quinn et al. [5] show in their case study in the UK, where political solidarity, particularly in response to financial claims, is often unrealized due to the individualized and potentially divisive nature of such claims. Most literature in CR resilience perceives solidarity as political solidarity, while social and civil solidarity are often using simultaneously with support and aid.

The third key characteristic of relationality in bottom-up CR is support. Support is defined as "social interactions that provide individuals with actual assistance and embed them into a web of social relationships perceived to be loving, caring, and readily available in times of need" [28]. However, there are differences in what support means and does referring to "received" and "given" support, as well as psychological and material support.

To illustrate how crucial support is for disaster survivors, Norris et al. [28] showed through the "social deterioration model" that the lack of support and resulting feelings of isolation and abandonment have an impact on mental health. One finding of studies about social support showed that victims who received high levels of support dealt with less severe mental health impacts after the disaster [28]. However, it is important to distinguish between received or given support, because receiving support is particularly important in the aftermath of disaster as a psychological safety net. But if people remain on the receiving end for too long, without the possibility of reciprocating, then it might lower self-esteem in the long run. Similarly, if people remain on the giving end for too long it might cause stress [28]. Therefore, it is necessary to include power relations in one's analysis of support.

Engaging with the shortcomings of the concept of support regarding power relations, Harrington and Cole stress the concept of "mutual aid" which includes support but emphasizes mutuality in the process and includes the material as well as the psychological level. Their conceptualization of mutual aid goes beyond spontaneous forms of social support, as they engage with institutional mutual aid networks, group-based self-help and social movement networks determining levels of reciprocity, solidarity, self-determination and resistance.

Bottom-up CR relies strongly on relationality, in this case on social bonds between community members expressed as agency, solidarity and support. All owhich need further differentiation particularly with regards to power relations and political goals. However, social bonds determine the level of community resilience which can be mobilized for disaster management. In this strand of literature, community is often understood as a political concept and as a space of shared identity. Resilience is understood as transformation and as helpful for overcoming hardships. Together both concepts, refer to how community members mobilize together to transform their fate in face of a disaster. To analyze relationality is particularly important, because it helps to answer questions such as how CR is constituted and mobilized when needed.

Information and Communication Technology in Shaping Relational Processes of Resilience.

Information and communication are important with regards to community resilience. Equally relationality matters with regards to communication and information processes. Recent research on community resilience and disaster risk communication point towards participatory methods to enable an "co-construction of risk knowledge" [47]. Relationality is reflected in these methods through their participatory character. In the following, I present the findings on information technology and risk communication with regards to CR in accordance with the conceptual findings outlined above. Information technology in CR literature invokes the same themes: it shows the relevance of relationality on a system-level as well as through bottom-up approaches, particularly with regards to agency, solidarity and support.

Regarding the relational factors of bottom-up resilience, research on information technology in CR shows that CR is best achieved through practices that reflect agency and solidarity. In a remarkable study by Pitidis et al. they show how citizens generate disaster relevant ant data and thereby enhance CR through this process of collective action. In this process, citizens generate the data themselves, for example through "dialogical participatory mapping" a process through which community members can share their risk perception in the area which can subsequently be shared in platforms like the OpenStreetMap. This practice exemplifies bottom-up resilience, as it includes agency through participatory practices taking the voices of the community members seriously, and it exemplifies solidarity as the results are shared and distributed to a wider network digitally. This shows how information technology can enable and enhance relational practices for community resilience.

Solidarity was also expressed as a symbolic gesture of shared grieve and commemoration in the Sewol ferry disaster in 2014. Hong et al. [48] show in their study about solidarity on social media, that platforms were used to share news and updates on the disaster, but also to sympathy, condolences and hope to provide emotional and physical support for the families of the victims. Thus, information technology is not only used to share relevant information on disaster, but also for emotional purposes strengthening a community of victims by showing support. As illustrated in the previous section, social support is crucial to mitigate mental health impacts of disaster affected persons.

To conclude, information technology is an important factor for CR and reflects relational approaches. Moreover, information technology questions assumptions about CR like if CR is still a place-bound concept, as information technology bridges distance and allows for relational bonds transcending geographical boundaries.

5 Conclusion

This article engagement with the question how relationality is conceptualized in community resilience literate regarding disasters. The first outcome was that the conceptualization of community resilience had to be clarified, and most authors agree that a socio-ecological definition of resilience, covering both social interactions and psychological factors as well as a system-oriented perspective is needed. Resilience is defined more as a transformation and improvement, rather than a return to a status quo or to a previous equilibrium. Second, authors note that CR is not as such a positive outcome, rather CR had to tied to a normative understanding of well-being, buen vivir or a good life. Third, CR literature conceptualizes relationality on different levels, one of which I called the system-oriented level engaging with the factors of relationality between institutions, organizations, nature and communities. Particularly decolonial and postcolonial approaches aim to include community-nature relations and they are sensitive to power imbalances. The second level of how relationality is discussed in CR literature is bottom-up resilience. In this case authors deal with interpersonal and intergroup level engagements, where the most used conceptualizations of relationality were agency, solidarity and support. Both levels were also important for information technology and disaster communication, where social media offers the opportunities for communities to participate actively in the disaster management effort and strengthens social bonds beyond geographical boundaries. Future research should place greater emphasis on the issue of trust, given its significant relevance to relationality.

References

1. Zebrowski, C., Sage, D.: Organising community resilience: an examination of the forms of sociality promoted in community resilience programmes. Resilience **5**, 44–60 (2017). https://doi.org/10.1080/21693293.2016.1228158
2. Spialek, M.L., Houston, J.B.: The influence of citizen disaster communication on perceptions of neighborhood belonging and community resilience. J. Appl. Commun. Res. **47**, 1–23 (2019). https://doi.org/10.1080/00909882.2018.1544718
3. Lam, L.M.: Asymmetrical power relationships in disaster reduction remain the key barrier to sustainable recovery: neoliberalism and Nepal's post-earthquake recovery experiences. Sustain. Dev. **32**, 1483–1495 (2024). https://doi.org/10.1002/sd.2683
4. Barrios, R.E.: 'Here, I'm not at ease': anthropological perspectives on community resilience. Disasters **38**, 329–350 (2014). https://doi.org/10.1111/disa.12044
5. Quinn, T., Adger, W.N., Butler, C., Walker-Springett, K.: Community resilience and well-being: an exploration of relationality and belonging after disasters. Ann. Am. Assoc. Geogr. **111**, 577–590 (2020). https://doi.org/10.1080/24694452.2020.1782167
6. Mulligan, M., Steele, W., Rickards, L., Fünfgeld, H.: Keywords in planning: what do we mean by 'community resilience'? Int. Plan. Stud. **21**, 348–361 (2016). https://doi.org/10.1080/13563475.2016.1155974
7. Holling, C.S.: Resilience and stability of ecological systems. Annu. Rev. Ecol. Syst. **4**, 1–23 (1973)
8. Werner, E.E.: Vulnerable but invincible: high risk children from birth to adulthood. Eur. Child Adolesc. Psychiatry **5**, 47–51 (1996). https://doi.org/10.1007/BF00538544

9. Kan, W.S., Lejano, R.P.: Relationality: the role of connectedness in the social ecology of resilience. Int. J. Environ. Res. Public Health **20** (2023). https://doi.org/10.3390/ijerph20053865
10. Lejano, R.P.: Relationality and social-ecological systems: going beyond or behind sustainability and resilience. Sustainability **11** (2019). https://doi.org/10.3390/su11102760
11. Chandler, D.: Decolonising resilience: reading glissant's poetics of relation in central eurasia. Camb. Rev. Int. Aff. **35**, 158–175 (2022). https://doi.org/10.1080/09557571.2021.1944984
12. Henly-Shepard, S.: Empowering the 'vulnerable': intergenerational solidarity for rights-based disaster resilience. J. Intergener. Relatsh. **11**, 330–333 (2013). https://doi.org/10.1080/15350770.2013.810052
13. Richmond, C., et al.: The Health Impacts of Social Distancing Among Indigenous People in Ontario During the First Wave of COVID-19 Author Info. https://doi.org/10.32799/ijih.v18i1.36933
14. Galway, L.P., Esquega, E., Jones-Casey, K.: "Land is everything, land is us": exploring the connections between climate change, land, and health in Fort William First Nation. Soc. Sci. Med. **294** (2022). https://doi.org/10.1016/j.socscimed.2022.114700
15. Kalra, P.: Locating central Eurasia's inherent resilience. Camb. Rev. Int. Aff. **35**, 235–255 (2022). https://doi.org/10.1080/09557571.2021.1993136
16. Ireni-Saban, L.: Challenging disaster administration: toward community-based disaster resilience. Adm. Soc. **45**, 651–673 (2013). https://doi.org/10.1177/0095399712438375
17. Gil-Rivas, V., Kilmer, R.P.: Building Community Capacity and Fostering Disaster Resilience (2016)
18. Broeckling, U.: Gute Hirten fuehren sanft. Ueber Menschenregierungskuenste. Suhrkamp Verlag, Frankfurt am Main (2017)
19. Alexander, D.E.: Resilience and disaster risk reduction: an etymological journey. Nat. Hazard. **13**, 2707–2716 (2013). https://doi.org/10.5194/nhess-13-2707-2013
20. Fooken, I.: Multidisziplinäre Perspektiven der Resilienzforschung. Multidisziplinäre Perspektiven der Resilienzforschung (2016). https://doi.org/10.1007/978-3-658-09623-6
21. Holling, C.S.: Engineering resilience versus ecological resilience. In: Engineering Within Ecological Constraints, pp. 31–44 (1996). https://doi.org/10.17226/4919
22. Werner, E.E.: Risk, resilience, and recovery: perspective from the Kauai longitudinal study. Dev. Psychopathol. **5**, 503–515 (1993)
23. Berkes, F., Ross, H.: Community resilience: toward an integrated approach. Soc. Nat. Resour. **26**, 5–20 (2013). https://doi.org/10.1080/08941920.2012.736605
24. Adger, W.N.: Social and ecological resilience: are they related? Prog. Hum. Geogr. **24**, 347–364 (2000). https://doi.org/10.1191/030913200701540465
25. Gunderson, L.: Comparing ecological and human community resilience. Environ. Stud. **5**, 35 (2009). https://doi.org/10.1017/CBO9781107415324.004
26. Korosteleva, E.A., Petrova, I.: What makes communities resilient in times of complexity and change? Camb. Rev. Int. Aff. **35**, 137–157 (2022). https://doi.org/10.1080/09557571.2021.2024145
27. Chaskin, R.J.: Resilience, community, and resilient communities: conditioning contexts and collective action. Child Care Pract. **14**, 65–74 (2008). https://doi.org/10.1080/13575270701733724
28. Norris, F.H., Stevens, S.P., Pfefferbaum, B., Wyche, K.F., Pfefferbaum, R.L.: Community resilience as a metaphor, theory, set of capacities, and strategy for disaster readiness. Am. J. Community Psychol. **41**, 127–150 (2008). https://doi.org/10.1007/s10464-007-9156-6
29. He, Z., Xiang, Y., Qi, C., Liu, X., Li, S.: The emergence and impact of community resilience initiatives during the COVID-19 pandemic: an exploration study from a Chinese urban community. Asia Pac. J. Soc. Work Dev. **32**, 262–277 (2022). https://doi.org/10.1080/02185385.2022.2136235

30. Teufel-Shone, N.I., et al.: Development of a culturally anchored qualitative approach to conduct and analyze focus group narratives collected in diné (Navajo) communities to understand the impacts of the gold king mine spill of 2015. Int. J. Environ. Res. Public Health **18** (2021). https://doi.org/10.3390/ijerph18179402
31. Pitidis, V., Porto De Albuquerque, J., Coaffee, J., Lima-Silva, F.: Enhancing community resilience through dialogical participatory mapping. Presented at the May (2022)
32. Acharibasam, J.B., Datta, R.: Enhancing community resilience to climate change disasters: Learning experience within and from sub-Saharan black immigrant communities in western Canada. Sustain. Dev. **32**, 1401–1411 (2024). https://doi.org/10.1002/sd.2677
33. Subroto, S., Datta, R.: Perspectives of racialized immigrant communities on adaptability to climate disasters following the UN Roadmap for Sustainable Development Goals (SDGs) 2030. Sustain. Dev. **32**, 1386–1400 (2024). https://doi.org/10.1002/sd.2676
34. Datta, R.: Relationality in indigenous climate change education research: a learning journey from indigenous communities in Bangladesh. Aust. J. Environ. Educ. (2024). https://doi.org/10.1017/aee.2024.13
35. Russo, A., da Rosa, C.: Acknowledge, elevate, and reclaim: a thematic review of critical and decolonial perspectives on contemporary disaster resilience. Adm. Theory Praxis (2023). https://doi.org/10.1080/10841806.2023.2282899
36. Gruber, B.: The Difference Resilience Makes: U.S. National Preparedness - From Civil Defence to Resilience. A Culture of Resilience Report (2017)
37. Fransen, J., Hati, B., Simon, H.K., van Stapele, N.: Adaptive governance by community based organisations: community resilience initiatives during Covid-19 in Mathare, Nairobi. Sustain. Dev. **32**, 1471–1482 (2024). https://doi.org/10.1002/sd.2682
38. Page-Tan, C., Aldrich, D.P.: Snowed in? An analysis of social and transportation networks in the 2015 Boston Snowmageddon. Sustain. Dev. **32**, 1446–1457 (2024). https://doi.org/10.1002/sd.2680
39. Shahidullah, A.K.M., Choudhury, M.U.I., Emdad Haque, C.: Ecosystem changes and community wellbeing: social-ecological innovations in enhancing resilience of wetlands communities in Bangladesh. Local Environ. **25**, 967–984 (2020). https://doi.org/10.1080/13549839.2020.1849077
40. Koshy, M., Smith, D.: Community resilience implications for institutional response under uncertainty: cases of the floods in Wayanad, India and the earthquake in Port-au-Prince, Haiti. Sustain. Dev. **32**, 1412–1427 (2024). https://doi.org/10.1002/sd.2678
41. Knearem, T., Jo, J., Alliyu, O., Carroll, J.M.: Solidarity not charity! empowering local communities for disaster relief during COVID-19 through grassroots support. Comput. Support. Coop. Work (2024). https://doi.org/10.1007/s10606-023-09484-5
42. Stotten, R.: The natural domain and its social representation in the community resilience concept. Sustain. Dev. **32**, 1458–1470 (2024). https://doi.org/10.1002/sd.2681
43. Brown, K., Westaway, E.: Agency, capacity, and resilience to environmental change: lessons from human development, well-being, and disasters. Annu. Rev. Environ. Resour. **36**, 321–342 (2011). https://doi.org/10.1146/annurev-environ-052610-092905
44. Harrington, E., Cole, A.: Typologies of mutual aid in climate resilience: variation in reciprocity, solidarity, self-determination, and resistance. Environ. Justice **15**, 160–169 (2022). https://doi.org/10.1089/env.2021.0046
45. Babayev, A., Abushov, K.: The Azerbaijani resilient society: explaining the multifaceted aspects of people's social solidarity. Camb. Rev. Int. Aff. **35**, 210–234 (2022). https://doi.org/10.1080/09557571.2021.2020214
46. Meriläinen, E., et al.: Examining relational social ontologies of disaster resilience: lived experiences from India, Indonesia, Nepal, Chile and Andean territories. Disaster Prev. Manag. Int. J. **31**, 273–287 (2022). https://doi.org/10.1108/DPM-02-2021-0057

47. Casas, E.V., Pormon, M.M., Manus, J.J., Lejano, R.P.: Relationality and resilience: environmental education in a time of pandemic and climate crisis. J. Environ. Edu. **52**, 314–324 (2021). https://doi.org/10.1080/00958964.2021.1981205
48. Hong, J.Y.J., Kim, N., Lee, S., Kim, J.H.: Community disaster resilience and social solidarity on social media: a semantic network analysis of the Sewol ferry disaster. Inf. Res. **23** (2018)

Author Index

Published by Springer Nature Switzerland AG 2026
W. Seböck et al. (Eds.): ITDRR 2024, IFIP AICT 752, p. 291, 2026.
https://doi.org/10.1007/978-3-031-97115-0

The manufacturer's authorised representative in the EU is Springer Nature Customer Service Centre GmbH, Europaplatz 3, 69115 Heidelberg, Germany. If you have any concerns regarding our products, please contact ProductSafety@springernature.com

Printed and bound by CPI Group (UK) Ltd, Croydon, CR0 4YY
01/10/2026
02225865-0010